MALTA

Roots of a Nation

THE DEVELOPMENT OF MALTA FROM AN ISLAND PEOPLE TO AN ISLAND NATION

EDITED BY
KENNETH GAMBIN

 Heritage Malta

**Malta – Roots of a Nation
The development of Malta from
an island people to an island nation**

Edited by
Kenneth Gambin

First edition 2004

© the Authors, 2004

Cover design by Josian Bonello

Produced by Midsea Books Ltd for
HERITAGE MALTA
and the
EU ACCESSION CELEBRATIONS COMMITTEE

Printed at Gutenberg Press, Gudja

ISBN: 99932-57-01-X (hardback)
ISBN: 99932-57-02-8 (paperback)

Since time immemorial man has travelled across Europe in search of new opportunities, to learn, to enrich himself materially and spiritually, or to acquire new ideas and techniques. The spread of culture across the European continent has never been hindered by language or by geographical barriers. This has made possible the creation of a wide European culture which – despite the differences between North-South and East-West – is the common heritage of all Europeans; not simply because we live on the same soil, but also because we broadly share the same values and expectations. By culture one understands a 'package' of shared beliefs, traditions, language, arts, knowledge, practices and aims.

In our present day and age, the globalisation of the economy, the ever-increasing social mobility, and the spectacular development of new technology, have transformed the world into one village. Yet at the same time, and perhaps as an unconscious psychological reaction to this standardisation process, there is an increasing trend towards the assertion of individual values and the strengthening of local, regional or national identities, which, while acknowledging common origins, tend to emphasise particular ethnic traditions, social perceptions and values.

It was precisely for these reasons that on the occasion of Malta's accession into the European Union on 1 May 2004, Heritage Malta was officially appointed by the EU Accession Celebrations Committee to set up an exhibition entitled 'Malta - Roots of a Nation', and to edit and publish a book with the same title.

The publication has a dual function. It is envisaged not only to act as a companion to the exhibition itself, but will also hopefully remain to be considered as a reference tool for all those interested in further research about Malta's fascinating history and culture both in Malta and abroad. It offers the possibility to millions of Europeans to discover other, perhaps less known aspects of their heritage, such as those originating from a tiny island and a frontier society such as Malta, lying on the southern-most border of Europe. It tries to create a concrete link between peoples in Europe, thus bringing them closer through the discovery of their common roots.

Malta is rich in culture. Considering its minute size and population one may say that its culture is disproportionate. Through millennia of history it has managed to distil traditional local characteristics with broader foreign influences. Yet Malta is definitely a consequence of its environment. There is no sense in trying to explore and understand, and ultimately to explain the cultural identity of a small island without keeping into consideration the wider context of the outside world.

For this reason a number of Maltese academics, experts in their particular field of research, have been invited to contribute a paper on their specific subject of study. Besides presenting a general history of Malta written by experts in one volume, this book also tackles some of the aspects that make up Maltese national identity, from art and architecture, to language and religion, from music and literature to geology and the natural environment. One can also find notes and references at the end of each paper to act as guidelines for those who wish to delve further into a particular subject. Neither the contributors nor the editor lay any claim to have presented a fully comprehensive picture of all aspects of Maltese history and culture through seven thousand years of history from prehistory to the present day. There are many more aspects of Maltese history that could have been examined. The final purpose of every author has been to focus on a particular aspect of Malta's history or culture and present what are his views on the subject or issue under discussion. There has been no attempt by the editor to bring the contributors to present one definite view of Malta and its cultural traditions. Nor do the authors necessarily agree on all topics.

There is however one underlying common theme in all contributions. A particular emphasis has been made on the contacts that Malta had with Europe through the centuries, and similarities or contrasts with other European cultures. The purpose is twofold: not only for Maltese culture to find its place in wider European culture, but also to emphasise the general contribution that Malta can make towards the enhancement of the culture and traditions of Greater Europe with its new typical and particular, local and regional perspectives. It thus stresses European cultural unity through its diverse manifestations, and seeks to stimulate a feeling of togetherness by highlighting a common European lifestyle, hopefully promoting a sense of responsibility to protect and preserve our national and European cultural identity.

The publication of this book would not have been possible without the support of the Malta-EU Information Centre and the technical help of the EU Accession Celebrations Committee, especially Mr Charles Galea, Head of the Economic and Cultural Affairs Department of the Ministry of Foreign Affairs, who originated the idea of both exhibition and publication. It would not have materialised, above all, without the co-operation and understanding of all twenty esteemed contributors, especially when I fired very tight deadlines. Any defects in consistency however are fully mine, especially where I did not always follow their valuable suggestions.

I also have to thank the Chairman of Heritage Malta, Dr Mario Tabone, and the Chief Executive Officer Mrs Antoinette Caruana for their unconditional support, not less in difficult times. Finally I have to thank a number of friends and colleagues, too many to mention individually, but among who I single out Pierre Bonello and Antonio Espisnosa Rodriguez who have helped me in various ways during the preparation of this book. To all of them I owe a deep debt of gratitude and wish to extend my sincere appreciation.

Kenneth Gambin
Heritage Malta
April 2004
kenneth.j.gambin@gov.mt

CONTENTS

Part III: Cultural Perspectives

Part IV: The Maltese Language

Part V: Historical Aspects

LIST OF ABBREVIATIONS

AIM	Archives of the Inquisition of Malta, Cathedral Museum
Anon.	Anonymous
AO	Acta Originalia
AOM	Archives of the Order of St John, National Library of Malta
CAM	Cathedral Archives Malta
CEM	Curia Episcopalis Melitensis, Cathedral Museum
ch./chs	Chapter/Chapters
Civ. Proc.	Civil Proceedings
Crim. Proc.	Criminal proceedings
CST	Cedula Supplicae et Taxationes
ed./eds	editor/editors
et al	With other authors
f./ff.	folio/folios
Ibid.	Same as above
Id.	Same author
Lib.	Library Manuscript Collection, National Library of Malta
MCC	Magna Curia Castellania
Ms./Mss.	Manuscript/Manuscripts
NAM	National Archives Malta
NLM	National Library of Malta, Valletta
No.	Number
passim.	In various places
Univ.	Università Manuscript Collection, National Library of Malta

PART ONE

GEOGRAPHICAL TRAITS

John J. Borg

THE GEOLOGY OF THE MALTESE ARCHIPELAGO

Introduction

Although a lot of work has been carried out on the geology of the Maltese islands, it is only now that we are beginning to understand the complex rock formations within our 'simple' geological structure. Adding to this the sister science of Maltese Palaeontology is still a vast source of information waiting to be fully tapped. The aim of this contribution is to give a general description of the main geological features of the Maltese islands and a chronological history of Maltese geological maps.

Maltese geology has always been a branch of science that was largely understudied by local scientists/naturalists and only a handful has ever taken up the subject in any consideration, namely Carmelo Rizzo and Dr George Zammit Maempel. On the other hand a fair share of foreign scientists carried out extensive studies on various aspects of Maltese geology and palaeontology. These include Dr Andrew Leith Adams, Admiral Thomas A. B. Spratt, John H. Cooke and Martyn Pedley.

The Maltese Islands

The Maltese archipelago, with a total surface area of a mere 316 square kilometres, lies in the middle of the Mediterranean Sea some ninety kilometres south of Sicily and 350 kilometres north of the Libyan coast. The islands, starting from the southernmost tip, are Malta, which is 245.7 km² long, Comino 2.8 km², and Gozo 67.1 km². From a geological point of view the Maltese islands are a relatively young

Globigerina Limestone quarries on the south-west side of Malta (Photo: John J. Borg)

Rock breakdown in Maghlaq Fault with Filfla in the background (Photo: John J. Borg)

Dolines, cliffs, quaternary deposits in the Dwejra area in Gozo (Photo: John J. Borg)

composition of rock formation. The limestone-based deposits are of late Oligo-Miocene age and started forming as sediments around thirty million years ago in a shallow sea on the Pelagian Spur. During this period in time, the Sicilian-Tunisian platform formed the northern margin of the African continent and the area where the Maltese islands would eventually emerge was situated a considerable distance from any land. This is one of the reasons why Maltese rocks are almost completely devoid of any terrestrial fossil remains but are almost entirely of marine origin.

The islands are tilted towards the south eastern side with places reaching less than one metre above sea level, while at the other end the greatest altitude is the Rabat plateau at 253 metres above sea level. On the island of Gozo the highest altitude is found at the Ta' Dbiegi plateau at a height of nearly 200 metres.

The Origin of Maltese Rocks

The rocks of the Maltese islands are of a marine sedimentary origin, deposited on the bottom of a warm sea, at various depths and distances from a continental mainland during the Oligo-Miocene Epoch of the Tertiary Period of Geological Time, during a period ranging from about thirty to seven million years before present. After several processes these marine deposits solidified and became rock. The collision of the African and Eurasian Plates brought up the once submerged seabed onto the surface of the sea. A submerged ridge was formed extending from Sicily to Tunisia dividing the central Mediterranean into two unequal hydrographical basins. The tips of this ridge are the Pelagian islands and the Maltese archipelago.

The Main Rock Formations

The stratigraphic succession of the islands is composed of five main layer formations. The names assigned to these five layers were given by Murray and continued to be in use up to this day. Starting from the lower most formation, the main rock strata are: Lower Coralline Limestone, Globigerina Limestone, Blue Clay, Greensand, and Upper Coralline Limestone.

Lower Coralline Limestone – The oldest rock formation exposed at the surface on the Maltese islands forms most of Malta's south and south-western coastline between Fomm ir-Riħ and Benghisa. This rock formation is composed mainly of massive white limestone beds of shallow marine origin, generally composed of shell debris derived from skeletal remains, among others, of calcareous algae, corals, brachiopods, molluscs and echinoderms. The formation is exposed through a thickness of up to 140 metres in the almost inaccessible vertical sea cliffs along the western coast of Malta and Gozo. The base of this formation is found below sea level and because of the overall regional 'dip' of the strata across the Maltese islands, this layer becomes covered by the upper layers towards the north and east and is only visible in the deeper cut valleys.

A characteristic and marked division between the Lower Coralline Limestone and the overlaying Globigerina Limestone is what is termed the 'Scutella Bed', a layer with a great concentration of large flat irregular sea-urchins. In some areas there are three different beds of this type, ranging in thickness from a few centimetres up to a metre. The concentration of fossils in this layer indicates that there was a period in which the sandy sediments were 'filtered' away by waves and currents, leaving only the larger and heavier fossil shells. It is thought that this was caused by a temporary shallowing of the sea before it deepened to create conditions for the Globigerina Limestone to accumulate.

Globigerina Limestone – Topographically this formation generally presents a rolling countryside with shallow valleys and low ridges. This rock formation varies in thickness from twenty metres to a maximum of about 250 metres. The Globigerina Limestone formation outcrops extensively in the south-eastern part of Malta, extending over two-thirds of the island's surface. The formation owes its present name to the abundance of the shells of Globigerina and other Foraminifera, single-celled animalcules that make up the bulk of the purer limestone beds. These show that it was originally deposited in deeper waters below wave actions. Lithologically and palaeontologically, the formation is divided into Lower, Middle and Upper subdivisions, with a conspicuous phosphatic 'nodule bed' marking an important non-sequence at the base of each subdivision. These nodule layers are indicative of effects of agitated waters on the seabed sweeping away all the fine sediments, which also indicate a lowering in the sea level at the time of deposition. The presence of a high percentage of phosphate in the cements also suggests that waters streaming over this shallow surface were rising from greater depths as an 'upwelling' current, and by mapping out the sizes of the pebbles in the conglomerates it is possible to see that they get smaller in size towards the east, implying that the currents were mainly from west to east.

The fine-grained limestone of the Globigerina layers is lightly cemented and is therefore, easily worked, as for example, for building purposes. The lowest of the three divisions has proved to be the most appropriate as building stone because of its uniform texture and also because of its property to 'case harden' the surface of the cut blocks when these are exposed to the natural elements.

Clays – What is usually referred to as Blue Clay actually includes a wide variety of predominantly argillaceous beds, which vary considerably in colour and composition. Like the Globigerina Limestone, the Blue Clay is also very fine-grained sediment with a large component of fine lime grains dominated by skeletal material from planktonic organisms. The darker beds contain only two or three percent of carbonate of lime, and, when wet, become dark blue grey in colour and thoroughly plastic. Topographically, clays produce 45° slopes and taluses that tend to slide over the underlying Globigerina Limestone formation. Clays form an impervious base to the water bearing Greensand and Upper Coralline Formations. They hold up all the rainwater that percolates downwards through the pores and fissures of these formations, thus forming, in the upland regions of the islands, perched water tables of perpetually fresh water. This layer varies in thickness from over seventy metres in the western side to a total absence in the easternmost areas of Malta. The clay content of this formation can only have come from a land source resulting from the progressive uplift of the mountain ranges of the north of Sicily induced by the convergence of the African and Eurasian plates. This led to intensive erosion of the uplifted areas and consequently detritus was shed into the surrounding seas.

Greensand – The abundance of minute dark-green, almost black, granules of the mineral glauconite constitutes the bulk of this rock formation. It is sand made up of fossil debris with brown phosphatic grains and rounded grains of Glauconite. The distribution of glauconite, however, is far from uniform within this lithologically complex accumulation. Some thin bands are practically pure glauconite sand. In other parts, however, it is only a minor constituent and fossil shells make up more than ninety percent of the rock, so it could be described as glauconitic limestone rather than greensand. This formation is not always present between the Clays and the Upper Coralline and is the thinnest of all the five main layers with a maximum thickness of up to eleven metres at il-Gelmus, Gozo. The Greensand represents a final shallowing after the deepwater situation in which most of the Blue Clay was laid down, and encompasses a period of active current activity which swept away all clay and fine lime particles and concentrated the larger particles, many of which were fossils or their fragments.

Greensand weathers by forming a thick crust on the surface beneath which cavities may form. Topographically it furnishes vertical exposures and it is often found as large detached boulders on the underlying clay slopes. Over much of the region the horizon is represented by only a few centimetres of thinly bedded glauconitic marl, transitory between the Clays and the marly basal beds of the Upper Coralline.

Upper Coralline Limestone – This is the youngest rock formation of the Maltese islands, outcropping a little less than a quarter of the total area of Malta and Gozo. On the high outcrops this formation reaches a maximum of thirty metres in thickness, but in general it is much less. On the other hand, in some areas such as the Victoria Lines, it reaches a maximum thickness of 162 metres in the Bingemma Syncline Borehole. On Comino, where about eighty metres outcrops at the surface, it may reach greater depths. This rock formation is divided into three major sub-divisions in the vertical succession, each of which displaying considerable lithological and faunal variation, when followed from west to east across the islands. The lowermost division is mainly composed of thinly bedded alterations of coralline

Extensive quaternary deposits along the south-west coast of Malta (Photo: John J. Borg)

Ta' Ċenċ limestone cliffs (Photo: John J. Borg)

Natural erosion at Qbajjar, Gozo utilised as saltpans (Photo: John J. Borg)

Common Tertiary fossils in Maltese rocks (Photo: John J. Borg)

algal bands (*Lithothamnum*) with yellow weathering marly bands containing an abundant fauna. An algal reef, up to six metres in thickness, extends widely through western Malta and eastern Gozo in a north-south division. The soft pure limestone of this division has been quarried extensively for the manufacture of lime. The upper division is composed of massive compact beds, largely of reef origin, with abundant corals associated with rock-boring bivalves (*Lithodomus*). Some of the beds appear to have accumulated in very shallow waters, possibly at times intertidal.

At this time, by the end of the Tertiary Epoch some seven to five million years ago, Africa and Europe were being pushed closer to each other and the pressure of these two land masses uplifted the seabed. As a consequence the Maltese archipelago emerged from underneath the surface of the sea.

The Quaternary Deposits

This is the most recent rock formation in geological time and extends up to and includes the present day. The Quaternary period comprises two epochs, the Pleistocene and the Holocene periods, and its formations are still operating today. It is the latest subdivision of the Cenozoic Era. There are still debates about when the Quaternary really started from, however most scientists agree that quaternary formations started about two million years ago.

During the Quaternary the climate changed constantly and rapidly. It has been considered that Quaternary deposits are synonymous with the Ice Age, which is a view that can be traced back to the time of Sir Edward Forbes, who in 1846 regarded Pleistocene to be equivalent with the 'Glacial Epoch'. The constant and rapid change in the climate was notably due to the results of the Milanchovitch factors, having alternating periods of glacial cold stadials and temperate periods similar to today (interglacials). It is for this reason that the Quaternary was divided into two unequal epochs, having the Holocene, which is the most recent epoch, comprising of the last 10,000 years of warm climate and the Pleistocene, which comprises the rest of the Quaternary before these 10,000 years. The Quaternary period is considered to be very important since the analysis of past environments may be a guide to what we may go through in the future. Disagreements on when the Quaternary period really started are still present, but D. Bowen and others have favoured the use of a timescale which was based upon deep sea coring system (V28-238) in the Pacific Ocean. In the last 2.5 million years, there were at least ninety-six major changes between cold and warm stadials.

At the time during which this layer started to form the climate was generally mild and denudations have uncovered older landforms. The Holocene Epoch, which is the second epoch of the Quaternary period, is also important since this period coincides with the first emergence of 'modern' man.

The Quaternary history of the Mediterranean is relatively poorly known when compared to areas such as North-western Europe and North America. The Maltese islands occupy a pivotal position in the central Mediterranean and they may be in a good position to link relatively well with the understood sequences of Italy. However, sequences in Tunisia and Libya are still relatively poorly known and therefore the sequence of environmental change is not clearly understood. Similar to other Mediterranean regions, the understanding of environmental change and of the quaternary deposits are still very limited in the Maltese islands.

The quaternary deposits provide evidence on which our reconstructions of past environmental change are based. One can literally learn how to 'read' quaternary deposits and analyse the different climates in the past since this can be visible on the deposit itself. The latter, together with dating of land snails and the dust itself, can help reconstruct past environment.

A modest amount of work has been carried out on the Maltese Quaternary fauna and studies have been conducted on the flora mainly through pollen analysis and leaf deposits. The main works focused mainly on the mammalian and avian fauna as well as on the mollusca.

The History of Maltese Geological Maps

The first systematic description of the geological features of the islands was presented by Commander (later Admiral) Thomas A. B. Spratt in the fourth volume of the Proceedings of the Geological Society in 1854. Spratt's contribution was supplemented with a small scaled map of Malta and Gozo and several coloured transversal geological sections of both islands. These diagrams highlighted the important geological faults and other features. Twenty-seven years later, when Andrew Leith Adams published his geological map of Malta in 1870, it was considered as a major improvement on Spratt's work. However but for the addition of two 'faults' to those marked by the Earl of Ducie's map, it can only be considered as a bad and inaccurate copy of the latter map, reproduced on too small a scale. In September 1890 the third geological map of Malta was published by Dr (later Sir) John Murray of the 'Challenger' expedition fame. Murray visited the islands on two occasions (1889 and 1890). Both his visits were of a short duration and the time at his disposal was inadequate for a detailed survey. Although at the time this was considered as the most complete map yet published, it was almost entirely based on the two previously published works, with several omissions and inaccuracies.

The next geological map which had to follow was that of Carmelo Rizzo in 1932, fifty-eight years after Murray's map. A detailed account of the island's geology, hydrology and natural resources was published, but unfortunately the accompanying maps were never published. Rizzo was the first to distinguish and to map the various sub-divisions of the Globigerina Limestone but these were never published. A team from the Royal Engineers produced another geological map soon after the Second World War. However, on account of the very limited number of copies prepared; this map is very little known. In 1957 another British team, this time from Durham University, produced another geological map on behalf of the British Petroleum Company prepared by M.R. House *et al*. In 1964 J.C. Wigglesworth prepared a detailed geological map of Gozo as part of his Ph.D. thesis. This map, showing the various sub-divisions of the Globigerina Limestone, was later published with some additions by Martyn Pedley in 1976. The latest version of the Maltese geological map is that published by the Oil Exploration Directorate of the Office of the Prime Minister of Malta in 1993.

References

Abela, G. F., *Della Descrittione di Malta isola nel mare Siciliano* (Malta, 1647).

Adams, A. L., *Notes of a Naturalist in the Nile Valley and Malta* (Edinburgh, 1870).

Borg, J. J., 'A Checklist to the Quaternary Avifauna of the Maltese Islands', in Mifsud, A. and Savona Ventura, C. (eds), *Facets of Maltese Prehistory* (Malta, 1999), 77-89.

Bowen, D. Q., *Quaternary Geology: A stratigraphic framework for multidisciplinary work* (Oxford, 1978).

Giusti, F., Manganelli, G., and Schembri, P.J., 'The non-marine molluscs of the Maltese Islands', in *Monografie XV* (Turin, 1995).

Hunt, C. O., and Schembri, P. J., 'Quaternary Environments and the biogeography of the Maltese Islands', in Mifsud, A., and Savona Ventura, C. (eds), *Facets of Maltese Prehistory* (Malta, 1999), 41-51.

Hunt, C. O., 'Quaternary deposits in the Maltese Islands: A microcosm of environmental change in Mediterranean Lands', *Geojournal*, 41, 2 (1997).

Lowe J. J., and Walker, M. J. C., *Reconstructing Quaternary Environments* (London, 1999).

Murray, J., 'The Maltese Islands, with a Special Reference to their Geological Structure', *The Scottish Geological Magazine* (1890).

Pedley, M., Clarke, M. H., and Galea, P., *Limestone Isles in a Crystal Sea. The Geology of the Maltese Islands* (Malta, 2002).

Pedley, M., House, M. R., and Waugh, B., 'The Geology of Malta and Gozo', *Proceedings of the Geologists Association*, 87, 3 (1976), 325-41.

Pedley, M., House, M. R., and Waugh, B., 'The Geology of the Pelagian Block: The Maltese Islands', in Nairn, A. E. M., Kanes, W. H., and Stehli, F. G. (eds), *The ocean basins and margins 4B. The Western Mediterranean* (1978), 417-33.

Rizzo, C., *Report on the Geology of the Maltese Islands including chapters on Possible Ground Water Tables and Prospecting for Mineral-Oil and Natural-Gas* (Malta, 1932), 1-37.

Spratt, T. A. B., 'On the Geology of the Maltese Islands', *Proceedings of the Geological Society*, IV (London, 1843), 225-32.

Spratt, T. A. B., *On the Geology of Malta and Gozo* (London, 1854).

Zammit Maempel, G., 'The Earliest "Treatise" on Maltese Fossils', *Melita Historica*, VIII, 2 (1981), 133-48.

Zammit Maempel, G., 'The Geology of Gozo', in Farrugia, J. and Brigulio, L. (eds), *A Focus on Gozo* (Malta, 1996), 5-25.

Zammit Maempel, G., *An Outline of Maltese Geology* (Malta, 1977).

Acknowledgments

My sincere thanks go to Nadia Fabri for her help and assistance, especially on the Quaternary period, and to Dr George Zammit Maempel for accepting me to work with him in the early stages of the new Għar Dalam museum and his inspiring comments.

Joe Sultana

THE BIODIVERSITY OF THE MALTESE ISLANDS.

Since the arrival of humans about 7000 years ago, the Maltese islands have seen great changes. Humans started using land to yield their sustenance and by time changed the landscape. Presently the terraced fields supported by many kilometres of rubble walls together with natural valleys and watercourses, bastion-like cliffs and a unique coastline carved through millennia, harmonise together to present us with a pleasant natural environment, relatively rich in biodiversity.

The Maltese archipelago consists of a small group of low-lying, mostly limestone islands, situated right in the central part of the Mediterranean Sea. They lie approximately 95 km south of Sicily and 290 km north of the Libyan coast, and are blessed with a typical, moderate, Mediterranean climate, with mild, wet winters and hot, dry summers. The islands are young in geological terminology; their oldest sedimentary rock, the lower coralline limestone, was formed between 25 and 30 million years ago. There are three main inhabited islands, Malta, Gozo and Comino, and a number of uninhabited islets, the most important being Kemmunett, Filfla, St Paul's islands and Fungus Rock. Their total surface area is approximately 322 square kilometres.

Geotectonic movements have moulded the islands by raising large tracts of land and subsiding other parts, creating hills, ridges and valleys. Malta, the main island, with a surface area of about 248 square km, ended up with an inclination from the south west rising to about 253 metres above sea level at Dingli Cliffs, to the northeast, where the land slopes gently into the sea.

Gozo, with a surface area of about 67 square km, and with an altitude of 191 metres at its highest point at Ta' Dbiegi, has a more complex topography. It is characteristically marked by a number of hilly plateaux, formed from upper coralline limestone, with the hillsides covered with clay slopes. Between the hills erosion has exposed the globigerina limestone forming plains, which slope down into winding valleys.

The total length of the shoreline of the Maltese islands is about 190 km. Mainland Malta has 17 percent of its coast made up of slopes with boulder screes and 22 percent consisting of cliffs. Gozo's coastline, which is about 40 km in length, has 14.5 percent composed of screes and 62 percent of cliffs. The coastline provides a good habitat to a variety of flora and fauna species. Here one finds sites of ecological importance, supporting unique habitats such as sea-cliffs, sand dunes, salt marshes, and coastal clay slopes, which host endemic or rare species.

The Flora

It is to be expected that the flora of the Maltese islands partakes of the Mediterranean plant life, and is most similar to that found in the south-eastern region of Sicily. The islands support some 1,100 vascular species, seventy percent of which are indigenous. About eighteen species of these are endemic, that is, they are confined to the Maltese islands and found nowhere else growing in the wild.

The evergreen wood, the maquis, the garigue and the steppe are the main four plant community types found in the Mediterranean. In the Maltese islands the woodland habitat, which was mainly dominated by large trees, such as the Evergreen Oak *Quercus ilex* and the Aleppo Pine *Pinus halepensis*, has been virtually exterminated since the arrival of humans. Only some remnants are left, such as the very old evergreen oaks' copse, which still survives at Wardija, with specimens possibly between 500 and 900 years old.

The maquis vegetation is still widespread and is mainly found at the base of cliff formations, and along the sides and bottoms of several valleys. It is characterised by Carob *Ceratonia siliqua*, Olive *Olea europaea*, Mediterranean Buckthorn *Rhamnus alaternus*, Lentisk *Pistacia lentiscus* and Bay Laurel *Laurus nobilis*, together with a number of climbers and large herbaceous plants. The Maltese national tree, the Sandarac Gum tree *Tetraclinis articulata*, is locally a rare tree, which also forms a maquis in a few rocky slopes. Mature specimens are present at Maqluba, a small ecological site, which is a relatively recent cave collapse structure. This tree's distribution extends through the Maghreb countries, but in Europe it is restricted to a few areas in Spain and in Malta.

Dense, low and aromatic plants, growing on large expanses of limestone, which have been eroded into numerous fissures and depressions, form the garigue vegetation. This is the most typical of Maltese communities, frequently characterised by Mediterranean Thyme *Thymus capitatus*, Mediterranean Heath *Erica multiflora*, olive-leaved Germander *Teucrium fruticans*, Shrubby Kidney Vetch *Anthyllis hermanniae*, and several other similar species. The Maltese Spurge *Euphorbia melitensis* is one of the garigue endemic plants, and it is frequently the dominant species.

Comino supports the least spoilt garigue areas in the Maltese islands. However one of the richest garigue localities is found in Gozo at Il-Qortin tal-Magun, a rocky limestone plateau protruding eastwards and flanked by the valleys of Daħlet Qorrot and Wied ir-Riħan. Here the garigue has developed into a dense covering of low-growing shrubs of a large variety of species, dominated by narrow-leaved Rock-Rose *Cistus monspeliensis*, Tree Spurge *Euphorbia dendroides*, African Wolfbane *Periploca angustifolia*, White Hedge Nettle *Prasium majus*, and other typical garigue species. Patches of the yellow and purple forms of the rare Southern Dwarf Iris *Iris pseudomila*, among several other scarce species, are also found here.

The most widespread of the plant community types, however, is the steppe vegetation, which is formed mainly by herbaceous plants, particularly grasses, umbellifers, legumes, and tuberous species such as the Sea Squill *Uriginea marittima* and the Branched Asphodel *Asphodelus aestivus*.

Cliff communities are mainly located on the southern and western coasts. There are many interesting plant taxa here including two, the Maltese Cliff-Orache *Cremnophyton lanfrancoi* and the Maltese Rock Centaury *Palaeocyanus crassifolius*, the national plant, both of which belong to monotypic genera, and are endemic to the Maltese islands. The western cliffs of Gozo and Fungus Rock also support an endemic species, the Maltese Everlasting *Helichrysum melitense*. It is an ornamental species, with greyish-white foliage and yellow flowers. The dense shrub, known as the Maltese Salt-Tree *Darniella melitensis*, is another endemic species. It also grows mainly on coastal cliffs, although it is found growing inland, particularly in Gozo. It is the only European species of the genus *Darniella*.

The flora of Gozo is essentially similar to that of the rest of Malta but there are several species which have been recorded only from the island. The Shrubby Campion *Silene fruticosa* is one of them. A very small population of this species still grows in the garigues of Mġarr ix-Xini and Xlendi. A number of typical dune species persist only on the sand dunes at Ramla, which are the least spoilt dunes in the Maltese islands. Here a unique sand dune habitat still supports a relatively rich coastal flora community, which includes several vulnerable and rare species of dune flora such the Sea Daffodil *Pancratium maritimum* and the Sea Holly *Eryngium maritimum*. The famed Malta Fungus *Cynomorium coccineum*, which was originally described from Fungus Rock, is another interesting plant. This stocky, very deep red, strange looking plant was formerly known only from this islet and it was believed to have medicinal and magical powers. Subsequently it was found growing in several other parts of the Mediterranean. It is not a fungus but a parasitic flowering plant, which grows on roots of halophytic plants.

The Fauna

The terrestrial fauna of the Maltese islands, apart from one amphibian, nine reptiles, about 380 birds, and some nineteen mammals, is largely made up of

Aerial view of Filfla islet (Photo: Joe Sultana)

Ta' Ċenċ Cliffs on the south coast of Gozo (Photo: Joe Sultana)

Simar – a restored wetland area (Photo: Joe Sultana)

The sand dunes at Ramla Bay in Gozo hold rare flora and fauna species (Photo: Joe Sultana)

invertebrates, with insect, arachnid and mollusc species being the most evident. As with the flora, the Maltese fauna has a great similarity with that of Sicily, and most Maltese species occur there too.

Insect species are the most numerous; the coleopteran fauna alone includes more than 2,000 species, while nearly 600 species of butterflies and moths have been recorded. There are several endemics, particularly among the invertebrates. Out of seventy land and fresh water molluscs, six have been recorded only from the Maltese islands. Some invertebrates are quite rare. The Sand Cricket *Brachytripes megacephalus* is one of them. This nocturnal, relatively large-sized sand-burrowing cricket is restricted to Għadira in Malta and Ramla in Gozo. Some insect families are represented by just one species. A case in point is the noisy Cicada *Cicada orni*.

In spite of having a rather long dry season one can still find a number of freshwater species, including a freshwater crab, whose few isolated populations belong to a distinct endemic subspecies *Potamon fluviatile lanfrancoi*. Temporary rainwater pools also support a number of other locally rare crustaceans such as the Fairy Shrimp *Branchipus schaefferi*, the Tadpole Shrimp *Triops cancriformis* and the Clamp Shrimp *Cyzicus tetracerus*.

The only amphibian found in the islands is the Painted Frog *Discoglossus pictus*, which is restricted to localities where freshwater is present. The Ocellated Skink *Chalcides ocellatus*, two geckos (the Moorish *Tarentola mauritanica* and the Turkish *Hemidactylus turcicus*), an introduced chameleon *Chamaeleo chamaeleon*, four snakes (the most common and widespread is the Western Whipsnake *Coluber viridiflavus*), and the Maltese Wall Lizard *Podarcis filfolensis* make up the terrestrial reptiles. The latter is the most interesting species due to its four endemic races, which have been described from the various Maltese islands. The fifth race is found on the Pelagian islands.

Of the 380 bird species recorded in the Maltese islands, approximately thirteen are resident, five summer visitors, 52 winter visitors, 112 more or less regular migrants and the rest rare and irregular migrants and vagrants. The resident Sardinian Warbler *Sylvia melanocephala* breeds in most habitats, including suburban areas, while the Short-Toed Lark *Calandrella brachydactyla*, which is a summer visitor, inhabits the open countryside, particularly in Gozo. The Zitting Cisticola *Cisticola juncidis*, which colonised the islands some thirty years ago, is now very common and widespread. Bird migration dominates the Maltese ornithological year, and in spring and autumn a consistent migration of birds occurs through the islands. Large numbers are frequently seen during adverse weather conditions.

The most interesting mammal species is the Sicilian Shrew *Crocidura sicula*, which has been recorded only in Sicily, Ustica, Egadi and Gozo. Its subspecies *calypso* occurs only in Gozo. On the other hand mammal species which are found on the island of Malta, such as the Weasel *Mustela nivalis* and the Pygmy White-Toothed Shrew *Suncus etruscus* are not recorded from Gozo. Of the ten species of bats recorded, five are residents. One of these belongs to a local race of the Lesser

Mouse-Eared Bat *Myothis blythii*. Another interesting mammal species is the Vagrant Hedgehog *Aterelix algirus*, which as in most species of mammals found here, other than bats, has been introduced after humans colonised the islands.

Areas of Natural Importance

Given the small size of the islands, approximately 7000 years of human occupancy, a relatively large population of some 400,000 people, 98.5 square km of developed land and 150 square km of land under cultivation, it is surprising to note that the islands still support several sites of natural importance. Foremost among these are the minor islands, particularly Filfla, Fungus Rock and St Paul's islands. There are also several other naturally important areas on the two main islands.

Buskett is the only site that represents a mature woodland ecosystem. It is actually semi-artificial woodland, fairly characteristic of a Mediterranean evergreen wood. The Aleppo Pines, Evergreen Oak, Olive and Carob are the dominant trees here, together with a number of smaller trees and shrubs such as Lentisk and Mediterranean Buckthorn, among several others. In the adjoining Wied il-Luq valley there is a narrow strip of deciduous woodland consisting mainly of Ash *Fraxinus angustifolia* and White Poplar *Populus alba*. It was in the thick vegetation along this valley and the nearby green area at Girgenti that the Cetti's Warbler *Cettia cetti* established itself some thirty-six years ago as a new breeding bird in the islands, from where it extended its breeding range to other suitable localities. Buskett is also an important roosting site for migrants, notably raptors, particularly the Honey Buzzard *Pernis apivorus* and Marsh Harrier *Circus aeruginosus*, as well as an important site for passage and wintering passerines.

The nature reserves at Għadira and Simar in the northern part of mainland Malta are the only two restored and engineered wetlands, both rich in biodiversity. Għadira is a saline marshland with several halophytic plants and supports a very diverse entomofauna, including a population of the fossorial Sand Cricket *Brachytripes megacephalus*. The Tamarisk, *Tamarix africana* and *Tamarix gallica*, are the dominant trees, while the lesser tassel-pondweed *Ruppia drapensis*, which grows submerged in the water, is only known from this site in Malta. Birds are the main attraction here with several waders and other water birds occurring regularly. The Little Ringed Plover *Charadrius dubius* has been breeding regularly here for the first time in Malta for the last five years. At Simar the Common Reed *Phragmites australis* provides suitable habitat for small populations of Moorhen *Gallinula chloropus* and Reed Warbler *Acrocephalus scirpaceus*, two newly established bird species since engineering works helped to create a permanent wetland. The Killifish *Aphianus fasciatus*, the only brackish water fish found in the islands, occurs at both wetland areas.

The 2.02 ha. islet of Filfla is a strict nature reserve and is important for supporting various interesting species. The endemic lizard *Podarcis Filfolensis*

The Filfla lizard is endemic to the islet of Filfla (Photo: Joe Sultana)

The hedgehog is one of the few mammals to be found on the islands (Photo: Joe Sultana)

Maltese Centaury – the endemic national plant which grows on the southern cliffs of Malta and Gozo (Photo: Joe Sultana)

The Maltese everlasting (Semprevyva ta' Għawdex) – an endemic plant found in the Dwejra area and on Fungus Rock (Photo: Joe Sultana)

filfolensis and an endemic subspecies of a land snail of the genus *Trochoidea* are known only from this islet. It also supports one of the largest known colonies of the Mediterranean race of the European Storm Petrel *Hydrobates pelagicus melitensis*, and smaller colonies of Cory's Shearwater *Calonectris diomedea* and Yellow-Legged Gull *Larus cachinnans,* the latter being the only colony of this species found in the islands. A large form of the Wild Leek *Allium commutatum*, grows profusely on the plateau surface of the islet. Another subspecies of the Maltese Wall Lizard, *Podarcis filfolensis kieselbachi*, is endemic to St Paul's islands, another site of ecological importance. St Paul's islands, which have an area of about ten hectares and are situated off Selmun, are also the only site for Cretan Pellitory *Parietaria cretica*.

Another important islet is Fungus Rock, which stands in front of one of the collapse depressions at Dwejra, Gozo.

Dwejra is a geological complex which is on top of the list of Gozo's ecological sites. Here one can find geological formations, slickensides, collapse structures, quaternary deposits, a unique topography, and a diversity of habitats, including a freshwater pool. Fungus Rock is not only the home of the famed Malta Fungus but also of another endemic subspecies of the Maltese Wall Lizard *Podarcis filfolensis generalensis*. This massive stack is known locally as Ħaġret il-Ġeneral or il-Ġebla tal-Ġeneral and is also a strict nature reserve.

Il-Qawra is also a subcircular collapse depression, which includes what is popularly known as the 'inland sea', surrounded by a couple of valley mouths, cliff sides, a steep sided ridge, clayey slopes and long uncultivated fields. The endemic Maltese Sea-Chamomile *Anthemis urvilleana*, a low-growing plant, which is frequent in seaside habitats, is one of the interesting flora species which grow in the area. Il-Qattara, a permanent freshwater pool fed by a perennial trickling spring, is also found in this depression. This permanent freshwater pool abounds with water life particularly in summer, when the surrounding area is parched dry. Close to the pool there are fine stands of Chaste-Tree *Vitex agnus-castus*. The rare Maltese Toadflax *Linaria pseudolaxiflora*, a Pelago-Maltese endemic, also grows in the Dwejra area.

Several species of insects, including diving water beetles and water boatman, dragonflies, and wasps, are common here. The richness of the pool's fauna includes a number of freshwater snails, which are found in the spring trickling into the pool.

The Corn Bunting *Miliaria calandra*, which has almost disappeared from the island of Malta and has decreased drastically in Gozo, still visits the pool during the summer months. The whole area of Dwejra is one of the few areas where one or two pairs of Corn Bunting still breed. This species, which prefers open country with a few or no trees, builds the nest on the ground among herbage. Dwejra is also one of the remaining posts where another declining species, the Spectacled Warbler *Sylvia conspicillata,* is still found breeding. It is a shy, resident species, frequenting open countryside, preferring low-growing shrubs as a nesting site.

Another site of ecological importance is the extensive rocky area at Ta' Ċenċ in Gozo. Apart from the beautiful landscape provided by the massive lower coralline limestone cliffs, the area is recognised for its garigue vegetation, parts of which are dominated by the Tree Spurge *Euphorbia dendroides* or the Mediterranean Thyme *Thymbra capitata*. The Common Pyramidal Orchid *Anacamptis pyramidalis*, the French Daffodil *Narcissus tazetta*, the Large Star of Bethlehem *Ornithogalum arabicum* and the Blue Stonecrop *Sedum caeruleum* are few of several common flowering plants that grow here, providing an extensive natural rock garden.

Ta' Ċenċ also qualifies as an international important bird area. The cliffs support the largest colony of Cory's Shearwaters *Calonectris diomedea* in the Maltese islands, and are a stronghold of the national bird, the Blue Rock Thrush *Monticola solitarius*. The cliff-top rocky area is a good breeding site for the Short-Toed Lark *Calandrella brachydactyla* and the Spectacled Warbler *Sylvia conspicillata*, while the Peregrine Falcon *Falco peregrinus* and the Barn Owl *Tyto alba* used to breed in the cliffs. Quite recently a small colony of the Mediterranean race of the European Storm-Petrel *Hydrobates pelagicus melitensis* has been rediscovered breeding in one of the numerous sea caves below the cliffs.

The valleys in Gozo harbour very interesting vegetation and support a wide variety of fauna species. The Xlendi valley system is among the most remarkable ones. It includes Wied il-Lunzjata and carries a permanent freshwater spring which supports a number of interesting flora and fauna species, including the rare Fresh Water Crab *Potamon fluviatile lanfroncoi*. The rare Dwarf Elder *Sambucus ebulus* can be found growing here. It is also the only place in the Maltese islands for the predatory leech *Haemopis sanguisuga*, as well as the breeding ground for the semi-aquatic grasshopper *Paratettetix meridionalis*. Towards Xlendi, one can also encounter the locally rare Sicilian Iris *Iris sicula*, an endemic plant to Sicily and Malta.

As can be seen from the above, the Maltese islands, in spite of their small size, a limited number of habitats, and an enormous pressure on their natural environment by a relatively high human population, are very rich in flora and fauna. The present Maltese generations hold this natural heritage in trust, and thus have a grave responsibility to conserve it for future generations.

References

Lanfranco, E., 'The Flora and Vegetation of Gozo', in Farrugia, J. and Briguglio, L. (eds), *A Focus on Gozo* (Malta, 1996).
Lanfranco, E. and Lanfranco, G., *Il-Flora Maltija* (Malta, 2003).
Lanfranco, S., *L-Ambjent Naturali tal-Gżejjer Maltin* (Malta, 2002).
Schembri, P. J., Lanfranco, E., Farrugia, P., Schembri, S. and Sultana J., *Localities with Conservation Values in the Maltese islands* (Malta, 1987).
Schembri, P. J. and Sultana, J. (eds), *Red Data Book for the Maltese Islands* (Malta, 1989).
Schembri, P. J., 'Current state of knowledge of the Maltese non-marine fauna', in *Malta Environment and Planning Authority – Annual Report and Accounts 2003* (Malta, 2003).
Sultana, J. (ed.), *Flora u Fawna ta' Malta* (Malta, 1995).
Sultana, J. and Falzon, V. (eds), *Wildlife of the Maltese islands* (Malta, 2002).

PART TWO

MALTA IN HISTORY

Anthony Pace

MALTA DURING PREHISTORY: AN OVERVIEW

The purpose of this brief overview is that of presenting a tentative bird's eye perspective of Maltese prehistory. The Maltese islands are blessed with an archaeological heritage that is steadily gaining more recognition and attention. Foremost elements of this important heritage are the megalithic structures that were constructed in their present form between 3600 and 2500 BC. The origin of these structures is still a matter of debate. But their mere presence in the Maltese landscape, and their survival after several millennia, has now captured the imagination of scholars and visitors alike. The Maltese megalithic structures are uniquely positioned in our understanding of the archipelago's prehistory. The stature of these monuments often obscures other important developments that left a mark on Malta's longest period of cultural development. Like many aspects of material culture, the Maltese megalithic buildings were a product of their socio-cultural context. The monuments were preceded by centuries of occupation, and were eclipsed by later developments that were geo-culturally broader than the immediate confines of the Maltese islands. An attempt to fully understand such developments will remain partial. The time spans involved are long. Permanent human occupation of the islands is known to have started during the closing centuries of the sixth millennium BC. Maltese prehistory came to an end some time during the seventh century BC.

A Prelude

The occupation of the Maltese islands during recent prehistory was the result of a number of interconnected developments that occurred unevenly over a series of centuries. These developments can be conveniently grouped into environmental changes, technological innovations and culture change. These simplified groupings represent a very broad and highly complex context that was the product of a particular era, the post-glacial period of recent prehistory. Central to these developments was cultural adaptation to environmental changes. Such adaptations were mostly successful because of important technological innovations, such as the consolidation of the domestication of a selection of plant and animal food resources, as well as maritime activity in various regions of the Mediterranean. Ultimately, these changes and innovations formed part of an important cultural development that saw hundreds of communities adopting farming and pastoral life-styles in preference to hunting and gathering economies. Scholars now believe that this transition, which took place over several millennia, was not simply a choice between diverse subsistence economies. It is well known that hunter-gatherer societies could achieve a sustainable subsistence economy, even though this may have conditioned demographic growth, the size of communities and the permanent settlement of landscapes. Agriculture allowed a different life-style that could combine farming with pastoralism as well as hunting and gathering. Requiring longer residence in strategic areas that had been transformed into farmsteads, agriculture encouraged longer seasonal occupation and permanent settlement, a prospect that was not always possible among hunter-gatherer societies. The increasing selection and use of arable soils enabled geographically focused settlement, and the intensive exploitation of land parcels. This possibility demanded less travelling and provided a technological mechanism that would transform food production that was not dependent on managed herding or the trans-geographical movement of large animal herds. Enabling the long-term occupation of land also meant that larger tracts of the ancient landscape could be permanently settled, thus allowing various environments to be used irrespective of their remoteness and geographic location. Such developments would in time enable the permanent colonisation of islands.

The environmental and climatic changes that led to the end of the last ice age set in motion long-term changes.[1] Between 25,000 BC and 7,000 BC, the edges of the ice caps created during the last ice age reached their maximum extent. The ice sheets had by then expanded all the way down to the European Alps. Europe and the Mediterranean were characterised by colder climates and were occupied by hunter-gatherers who exploited animal herds and plant resources. Everywhere, the cold climate led to a significant lowering of sea levels. As the ice sheets expanded, large amounts of water evaporated and turned into ice. The lowering of the sea levels is believed to have averaged about 120 metres throughout the Mediterranean.[2] Around this time, the Maltese islands formed part of the continental land mass, effectively the southernmost tip of what is now Sicily.[3] It is quite plausible that hunter-gatherers would have ventured all the way down to present-day Malta at this juncture. Evidence for such a possibility is, however, lacking.

The thawing of the ice and the rapid refilling of the Mediterranean was relatively rapid in terms of geological time. The effects of this phenomenon would have been extremely conspicuous, and witnessed by many generations of hunter-gatherers. The loss of land would have been dramatic, with all low-lying land being steadily drowned. Given the time spans involved, one cannot exclude the possibility that rising waters would have persisted in collective memory. Could such memories, however vague and legendary, linger long enough to implant themselves on later creation myths and other stories? The melting of the ice was linked to global warming. Around 12,000 BC, climatic conditions began to change rapidly. Oceanographic research suggests that a major influx of melt water left a mark on seas and oceans. By about 7,000 BC, the Mediterranean land bridges and lower grounds had almost totally disappeared, almost giving the sea much of its present-day configurations.[4] The rise in sea level may have slowed down around this time. By the Għar Dalam phase (5200 BC) the Maltese islands would have been cut off from Sicily, but may still have retained the last remaining areas of low-lying territory, especially on the north coast of the archipelago.

These dramatic climatic changes invariably led to significant transformations of the environment. These changes can be characterised in many ways. On the one hand, a certain degree of environmental stress could be envisaged, although the precise impact of such forces on existing global and regional populations may now be difficult to ascertain.

It was during these post-glacial developments that the management of selected plant and animal food resources became more important. Now associated with the terms agriculture or the Neolithic, the domestication of plants and animals provided a sustainable subsistence economy that would allow the settlement of difficult and remote parts of the world. The spread and adoption of agriculture was gradual and uneven.[5] By the eighth millennium BC, the new life-style had arrived in the central Mediterranean.

The First Millennium of Permanent Occupation 5200-4000 BC

Impressed pottery associated with a Neolithic life-style, and assigned to the Għar Dalam phase (5200 BC) marks the arrival of agriculture in the Maltese islands.[6] As often is the case for the prehistory of humankind, the identification of a specific event is a rare occurrence. Indeed, there is no reason to exclude the possibility that the adoption of the Neolithic was a prolonged affair. The Maltese Early Neolithic can be characterised as having involved a period of initial contact followed by the establishment of a more permanent use of the archipelago. Geographically and culturally, the Maltese islands may not have been so foreign and aloof to the inhabitants of nearby Sicily. Contact with the Maltese islands may have been motivated by a number of factors. The possibility of prospecting for mineral resources or lithics, the seasonal or periodical visits by hunters, sea-craft thrown off course and many other causes, would have been a prime mechanism for contact. Navigation would not have been free of risk, but a number of important factors

The central chamber of the Ħal Saflieni Hypogeum (Photo: MTA)

Aerial view of Ġgantija temples, Gozo, the most impressive of all temples (Photo: MTA)

served to improve sea voyages in the Sicily-Malta channel. From Sicily, the position of Malta and Gozo would have been highlighted by cloud cover. It would have been possible to keep a landmark in sight for substantial parts of the channel crossing. On exceptional days, depending on the number of rowers, favourable winds and sea currents, the voyage to Malta would have probably been achieved in about a day. The risk of longer and unpredictable crossings was however, always present. Communication was physical. Once out of earshot and eye contact, mariners would have been out of contact. Communication was therefore time consuming and unpredictable. Careful planning and sailing between late spring and autumn, would have improved seafaring opportunities. Although sea craft of the period have not yet been discovered, one can expect that these would have been advanced enough to transport cattle, and other animal farms as well as wheat stocks along with people.

Judging by imports and a number of similarities in pottery design between Maltese and Sicilian wares from the Għar Dalam to the end of the Skorba phases (5200 – 4000 BC), it would seem that contacts across the Sicily-Malta channel were maintained[7] even if such contacts cannot be characterised in terms of frequency and volume. From the very beginning, the farming communities of the Maltese islands lived in 'an in-between' reality of land and seascapes. The Sicily-Malta channel provided the main corridor of communication because it provided the shortest crossings as well as the only visual contact with landmarks. Once on the Sicilian coast, Malta's prehistoric mariners could interact with a broader world of fellow travellers, even visiting other important centres if circumstances permitted. A striking feature of the Maltese Early Neolithic is the importation of raw materials from an extensive geographic area. Whether this involved direct contact between Malta and other outlying islands is a matter of debate. But it is clear that a certain degree of trans-regional contacts and communication filtering took place via inter-connected exchange networks. After the passage of so many millennia, these networks are now represented by a limited but very indicative repertoire of imported materials. A few likely sources for imported flint, such as the grey-buff coloured type may have originated from sources found in the Monti Iblei. Etna may have been a likely source for lava, which was locally used in querns. Hard stones used in making polished stone axes may have been originally extracted from Sicily's Monti Peloritani or from Calabria's Aspromonte ranges.[8] Finally, fine obsidian cores made their way to the Maltese islands from Pantelleria in the west, or from Lipari, located to the north of Sicily.[9] Beyond the navigational corridor of the Sicily-Malta channel therefore, the inhabitants of early Neolithic Malta established patterns of travelling, communication and exchange that were in themselves linked to a much broader area than the immediacy of the central Mediterranean. In later centuries, such networks would leave an impact on the development of Maltese prehistory. Closer to home, Malta's Early Neolithic farmers embarked on establishing and consolidating settlements. An understanding of this period still lacks a general regional analysis, so that it is often difficult to characterise the period in terms of demography, the use of field systems, the possible seasonal use of different settlements, pastoralism and its effects on the archipelago's environment. Some evidence for cave settlements has been retrieved from such sites as Għar Dalam and Għajn Abdul. The village of Skorba, the sites of Taċ-Ċawla and Is-Sruġ (Gozo) and a few other locations suggest that open villages were also established in strategic locations. At Skorba, the survival of walls and hut floors suggests that these early villages had been laid out with a degree of complexity that may have included enclosures around domestic buildings. Other sites of the Early Neolithic may have been partly buried by the later construction of the megalithic structures during the Later Neolithic. This appears to be the case at Ta' Ħaġrat, where J.D. Evans counted Għar Dalam sherds among the surviving pottery residues.

The archaeological record for the centuries 4500 to 4100 BC following the Għar Dalam phase, provides a clearer picture of the next stages of the Maltese Early Neolithic. At Skorba, David Trump excavated a megalithic site that had already been discovered by Sir Temi Zammit[10] and partially investigated by Captain C. Zammit.[11] Initially, Skorba attracted attention because of the site's upright megaliths. Trump uncovered the remains of a village, or a complex arrangement of buildings. Skorba provides insights into the environment, as well as some socio-cultural aspects of the time. Broadly speaking, the village of Skorba reflects a diversified use of rudimentary architecture in a setting that was experiencing profound environmental changes. Inevitably, agriculture and related technology meant a transformation of the landscape. Farming and pastoral activity required field management and the probable clearing of original vegetation. Pastoral activity would have hastened the clearing process. At Skorba, the discovery of pollen grains of the Judas tree (*Cercis siliquastrum*), hawthorn (*Crataegus*) and ash (*Fraxinus*) suggests some of the tree species that made up Malta's ancient woodlands.[12] Future research will no doubt shed more light on the extent, thickness and nature of such woodland. The Skorba discoveries also suggest that as early as the Għar Dalam phase an Anatolian type of lentil, barley, emmer and Field Madder[13] also characterised the archipelago's landscape. The most significant discovery from Red Skorba village phases was that of a complex building which yielded a number of figurines, as well as a number of goat skulls that had been treated in a distinctive manner. The find-spot of these items was interpreted as a shrine by David Trump. Whatever the case, the figurines and treated goat skulls suggest that distinct spaces were set aside specifically for ritual or religious purposes. The distinction between the sacred and the secular was one of the main factors that was then to flourish during the Later Neolithic. Throughout this period, the Skorba villagers participated in exchange systems, initially internal, but ultimately linked to Sicilian and central Mediterranean networks. The village of Skorba was established within easy reach of the protected port of Ġnejna bay. The village commanded a strategic location and had easy access to one of the archipelago's fertile valleys. Access to the sea, the command of natural resources such as springs, lithic and clay sources as well as the land that was well-suited for cultivation, became some of the main qualities that were to characterise many of the megalithic structures of the Later Neolithic.[14] In effect, Skorba may be symptomatic of land use during Maltese prehistory, in the sense that many of the archipelago's strategic locations were already occupied within the first millennium of Malta's Neolithic.

The Rise of Megalithic Malta (4200-2500 BC)

The rise of 'megalithic Malta' marked a distinct development in Maltese prehistory. In terms of carbon dates,[15] the period appears to have covered over a millennium and a half. The archaeological repertoire of the period is complex and reflects a diversified worldview of the archipelago's communities. This worldview can only be partially reconstructed. However, from an impressive array of chamber tombs, buildings and works of art, one can get a sense that the islanders were equally at home expressing belief systems, undertake astronomical measurements, organise large scale construction projects along with the mundane requirements required for survival. As a convenient point of departure, the period can be characterised in terms of three very broad inter-related groups of archaeological remains. The first group comprises rock-cut tombs and underground cemeteries; the second covers a range of megalithic monuments spread across the landscape; the third, comprises diverse repertoire of art works and objects that were discovered in both chamber tombs and temples.[16]

The period opens with the Żebbuġ phase (4000 - 3800 BC), which is reflected in new ceramic designs as well as the adoption of rock-cut chamber tombs. These chamber tombs were related to central Mediterranean broader mortuary practices.[17] In Sicily, rock chamber tombs were associated with material of the San Cono - Piano Notaro region. Żebbuġ phase pottery is believed to reflect ceramic designs of this Sicilian region. The introduction of rock-cut chamber tombs is a reflection that the Maltese islands were still very much connected to the cultural realities of the central Mediterranean. However, the Maltese experience took on a highly localised evolution. Two general trends are conspicuous above others. Firstly, Maltese chamber tombs formed the nucleus of a process that saw the gradual expansion of particular tombs into large underground cemeteries. Secondly this process, which followed a stage-by-stage development, was linked to the development of the megalithic temples.[18] Originally rock-cut chamber tombs consisted of underground chambers that were accessed through shafts. Tombs of this type were discovered in groups as in the case of Xemxija or at the Xagħra Circle. At Ta' Trapna and San Pawl Milqi, burials of this period appear to have taken place in shallow hollows. Burial chambers were used repeatedly for collective inhumations over several centuries, suggesting that generation after generation of inhabitants chose to use the same chamber tombs. Chambers served for primary burials as well as ossuaries. The dead were buried with votive offerings that

Aerial view of the entrance to Ħaġar Qim temple (Photo: MTA)

Mnajdra Temples in Qrendi (Photo: MTA)

consisted primarily of personal embellishments, pots and other small objects. In time, burials became more complex with more elaborate artworks, such as statuettes and highly decorated ceramic vessels, flint and chert blades, obsidian flakes, as well as imported materials. The votive offerings may have been related to the social standing that the deceased may have commanded in life. The significance of collective burials may have assumed particular social significance. Rather than cutting hundreds of different tombs across the landscape, the archipelago's inhabitants concentrated their burials in carefully selected locations, a physical manifestation of a collective funerary concern.[19] Was this practice a reflection of social identity? The repeated use of chamber tombs may have also been a way to assert a sense of the past as well as an active mechanism to maintain kinship ties. In Malta, such customs led to the development of central cemeteries and the disappearance of smaller outlying ones, a phenomenon that is reflected in site and settlement patterning across the Maltese landscape.[20] The elaborate spaces of the Ħal Saflieni Hypogeum and the Xagħra Circle appear to have been a product of this process. The elaborate monumentality of underground cemeteries reflects a profound commitment to a belief system that structured concepts of the underworld that could literally be accessed during ceremonies and rituals.

Beyond the complex belief system that may have influenced perceptions of the underworld, an equally complex social structure of customs and rules was required in order that a series of elaborate megalithic buildings could be constructed in various locations of Malta and Gozo. Some scholars now believe that once established, this series of megalithic buildings may have in turn asserted a momentous influence on prevailing social structures and customs. Thus whether influenced or not by utilitarian needs, the construction or destruction of buildings are phenomena which convey social statements.

The second phenomenon of Malta's Late Neolithic comprises the building of a series of megalithic structures across the archipelago's landscape. The origins of Malta's megalithic architecture are a matter of discussion. In the 1950s, J. D. Evans suggested that the plans of the temples may have been derived from rock-cut chamber tombs found at Xemxija. Evans based his theory on presence of lobed spaces in both temples and the Xemxija tombs. This link is, however, only typological.[21] The Early Neolithic levels at Skorba suggest that the building of shrines had already been established. This building tradition may have eventually evolved into the megalithic architecture of the Late Neolithic period. However, these evolutionary steps may have been obscured by periodical alterations and enlargements. Skorba itself appears to have experienced many of these stages. David Trump's excavations revealed a series of floors and other structural features that have been dated to both the Early and Late Neolithic. Around 3600 BC, Malta and Gozo appear to have experienced a wave of construction that led to the building of several megalithic monuments in various locations of the islands. Was this a single combined effort, representing a single event? Time and the limitations of archaeology, unfortunately preclude a clear resolution of this question, although a refinement of available information in the future may throw more light on this matter. In any case, the carbon date of 3600 BC, provides a convenient landmark. This megalithic architecture, often referred to as temple architecture, was meant to be exceptionally monumental and complex in design. The temples would have served several purposes. Monumentality requires durable structures that could have a long-term impact on the landscape. The monuments would therefore have served a primary function of public building that would have symbolic meaning across the landscape. The choice, transportation and use of megaliths cannot be underestimated. Construction required the mobilisation and organisation of human resources. Such a mobilisation would have been successful if a good degree of social stability and coherence prevailed across the islands. Although it is now difficult to establish whether such communal projects had been forced or negotiated,[22] the building of so many megalith buildings still reflects a level of widespread success in a social system that could create such an infrastructure. Some scholars look upon the Maltese temples as central focus points for regional or territorial divisions.[23] Other theories have elaborated this theme, suggesting the possibility that the temples radiate intra-community rivalry and competition.[24] Whatever the cause behind the success of megalithic Malta, one can hardly imagine that small communities would refrain from providing building services wherever this may have been needed. One conspicuous characteristic of the Maltese temples is their coherent use of common architectural forms, structural engineering, aesthetics and repertoire of objects. Although particular temples exhibit specific design peculiarities, the structures still exhibit a coherent philosophy. This may be a reflection of successful social cohesion and co-operation rather than rivalry. The overall population of the two islands has been estimated as possibly not exceeding a figure of 7,000 or 10,000.[25] Although dispersed across the two islands, communities would have been linked through lineage and other social bonds. The function of the temples remains a matter of speculation.[26] Temple construction followed a few basic principles. First, the Late Neolithic structures were supposed to be visually impressive. Temple facades were designed to dwarf spectators without losing a comfortable human scale. Facades were also laid out to a concave alignment. Entrances were strategically placed in the middle of the concave facade. A temple facade delineated a line between the interior and exterior of the buildings. The facade could deflect attention from the interior of the buildings. Temples were also served by a plaza, where public gatherings may have taken place. One intriguing question still revolves around whether access and movement within the buildings was regulated. Temple interiors were decorated with refined carvings of abstract spirals or animal representations. Beautifully hand-crafted altars, niches and other installations were important elements of a temple interior.[27]

The art of Late Neolithic Malta is the third group of attributes which help us to understand the period.[28] The art of the temple period is varied and reflects a diversified cosmology. Art works were normally small, almost domestic-like. Exceptions to this rule were those statues, carved altars and megaliths that were placed in temples for public use. The temple period art repertoire can be classified in various categories. Convenient starting points are such categories as abstract art, the representation of animals, the representation of astrological bodies, ceramic design and the representation of the human figure. The more conspicuous elements of abstract art are the renowned spirals. These designs come in a number of variations and sizes. No set of spirals looks alike. In addition a number of variations on the spiral theme were also created. With a few exceptions, the spirals were not incised. Each design required careful planning and execution. The stone face chosen to receive the spiral decoration was first dressed down to a uniform finish. In some cases the edge of the entire composition was defined. The spirals themselves were carefully measured and possibly drawn out. Craftsmen then scooped out the stone around the prepared design so that the spirals emerged as an embossed carving. The spirals are invariably set in a strict composition, normally a two-tier layout. Typically, Maltese spirals are not organic in appearance, as is often the case with other examples known from elsewhere in the ancient world. Animals in art is of course a dominant category of Maltese Late Neolithic art. The repertoire of animal representations covers a series of farm animals, birds, fish, snakes and reptiles. The representations are remarkably realistic. Understandably, the presence of cattle, pigs and goats loomed high in the lives of the archipelago's inhabitants. The iconography of farm animals was therefore given prominence not only on personalised items such as decorated pots and ceramic vessels, but more importantly on megaliths that were given a prominent function within the temples. At the Tarxien temples, large carvings of bulls were cut on huge megaliths within a particular chamber, while two low-lying altars found in one of the outer apses of the temple complex showed herds of goats and pigs. Such animals were of course valuable resources. Their loss would have spelt serious problems for the islanders who would have had to replenish their stock from Sicily. At worst, the loss of farm animals would have increased the risk of famine. Another source of artistic inspiration was of course the human figure. The oldest representation of the human figure so far known in the Maltese islands, dates back to the Red Skorba phase of the Early Neolithic. During the Żebbuġ phase stylised figures were painted or incised on ceramic ware, while statue menhirs were carved as part of the funerary ensembles of burials. Later, the human representations become more varied. The more conspicuous figurines and statues represent obese figures. However, a number of other small statues reflect a certain degree of realism, some reflecting deformities and possible medical problems, others showing simply a high degree of modelling. The statues were in the main part discovered without heads. In some cases heads were intentionally broken off; in other cases statues were provided with a shaft in which heads could be fixed. The removal of heads, or the temporary nature of heads may have been tied to specific ceremonies. Figurines have been discovered in burial contexts as well as in megalithic structures. With a few notable exceptions, figurines were small and portable. In many cases figurines were made of local stone and clay; in a few cases figurines were made of imported

The Xagħra Circle in Gozo (Photo: MTA)

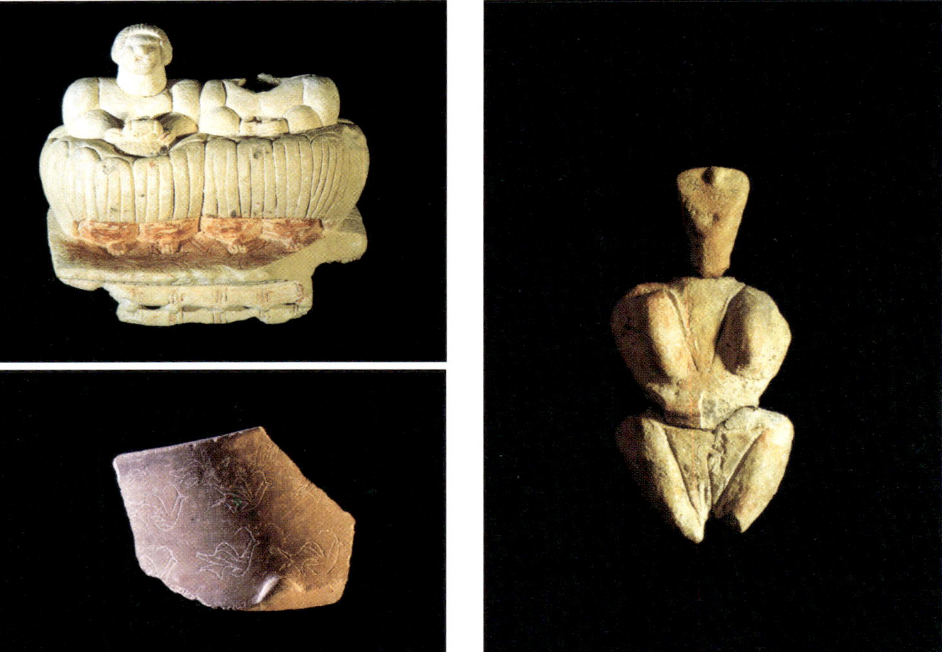

Top: Seated figures from the Xagħra Circle; above left: birds on a sherd from Ġgantija; above right: a stylised figurine from Skorba (Photo: MTA)

materials. The design of ceramic vessels has often been reduced to a non-art status. While vessels were primarily meant to be functional, their actual manufacture and decoration was a highly personalised task. Forms were created and given distinctive decorations that were either finely incised or painted. During the Tarxien phase, ceramic designs reached their most complex forms. Finally, apart from the more day to day themes of iconography, one or two items point to other interests, such as the representation of astronomical bodies. Although using rudimentary technology, the islanders are thought to have been well-versed in charting astronomical phenomena. Seasonal measurement of critical annual intervals, such as the solstice and equinox, would have been important not only to map the passing of time, but also for agricultural purposes, the beginning of the sailing season and various other social and ritual events.

The Age of Metal and the Demise of Megalithic Culture

The demise of the megalithic culture in the Maltese islands, is marked by changes in the archaeological remains that are dated to about 2500 BC.[29] The changes are diverse and particularly distinct as to suggest a complete break with the Maltese Later Neolithic. Traditionally, some scholars have characterised this period of change as one that involved an immigration of newcomers who found a deserted archipelago. A 'sterile' layer covered by a cremation cemetery noted at the Tarxien temples by Temi Zammit has often been invoked as the best evidence for this. This over emphasis on a single stratum, has historically coloured studies in Maltese prehistory with claims of abrupt cultural discontinuity. However, it is doubtful whether discontinuity, the total abandonment of the Maltese islands or, to that matter, continuity, can be easily illustrated archaeologically. Cultural change can often be distorted by the prolonged use or reuse of sites, effectively, a distortion of an already distorted past as a result of centuries-old taphonomy. Change itself is an elusive phenomenon, precisely because it embodies both continuities and discontinuities. At the same time examples of abrupt events, such as the destruction of Akrotiri on the Greek island of Thera, or the destruction of Pompeii, are rare occurrences in archaeology. Can changes, such as the sudden abandonment of an entire archipelago, or the sudden annihilation of an entire population be grasped from archaeology? How and to what extent can catastrophe theory be illustrated archaeologically? Was the demise of the temple period really so sudden, as we have traditionally believed? Such questions will continue to colour archaeology, often awaiting future refinement of available information.

To begin with, the end of the temple period took place at a particular juncture of Mediterranean history, in a manner that was not unlike the spread of agriculture so many millennia before. This time, the end of the Neolithic was marked by the emergence of the metal ages,[30] an oversimplification of change which is still in use for want of a better terminology. By the end of the Neolithic in Malta and Gozo, important centres of metal production were steadily leaving a mark on other regions of the Mediterranean. The period has often been characterised by a sense of increased transhumance and the transformation of social and cultural values. Identity and cultural significance came to be understood in ways that were clearly different, and less dependent on large-scale communal undertakings such as the building of megalith temples. The Maltese Bronze Age is characterised by a material culture that is distinct from that of the temple period. The old temples were used for different purposes. Smaller monuments were built across a different landscape. Ceramic designs bore a distinct departure from existing designs. Prestige and value were now marked by copper and metal axes. Connections with the metal producing centres of the Mediterranean became more pronounced as the islanders participated in new exchange networks. Networking, maritime travel, geography, environmental realities, and a strong agricultural base remained important components of the ancient world, so that in reality factors of continuity may have been extremely strong, forming a backbone of prehistoric societies.

What was the general background to the Maltese Bronze Age? At the end of the third millennium BC, the importance of metallurgy became more important. Metal had already been in use in several uneven forms, during preceding centuries. Across Europe and the Mediterranean, the circulation of copper and bronze objects steadily became more widespread as extraction and pyrotechnical innovations were perfected. The manufacture of metal objects, their possession, use, circulation and control coincided with the emergence of new symbols, belief systems, technological innovation, commerce, and social customs.[31] It is now believed that prestige, hierarchy and a new sense of wealth began to leave a mark on agrarian and pastoral society. Across Europe and the Mediterranean, these changes may have also accelerated trade, exchange and maritime activity. New exchange systems emerged with the increasing circulation of prestigious objects made of bronze, gold, ceramic and other materials, among leading communities and major village settlements. The Bronze Age is also marked by the emergence and consolidation of the first urban communities that, in various parts of Europe and the Mediterranean, were concentrated in townships. Such developments were uneven, with the most spectacular achievements being those reached in the Aegean. Here, communities adopted and developed writing, language, the arts and, many believe, political structures. Such developments are thought to have been accompanied by demographic increases, which although geographically uneven, were beginning to have an impact on larger regions. In the Maltese islands this phenomenon is reflected in the establishment of large settlements, on hilltops or defended promontories, during the Borġ in-Nadur phase.

Like the Neolithic, the Maltese Bronze Age was an extremely long period, spanning the period between 2500 BC and the eighth century BC. For over a millennium and a half, the Maltese islands experienced at least three phases of innovation, which are traditionally referred to as the Tarxien Cemetery (2500-1500 BC), Borġ in-Nadur (1500-900 BC) and Baħrija (900 BC to about 870 BC). This long period can also be approached in terms of two very broad phases, an Early Bronze Age and a Later Bronze Age. A number of foreign connections improve our characterisation of the Maltese Bronze Age. The islanders maintained links with Sicily, but there are numerous hints of broader connections with Southern Italy, Greece and the Aegean. Unlike the Neolithic, during which connections appear to have been mostly concentrated on the immediate neighbouring lands and islands, the Bronze Age is characterised by links with the East, particularly with the Aegean. Pottery from far away as Thermi in the north-east Aegean, has been located in Late Neolithic levels at Skorba[32] and at the Tarxien temples.[33] As usual the intensity and general character of foreign contacts is problematic. The Maltese islands may have been peripheral to the growing trade centres that were steadily dominating the Aegean, Greece and Italy. These centres, along with many others, foreshadowed the emergence of the city-state and proto-urban societies. What was the role of small islands in this new world order? In particular, what were the characteristics of island life for the inhabitants of the Maltese islands? Was the emerging world order of the metal ages more far-reaching than the cultural and economic forces of the preceding Neolithic?

The Maltese Early Bronze Age began with the long Tarxien Cemetery phase. The period is named after Zammit's discovery of a cremation cemetery at the Tarxien temples. The more spectacular discoveries of this cremation cemetery consisted of new types of pottery and votive copper axes and daggers. Elsewhere across the archipelago, a new type of megalithic structure, the dolmen, made an appearance. At Tarxien, the upper layers of the existing megalithic structure had been partly used as a cremation cemetery. Zammit encountered a grey ashy deposit in which he found a number of cremated human remains which had been placed in urns. Together with these burial urns, a series of offerings consisting of ceramic vessels, personal ornaments and, in some special cases, axes and daggers were buried.

The Tarxien cremation cemetery represents a clear departure from the long established custom of collective inhumations in underground tombs, a cultural trait of the Maltese Later Neolithic. The undisputed use of metal fortified the idea of change and innovation. The preoccupation with megalithic monuments, albeit a different one, persisted. Scholars have recorded the residues of Tarxien Cemetery pottery at almost every Late Neolithic megalithic site. In the case of Tal-Qadi, a grey ashy deposit was also noted. The nature of the re-use of older megalithic buildings requires future research, but even a quick look at settlement distribution patterns across the Maltese landscape will show a persistent re-use of older temple period sites. Can this be a reliable indication of continuity and innovation?

What were the origins of the Tarxien Cemetery? As so often happens in Maltese archaeology, explanations of culture change and innovation are framed within the context of foreign contacts. In their extreme, such explanations still consider external contacts as a *deus ex machina* element of change. For instance it has traditionally been easier for some scholars to see the Tarxien Cemetery as the arrival of invaders and the destruction of the temples, without giving any consideration to the possibility of change being also a local response to regional innovations. Often, islanders are viewed as being isolated occupants of remote islands, immune to changes that occur elsewhere. Indeed, such a process is not unusual especially for a region that has for millennia experienced transhumance on large scales. The Tarxien Cemetery phase provides a sense of broader contacts between Malta and the central Mediterranean and the Aegean as far north as its north-eastern reaches. Another source of foreign influence is reflected in the similarity that exists between the Maltese dolmens and those found in the South Italian Apulia region around Otranto.[34] Dolmens were small monuments that consisted primarily of a raised capstone. The 'classical' dolmen would consist of a capstone supported by one or two low-lying megaliths or boulders. Variations occur however. Current research is showing that some dolmens simply consisted of a megalith raised at on end by an underlying stone. This method of building megalithic monuments marks a distinct break with the past. Dolmens are invariably less conspicuous than Late Neolithic monuments. In comparison to temples, dolmens were relatively easier to build, requiring large smaller groups of builders who could complete construction in one or two days at most. John Evans managed to date one particular dolmen, that located at Ta' Ħammut, after discovering Tarxien Cemetery pottery underneath the capstone.[35] Often, dolmens have been linked to funerary rituals, but clear evidence for this is lacking. The monuments may have indeed been linked to a form of ritual that may have been tied to valleys, watercourses and the sea. Invariably, the location of these monuments appears to have been strategically chosen. In the case of the dolmens found at Ta' Ċenċ, Ta' Ħammut, Wied Żnuber and Mosta, the use of landscape and seascape as a backdrop may have played an important role. The symbolic use of landscape therefore appears to have been of some significance. Finally, ceramic designs and a few odd objects associated with the Tarxien Cemetery are thought to reflect design elements that may have originated in Early and Middle Helladic Greece as well as Sicily and Capo Graziano on Lipari. The Xagħra Circle excavations suggest that the old obsidian trails of the central Mediterranean were still active to a point. Then there is the presence of the 'bossed bone plaque' fragment found at Tarxien, which more than any other object reflects Malta's links to other Mediterranean regions. Examples of the bone plaque have so far been found exclusively in south-east Sicily, south Italy, Greece and Troy. The elements of change introduced during the Maltese Early Bronze Age, therefore suggest a link to an Aegean-South Italian axis of communication, in which Apulia and Sicily played a dominant role.

The Borġ in-Nadur phase (after c. 1500 BC) marks the second major period of development of the Maltese Bronze Age. Borġ in-Nadur reflects local as well as external changes on a scale that appear to have been different from preceding ones. The Borġ in-Nadur phase was marked by a change of settlement patterns and the emergence of fortified townships, which occurred against the backdrop of a changing Mediterranean that now came to be dominated by palace-like complexes. The remains of complex buildings and citadels suggest that at Thapsos on Sicily, and certainly throughout the Mycenaean world, the proto-urban phenomenon was taking root. In the central Mediterranean, South Italy and Sicily appear to have provided a major destination for Aegean trade.[36] The South Italian –Aegean axis of trade and interaction was a dominant force that may have eclipsed the role of small islands. The small islands may have been marginalised, with places such as Malta and Gozo being for the most part excluded from main shipping lanes. But far from being isolated, islands such as Malta and Gozo may have resorted to maritime activity, possibly to capitalise on the major trade routes that were now setting the commercial pace in the Mediterranean. Such ideas are of course tentative, but the discovery of the Borġ in-Nadur ceramic vessels in tombs at Thapsos, in Sicily, is suggestive of the degree of interaction by the islanders. One theory has also suggested the possibility of migration of a group of people of Borġ in-Nadur origins.

Maritime activity may have been accompanied by a sense of insecurity. From this period, stories of piracy, warfare and illicit maritime activity have been immortalised in Homeric mythology and a number of other famous sea myths. Archaeology has so far failed to provide any direct evidence of violence during the Borġ in-Nadur phase. Nevertheless, fortified villages may have played an important role. On the south-west coast of Malta, the hill region running from Wardija ta' San Ġorġ near present day Siġġiewi, through Mdina, Mtarfa all the way to Baħrija, experienced a widespread establishment of villages. Hilltops were chosen for their defensive and strategic qualities. In some locations fortifications had to be built around village settlements, suggesting that the strategic location of a settlement had to be defended at all costs. A good example on Malta is the fortified wall at Borġ in-Nadur. On Gozo, the hills of Nuffara and the Cittadella were chosen for settlement purposes. In many of the Borġ in-Nadur settlements, a number of bell-shaped storage silos for grain, water reserves or general provisions, were cut in the rock. The extent and number of these village settlements suggest that the population of Malta and Gozo may have reached significant figures.

From the closing centuries of Maltese prehistory come the enigmatic cart-ruts. These curious features, running in sets of parallel rock-cut channels, have still not been properly explained or dated with certainty. At a number of sites, cart-ruts were cut by later, Punic tombs suggesting a date that would have at least been contemporary with Phoenician - Punic occupation. The cart-ruts would have been abandoned by that time. Some scholars have argued that many cart-ruts are known to lead directly to Borġ in-Nadur settlements, an argument which has been used to date the ruts to the Bronze Age. The lack of evidence of similar features in the rest of the Phoenician world appears to emphasise the local character of the ruts. Ruts have been noted in various Mediterranean localities, normally sites of classical origin, but parallels with the local features have remained tentative. The widespread absence of cart-ruts in the Phoenician world may be a reflection that cart-ruts did not in fact form part of the customary Phoenician infrastructure.

Maltese prehistory passes on into history at yet again another important juncture of Mediterranean history, the great colonising period of the eighth century BC. Once again, it is difficult to draw clear conclusions on where prehistory is supposed to end. The seventh century BC saw the Greeks establishing their colonies in the West, accompanied by Phoenician colonisation of the south. One would imagine that the Phoenicians began pioneering contacts with the Maltese islands some time around this period, judging by the presence of early Phoenician red-slipped ware. The last centuries of the Maltese Bronze Age are also marked by the Baħrija type of pottery, possibly marking the third phase of the Bronze Age. The Baħrija pottery is linked to the Iron Age ceramic developments of South Italy. The Baħrija development may have been a limited one. Recent discoveries at Tas-Silġ and at Mdina suggest that the Borġ in-Nadur ceramic tradition may have survived well up to the arrival of the first Phoenicians. The Baħrija wares have always been found in Borġ in-Nadur settlements, suggesting that the new wares may have been the result of trade. Many Phoenician townships and religious centres are located close to Borġ in-Nadur settlements. In some cases, such as Mdina, such townships appear to have evolved out of Bronze Age settlements. It would have been impossible for Phoenician settlers to avoid local inhabitants, who, in their townships, would have already provided an attractive market for trade and exchange. Gradually, the Phoenician-Punic landscape followed trajectories that marked a slow but final end to the Bronze Age. The old Borġ in-Nadur villages were abandoned in favour of the new towns. With the exception of centres such as Mdina, Punic rock-cut tombs, temples and public buildings reflect a movement away from older prehistoric centres of the Borġ in-Nadur period. Other than a few citadels, such as Mdina, hilltops were mostly taken over for other uses. In many places, industrial buildings and farmsteads spread as land was taken over for the type of agricultural production that is now associated with the ancient classical world.

Notes

1   T. Champion, C. Gamble, et al, *Prehistoric Europe* (London, 1997).
2   J. C. Shackleton, T. H. Van Andel and C. N. Runnels, 'Coastal Paleogeography of the Central and Western Mediterranean during the last 125,000 years and its Archaeological Implications', *Journal of Field Archaeology*, 11 (1984), 308-14.
3   M. Pedley, M. Hughes Clark and P. Galea, *Limestone Isles in a Crystal Sea. The Geology of the Maltese Islands* (Malta, 2002).
4   Shackleton et al, 'Coastal Paleogeography'.
5   B. Cunliffe, *The Oxford Illustrated Prehistory of Europe* (Oxford, 1994); M. Zvelebil, *Hunters in Transition* (Cambridge, 1986).
6   J. D. Evans, *The Prehistoric Antiquities of the Maltese Islands: a survey* (London, 1971); D. H. Trump, *Skorba* (London, 1966); C. Renfrew, 'Malta and the calibrated radiocarbon chronology', *Antiquity*, 46 (1972).
7   Trump, *Skorba*.
8   Ibid.
9   A. C. Renfrew and J. R. Cann, 'The characterisation of obsidian and its application to the

Mediterranean region', *Proceedings of the Prehistoric Society*, 30 (1964).
10   *Museum Annual Report*, 1914-15.
11   *Museum Annual Report*, 1937-38.
12   Trump, *Skorba*.
13   Ibid.
14   A. Pace, 'The Development of Megalithic Structures, Mortuary Facilities and Site Location patterning during the Maltese Late Neolithic and Early Bronze Age. Some Reconsiderations', (Unpublished M.Phil Thesis, Cambridge University, 1992).
15   Renfrew, 'Malta and the calibrated radiocarbon chronology'.
16   Pace, 'The Development of Megalithic Structures'.
17   Whitehouse, R., 'The rock-cut tombs of the Central Mediterranean', *Antiquity*, XLVI (1972); *Id.* 'Megaliths of the Central Mediterranean', in *Antiquity and Man: Essays in honour of Glyn Daniel*, ed. J. D. Evans, B. Cunliffe and C. Renfrew (London, 1981).
18   Pace, 'The Development of Megalithic Structures'; *Id.*,'The Archaeology of Collectivity', *The Archaeological Review* (Malta, 1997).
19   Pace, 'The Archaeology of Collectivity'; A. Pace and D. Cilia, *Melit et Gaul* (Malta 1995).
20   *Id.*, 'The Development of Megalithic Structures'; *Id.*, *The Hal Saflieni Hypogeum* (Malta, 2000).
21   Ibid.
22   C. Renfrew, *Before Civilization* (Harmondsworth, 1973); S. Stoddart, et al., 'Cult in an Island Society: Prehistoric Malta in the Tarxien Period', *Cambridge Archaeological Journal* 3, 1 (1993), 3-19; Pace, 'The Archaeology of Collectivity'.
23   Renfrew, *Before Civilization*.
24   Stoddart et al, 'Cult in an Island Society'; C. Malone, A. Bonanno, T. Gouder, S. Stoddart and D. Trump, 'The death cults of prehistoric Malta', *Scientific American*, 269, 6 (1993), 110-17.
25   Renfrew, *Before Civilization*.
26   J. D. Evans, 'The "dolmens" of Malta and the origins of the Tarxien Cemetery Culture', *Proceedings of the Prehistoric Society*, XXII (1956).
27   M. Ridley, *Corpus of the Megalithic Art of the Maltese Islands* (Hampshire, 1971).
28   Evans, *Prehistoric Antiquities*; Ridley, *Corpus*; Pace, 'The Archaeology of Collectivity'.
29   T. Zammit, *Prehistoric Malta, The Tarxien Temples* (Oxford, 1930); Evans, *Prehistoric Antiquities*; Trump, *Skorba*.
30   A. F. Hardy, *European Societies in the Bronze Age* (Cambridge, 2000).
31   Ibid.
32   Trump, *Skorba*.
33   *Museum Annual Report* 1956-57.
34   Evans, 'The dolmens'.
35   Ibid.
36   R. Leighton, *Sicily Before History* (London, 1999).

Thanks go to Michelle Buhagiar and Nathaniel Cutajar for their useful suggestions.

References
Bonanno, A., Gouder, T., Malone, C. and Stoddart, S., 'Monuments in an island society: The Maltese context', *World Archaeology*, 22 (1990).
Champion, T., Gamble, C., et al, *Prehistoric Europe* (London, 1997).
Cherry, J. F., 'Pattern and Process in the earliest colonisation of the Mediterranean islands', *Proceedings of the Prehistoric Society*, 47 (1981), 41-68.
Cherry, J. F., 'Early settlement in the Western Mediterranean islands and the peripheral areas', in *The Deya Conference of Prehistory*, ed. W. H. Waldren, R. Chapman, J. Lewthwaite and R. C. Kennard (Oxford, 1984), 7-23.
Cunliffe, B., *The Oxford Illustrated Prehistory of Europe* (Oxford, 1994).
Evans, J. D., 'The Prehistoric culture-sequence in the Maltese archipelago', *Proceedings of the Prehistoric Society*, XIX (1953), 41-94.
Evans, J. D., 'The "dolmens" of Malta and the origins of the Tarxien Cemetery Culture', *Proceedings of*

the Prehistoric Society, XXII (1956).

Evans, J. D., *The Prehistoric Antiquities of the Maltese Islands: a survey* (London, 1971).

Evans, J. D., 'Islands as laboratories of culture change', in *The Explanation of Culture Change*, ed. C. Renfrew (London, 1973).

Hardy, A. F., *European Societies in the Bronze Age* (Cambridge, 2000).

Leighton, R., *Sicily Before History* (London, 1999).

Malone, C., Bonanno, A., Gouder T., Stoddart, S. and Trump, D., 'The death cults of prehistoric Malta', Scientific American 269, 6 (1993), 110-17.

Museum Annual Report, 1914-1915.

Museum Annual Report, 1937-1938.

Museum Annual Report, 1956-1957.

Pace, A., 'The Development of Megalithic Structures, Mortuary facilities and Site Location patterning during the Maltese Late Neolithic and Early Bronze Age. Some Reconsiderations' (Unpublished M.Phil Thesis, Cambridge University, 1992).

Pace, A., 'Art Forms from Megalithic Malta', *Treasures of Malta* (1994).

Pace, A. and Cilia, D., *Melit et Gaul* (Malta, 1995).

Pace, A., 'The Archaeology of Collectivity', *The Archaeological Review* (Malta, 1997).

Pace, A., *The Hal Saflieni Hypogeum 4000 BC – 2000 AD* (Malta, 2000).

Pedley, M., Hughes Clark, M and Galea, P., *Limestone Isles in a Crystal Sea. The Geology of the Maltese Islands* (Malta, 2002).

Renfrew A. C. and Cann J. R., 'The characterisation of obsidian and its application to the Mediterranean region', *Proceedings of the Prehistoric Society,* 30 (1964).

Renfrew A. C., 'Malta and the calibrated radiocarbon chronology', *Antiquity,* 46 (1972).

Renfrew, C., *Before Civilization* (Harmondsworth, 1973).

Ridley, M., *Corpus of the Megalithic Art of the Maltese Islands* (Hampshire, 1971).

Shackleton, J. C., Van Andel, T. H. and Runnels, C. N., 'Coastal Paleogeography of the Central and Western Mediterranean during the last 125,000 years and its Archaeological Implications', *Journal of Field Archaeology,* 11 (1984), 308-14.

Stoddart, S. et al., 'Cult in an Island Society: Prehistoric Malta in the Tarxien Period', *Cambridge Archaeological Journal,* 3,1 (1993), 3-19.

Trump, D. H., *Skorba* (London, 1966).

Whitehouse, R., 'The rock-cut tombs of the Central Mediterranean', *Antiquity,* XLVI (1972).

Whitehouse, R., 'Megaliths of the Central Mediterranean', in *Antiquity and Man: Essays in honour of Glyn Daniel*, ed. J. D. Evans, B. Cunliffe and C. Renfrew (London, 1981).

Zammit, T., 'The Hal-Tarxien Neolithic Temple, Malta', *Archaeologia,* LXVII (1916), 127-44.

Zammit, T., *Archaeological Field Notes*, Note Book 13 (Unpublished, National Museum of Archaeology, Malta, 1915-19).

Zammit, T., *Prehistoric Malta, The Tarxien Temples* (Oxford, 1930).

Zvelebil, M., *Hunters in Transition* (Cambridge, 1986).

Anthony Bonanno

MALTA DURING PHOENICIAN, ROMAN AND BYZANTINE TIMES:
OUTSIDE INFLUENCE AND ORIGINAL TRAITS

The Geography

Malta occupies a distinctive place in the geo-scape[1] of the central Mediterranean, right in the centre of that sea, almost at equal distances from the sea's east and west boundaries, and its north and south continents. That is a reality that humans have not been able to change. Whether Malta's geographical identity is African or European - or neither, or both - depends on its geological formation, its position on the map, and on its climate; all of which determine the bio-environment (including the flora and fauna) of a place. The African geological identity of Malta has been firmly established by the geologists.[2] Malta forms part of the African tectonic plate that incorporates the southern tip of the Sicilian triangle, up to the southern fringes of Etna. Malta's position on the map makes it closer to Europe (only 90 km from the southern tip of Sicily) than to any point on the African littoral (300 km or more), though it should be kept in mind that Malta lies on a more southerly latitude than parts of the north African countries of Tunisia and Algeria. The present climate, which has probably changed to some degree over the millennia, is neither European nor African; it is, we are told by geographers, typically Mediterranean; and so is its bio-environment, characterised as it is by its semi-arid, typically Mediterranean maquis. Comprehensively, Malta's geographical identity is fundamentally Mediterranean. No human can change that.

What humans have been able to change, and have in fact moulded, is the geopolitical-scape of the archipelago and, as a result of that, they also shaped its geocultural-scape. As we shall see, the Phoenicians introduced the Oriental Semitic cultural element as from the second half of the eighth century BC and incorporated the islands into a predominantly western Mediterranean political sphere from the fifth century BC. This was interrupted in 218 BC by Malta's incorporation within the Roman Empire, which gravitated on Rome as its centre of power but in time incorporating all the lands washed by the Mediterranean and extending deeply into the European continent at its western end and, at times, deeply into southwest Asia (that area we are now accustomed to refer to as the Middle East) on the east end. This situation lasted for almost eight centuries, until Malta was annexed to the Eastern Roman Empire, better known as the Byzantine Empire, in AD 535. An important cultural factor, which must have started in the last two centuries of Roman rule - at the latest - but reached its zenith in the Byzantine period, is the Christianization of the islands. All this was brought to an abrupt end with the Arab invasion of AD 870.

The Ancients' Perception

It is hard to tell whether ancient geographers were influenced by the political vicissitudes of the archipelago, and if so to what degree, when they classified them geographically. Diodorus Siculus most certainly was (Diod. v, 12, 1-4). Writing in the first century BC, when Malta had already been integrated into the Roman empire for two whole centuries, this Sicilian historian was still referring to Gozo and Malta as 'Phoenician colonies' (*apoikoi*). We can consider Diodorus' statement as a historical anchronism, but it must surely reflect an ingrained, long-lasting perception among certain quarters of Republican Roman society of the archipelago's role in Rome's wars of conquest.[3] Diodorus' predecessor, Skylax of Caryanda, better known as Pseudo-Skylax, writing in the fourth century BC, was much more correct when he placed the islands in the political sphere of the western Phoenician colony of Carthage. Skylax is the first ancient writer to associate Malta and Gozo with Africa since he mentions them in the last section of his work, the section dedicated to Libya (i.e. North Africa), precisely under the subsection dedicated to Carthage. He gives the geographical position of the two small islands, 'to the east of Cape Bon' (Skylax 111).

A later Greek geographer, Strabo (64 BC - after AD 24), shifts his perception somewhat and gives the distance (500 stadia) between Malta and Cossura (Pantelleria) (*Geog.* XVII, 3. 16), and the distance that separates Malta and Gozo (88 miles) from Cape Pachynus (*Geog.* VI, 2.11). His points of departure are, in fact, Africa in the first instance, and Sicily in the second one. In the author's words, his geography was intended for political leaders and to impart practical wisdom, such as distances between landfalls for the sake of navigators. From this we may assume that there were frequent connections between Malta and these two destinations.

Ptolemy, the best known ancient geographer, writing his *Geography* in the second century AD, lists five landmarks concerning the Maltese islands and gives their latitudes and longitudes (Ptol. *Geogr.* 4.3.13). These were: two cities, Melite for

Malta and Gaulos for Gozo; two sanctuaries, one dedicated to Herakles and the other to Juno; and a place called '*Chersonesos*' meaning 'headland', to which some editions add, in my view erroneously, the word '*polis*', implying that there was a third city by that name. But what interests us in this context is Ptolemy's treatment of the Maltese islands in his section dedicated to Africa, as Skylax had done before him. Contemporary with Ptolemy is the *Itinerarium Antoninianum* (or *Antonini Augusti*). It only mentions Malta as a station for ships plying from Italy to Africa.[4] So does Lucian of Samosata who in his *The Ship* suggests that Malta was a port of call for heavy cargo vessels carrying corn from Egypt to Pozzuoli in Italy.[5]

The Historical and Archaeological Records

Had Malta been colonised by the Greeks the whole course of history of the archipelago would have been different.[6] Why the Greeks failed to do so is difficult to tell: probably because they were preceded there by the Phoenicians; possibly because the topography of the islands, lacking the extensive fertile plains they preferred for the cultivation of grain, did not attract them sufficiently. Whatever the reason, there is no evidence of a Greek colony here. Had it been so, the archaeological heritage of the first five centuries of Malta's ancient history would have been very different. The artistic and artisanal repertory would have been to a great extent identical to that found in neighbouring Sicily and southern Italy to our north and in Cyrenaica, Libya, to our southeast. With the strongly Classical bias of my professional formation, I find that I deeply miss the refined and elegant products of Greek art of the Archaic and Classical age. Can you imagine the beauty of typical Greek temples, in typical Malta stone, standing against the silhouetted heights of Rabat, or on the side of one of the hills against the typical Maltese landscape, green in winter and glaring white in summer?

On the other hand, you might say, this would have made us merely a part of Sicily, a micro-insular cultural extension of that largest island of the Mediterranean. What in fact happened, you might add, is even more significant because, as had already happened 3000 years earlier, Malta underwent a cultural development which distinguished it from the cultural destiny of neighbouring Sicily. The way things turned out, Malta was given, once more, the opportunity of asserting a different cultural identity from that of its immediate neighbours to the north. This cultural identity is marked by its Semitic Phoenician character, a cultural legacy that, we should not forget, is shared by Sicily,[7] by today's Italy itself,[8] and, further afield, Spain,[9] not to mention the western half of our north African neighbour to our south, namely, Libyan Tripolitania.[10]

Malta's Phoenician legacy, apart from the language which survived well into the Roman rule, consists of a whole array of underground rock-cut tombs that are scattered throughout the landscape of the two islands, with a concentration in the collective cemeteries just outside their two urban centres. These tombs have yielded

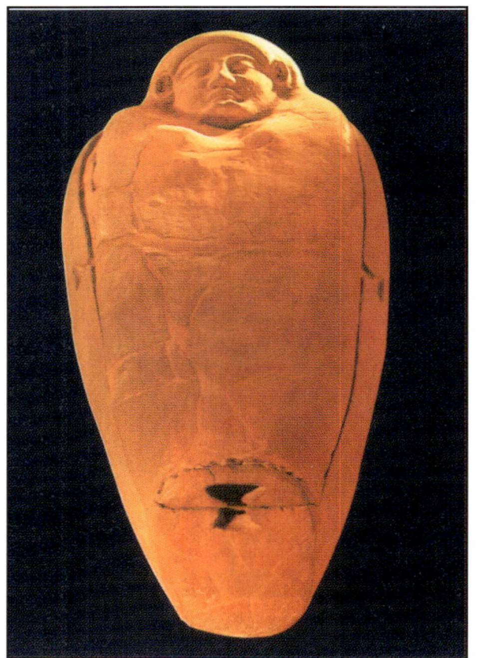

Clay anthropomorphic sarcophagus (fifth century BC) from Għar Barka, Rabat

Clay amphora of the seventh century BC

Gold amulet of Horus and Anubis (seventh-sixth century BC) from Għajn Klieb, Rabat

Phoenician papyrus from Tal-Virtù, Rabat

a rich repertory of ceramic furniture, obviously buried with the deceased for some purpose in the afterlife. Occasionally, this characteristically Phoenician (or Punic) ceramic repertoire included the odd Greek import, certainly treasured for its fine quality and painted decoration. The best known are the proto-Corinthian kotyle and eastern Greek 'bird bowl' found in a tomb at Għajn Qajjet. Unmistakable are also the occasional pieces of personal jewellery, the golden ones being rare but of immensely high aesthetic and religious symbolic value. Foremost among these is the solid gold pendant from a tomb at Għajn Klieb, representing two Egyptian gods (Horus and Anubis) soldered together back to back. This jewel, together with another pendant from a tomb at Tal-Virtù, this time of bronze but containing a small sheet of papyrus with a prayer written over a drawn figure of the goddess Isis, represent an early introduction of the Egyptian cultural component into Maltese Phoenician art and religious thought.[11]

Although virtually no structures have come to light belonging to the two Phoenician urban centres of the islands,[12] their existence is corroborated by the ancient writers (mainly Pseudo-Skylax). Their location, corresponding to Mdina and part of Rabat for Malta and to part of modern Victoria/Rabat and its Citadel for Gozo, is indicated by the distribution of tombs. These urban centres were the precursors of the two cities that were attributed by later writers to the two islands in the following, Roman period.

Undoubtedly, the two urban settlements had their own religious establishments to cater for the spiritual needs of the community, but no trace of them has yet come to light, except perhaps the reported find of a large number of pots containing bones of animals and birds (one version states 'of children and small animals'), made inside a cavity in the vicinity of Mdina in 1819. This find seems to have resuscitated the possibility of the existence of a tophet in this area, near the Dominican monastery of Rabat, the same area from which two inscriptions mentioning a sacrifice to Baal Hammon originate.[13] But a more prominent sanctuary was set up by the Phoenicians away from the town, on top of a small hill on one side of Marsaxlokk harbour. The Tas-Silġ sanctuary was dedicated to the goddess Ashtart and must have been frequented by mariners visiting this harbour, as well as by the local inhabitants. The archaeological contents of this period, unearthed by excavations conducted in the 1960s and the ongoing ones, show three major cultural components, which are representative of the prevailing culture of the island, namely, the dominating Phoenician-Punic one, mixed with a sprinkling of Egyptian (or Egyptianising) imports, as well as the Hellenic and, later, Hellenistic one.

The Romans took the islands in 218 BC, the first year of the Second Punic War, the long war the Romans sustained against Carthage, the latter championed by her greatest general, Hannibal. The Roman navy had visited Malta at least once during the First Punic War, but on that occasion they limited themselves to pillaging and burning whatever they could. For the second time, they met no resistance, even though a Punic garrison of 2000 soldiers was stationed there. This time, the Roman invaders realised the strategic value of the islands, even if a negative one, and annexed them, incorporating them in their first overseas province, that of Sicily. This attachment to Sicily accounts for a much more intensive commercial and cultural intercourse with the larger neighbouring island throughout Roman and the Byzantine rule, including the use of the Greek language in the coin legends and in inscriptions.

With notable exceptions, when they meted out harsh punishments for stubborn resistance, the Romans were quite liberal in their treatment of conquered peoples. They were not interested in eradicating local customs, religious beliefs and cultures, as long as their subjects behaved themselves, paid taxes and respected the laws of Rome. Their treatment of Malta was no exception; they gave it the same treatment as to most Sicilian cities. They even allowed it to mint coins, albeit only of bronze, of small denomination and for internal circulation, for the first two centuries of their domination, practically throughout the late-Republican age. What is strange, but not entirely surprising, is the fact that the figurative motifs on the earlier coins were Orientalising (in fact, mostly Egyptianising) and the legends in Punic.[14] This is only symptomatic of the general survival of Punic culture in the first two centuries of Roman rule. Such continuity can be traced also in the religious worship, the burial customs, the use of the native language, and in the pottery production.

According to the orator Cicero, where taxes were concerned, the cities of Sicily, including Malta, were accorded a special treatment: instead of becoming *stipendiarii*, they were allowed to continue to pay taxes under the tithe system they had been accustomed to before the Roman conquest. The Maltese islands were administered by the governor of Sicily, who represented Rome and was assisted by other officials. One such governor, Verres, made a name for himself for the corrupt style of his administration and caused Malta to be mentioned repeatedly by the lawyer Cicero in the prosecution speeches against him in Rome. Through them we know that Malta produced fine draperies that found an appreciative market abroad. We also learn of the international fame, veneration and respect enjoyed by its sanctuary of Juno, comparable to that of the same divinity on Samos; and of its rich treasure, most of which was pillaged by Verres during his term of office in 73-71 BC. It is possible that the inhabitants of Malta, along with those of the other cities of Sicily were given full Roman citizenship, soon after 44 BC, by the triumvir Antony who was, in the immediate aftermath of Caesar's assassination, the most powerful man in Rome. But this privilege was short-lived because Octavian, the future first emperor, rescinded that privilege in 26 BC.[15]

Things started to change after the fundamental constitutional reform in Rome in 27 BC when the Republic was replaced by a monarchic regime. The metropolis and, consequently the whole empire, started to be ruled by one man, the Emperor. This change is reflected in the Maltese epigraphic and archaeological documentation from the first century AD onwards. The Maltese continued to pay taxes to their Roman masters but seem to have lived in relative prosperity brought about by the *pax romana*. A scatter of villas, often enjoying beautiful scenery in the

Maltese countryside, may have belonged to wealthy locals or foreign, probably Italian, settlers.[16] Most of them had olive groves attached to them, whose product was processed for the production of olive oil in a specially designated part of the villas. The most spectacular of such agriculturally-oriented villas is the one of San Pawl Milqi. That at Ramla Bay, on the other hand, located only a few metres from the sea shore, seems to have been of a purely residential type.

The town house of Rabat, built to high specifications around 100 BC, with floors covered by a rich cycle of mosaics of the highest quality, continued to be inhabited by prominent members of the community.[17] Around AD 50, the last occupier of the house had enough means and sufficiently strong motivation to furnish it with a cycle of imperial portrait statues representing the reigning emperor Claudius and some members of his family. At about the same time, ten years later in fact, the chief man of Malta (the *protos*) offered hospitality to St Paul when the latter was shipwrecked on the island, according to tradition an episode of tremendous importance in the islands' history.[18] As there is no specific mention of conversions to Christianity in the account of Paul's three-months' stay on the island, and as the earliest archaeological evidence of widespread Christian cult dates only to the fourth century AD, the claim of an early, apostolic Christianisation of Malta can only base itself on the strong personality of Paul and his proselytising track record.

It is in imperial times that the central power at Rome judged certain religious sects, especially the Christian one, as a threatening force to the stability of the imperial authority. Christianity was banned and subjected to extended episodes of organised, cruel persecution. It is difficult to tell whether these persecutions affected the Maltese population in any way, simply because we have no idea how strong the Christian following was, if any, before the emperor Constantine embraced Christianity and encouraged its proliferation throughout the empire by the Edict of Milan (AD 313).

Malta is thought to have been absorbed by the Byzantine empire in AD 535 when Sicily and its islands were conquered by Justinian's general Belisarius. In the period spanning the second half of the fifth century and the Byzantine conquest, Malta might have been occupied by barbarians, Vandals from North Africa and Ostrogoths from Italy.[19] All the early Christian tombs and catacombs date to the period that spans from late Antiquity (fourth-fifth centuries) to Byzantine times. Among them were a few family hypogea which were used by a sizeable Jewish community. A few inscriptions, in Greek, refer to members of this community, including the head of the council of elders (*gerousiarch*) and his wife (Eulogia) who held the office of elder (*presbytera*) in the Jewish synagogue.[20] Associated archaeological material originates in North Africa (Tunisia and Tripolitania), Italy and the eastern Mediterranean. A Christian basilica was built over the courtyard of the preceding pagan sanctuary of Juno at Tas-Silġ sometime in the fifth century. Its baptistery had a drain hole at the bottom through which a group of coins of several Byzantine emperors found their way. One of them, with the effigy of emperor Constantine IV (AD 654-668), was of gold.

The central mosaic of the Roman domus at Rabat (first century BC)

The tepidarium mosaic at the Roman Baths in Ghajn Tuffieha

General view of St Paul's catacombs at Rabat (Photo: MTA)

The Arab invasion of 870 brought about the end of a millennium, during which the Maltese islands formed part of the Greco-Roman world, and the beginning of another era, characterised by a different civilisation based on another religion of the Book, Islam.

Notes

1   I request the reader's indulgence on the adoption of this and two other neologisms - I believe they are so. The words geo-scape, geopolitical-scape and geocultural-scape have been adopted to express the respective extension of the concept of 'landscape' in the English sense, the lay of the land.

2   M. Pedley, M. Hughes Clarke and P. Galea, *Limestone Isles in a Crystal Sea* (Malta, 2002), 23-34.

3   A. Bonanno, *Roman Malta: the Archaeological Heritage of the Maltese islands - Malta Romana: il Patrimonio Archeologico delle isole Maltesi* (Rome, 1992), 13, n. 2. This anachronism may also be attributed to the historian's uncritical, sometimes confused use of his sources.

4   O. Cunta, *Itinerarium Antonini Augusti* (Leipzig, 1929), 518.

5   J. Busuttil, 'Maltese harbours in Antiquity', *Melita Historica* V, 4 (1971), 305-07.

6   This statement is correct, but to a limited extent, in the sense that Roman domination would have been inevitable, whether Malta was previously Greek or Phoenician. What would have changed was the ethnic composition of the islands and their culture, both of which endured long beyond the Roman conquest.

7   Albeit limited to its north-western tip (consisting of Palermo, Motya and Solunto) which was Phoenician to all intents and purposes.

8   Italy's western island of Sardinia (the second largest island of the Mediterranean Sea), was also colonised and accultured by the Phoenicians.

9   Most of south and southeast Spain, up to the Ebro river, was in the Phoenician political, *ergo* cultural, sphere.

10   Even today Libya is geographically and culturally divided into distinct parts, Tripolitania in the west, marked by three Phoenician colonies (Leptis Magna, Sabratha and Oea), and Cyrenaica in the east, named after the main city (Cyrene) of a group of Greek colonies.

11   See T. C. Gouder and B. Rocco, 'Un talismano bronzeo da Malta contenente un nastro di papiro con iscrizione fenicia', *StMagreb*, VII (1975), 1-18, and N. Cutajar, 'Recent discoveries and the archaeology of Mdina', *Treasures of Malta*, VIII, 1 (Christmas 2001), 79-85.

12   Recent investigations under the Xara Palace Hotel have reportedly uncovered a Phoenician wall (Cutajar, 'Recent discoveries').

13   Shortland Jones, 'The Phoenician connection', *Treasures of Malta*, V, 1 (Christmas 1998), 92. See A. Frendo and N. Vella, 'Les îles phéniciennes du milieu de la mer', *Dossiers d'Archéologie* 267 (October 2001), 55.

14   Not surprising, because other cities like Palermo and Pantelleria did the same.

15   A. Bonanno, (forthcoming). *Phoenician, Punic and Roman Malta* (Malta).

16   For an account of these villas and their contribution to the Maltese economy in the Roman period, see A. Bonanno, 'Distribution of villas and some aspects of the Maltese economy in the Roman period', *Journal of the Faculty of Arts*, VI, 4 (1977), 73-81.

17   On the architecture, mosaic decoration and sculpture of this house see Bonanno, *Roman Malta*, 21-24.

18   *Acts* xxvii, 37-44; xxxviii, 1-11. The controversy over the Christianisation of Malta is discussed in M. Buhagiar, 'The St Paul shipwreck controversy: an assessment of the source material', in K. Sciberras (ed.), *Proceedings of History Week 1993* (Malta, 1997), 181-213.

19   The most comprehensive account on this period remains T. S. Brown, 'Byzantine Malta: A Discussion of the Sources', in A. T. Luttrell (ed.) *Medieval Malta* (London, 1975), 71-86. See also

C. Dalli, *Iż-Żmien Nofsani Malti* (Malta, 2002), 9-24.

20   R. S. Kraemer, 'A new inscription from Malta and the question of women elders in the Diaspora Jewish communities', *Harvard Theological Review* 3-4 (1980), 431-38.

Nathaniel Cutajar

THE ARCHAEOLOGY OF MALTA'S MIDDLE AGES: DOCUMENTING CULTURAL CHANGE BETWEEN THE TENTH AND THIRTEENTH CENTURY

A historiographic debate

Between the ninth and the thirteenth century Malta experienced a succession of profound, even traumatic episodes of cultural transformation. In a relatively short time, Malta swung through three major cultural, religious and linguistic changes – from Greek Byzantine rule, to Arab and Latin Norman dominion.

In view of the absolute lack of local archival records, historians have had to rely heavily on the testimony of a few scattered accounts in the works of foreign medieval chroniclers and administrators. Most of these authors had no direct experience of the Maltese context, being rather concerned with political and dynastic issues quite alien to the insular situation.

Malta's High Middle Ages therefore read like a history of the foreigner, a narrative of what non-Maltese potentates did in the course of their bid for Mediterranean dominance.[1] Inevitably we are given a picture of local passive acceptance of a too powerful surge of foreign military and cultural influences. Not surprisingly this pessimistic image has been mainly advocated by twentieth century historians who had before their eyes the image of an island securely in the grip of colonial rule. It is therefore difficult to avoid the suspicion that modern colonial realities have been too uncritically projected onto the medieval past.

Earlier historical works of the seventeenth and eighteenth centuries used similar sources to reach quite different conclusions.[2] For these earlier authors and antiquarians, the history of Arab and Norman Malta was a monument to local achievement, a saga of autochthonous resistance in the face of mounting foreign threats to native identity and political liberties.

A filter jug (left) at a sprouted jug (above) dating from the Arab period (Photo: Nathaniel Cutajar)

Remains of an Islamic decorated amphora (above left), a deep bowl (above right) and amphorae rims (below) (Photo: Nathaniel Cutajar)

Interestingly however both the Baroque antiquarian and the twentieth century historian share a common paradigm. Both sets of history writers ultimately describe the Middle Ages in terms of a dualistic confrontation between an autochthonous element and an intruding foreigner. What they disagree on is the actual perspective of the interpretation – one is partisan to the presumed claims of the locals, while the others identify the foreigner as the principal catalyst of historical change.[3]

Research into the medieval archaeology of Malta has in the 1990s added much data to this ongoing historiographic debate.

Baroque scholarship was the first to rely on archaeological remains in an effort to reconstruct an image of the islands' more distant medieval past. Giovanni Francesco Abela in his *Descrittione* of 1647 made important observations on a number of now lost medieval monuments. These include accounts of abandoned 'raħal' sites in the Maltese countryside, or the precious description of the now lost Jewish cemetery at Mtarfa. Marchese Barbaro's eighteenth century account of the archaeological remains he investigated in 1794 on Jesuit Hill,[4] similarly included insightful considerations on the site's destiny during the Byzantine and Islamic occupation.

The political situation in the colonial period, with its emphasis on the language and religious questions, heavily influenced historical and archaeological debate in the nineteenth and twentieth century. This situation polarised the attention of scholars, whose main agenda with regards the Middle Ages was diverted towards the frankly vexing issue of 'cultural continuity'. Passions were roused by debates on whether Christianity in Malta, or the Maltese language and 'race' had actually originated in antiquity or in more recent times. Much of this debate was influenced by partisan politics and led to a drying up of the intellectual vein that had animated earlier scholarship.

This notwithstanding the nineteenth and early twentieth century did witness some notable advances in the area of medieval archaeology, most notably in the study of the island's important corpus of late Roman and early medieval catacombs. These sites were prized almost exclusively as a source of information for the early stages of Christian community life in Malta. Typical of this line of research was the impressive inventory work of A. A. Caruana or the philological and typological work of A. Mayr.[5] However the most spectacular discovery in medieval archaeology in this period was the uncovering of a large Muslim cemetery just outside the walls of Mdina by Themistocles Zammit in 1921. At this site various limestone tombstones with incised decorations and Cufic inscriptions were found, providing for the first time a tangible insight into the existence of an urbane and literate Islamic society in high medieval Malta.

The archaeology of the tenth to thirteenth centuries in the Mediterranean has for the last two decades progressed very rapidly. In particular detailed ceramic typologies now exist for various ceramic classes of production of the period, most importantly those pertaining to amphora, glazed wares and proto-majolica. The great improvement in archaeological field techniques has also resulted in a much greater yield of information from the excavation of new medieval sites, both on land and at sea.[6] The Maltese islands have benefited from these advances in medieval archaeology, together with the rest of the region. What follows is an overview of the major issues emerging from this fast changing picture of medieval Maltese life and culture.

The Archaeological Evidence - Arab Malta

The Arab occupation of Malta was one episode in the prolonged war that raged between the Aghlabid rulers of Tunisia and the Byzantine Greeks from 827 to 902 over the possession of Sicily. The war was a desperate affair during which various Sicilian towns were reportedly wiped out, and their original inhabitants replaced by the victorious Arabs. This is said to have occurred at places where Byzantine resistance was most determined as at Enna, Syracuse and Taormina.

The Arab invasion of Malta seems to have been similarly destructive. The event as chronicled by medieval Arab authors developed in two phases.[7] The first phase involved the arrival from Tunisia of an Arab expeditionary force in 869. A staunch Byzantine counter-offensive threatened to destroy the invading army. The second phase of the invasion settled the conflict in favour of the Arabs with the arrival, in 870, of additional reinforcements from Sicily. Following the over-running of the islands, the Arabs are reported to have punitively razed the Byzantine stronghold to the ground.

According to some sources the islands were left as uninhabited territories up to 1045 AD, when fresh colonisers supposedly established a new Islamic polity on Malta. This report seems to be confirmed by a striking linguistic parallelism. It has been pointed out how the modern Maltese idiom is directly descended from a medieval form of Arabic. No linguistic substratum appears to have survived from earlier occupations of the islands.[8] No trace of Punic, Latin or Medieval Greek can be securely identified in the Maltese language. This feature may suggest that the Arabs did indeed carry out a rapid and violent take-over of the islands – as suggested by the sources – possibly entailing a complete ethnic turnover.

The emerging archaeological record for this period suggests however a decidedly more complex scenario than that indicated by the written sources. Ceramics of the late tenth to eleventh century have been heavily attested at the town of Mdina.[9] Smaller quantities of ceramics from this period have also been sporadically documented in the urban centre of the Cittadella in Gozo, as well as at a number of rural and coastal settlements in Malta.

The ceramic record for this period includes very typical forms and productions that have been widely studied and published, particularly in relation to the Islamic archaeology of Sicily.[10] Most of the forms documented seem to belong to the more archaic typologies (late tenth to mid-eleventh century) of the published ceramic sequences from Sicily. The most typical glazed forms include the various typologies of carinated bowls (particularly characteristic are the forms with thickened, grooved rims), deep cups with straight sides and a ring-handle, and oil-lamps with closed basin and elongated nozzle. The decoration consists primarily of polychrome glazes, as well as floral and geometric motifs. Besides the glazed wares, one also finds wheel-turned wares with painted decoration – mainly amphorae – sometimes decorated with pseudo-calligraphic motives. Also typical are unglazed water-jugs with fine, thin bodies and with in-built ceramic filters.

The evidence suggests that Arab Malta was heavily engaged in the prosperous commercial networks linking the Maghreb and Sicily under the Kalbid Dynasty up to the mid-eleventh century. All the ceramic typologies described above consist of imports, mainly from Sicily and from Tunisia. A few shards seem to indicate that commercial links with the Eastern Mediterranean persisted as well. Similarly, the commerce in edible goods within amphorae – sparsely documented in the central Mediterranean during this period – is also well documented in Mdina.

Another index of the healthy level of commercial activity carried out in Arab Malta is the frequent presence of glass fragments in the strata of this period, especially at Mdina. One site at Mdina has produced a hundred glass fragments from a great variety of vessels.

Besides the imported glass and ceramics, a range of coarse, hand-made kitchenware is also attested in the strata of the Arab period. These forms – probably local products - include open dishes and pans, as well as deep, bell-shaped stewing pots. Unlike later medieval Maltese hand-made wares, none of these Arab-period productions employ slips or burnish.

The Arab presence in Mdina is characterised by a re-occupation of spaces and structures formerly used by the Byzantines.[11] In two instances we may have evidence pointing to a simple Arab upgrading of pre-existing Byzantine urban defences. A similar situation could mark the large Islamic burial grounds just outside the walls of Mdina. The possibility that the Arabs simply carried on with a pre-existing Byzantine land-use is suggested by the fact that two late Antique/Byzantine funerary epigraphs are reported to have been found in the site's immediate vicinity.[12]

As far as Mdina is concerned, it is possible to hypothesise that the Arabs simply took over the urban infrastructure vacated by the Byzantine troops. There is so far nothing in the archaeological evidence to justify the idea that the town lost its former population in a rapid and violent manner. In fact the inverse may actually be the case, with an increase in the town's size, particularly towards its northern end. It is also true that the material culture of the township shows a radical shift away from the former Byzantine long-distance links with the Aegean and the Adriatic, in favour of more intensified links with the Maghreb and Sicily.

A different pattern seems so far to characterise the rural landscape. Late Byzantine rural settlement is limited to a few defended or defensible coastal sites next to the island's major harbour systems. No inland late Byzantine settlements of the *villa* or *vicus* typology have been documented in Malta so far.[13] This situation starts to be reversed with the Arabs. There is documentation for at least one large late tenth/eleventh century rural cluster in the Għajn Klieb / Ġnien is-Sultan area.[14] Small, but significant ceramic scatters are also documented on the hilltop sites of Ta' Ċieda and Tas-Silġ.

The scarcity of documented rural settlement during the Byzantine and Arab periods are perplexing, particularly when compared with the flourishing situation noted at Mdina and to a lesser extent at the Cittadella. This negative archaeological datum suggests indeed that the Maltese rural landscape was up to the eleventh century relatively unencumbered with human settlement. This may indeed have occasioned the perplexing comment made by some Arab sources that Malta was uninhabited during part of the High Middle Ages.

It is possible to suggest that the islands were in this period not pursuing the intensive arable agricultural practices normally associated with the early Roman or late medieval situation. Malta's economy may rather have been geared to extract primary raw materials from an uncultivated rural hinterland, with its relatively wide-open spaces and its range of natural environments. In fact products such as timber for shipbuilding, herds, honey, fruit and fish are repeatedly associated with Islamic Malta in the surviving sources.

The extraction of these primary raw materials from the rural hinterland provided the local economy with a range of products with which to tap the long-

Islamic cooking pots

Fragments of Islamic oil lamps (left) and cooking pots (right) (Photo: Nathaniel Cutajar)

Fragments of Norman glazes (left) and late Norman Majolica (right) (Photo: Nathaniel Cutajar)

distance trade routes traversing the medieval Mediterranean. This could possibly explain the presence of such a variety of imported materials in Byzantine and Islamic strata - coinage, glass, fine ceramics, cooking ware, amphorae – within the context of a society that seems to have invested so little in rural settlement.

Norman Malta

In 1061 the Normans under Count Roger started a successful thirty-year long invasion of Sicily. The political link with Sicily was destined to grow closer when, in 1091, Count Roger led in person a military invasion of the Maltese islands. A second more thorough occupation was carried out by his son Roger II, in 1127.

As in Sicily, the Normans forced a number of typical western institutions upon the largely Islamic population of Malta. This included the introduction of the Latin Church and the re-establishment of a local diocese. These measures formed part of a determined and effective drive at re-christianising the newly conquered territories. The pace of this process of cultural imposition and the actual social and economic mechanisms employed in the process are still far from clear.

Feudal notions were introduced in the management of the island, particularly with the creation of the county of Malta. However, the feudal set-up was not allowed to jeopardise the monarchy's control over the islands. Malta appears to have been transformed by the Sicilian monarchs into a closely controlled base from which to conduct operations against North Africa and the Eastern Mediterranean. Indeed the title of Count of Malta and that of Admiral of the Sicilian fleet were often synonymous.

The Norman dynasty endured up to the late twelfth century. On its extinction, the kingdom passed on to the Hohenstaufen or Swabian dynasty, heirs to the Sicilian Crown. The new German rulers pursued with great energy the centralising policies experimented by their Norman predecessors. Particularly relentless was their struggle against the ever-rebellious Arabs and the fractious feudal lords of Sicily. It is indeed under the Swabians that the last Maltese Islamic communities are documented to have been forced out of the islands.

The commercial links enjoyed by the Maltese islands from the twelfth to the early thirteenth century are archaeologically amply documented. In the twelfth century the main bulk of glazed wares appear to be reaching Malta from Sicily, together with minor contributions from Campania and from the Eastern Mediterranean. From the end of the twelfth century, glazes and proto-majolica start being imported from a wide-range of locations across the Mediterranean: Tunisia, Puglia (Brindisi and Taranto), Campania, south-west Sicily, possibly Spain and the Eastern Mediterranean. Less fine ceramic products – such as glazed cooking wares and amphorae – arrived from Sicily throughout this period.

The pattern of ceramic importation in Malta during the Norman period is highly compatible with the recorded situation in Sicily. A radical change is noticeable in the trade patterns favoured by the Normans, compared to the older Arab routes. The major difference lies in the slowing down of commercial links with the Maghreb, in favour of a Tyrrhenian connection. The documented political ascendancy over the Siculo-Maltese region by Genoese and Pisan mercantile interests helps explain this switch in trading partners during the Norman and Swabian period.

The impact of the Norman occupation at Mdina is difficult to assess due to a surprising dearth of twelfth and thirteenth century remains. An important exception is the discovery of a massive stone ashlar structure – possibly the foundations of a tower – built over what appears to be Arab period defences in the area fronting the Carmelite Convent at Mdina. This later construction is tentatively dated to the twelfth/thirteenth century.

Archival references confirm that the Normans carried out some degree of re-fortification at Mdina. These sources refer to the existence of a *Castellu di la Chitati* (town castle) at Mdina,[15] as well as to a companion *Castrum Maris* (castle by the sea) situated at the Grand Harbour. A third castle dominated the town centre of Gozo. These three royal garrisons were entrusted with the policing of the islands as well as with securing a home base for the Sicilian fleet.

The construction of the Mdina Castello may have incorporated the entire upper ridge of the hill, creating a sort of feudal acropolis or upper town. It seems probable that the footprint of this enclosure followed closely that of the earlier Byzantine and Arab town fortifications. The Norman Cathedral would have formed an integral part of this large military enclosure – a measure necessitated by the atmosphere of military insecurity that existed at this frontier fortress. These military developments must have necessitated the removal of older Arab quarters and constructions from the summit of the hill, with the consequent creation of new suburbs at the margin of the town.

The archaeological evidence for rural settlement in the twelfth and thirteenth centuries shows a marked increase in the number of documented settlements. Ceramics from this period have been noted at the sites of Tas-Silġ, Ta' Ċieda, Marsa, San Pawl Milqi, Wardija ta' San Ġorġ and Baħrija. Interestingly all these sites are set on naturally defended hilltop locations, suggesting that they actually consisted of fortified units. Judging from the Sicilian context, these fortified settlements could have housed either feudal tenants or may have provided refuge to peasant communities in times of crises. Considering the toponomastic evidence, fortified rural settlements – identified by the use of terms as 'qalat', 'klija' 'qroq', 'qortin' and 'wardija' - must have been more common in the Maltese landscape than is currently suggested by the archaeological data.

The existence at this early date of open, undefended rural settlements is difficult to assess. The use of toponomastic terms such as 'raħal' or 'ħal' suggests that many such open rural sites come into existence and were abandoned in the High and Late Middle Ages.[16] We lack however positive archaeological proof to indicate that any of these 'raħal' sites were actually occupied from as early as the twelfth century.

The only recorded excavation at an open 'raħal' site – at the village site of Ħal Millieri – has not located any remains older than the thirteenth century.[17]

Clearly more fieldwork is needed in the areas of rural medieval settlement. All in all however the available evidence points to a dramatic increase in the range and number of rural settlements operating in Norman and Swabian Malta. This tendency towards intensified rural settlement was already noticeable in the Arab period. This trend may have been dictated by a rise in population, as well as by a re-distribution of the existing population according to the needs of the island's new feudal type of land management. This trend also indicates a radical change in the agricultural basis of the island's economy.

The documented references as from the twelfth century to wheat and cotton production may throw some light on the island's new economic basis under the Normans/Swabians. Cotton was a particularly critical introduction, providing the islands with a cash product that – in its raw or worked state – could be easily traded on the Tyrrhenian markets.

The introduction of new agricultural practices would however have necessitated the destruction of the early medieval landscape as more and more terrain formerly given over to animal husbandry and forestry were reclaimed by means of terracing and land-drainage works. The documented silting up of the lower reaches of Malta's valley systems provides us with an index of this transformation. In fact archaeological data exists indicating that a deep stratum of alluvium was deposited within the lower valley systems of Burmarrad and Marsa at some time after the eighth century and probably before the early-thirteenth century. The origin of these silts could be sought in the erosion of the old rural landscapes as a result of the introduction of new agricultural practices in the course of the High Middle Ages.

Conclusions

The archaeological investigation of the Maltese High Middle Ages has so far failed to produce a clear-cut differentiation between 'local' and 'foreign' elements in the material culture of the period. What has emerged instead is the image of a society engaged in a process of rapid, dynamic and holistic transformation within a broader context of Mediterranean development. This process of change in High Medieval Malta was furthermore not only limited to language and religion, but also affected the very physical appearance and economic infrastructure of these islands. The continuation of these studies promises to provide us with an interesting archaeological model for comprehending the phenomenon of cultural change and cohabitation in the medieval Mediterranean.

Notes

1   A thorough historical synthesis of the Maltese Middle Ages is presented in A. Luttrell (ed.), *Medieval Malta. Studies on Malta before the Knights* (London, 1975).

2   The principal work in this Baroque strain of history writing is undoubtedly that of the seventeenth century humanist and statesman G. F. Abela, *Della Descrittione di Malta Isola nel Mare Siciliano* (Malta, 1647), facsimile edition 1984. Followers of the 'Abela genre' of history writing can however be traced well into the nineteenth century.

3   Important exceptions to this dualistic model are the works of authors such as R. Valentini, 'Feudo e commune in Malta fino alla caduta della dominazione Angioina', *Archivio Storico di Malta*, VI, 6 (1935), 1-33, as well as that of C. Dalli, 'Capitoli: voice of an elite', in S. Fiorini (ed.), *Proceedings of History Week 1992* (Malta, 1994), 1-18 – both of whom interpret the local socio-historic datum within the Sicilian context.

4   C. Barbaro, *Degli Avanzi d'Alcuni Antichissimi Edifizi Scoperti in Malta l'Anno 1768* (Malta, 1794).

5   For an account of Mayr's work in this area see H. Stoger, 'Albert Mayr (1868-1924)', *Malta Archaeological Review*, 4 (2000), 3-9.

6   The first medieval Maltese site to benefit from the use of stratigraphic excavation was the 1977 investigation of the late medieval chapels of the Annunciation and of the Visitation at Hal Millieri.

7   The key commentary on the Arab documentary sources for Malta remains G. Wettinger, 'The Arabs in Malta', in *Malta: Studies of its Heritage and History*, Mid-Med Bank (Malta, 1986), 87-104.

8   The interplay of language and history in medieval Malta has been discussed in most detail by J. M. Brincat, *Malta 870-1054: Al-Himyari's Account and its Linguistic Implications* (Malta, 1995). Brincat also presents the most complete account regarding the Arab invasion of 869-70.

9   M. Molinari and N. Cutajar, 'Of Greeks and Arabs and Feudal Knights - a preliminary archaeological exposure of Malta's perplexing Middle Ages', *Malta Archaeological Review*, 3 (1999), 9-16.

10 See for example L. Arcifa, 'Contributo allo studio della ceramica comune medievale in Sicilia (Sec. X-XII): Problemi di classificazione e temi di ricerca' in Feller, Mane and Piponnier (eds), *Le Village Medieval et son Environnement* (Paris, 1998), 273-89, and A. Molinari, 'Momenti di cambiamento nelle produzioni ceramiche siciliane', in *La Ceramique Medievale en Mediterranee*. Actes du 6e Congres (Aix-en-Provence, 1997), 375-82.

11 N. Cutajar, 'The archaeology of Mdina – Recent Discoveries', *Treasures of Malta*, VIII, 1 (2001), 79-85, 117.

12 See V. Grassi, 'Materiali per lo studio della presenza Araba nella regione Italiana - L'Epigrafia Araba nelle Isole Maltesi', in *Studi Magrebini*, XXI (1989), 9-92, for the most detailed publication of the Islamic cemetery and A. A. Caruana, *Report on the Phoenician and Roman Antiquities in the Group of the Islands of Malta* (Malta, 1882), 153, 155-56 for notices on the discovery of the late Antique and Byzantine funerary epigraphs.

13 B. Bruno, and N. Cutajar, 'Archeologia Bizantina a Malta: primi risultati e prospettive d'indagine', in Amadasi Guzzo, M., Liverani, E. and Matthiae, P. (eds), *Da Pirgi a Mozia – Studi Sull' Archeologia del Mediterraneo in Memoria di Antonia Ciasca*, Vicino Oriente, Quaderno 3 (Rome, 2002), 109-38.

14 Glazed ceramics from this period were encountered by T. Zammit in the course of his investigations of an ancient tomb at Għajn Klieb (Museum Annual Report 1906-07, 2-3), and of a silo pit at Ġnien is-Sultan (Museum Annual Report 1925-26, iii), as well as in the 1981-82 investigation of the chapel of San Cir, also in the Ġnien is-Sultan area.

15 The best discussion on the medieval castle at Mdina is presented in S. C. Spiteri, 'Castellu di la Chitati – the medieval castle of the old town of Mdina', *Malta Archaeological Review*, 4 (2000), 15-25.

16 See G. Wettinger, 'The Lost Villages and Hamlets of Malta', in A. Luttrell (ed.) *Medieval Malta* (London, 1975), 181-216.

17 See T. Blagg, A. Bonanno, and A. Luttrell, *Excavations at Hal Millieri, Malta* (Malta, 1990).

Charles Dalli

SICULO INGENIO, AFRO CONFUSO:
MALTA IN THE LATER MIDDLE AGES

'The people have a Sicilian character, with a mixture of African', exclaimed Jean Quintin d'Autun in his *Insulae Melitae Descriptio* (Lyons, 1536); 'they are not strong enough for nor adapted to warfare. I would not have mentioned that had not the very Battus, king of the Maltese, admitted it about himself and his own people in the words of Ovid. The women are not at all ugly, but live very much as if they were uncivilised; they do not mix with other people; they go out covered in a veil, as if to see a woman is here the same as to violate her.' A member of the Hospitaller Order of Knights who took charge of Malta, Gozo and Tripoli from the emperor Charles V in 1530, Quintinus was not the first visitor to remark on Malta's 'African' qualities. Nor would his words go unechoed, for a string of early modern travellers commented on the inhabitants' 'Moorish' tongue and ways. Latin Christian expansion across the Mediterranean world in the high Middle Ages had enhanced the strategic location of the Maltese islands at the crossroads between Christian southern Europe and Muslim North Africa; the sea south of Malta was generally known as the 'African sea'. The islanders' humble cotton crop, which was listed by Francesco Pegolotti in his fourteenth century trader's manual, found its way to European marketplaces, which in turn supplied the Maltese population with a wide range of goods. A number of pilgrims touched at Malta on their way to the Levant and inserted a mention of the island in their travel diaries, while interest in the island's connection to Paul the apostle developed. Pirates sought shelter in Maltese waters as well as onshore, especially on the tiny island of Comino midway between Gozo and Malta, whereas raiders both Moorish and Christian carried away captives to the lucrative slave markets of the Mediterranean; Malta-based privateers often joined forces with other corsairs to launch extended raids along the Barbary coast or target the ships which plied the trade routes between Sicily and the southern Italian mainland, Tunisia and Tripolitania.

The Maltese islands shared, by and large, in the turbulent political history of the Kingdom of Sicily in the second half of the thirteenth century. A militant Roman Church determined the elimination of the successors of Frederick II from the southern kingdom, leading to the establishment of St Louis' warlike youngest brother on the throne of Roger II. Charles of Anjou's fifteen year rule in Sicily, from 1268 to 1282, was brought to an abrupt end in the same belligerent way as it was born; for decades, war became very much a way of life. The War of the Vespers opened the way for Catalan-Aragonese rule in Sicily (but not in the southern Italian mainland, which remained Anjevin-controlled). Both Ramon Muntaner and Bernat D'Esclot provide vivid descriptions of a major sea battle fought outside the Maltese harbour between the Catalan and Provencal fleets in July 1283; Roger of Lauria won the day, sealing Catalan-Aragonese mastery of the central Mediterranean sea lanes. Later the famed Admiral of Aragon switched sides and even obtained from Charles II of Anjou the concession of the Maltese islands as his county, in the style of earlier, mainly Genoese-born admirals like Henry of Malta, Frederick II's famed naval commander. It was, of course, a theoretical grant, like the Maltese title later on sported by Nicolo Acciaiuoli, the celebrated Florentine Grand Seneschal of the Kingdom of Naples, and his successor. Catalan-Aragonese government in the Maltese islands fluctuated between periods of feudal tenure and direct Crown rule, in which royal appointees like the town captain and the castellans of the Maltese sea-castle, or *castrum maris*, and the castle on Gozo, were counterbalanced by a council of citizens. Both Malta and Gozo had a town-based citizen body and governing council, or *universitas*, which met regularly and elected public magistrates who took charge of the islands' everyday administration. Malta was also the seat of a bishopric, and the Church had its own network of parishes, posts and tribunals firmly in place by the end of the fourteenth century. In the early fourteenth century the Kings of Sicily established a cadet branch of the House of Aragon as counts of Malta, with strong links to the Catalan Duchies of Athens and Neopatras in Greece, notably Alfonso-Fadrique. By the mid-fourteenth century a Catalan consul was resident in Malta, and Genoese and other Italian traders frequented the islands' waters on their way to Tripoli, Alexandria and elsewhere. The islands were a coveted prize during the decades of near-anarchy in Sicily, which sometimes flared into open warfare between the chief aristocratic families in the mid- and later- fourteenth century. In particular, the ambitious Sicilian magnate Manfred Chiaromonte annexed the islands to his burgeoning domains in Sicily, and it required a fully-fledged Catalan-Aragonese armed invasion of Sicily from 1392 to 1397 to bring the feudal clans to heel. From 1397 to 1530 the Maltese islands experienced an extended period of Crown rule during which a handful of families, pertaining to the local town-based nobility, enjoyed a near-monopoly of feudal grants and municipal appointments. A number of foreign-born servants of the Crown, traders and adventurers settled in the islands and soon integrated themselves into the local communities; Spanish or Sicilian ancestry apart, the real measure of their success lay in the extent of their landholdings and their ability to translate royal service into personal profit. In particular, at the start of Alfonso V's campaign to conquer the Kingdom of Naples, his Castilian galley captain, Gonsalvo de Monroy, forwarded the Aragonese monarch the lavish sum of thirty thousand florins, accepting in return the Maltese islands as collateral. Six years into Monroy's quasi-feudal administration, the inhabitants of Gozo and Malta were already up in arms; the cash-strapped king re-established direct rule in the islands by granting the islanders the right to repay the money themselves!

An Italian pilgrim on his way to the Holy Land in 1394, the notary Nicola Martoni, reported his astonishment at finding the islands well populated. At least a quarter of the islands' population, some ten thousand in all in the early fifteenth century, lived in the town, or Mdina (from the Arabic *madina*) and three suburbs: the *rabat* which grew outside the Castle on Gozo, the *rabat* outside Mdina on Malta, and the 'maritime suburb', popularly called Birgu or the *borgo*, which developed next to the sea-castle at the Maltese harbour. These centres accommodated shopkeepers and artisans, traders and administrators; within the Arabic streetscape of Mdina there evolved a town square adjacent to the Cathedral complex, as well as the 'lords' quarter', or the main street where some of the principal families of the island resided in their relatively spacious, 'European' style townhouses.

Sheltered by the sea-castle, the island's major stronghold, Birgu's castle garrison and mix of local and foreign seafarers distinguished that seaside community from the rest of the island, which was mainly agrarian in character. The urban centres included substantial Jewish communities which enjoyed a degree of autonomy, were largely self-governing 'servants of the Crown', and paid their taxes separately. Some of the earliest records of the native Arabic tongue spoken on Malta by Christian and Jewish inhabitants alike survive in late fifteenth century fragments of Judeo-Arabic script. A number of Jewish medics provided their services as town doctors. The Jewish communities were expelled from Malta and Gozo in 1492 following the decree of expulsion issued by Ferdinand and Isabella; ironically, the Jewish connection with the islands is best known through the artistic imagination of Marlowe's 'Jew of Malta', though scholars of Jewish medieval philosophy are familiar with the presence on Comino, in the late 1280s, of the Jewish exile from Sicily Abraham Abulafia, where allegedly he composed his *Sefer ha-Ot* or 'the Book of the Sign'. Mdina was the seat of largely absentee bishops, who enjoyed extensive estates near Lentini in Sicily, but the Church played a prominent role in public life, attracting endowments and fostering community life. By the fifteenth century most ecclesiastical posts were reserved for native churchmen who spoke the language; they were, nonetheless, generally barred from town politics. Learned clerics took charge of the publicly-financed grammar school at Mdina, while a number of citizens boasted varying degrees of legal learning, practised as public notaries or took their seat on several public tribunals. The town councils organised

Aerial views of Mdina (above) and the Citadel, Gozo (below) (Photo: MTA)

the island's militias composed of able-bodied male citizens and villagers, charged with the night watch in the countryside and along the coasts.

The rest of the population were largely clustered into dozens of tiny to medium-sized villages and hamlets spread out across the Maltese countryside; frequently the *rahal*, or Arabic for village, was more than just a grouping of farmsteads, as the term originally implied in Sicily and al-Andalus. By the late fourteenth century the Maltese islands were subdivided into parishes, or *cappelle*: twelve on Malta, with another four on Gozo. Malta's late medieval villagers participated in the island's political life by appointing parish representatives to the island's general assembly, which met infrequently; village constables oversaw the militia, while bailiffs were frequently called to settle disputes among peasants. Mdina's royal and municipal officials took charge of most public aspects of village life, to the chagrin of castellans whose intervention in village life, and the profit they could derive thereof, was mainly limited to the *borgo*. Most households lived in ground-floor farmsteads built around internal courtyards; to be sure, Quintinus called them *Africana magalia* or 'little African dwellings', and several features of late medieval architecture underline Malta's character as a cultural crossroads. As the author from Autun discovered, quite a few inhabitants made use of natural caves and rock-cut structures for their abode; likewise some of the islands' numerous late medieval churches and chapels were troglodytic in character, with a few surviving to this day.

The villagers, called *biduini* in a fifteenth century document, were mainly small landowners who cultivated cotton, cumin and other crops; animal husbandry ensured the islands of their fresh supply of meat and dairy produce, but the demand for grain could only be met through substantial imports from Sicily. Noblemen and fief holders, as well as the leading ecclesiastics, leased their own estates, vineyards and orchards and drew rent in cash and kind. Little of the material culture of late medieval Malta and Gozo has survived; the study of marriage contracts, last wills and testaments which survive from the late fifteenth century onwards lets us peek inside the homes of villagers and townsmen. The poor household's meagre furnishings were often passed on from one generation to the next; fold-away mattresses, richly quilted cotton and linen blankets, and female jewellery were prized possessions in the family's heirloom, and testified to the skills of local craftsmen – and women. Hunting was a leading pastime for townsman and peasant alike, while proceedings in the Bishop's Court, as well as municipal admonitions, mention taverns and wine shops in the villages and suburbs as familiar settings for drunken revelry and quarrels, gambling and prostitution.

The Maltese islands bore the brunt of Moorish raids, particularly the attack of 1429 in which, according to some sources, several thousand inhabitants were carried off into slavery. The islands' weak defences must have invited the preying eyes of slave-ships to their shores, while the records of late fifteenth century town council meetings are interspersed with fearful references to coming attacks.

Fifteenth century captives included the islands' bishop and several noblemen; these, at least, had a greater chance of getting themselves redeemed from their captivity in Barbary or elsewhere than villagers who often died in captivity. In 1488 a squadron of Turkish ships sacked Birgu, capturing a number of residents. No wonder the Hospitaller commissioners sent in 1524 to report on the island's poor defences sought to discourage their brethren from pursuing the idea of establishing the Order there. Religious foe and political enemy, yet also commercial partner and client, the Muslim - or 'Moor' – was by the fifteenth century the subject of collective fear and – by modern standards - racial hatred. This seems odd today (but not then), considering that Malta's inhabitants shared with North Africa the same common tongue; in an isolated instance, a notary public and cleric recorded a *cantilena*, or song, composed by his relative Peter Caxaro, a prominent notary public and townsman of late fifteenth century Mdina.

According to Bartholomew of Neocastro, a chronicler from Messina, an old Muslim on Gerba was asked in 1284 to explain the ancestry of the inhabitants of the Maltese and other central Mediterranean islands. The old man insisted they were the children of Byzantine women exiled from Sicily, who had had relations with the Egyptian oracle god Ammon; subsequently their offspring had adopted the Arabic tongue and the Muslim faith but vaguely recalled that their mothers spoke Greek. When Quintinus questioned the inhabitants about their language soon after the arrival of the Order in Malta, they claimed they could understand most of the Punic words uttered by Hanno, a Carthaginian character in Plautus' *Poenulus* or 'The Puny Punic', as well as the Semitic words in the Gospels. The Frenchman was also entertained with an explanation of the prevailing winds in Maltese waters, and how these correspond exactly to the winds mentioned in the account of Paul's shipwreck. 'The inhabitants are as firmly convinced that Paul has been in Malta as they believe that Peter has been in Rome.' Attachment to the Christian faith and the struggle against the Moor – around which an early modern Maltese collective self-image would evolve – were natural elements in the self-definition of a people which bridged the cultural divide across the two sides of the Mediterranean world.

References

Jean Quintin d'Autun's *Insulae Melitae Descriptio* (Lyons, 1536) was translated by Horatio C. R. Vella, *The Earliest Description of Malta* (Lyons 1536) (Malta, 1980). For a general account of the medieval history of Malta (in Maltese) see Charles Dalli, *Iż-Żmien Nofsani Malti* (Malta, 2002). The collections of essays published by A. T. Luttrell (ed.) *Medieval Malta: Studies on Malta before the Knights* (London, 1975), is still a useful starting point for the exploration of medieval Maltese history; see also A. T. Luttrell, *The Making of Christian Malta* (London, 2002), Godfrey Wettinger's study on *The Jews of Malta in the Later Middle Ages* (Malta, 1985), as well as the author's numerous articles on late medieval Maltese history which have been listed in Paul Xuereb (ed.), *Karissime Gotifride. Historical essays presented to Professor Godfrey Wettinger on his seventieth birthday* (Malta, 1999). Several articles by Godfrey Wettinger, Mario

Buhagiar, Stanley Fiorini and other contributors have been published in *Melita Historica* and in the annual *Proceedings of History Week*. Published primary sources include: Godfrey Wettinger, *Acta Iuratorum et Consilii Civitatis et Insulae Maltae* (Palermo, 1993). The series of *Documentary Sources of Maltese History* published by the University of Malta to date includes two volumes of notarial acts of Notary Giacomo Zabbara (1486-88 and 1494-97) edited by Stanley Fiorini (Malta, 1996, 1999). Stanley Fiorini has also edited *Documents in the State Archives, Palermo, 1259-1400* (Malta, 1999) to be followed up by a forthcoming volume of fifteenth century documents; while Julio del Amo Garcia *et al*, *Documents of the Maltese Universitas* (Malta, 2001) edits a collection of municipal documents at Mdina Cathedral Museum from 1405 to 1542. Godfrey Wettinger, *Place-Names of the Maltese Islands ca.1300-1800* (Malta, 2000) documents some six thousand medieval and early modern Maltese place-names.

Carmel Cassar

THE SOCIO-CULTURAL TRANSFORMATION OF MALTA: 1530-1798

The Advent of the Order of St John

Until the advent of the Order of St John in 1530, Malta was considered as one of the many communes of Sicily, a state of affairs that was not altered in the first part of the sixteenth century. This explains why in 1536, Jean Quintin d'Autun, a priest and a French member of the Order of St John, described Malta as,

> ...part of Sicily and has its same customs, Malta became Roman along with Sicily, and since that time it has always had the same rights and the same government.[1]

In what ways can we say that the drastic changes brought about by the Knights effected the everyday life of the inhabitants? Anyone who browses through the rich archival records of the time cannot help noticing that continual transformations were taking place in the lives of the Maltese throughout the sixteenth and seventeenth centuries.

The first Grand Master L'Isle Adam established the Magisterial Law Courts in 1533 and by the time of Grand Master d'Homedes (1536-53) the Order was allowed to enjoy the sovereign prerogative of coining money.[2] However the Grand Master continued to exercise very limited authority at first, and it was only with the passage of time that the Grand Master became conscious of his dual position. On the one hand, as head of the Order of St John, he was subject to the Order's statutes and was considered a *primus inter pares* by the other members of the Order. In such circumstances, a Grand Master was expected to rule according to the advice of the Grand Council. At the same time, the Grand Master ruled Malta as feudal overlord.[3] The Maltese became so dependent on their ruler that by the time of Grand Master La Valette (1558-68), the areas that remained free of his control were indeed very limited. In fact, the more intensively the Grand Master dominated the local administration, the more the Maltese shifted their allegiance from their *Università* to the Grand Master.[4] The more energetically the Grand Master's sovereign rights were exercised, the more restrictions there were on all sorts of common customary rights.[5]

Little heed was paid to the ancient privileges and liberties of the Maltese. In exercising its functions, the *Università* continually appealed for justification of its position. This argument was often based on antiquity, custom and traditions as a source of authority, and intended to hedge the encroaching demands of the Grand Masters.[6]

By the late sixteenth century, the *Università* became so weak and enfeebled, that it busied itself with small measures, particularly the distribution of grain, and generally played second fiddle to the Grand Master's rule.[7] Yet it remained the organ that vested the Maltese elite with oligarchic pretensions. It also served as a symbol of Maltese traditions of liberty.[8]

In order to survive and grow, the *Università* had to depend on its usefulness as an instrument of the Grand Master's government. As such, the latter did not wish to get rid of the 'people's representatives', but he expected them to be cooperative and acquiescent, consenting to money grants when asked, offering constructive counsel, and not directing their energies to criticism or obstruction.[9]

Work and Social Life

It may be said that the siege of 1565 brought about a radical transformation to life in the island. For most people it marked the end of an old era and the beginning of wider horizons. This break with the past manifested itself at all levels. Immediately after the siege, increased migration to Sicily coupled with the continual abandonment of the countryside by a peasantry attracted to city life, led to extensive rural depopulation. The widespread destruction of houses, fields, and livestock changed the villages physically. New buildings and churches in a different style were set up.[10]

The new system created a dual social structure that becomes sensible immediately after the Knights Hospitallers set foot on Malta and becomes even more apparent after the siege of 1565 and the building of Valletta. This duality did not exist at the social level only, but it also pervaded the mental and cognitive structures of Maltese society. Two different cultural blocs, strictly separated from each other, formed two opposing camps, namely, Mdina and its suburb of Rabat at the head of the countryside; Birgu (Vittoriosa after 1565) - and later Valletta - the seat of the urbanised harbour area.

On the one side there were the typical classes of an agrarian society, consisting of landowners, a small class of notaries, priests and clerks, and a mass of peasants. These had their own 'cultural traditions', to which they were strongly attached.

On the other side, there were the new town dwellers and other settlers, often in the direct employment with the Order, who were 'alien', lived in the city, cosmopolitan in their orientation and with no 'ancient culture' of their own. Yet in the harbour towns social distinctions prevailed, the fundamental difference based on economic affluence. The property owners and independent members of the town such as merchants, craftsmen, shopkeepers and professionals spurned those who were subservient or economically dependent by virtue of being labourers, apprentices and servants.[11]

The Order came to represent a concentration of international capital, which coupled to an incredible reserve of human resource, made possible a vast programme of urbanisation, successfully carried through from the moment the Order set foot on Malta in 1530. Even so, it is surprising to realise that all this could be achieved from an island with a population-base of merely 30,000 in 1590.[12]

The creation of a new urban area around the Grand Harbour had effectively revolutionised the human geography of Malta and the life of its people. But the factor that dominated and conditioned Maltese life after 1565 was the emergence of Valletta as the administrative capital of the Maltese islands. Urban theory recognises cities to be, not merely dense concentrations of people, but above all, concentrations of people doing different things, where the urban character derives more from that variety of activity than it does from sheer numbers.[13]

In reality, to speak of the harbour area is to speak of a conglomeration of four towns: Valletta was the political and economic capital. In the upper part of the city, the Grand Master, the Grand Council and high society lived and exercised their authority. The common people lived mostly in the lower districts. On the south bank of the Grand Harbour, there were the 'Three Cities' of Vittoriosa (known as Birgu before 1565), Senglea (or Isola) and Cospicua (previously known as Burmola). Between them the four towns had a population of around 10,000, that is, approximately one-third of Malta's population in 1590.[14] The 'Three Cities' eventually came to form part of the popular district, together with lower Valletta with their narrow streets packed with foreigners, merchandise, sailors and slaves.

The entire economy of Malta was orchestrated from Valletta. The political influence of the harbour towns on the countryside, the power of the Grand Master, the highly concentrated nature of trade, all combined and contributed to the vast development of the harbour area. This growth imposed an order on the area it dominated, and established a wealth of administrative and trading connections. As well as being a very busy area, handling practically all Malta's foreign trade, the harbour zone had by the early seventeenth century developed into a cultural centre of some value.[15]

The harbour towns were multifunctional and together they performed roles that were essential for the whole society. The creation of an efficient and well-organised bureaucracy was to form the basic organ for the economic and political dependency of the countryside. Thus the more technically efficient the harbour towns became, the more they increased the potential dependency of the countryside.[16] The virtual

Grand Master L'Isle Adam (1530-34) welcomed at Mdina in 1530 (Photo: MTA)

Grand Master La Valette (1557-68) the victorious leader of the Great Siege (Photo: MTA)

monopoly of Valletta, over importation of all commodity items and over exports including that of cotton (the major cash crop) enabled the new capital, from very early on, to control all the production and redistribution within the Maltese islands: it was, above all, the central sorting station.[17] Whether bound inland or abroad, everything had to filter past through the Valletta harbour.

The harbour town dwellers were well aware of the influence that the state had on their daily existence. The intensification of traffic and trade, the new technical possibilities of administration, and the economic development of the harbour area, is part of the picture of the systematisation of authority and the strengthening of the Grand Master's political role.

Urban Culture and the Influx of Migration

The heavy influx into the new urban areas of foreigners and people from the countryside, starting from the sixteenth century onwards, altered the ethnic character of the population of Malta. Even if the newcomers did not bring a distinctive culture of their own, as the case seems to be, their physical preponderance managed to transform the distinctiveness of the Maltese lifestyle. One may rebut that cultural patterns, exclusively attached to urban dwellers, may be grouped together and defined as urban culture.[18] After all, what is essential here are not the internal contrasts of urban culture, but its different character from peasant mentality. It was common for the early modern middle classes to mingle with the ordinary folk on account of the ever-growing demographic pressures. Thus, both wealthy Maltese and the Knights often occupied sumptuous buildings, while the workers were housed wherever space was available. The ground floor of these imposing edifices usually contained stables, stores and workshops with an entry from the street, sometimes with displays extending into the street itself.[19]

Very often a number of families had to share the same dwelling in order to be able to pay the rent bill. Matrimonial contracts indirectly refer to the shortage of space within the harbour towns. Thus, whereas it was normal for peasants to own a normal house, maybe consisting of some rooms at ground floor level,[20] it was common for poor artisans to live in one-room cellars, whose only means of light and air was the street door. The *mezzanini*, constructed above them, were likewise small and ill-ventilated.[21] Except for the houses of the rich, tenements in the harbour area were economically planned. Such an atmosphere made family life difficult, and therefore most of the socialisation processes took place not in the family, but at public levels.

Urban culture did not simply renew or transform earlier cultural practices, but organised them according to fundamentally new principles based on a 'market economy'. Obviously city life was looked upon as 'alien' by the indigenous population right from the very beginning of the Order's rule, independently of class attachments, ethnic identity and other traditional prejudices. The immense surge of activities generated both by the foundation of Valletta and by the Order's presence, with its manifold interests, made the island one of the busiest centres of the Mediterranean. It served to create a cosmopolitan atmosphere that impressed itself on the character of Valletta and helped to enrich the country especially in the more creative activities.[22] The Order of St John had thus managed to establish a ruling system that seeped down the social scale and gave character to the harbour area.

But these dominant cultural patterns failed to infiltrate the entire structure of peasant society. Philip Skippon, writing in 1664, could visibly distinguish city dwellers from villagers. He sums up the situation, by noting that while most city dwellers speak Italian well, the natives of the countryside speak a kind of Arabic.[23] Godfrey Wettinger tends to agree with Skippon's view. He argues that,

> ...Gradually the townspeople became largely indistinguishable in outlook from the inhabitants of other towns in southern Europe ... In the countryside, however, old forms of cooking, old musical instruments, much of the old types of houses ... remained very much in use. There they still repeated the same old Maltese proverbs ... worked the land in largely the same old way, hunted ... and held homely festivities.[24]

In practice, however, the Great Tradition certainly influenced village life that went on to absorb and adopt elements of city life in a way to make it its own. The cosmopolitan character of Valletta helped enrich the island-state, especially in the more creative sectors. The architectural boom spilled from the new city into the surrounding countryside and by the early seventeenth century, the parish churches of larger villages like Qormi and Birkirkara, as well as, smaller ones like Balzan, Lija, and Attard, could boast of a parish church that was built on a magnificent scale.[25] Thus one could say that urban culture possessed such a great integrating force that it quickly achieved hegemony. It was able to create a mode of behaviour and a way of life by and largely acceptable to the whole society.

The cultural magnetism of the city was underlined by its political centrality. Functioning as an administrative capital, Valletta broadcasted the fashions and values of the Grand Master's court.

Ideas and styles, fashions, manners, and habits, artists, architects, and Belgian tapestries, were all imported from 'trading Europe', and paid for by the Order's accumulating capital.

It attracted litigants to its Law Courts, and passed on the government's proclamations to the rest of the island. In the economic field, the city became the harbinger of modernity with markets that

> ...were as much a meeting place for social intercourse as they were for business transactions.[26]

Artistic and cultural influence, information, and news were thus disseminated to the country. Valletta, like any other early modern European capital, was the power house of cultural change. Together with the other towns of the harbour area, it monopolised the economic and administrative resources of the new state. The influence of the new capital was so strong that the rural way of life in all its manifestations became symbolically equated with a lack of cultural accomplishment, a view particularly diffused among the intellectual elites.

In short the aggressive policies of the Order of St John vis-à-vis the neighbouring Muslims, coupled with the cosmopolitan atmosphere created in the harbour area, had drastically transformed Maltese socio-cultural values. By the middle of the seventeenth century, the Vice Chancellor of the Order Gio. Francesco Abela (1582-1655) could point out that apart from being overpopulated Malta was frequented by a multitude of foreigners who eventually settled there.[27] These settlers often declared themselves to be citizens of Valletta or inhabitants of Malta, suggesting that early modern Malta was a haven teeming with foreigners.

Meanwhile many Maltese, attracted by the good work opportunities, the abundance of food, and the relative safety of nearby Sicily from Turkish incursions, were induced to settle there before and after the siege of 1565. This tendency often verged on mass migration, especially in times of danger, and it was only during the reign of Grand Master Lascaris Castellar (1636-57) that special measures to check the outflow were enacted. Lascaris decreed that a special licence had to be sought by those intending to emigrate from Malta. The Grand Master even enacted regulations prohibiting the continued ownership of landed property by Maltese living abroad and who showed no intention of returning to Malta.[28] Yet this phenomenon of native Maltese leaving their island home was more than compensated by the uninterrupted inflow of foreigners and returning migrants.

When the Hospitaller Order of St John set up their convent in Malta, it found a population who considered the Sicilian communes as sister-entities, in which it was therefore natural for Maltese to set up home if so inclined.[29] At the time, the majority of individuals viewed their commune with a loose transferable sense of loyalty. This attitude facilitated the movement of people to and out of Sicily. It seems that, even until the early seventeenth century, there was little feeling among the Maltese themselves that their commune was in any way distinct or unique from others in Sicily. Malta kept its representatives or consuls in the principal Sicilian towns, whose job was to ensure a regular supply of goods, particularly commodities, to the island. On the other hand, Sicilian businessmen had their representatives in Malta, and artisans were engaged side by side in all activities.[30]

Human traffic continued to flow into Malta from Mediterranean Europe, coupled with enforced settlers or slaves throughout the Order's rule. Slaves were captured in warring and corsairing activities, mostly during swift raids carried on the coasts of North Africa, and came to form an important labour force, employed especially as galley-rowers, stone-carriers, builders and domestic servants. Slaves were relatively free to mix with all strata of Maltese and resident society and were allowed to take part-time jobs in order to gain money for their eventual redemption. Yet, it was not uncommon for some of these slaves to accept

Contemporary and early modern views of Valletta and the harbour area, which developed into a cosmopolitan centre during the Order's rule (Photo: MTA and the National Maritime Museum)

Christianity, marry locally and in their turn become integrated within Maltese society.

Population shifts, and the continual increased rhythm of trade and communications made it necessary for the urban dwellers in the harbour area to acquire the *lingua franca* which, in the early modern Mediterranean, consisted primarily of Italian words.

The Spoken Word and Literacy

The Knights kept strong communications with Europe and strengthened both the merchant fleet and the navy. At the same time, Malta served as a base for corsairs against the Muslims of the Maghreb and the Turks in the Levant. Finally, one should include the multitude of foreign men who contracted marriages with Maltese women, notably in the harbour towns. It was therefore natural for Margarita Bonnici of Vittoriosa, to refer to a herb she used for a love potion both in Maltese and in *franco*.[31] Concurrently Minichella de Patti from Vittoriosa apparently communicated with her French husband Antonio Gontier in Italian.[32] 'Italian' was then the language of trade in the Mediterranean[33] that Godfrey Wettinger argues to have spread in the Maltese harbour towns at the expense of Maltese, then reduced to the status of a local dialect spoken by servants, peasants and the lower orders of society.[34]

Yet it seems that up to the end of the eighteenth century, the Maltese language was practically the exclusive language for daily communication used in the countryside, and to a large extent it continued to be employed by the townspeople too. People of all social conditions, including the learned and the rich, spoke Maltese.[35] The evidence of Georgio Scala given in September 1598 further confirms this view. Scala went to confess at the chapel of the Grand Master at the crypt of the Conventual Church of the Order in Valletta and then went to receive communion at the church of the Franciscan Minors. There he met a friar whom Scala assumed to be a foreigner because he spoke Italian rather than Maltese.[36] The case of Dr Melchior Cagliares, a well-known judge of the Grand Master's court, who took the Grand Master's side in a quarrel between his master and Bishop Gargallo, strengthens this point further. In 1579 the Bishop excommunicated Cagliares, so that no good Catholic was supposed to have dealings with him. The Inquisition records refer to Cagliares' reaction to the sentence. When the Rector of St Paul's Parish Church in Valletta, presumably a friend of his, one day failed to greet the Judge whom he encountered in the town-square, Cagliares called out in Maltese,

Le tibzax hecde kif fixkilt lohrayn infixkil lilik
[Do not worry, I will confound you as I did others].[37]

Thus, even the Maltese educated elite communicated in the local tongue between them. At the same time, Maltese was often associated with ordinary people and popular culture.

By the late eighteenth century, this jargon seems to have developed into what M. A. Vassalli labelled, *dialetto della città* (city dialect), which he considered as the most corrupt dialect of Maltese, due to the large number of foreign words it contained. The presence of a great number of foreigners, as well as the use of foreign languages, notably Sicilian, Italian, French and other European vocabulary, led to *barbarizzare l'idioma nativo* (the 'barbarization' of the native idiom).[38]

This development induced Vassalli in 1796 to insist on the social need to cultivate *la lingua nazionale* (the national language). Vassalli reflected upon the attitudes of his times and admitted that Maltese seemed undignified and abounding in 'barbarisms' which, he concluded, were the result of the long neglect of the language.[39] Vassalli's ideal perspective of a defined Maltese culture and language was to take root over a century after his death. His dream of Maltese consciousness could only materialise with the widespread use of literacy.

At the end of the eighteenth century, a little before Vassalli put ink to paper, very few Maltese could read and write and this seems to have been more evident in the rural areas. For instance, at Qormi in 1773, out of 226 heads of households, only 22 or 9.7 percent could sign their name.[40] And a signature does not qualify an individual as literate. Written works were accessible only to the educated few, the majority of whom were clerics. Hence, in spite of the theoretical existence of writing and printing, only a limited elite could fully utilise the written word. The net result was that oral culture continued to dominate the scene at least until the early nineteenth century.[41] Malta, like the rest of the Mediterranean, possessed a definite literary class whose compositions were often transmitted to the illiterate mass of the population in oral form.

Several authors have stressed the idea that writing could be an instrument in the hands of the powerful, and employed to control and communicate. It has been argued that in early modern Europe, writing was used to bolster up the power of the clergy, the administrative class that exercised power, and a small cultural elite.[42] It all becomes evident when one realises the importance that was attached to notarial deeds. Indeed the Maltese, from all walks of life, had ever since the fifteenth century resorted to the notarisation of all-important acts in both private and public life.[43] Notaries, who were experts in legal formulas and terminology, drew up a great mass of documentation, ranging from marriage contracts and powers of attorney to official ordinances and petitions.

The differentiation into high culture (written) and low culture (oral) was not simply a cultural division that created also a distinction between two kinds of work. Administrative, academic and professional work could only be aspired to through the acquisition of a literary education; manual work required considerable experience in the craft performed. This means that manual workers generally had no motivation whatsoever to learn how to write. This seems to have applied to the gifted like the local engineer Mastro Thomaso Dingli, engineer in church architecture of several important parish churches during the first half of the seventeenth century. Dingli concluded his deposition in front of the inquisitor by marking the sign of the cross rather than signing his name.[44] Thus writing created a radical distinction between the literate and illiterate elements of society.[45]

In the end, the kind of knowledge obtained from the literary tradition tended to be more highly valued than the practical knowledge and experience acquired by some form of manual participation.[46] Hence written literature was considered to be the highest form of expression, even though oral culture remained the only accessible form of expression for the majority of the people. The frequent promulgation of *bandi* (edicts), which were read out aloud in town and village streets for the information of those present, was the only official way news filtered to the masses.[47] In such circumstances, literacy comes to be considered as the established and respected tradition, while orality is transformed into a living art. Nonetheless, there is a constant interplay between oral and written forms.[48]

Official Religion and Popular Religious Beliefs

Another influential literate group were the clergy. They had long been expected to be literate in order to celebrate mass, since this oral performance was in fact 'a public reading from the service book, the Missal'.[49] The clergy were obliged, or at least expected, to recite other daily prayers, mostly readings from the Breviary. They had to keep themselves up to date in their pastoral care by reading other books as well 'whether they were theological, devotional, or practical'.[50] Occasionally priests could be insufficiently educated, at times even illiterate, a situation revealed by Dusina's Apostolic Visitation Report of 1575, that brings out clearly the poor state of education among a large number of sixteenth century Maltese clerics.[51]

Most of those examined by the apostolic visitor had received their education a generation or so before the closing of the last session of the Council of Trent (1564). On several occasions Dusina had to remark that the priest concerned knew no grammar, or that he only had a smattering of Latin, or that he could read, but understand Latin very imperfectly. The priests' knowledge of theology was just as bad, so that in the end the apostolic visitor could express satisfaction with a mere ten out of the forty priests he examined.[52] Access to the ranks of the clergy appears to have been rather effortless since candidates did not seem to require anything more than a 'right intention' and a minimum capacity needed to fulfil the appropriate duties.[53] Low standards were required from the candidates and many clerics received their rudimentary clerical apprenticeship from their own parish priest.

Dusina was sent to Malta expressly to reform the diocese, and to upgrade the standards according to the instructions of the Council of Trent. He therefore

Grand Master Pinto (1741-73) (above), Grand Master Vilhena (1722-36) (bottom left) and Grand Master Hompesch (1797-98) (Photo: Heritage Collection)

insisted that a seminary be set up to train the secular clergy. Nevertheless, the proposal of the apostolic visitor was not discussed prior to the meeting of a Diocesan Synod called in 1591. On that occasion Bishop Gargallo decreed the foundation of a seminary, but the proposal got temporarily shelved. Instead, a Jesuit College was established in Valletta on the insistence of the bishop himself. Early evidence of the services provided by the Jesuit College is provided by the cleric Andrea Caruana of Qormi who was summoned before the Inquisition on New Year's Eve of 1603. In his evidence Caruana declared his ignorance of village matters since he attended the Jesuit College and only returned to the village at night time.[54] The Jesuit College must have served the diocesan requirements well since it took more than a century before Bishop Cocco Palmieri finally set up a seminary in 1703.[55]

Until the eighteenth century the priesthood often constituted the only literate system of the community at village level. The clergy also served as a link between the government of the Order of St John and the mass of the villagers. The position of the parish priest was so strong that sometimes he took the place of the notary when a will had to be drawn. It also shows the social control exerted by the Church over the majority of illiterate inhabitants.

In spite of this, there existed a fundamental tension between written and oral cultures. The literate elite was increasingly inclined to have recourse to the written word both in the public and private spheres; oral traditions were based 'on nostalgic and utopian esteem for a society without writing, governed by words that everyone could hear and signs that everyone could understand'.[56]

Inquisition records in Italy likewise reveal the importance of the written word in the equipment of the cunning men and wise women in town and countryside alike, and the belief in its power to cure the sick. Amulets, with writings on them, were so common, that diocesan synods frequently denounced the 'superstitious words' inscribed on sheets of paper.[57] The inquisitors frequently admonished people who believed in such practices, but apparently they were very much aware that old habits diehard. In 1625 in an attempt to eliminate these beliefs, the clergy were obliged to denounce anyone who practiced magic either to the bishop or the inquisitor - a directive that was repeated in 1646.[58]

This approach explains why techniques employed by witches in sixteenth and seventeenth century Malta were still in use till 1798 and perhaps beyond. Muslim slaves and wise women were still preparing concoctions, reciting prayers and other rites and formulas, making omens, and suggesting the use of talismans and amulets for protection against the evil eye.[59] Indeed, some forms of magic still persist among some sections of the population.[60] While the literate public had to be guided and kept under control in order to avoid any incipient 'heretical behaviour', the illiterates presented a different problem due to their propensity towards and belief in popular religion.

Some Inquisition cases refer to the writing of books on magic, some of which appear to have been manuals on magical practices, like the one found by two priests when still aged sixteen. Among other recipes, the book in question contained suggestions on how to acquire immunity against fire-arms, and others on love magic which the two accused tried to procure for themselves.[61]

Books on magic could also be found in the libraries of learned gentlemen like Notary Jacobo Baldacchino, who owned a collection of books on necromancy. His accuser recalled some six of them with titles as: *Centum Regnum, La Clavicola di Salomone, il Ragiel, il libro delli esperimenti Cornelio Agrippa, Li Prestigii,* and *La compositione di quattro anelli*; the denouncer was positive that Baldacchino possessed a much larger collection.[62]

The existence of books on necromancy suggests, not only that the literate were keen on witchcraft, but they also found time to risk writing on prohibited topics. Among such individuals, we learn about a certain Dr Galeazzo Cademusto, a resident of Valletta, accused in 1579 of witchcraft practices, and even of having written a book on necromancy described as *libro di diavoli* (book of devils).[63]

Evidence from the Inquisition archives suggests that oral and literate cultures not only coexisted, but they also interacted. Thanks to the widespread general illiteracy, books and written papers were attributed an aura of mystery. Yet it would be misleading to assume that the uneducated were the only ones who resorted to such practices. Whereas a sound education could control excessive credulity, it did not completely destroy faith in popular beliefs. Thus, the literate were sometimes so keen about magical practices that they possessed whole sections of their private libraries dedicated to the topic. In a general overview of the Reformation sympathisers in Malta the Cambridge anthropologist Jack Goody points out that the dissemination of ideas, contrary to the teachings of the Catholic Church, was only partly aided by the advent of printing and the circulation of the book. He argues that the radical ideas themselves 'struck chords in the minds of the inhabitants because they corresponded to existing doubts'.[64]

The Makings of a Maltese Culture

The developments which took place in Malta in the century following the advent of the Order of St John, and especially after the siege of 1565, can be said to have profoundly transformed Maltese society, as well as the cultural values of its inhabitants.

Around the harbour area, the Order created a new urban environment within which was concentrated most of the Order's attention and activity, intensified after the foundation of Valletta in 1566. The division between the urban centres around the harbour and the *campagna*, as the rest of rural Malta was called, was to remain a permanent feature throughout the Order's rule and after. These drastic and rapid changes were accompanied by the rise of a social class of subjects or *familiares*, on whom the Order tended to rely heavily for the running of its bureaucratic machine. Undoubtedly, events were able to take this determinate course because the geography that really counted was the one established by the lanes of communication. As a consequence, Malta was drawn nearer to Europe, simply because it happened to lie nearer to the communication lane running along the southern coast of Europe. Its old and intimate ties with Sicily are an inevitable corollary of this situation.

The old isolation of Malta melted into thin air, when in 1530 the Hospitaller Order of St John were granted the Maltese islands - originally together with Tripoli - as a fief on such generous terms that the Order turned the island into a sovereign state in all senses of the word. Various categories of foreigners, attracted by good work opportunities, settled in Malta, importing social, cultural and ideological components, which were different from those originally predominating in the island.

Consequently early modern Maltese culture cannot be considered as some kind of uniform, homogeneous structure. Rather one has to think in terms of various culturally distinct groupings, that simultaneously managed to create a cultural hegemony under a dominant elite on the lines propounded by Roland Mousnier for seventeenth century France. Mousnier argues that, in a society of orders, social groups are arranged hierarchically, in a descending scale of status and privilege. The organising principle in such societies is the social esteem accorded to the group's economic role. This system, points out Mousnier, is different from a 'society of classes' in which individuals are legally equal, formal privileges do not exist, and social stratification follows one's function in the economy.[65]

By contrast medieval Malta had essentially been a peasant society. Mdina served primarily as a small fortified 'urban' centre that carried on the whittled-down function of the old *civitas*, where the old municipality met, where it held its law courts, and where most of the notables kept an official place of residence. Farming was practically the sole capital resource of the islands, coupled with some shipping activity, and corsairing on the side. The land was roughly equally shared out between the Church, the landowners, and the peasants themselves.

With the establishment of the Order of St John in Malta in 1530, the island immediately entered a phase of transformation. Overnight, the texture of society took on a cosmopolitan character with the insertion of more refined social standards, and of a more numerous class of highly skilled artisans. The Order kept a small but highly efficient navy; so that the overall effect of vastly increased maritime exchanges, together with the flourishing practice of corsairing, exerted a beneficial influence upon the backward rural economy of tiny Malta. In short the Hospitallers had introduced a European style urban civilisation into Malta.

Notes

1   J. Quintin d'Autun, *Insulae Melitae descriptio. The Earliest Description of Malta (Lyons 1536)*. Translation and notes by H. C. R. Vella (Malta, 1980), 19.

2   M. Sant, 'Minting and attempted recalling of fiduciary copper coinage in Malta', *Melita Historica*, VI, 1 (1972), 60.

3   D. Cutajar and C. Cassar, 'Malta and the sixteenth century struggles for the Mediterranean', in *Mid-Med Bank Ltd., Report and Accounts 1985* (Malta, 1985), 51.

4   G. Wettinger, 'Early Maltese popular attitudes to the government of the Order of St John', *Melita Historica*, VI, 3 (1974), 261.

5   Ibid., 269.

6   NLM, Lib. 1220 is a treatise by notary Vittorio Griscti, member of the Harbour *Università* in the late 1740s, 191-93; see also NLM, Lib. 148, ff.39v, 55.

7   NLM, Lib. 148, ff.39v, 55; Dal Pozzo, *Historia della Sacra Religione Historia della Sacra Religione Militare di San Giovanni Gerosolimitano, detta di Malta*, I (Verona, 1703), 241-42; NLM, AOM 453, f.277.

8   G. F. Abela, *Della descrittione di Malta Malta isola nel mare siciliano, con le sue antichità ed altre notitie* (Malta, 1647), 260, 262; NLM, Lib. 1220, 197-98.

9   An insight of this kind is found in I. Bosio, *Dell'Istoria della Sacra Religione Religione et ill.ma militia di S. Gio. Gerosolimitano*. Tome III (Rome, 1602), 516. On its arrival in Malta on 18 May 1565 the Ottoman armada was anchored off Mgarr for the night. The country people who had found refuge at Mdina jumped to the conclusion that the Ottomans' first objective was Mdina. The result was a concerted move by the country people to seek refuge in the harbour enclave that seemed to offer better security. In a state of panic, the *Università* despatched an envoy to the Grand Master choosing for the delicate task Luca de Armenia. He travelled in the night of 18 May to Birgu and presented to the Grand Master the views of the municipality, namely that if Mdina was going to be abandoned, he asked for shelter to be provided for the people then at Mdina; if on the other hand, the Old City was to be held, then the *Università* felt it ought to be garrisoned by a contingent of professional soldiers and be supplied with arms and ammunition. The mental anguish of the Maltese at the fate of Mdina can be gauged from the intense melancholy evinced by a Latin poem written by Luca de Armenia himself in the interval between the Ottoman fleet's appearance and La Valette's reply to de Armenia's embassy. Luca de Armenia's poem *Ad Patriam* was discovered by C. Cassar in NAM, MCC, CST, II (1565-1566), unpaginated, and published as 'O Melita Infelix' in *Melita Historica*, VIII, 2 (1981), 149-55. A more recent discussion of de Armenia's poem is to be found in C. Cassar, *Society, Culture and Identity in Early Modern Malta* (Malta, 2000), 201-203, 289.

10 L. Mahoney, *A History of Maltese Architecture* (Malta, 1988), part iii.

11 Cassar, *Society, Culture and Identity*, 237-53.

12 NLM Univ. I, ff.187-88; C. Trasselli, 'Una statistica maltese del xvi secolo', *Economia e Storia* (1966), 477.

13 E. Lampard, 'Historical aspects of urbanisation', in P. M. Hauser and L. F. Schnore (eds), *The Study of Urbanisation* (New York, 1965), 520-23.

14 NLM Univ. 1, ff.187-88; Trasselli, 477.

15 Cassar, *Society, Culture and Identity*, 91-94.

16 I. Wallerstein, *The Modern World System* (New York, 1974), I, 102-03; C.K. Wilber, 'Introduction: Economic development and underdevelopment in historical perspective', in C. K. Wilber (ed.), *The Political Economy of Development and Underdevelopment* (New York, 1973), 57-59.

17 V. Mallia-Milanes, 'Valletta: 1566-1798. An epitome of Europe', *Bank of Valletta Annual Report and Financial Statements* (Malta, 1988), xxiv-xxx.

18 Cassar, *Society, Culture and Identity*, 106-25.

19 P. Cassar, *Medical History of Malta* (London, 1964), 328-29; C. Cassar, 'Popular perceptions and values in Hospitaller Malta', in V. Mallia Milanes (ed.), *Hospitaller Malta, 1530-1798. Studies on Early Modern Malta and the Order of St John of Jerusalem* (Malta, 1993), 453.

20 Mahoney, 82.

21 P. Cassar, *Medical History*, 328-29.

22   Cassar, *Society, Culture and Identity*, 91-94, 106-113, 131-140.

23   Ph. Skippon, 'An Account of a Journey thro' part of the Low Countries, Germany, Italy and France [c.1664-1680]', in J. Churchill, and A. Awnsham and John (eds), *A Collection of Voyages and Travels* (London, 1732), 632.

24   G. Wettinger, 'Aspects of Maltese life', in G. Mangion (ed.), *Maltese Baroque* (Malta, 1989), 62.

25   Mahoney, ch.8.

26   Mallia-Milanes, 'Valletta 1566-1798', xxxii, xxv.

27   Abela, 75.

28   NLM Lib. 148, f.77v.

29   Antonio Coniglio alias Fenech a Maltese resident of Licata, who dictated his will on 21 December 1630, declared himself *fedelissimo cristiano, cittadino di questa città della Licata* (Most faithful Christian, citizen of this town of Licata). G. Bonello, 'The last will of Antonio Coniglio', *The Sunday Times (Malta).* 7 February 1993, 32.

30   R. Valentini, 'I cavalieri di S. Giovanni da Rodi a Malta. Trattative diplomatiche', *Archivum Melitense*, IX (1935), 177.

31   In August 1617 Margarita Bonnici, sive *La Bruna*, stated that among other remedies for love magic, Margarita Bertone advised her to mix four pepper grains and a herb called *reheuma* in Maltese or *musco marino in franco* (i.e. *lingua franca*) or Italian. CAM, AIM, Crim. Proc. 40A, f.161v. Such indications help to confirm the widespread use of *lingua franca* among the lower echelons of the Harbour area at least since the early seventeenth century.

32   Catherina wife of Vincentio Xerri reported that, *Minichella con furia et collera iniuro a decto suo marito dicendoli cornuto... et molti altri iniuri quali io non posso sapere perchè non intendo della lingua Italiana stando che lei parlava Italiano.* (With fury and anger Minichella offended her husband by calling him 'horned'... and many other insults which I could not know because I do not understand the Italian language since she spoke in Italian). CAM, CEM, AO 480, f.115: 21 October 1602.

33   K. Whinnom, 'Lingua franca: historical problems', in A. Valdam (ed.), *Pidgin and Creole Linguistics* (Bloomington and London, 1977), 297.

34   Wettinger, 'Aspects of Maltese life', 61.

35   Cassar, *Society, Culture and Identity*, 159.

36   AIM, Crim. Proc. 16A, case 5, f.112.

37   AIM, Crim. Proc. 144, case 7, ff. 94v-95. See also Cassar, *Society, Culture and Identity*, 160; C. Cassar, 'The first decades of the Inquisition: 1546-1581', *Hyphen – A Journal of Melitensia and the Humanities*, IV (Malta, 1985), 225.

38   M. A. Vassalli, *Ktyb yl klym malti mfysser byl-Latin u byt-Taljan... sive liber dictionum Melitensium... lexicon Melitense Latino-Italum* (Rome, 1796), xvi.

39   Ibid., xix.

40   CAM, AIM, Civ. Proc. 5, ff.190-208; F. Ciappara, *Marriage in Malta in the Late Eighteenth Century* (Malta, 1988), 16.

41   W. J. Ong, 'Is literacy passé?', in D. Potter and P. Sarre (eds), *Dimensions of Society: A Reader,* (London, 1974), 97.

42   P. Burke, 'Introduction', in P. Burke and R. Porter (eds), *The Social History of Language* (Cambridge, 1987), 2.

43   G. Wettinger, 'The village of Hal-Millieri', in A. T. Luttrell (ed.), *Hal-Millieri: A Maltese Casale, its Churches and Paintings* (Malta, 1976), 58-59.

44   K. Gambin, 'Fabio Chigi: Inquisitor-Missionary and Tridentine Reformer. A man of culture in Malta 1634-1639', (MA unpublished thesis, University of Malta, 1997), 22. cf. AIM, Crim. Proc. 51, case 14, f.40: 19 December 1634.

45   J. Goody, *The Logic of Writing and the Organization of Society* (Cambridge, 1986), 121.

46   *Id.*, *The Interface between the Oral and the Written* (Cambridge, 1987), 162-63.

47   Collections of *bandi* of the sixteenth and seventeenth centuries have been preserved. See for example: NLM Lib. Mss. 149, 429, 430 and 641.

48   H. J. Chaytor, *From Script to Print* (Cambridge, 1945), ch. 6. When referring to post war peasants of Locrorotondo in Apulia (Italy), H. Galt points out that, 'Many peasants' lack of language facility and literacy limited their access to information emanating from administrative centres, such as

the municipal and provincial levels of government. Information was diffused by word of mouth, often subject to distortion, as it passed from family to family through faulty understandings. Participation in town events, such as saints festivals and the Sunday mass, brought country folk closer to sources of information like posters, but these were written in Italian "bureaucratese", and not always accessible'. *Far from the Church Bells: Settlement and Society in an Apulian town* (Cambridge, 1991), 205-06.

49   P. Burke, *The Historical Anthropology of Early Modern Italy* (Cambridge, 1987), 120.

50   Ibid.

51   NLM Lib. Ms. 643, 507-30; The Visitation Report has recently been published by G. Aquilina and S. Fiorini (eds), *Documentary Sources of Maltese History. Part IV Documents at the Vatican. No.1 Archivio Segreto Vaticano Congregazioni Vescovi e Regolari. Malta: Visita Apostolica no.51 Mgr Petrus Dusina, 1575* (Malta, 2001).

52   Ibid.

53   A. Torre, 'Politics cloaked in worship: State, church and political power in Piedmont 1570-1770', *Past and Present*, 134 (1992), 46.

54   Ibid., f.173: 31 December, 1603.

55   V. Borg, 'Developments in education outside the Jesuit "Collegium Melitense"', *Melita Historica*, VI, 3 (1974), 216.

56   R. Chartier, 'The practical impact of writing', in R. Chartier (ed.), *A History of Private Life*, III. Eng. trans. (Cambridge Mass and London, 1989), 123.

57   Burke, *Historical Anthropology*, 121-22.

58   P. Cassar, *Medical history of Malta*, 426.

59   Cassar, 'The first decades of the Inquisition', 207-38; A. Bonnici, *Il-Maltin u l-Inkizizzjoni f'Nofs is-Seklu Sbatax* (Malta, 1977), 71-122; F. Ciappara, 'Lay healers and sorcerers in Malta (1770-1798)', *Storja '78* (Malta, 1978), 60-76.

60   J. Cassar-Pullicino, *An Introduction to Maltese Folklore* (Malta, 1947), 35.

61   CAM, AIM, Crim. Proc. 61A, case 45, f.219.

62   Ibid., 2B, case 31, f.338v: 19 September, 1574.

63   Ibid., 6C, case 48, f.1037: 2 November, 1582.

64   Concluding remarks by J. Goody on C. Cassar, 'The Reformation and sixteenth century Malta', *Melita Historica (New Series)*, X, 1, 65 in J. Goody, *Representations and Contradictions. Ambivalence towards Images, Theatre, Fiction, Relics and Sexuality* (Oxford, 1997), 267-69.

65   R. Mousnier, *Les hiérarchies socials de 1450 à nos jours* (Paris, 1965), esp., chs. 1 and 2.

Frans Ciappara

THE FRENCH IN MALTA

In spite of the preoccupation of some historians with historical origins, the French Revolution happened by accident. Following its intervention in the American War of Independence France was bankrupt, and to put its finances in order Louis XVI summoned the long-forgotten Estates General. Once at Versailles the Third Estate swore not to return home without having given France a new constitution. The result was momentous. The gates of history were flung open and an unstoppable deluge carried all before it, both throne and altar.

The adherents of the 'the most beautiful revolution that has ever been enacted on the world's theatre' championed the rights of the middle classes and harboured Rousseau's ideas of a contract between the ruler and the ruled. These maxims fitted with the aspirations of the Maltese bourgeoisie, rich but devoid of political rights firmly held by the Hospitallers.

The Maltese middle class owes its origin to the demilitarisation of the Mediterranean after the battle of Lepanto in 1571. The age of formal war was over and the 'tired giants', as Braudel refers to Turkey and Spain, were replaced by such upstarts like Algiers and Malta, practising another form of war – corsairing. Lying in the bottleneck between Sicily and North Africa, Malta was perfectly placed to act the part of 'the capital of Christian piracy'. The lure of profit attracted not only Maltese but also foreigners, who established themselves in the four towns round the grand harbour. Between 1590 and 1716 the population of this conurbation increased to about one-half of all the Maltese population.

By the middle of the seventeenth century the *corso* had started its decline. But now, and especially in the eighteenth century, Malta established itself as an important mercantile centre. This activity started with the building of the lazaretto in 1643. With the cheapest rates in the Mediterranean it rapidly became a depot

The French Army disembarking after the Order's capitulation

Allegory of the French Republic (Photo: Cathedral Museum, Mdina)

General Napoleon Bonaparte

for merchandise, so that in 1752 Grand Master Pinto had to build nineteen new stores.

A strong commercial class came into being, Cospicua in the eighteenth century being described as *popolatissima, particolarmente di persone che hanno negozi marittimi*. During the period 1750-60 a total of 307 *literae patentes* were issued to masters of sea-craft to travel to the 'four parts of the world'. Maltese merchant ships plying between Malta and southern Europe brought grain, wine, cheese, tuna, meat, coal, and snow. The most important item though was *specie* and several Maltese left the island with considerable sums of money belonging to many individuals *ad effetto di negoziarli nel viaggio ... per Marseglia, Barcellona, ed Allicanti.*

This wealthy class aspired for a share in the government and welcomed the French Revolution with its castigation of birth and its motto *la carrière ouverte aux talents*. A letter dated 19 May 1792 informed the Maltese government that a conspiracy was being hatched. It was financed by the rich merchants of Burmula and Żejtun who carried on their trade with Barcelona. The 'worthy' Charles Zammit had divulged it to Virieu; and it had been allegedly revealed to him by one Buhagiar, a Maltese merchant from Burmula. The leaders were supposed to be Samuel Caruana, a former public prosecutor dismissed from his post for venality, and one Dr Gatt, a lawyer. For the last year the two had exchanged their correspondence with Basire, vice-president of the *Comité de Surveillance* in Paris every twenty days. The revolutionaries sang the revolutionary song *Ca ira* under the bastions of fort St Elmo and boasted that soon they would lie down in the shadow of the tree of liberty. The rights of man would establish equality while destroying the Order, the grand master and its council, to the great benefit of the Maltese people who suffered slavery, tyranny and poverty at the hands of their government. The adherents of the revolution increased every day and some 250 people had already joined. The inhabitants of *casal* Żebbuġ were almost all adherents of the revolution; and one of them was mentioned by name, a certain Dimech, who even was in correspondence with Basire.

Grimaldi, the *chargé d'affaires* of Naples in Malta, did not believe Zammit's revelations; the persons mentioned in the letters were either dead or else fell under no suspicions at all. Inquisitor Scotti was not impressed either by this 'unjust gossip'. He believed there were no grounds for this 'mere invention', which he considered false and unfounded. His successor Mgr Giulio Carpegna thought likewise, even though there were not lacking, both among the Maltese and the Hospitallers, those who sympathised with the French and their 'detestable maxims'. So did he write to the cardinal secretary of state on 30 March 1797. However, only three months later, in June, a revolt was discovered.

If this influential class, though, welcomed the French revolutionaries, the rest of the population hated them for their anticlericalism. News of what was happening in France soon reached Malta either through travellers' reports or, more often, through correspondence: the nationalisation of church lands, the civil constitution of the clergy, the introduction of civil marriage and divorce, the massacre of several priests. The pope's effigy was burnt in Paris, and at Marseilles the coat of arms of His Holiness was removed from atop the residence of the papal consul and smashed.

Attached as they were to their church, the inhabitants were inflamed with hatred towards the 'so-called French republic'. Anger increased when the French armies invaded Italy. On 17 May 1796 Cardinal de Zelada informed Inquisitor Carpegna in Malta that Italy could not have been in a more critical situation: 'rapid and significant have been the victories of the French army'. The king of Sardinia had been made to ask for an armistice, by which he ceded the most important fortresses to the French. Parma and Modena paid heavy contributions and Milan was occupied. Fear invaded the land. The pope tried to reach an agreement with the French and sent Azara, the Spanish minister plenipotentiary in Rome, to Bologna. An armistice was concluded with Bonaparte on 23 June 1796 but negotiations for a definitive treaty broke down. The pope, who at one point thought of coming to Malta, called for a general mobilisation, asked the grand master for 10,000 guns and had two *mezze-galere* built at the shipyard, on which one hundred Maltese sailors were to serve.

From his headquarters at Milan Napoleon foretold that Liberty would soon be proclaimed for all Italy, and on 31 January 1797 declared war on the Papal States. A peace treaty, signed on 19 February 1797, and which made the pope pay a huge indemnity, was only a prelude to the final reduction of Rome, which fell on 15 February 1798. A Roman Republic was declared and a huge tree of liberty was planted at the Campidoglio. The pope's temporal sovereignty came to an end, and Pius VI started on his journey north to die later at Valence.

Of all European powers only Great Britain remained to be dealt with. In this situation there emerged the plan of an expedition to Egypt and in May the Army of the East sailed from Toulon. Napoleon intended to turn Egypt into a French colony, as well as using it as a base for the destruction of English commerce and a stepping-stone to the creation of a French empire in the East. On the way he captured Malta both to forestall Austria and Great Britain and to make France master of the whole Mediterranean.

As a prelude to attack he asked the Maltese government to let his ships enter the Grand Harbour to take water. When this peremptory demand was refused troops were landed. Opposition was ineffectual since strategic places were in the hands of traitors and it only took two days to subdue the strongest place in Europe. The first troops landed at 4 am at St George's Bay but the French knight de Preville, who was in charge there, waved a white handkerchief and went to meet them as if they were his friends. The Maltese defenders, who included 1200 men of the Birkirkara peasant militia, fled for safety. These incidents of treachery were repeated in several engagements and the Maltese soon realised they had been betrayed.

By Sunday 10 June the French were in possession of the greater part of the Maltese countryside and the cities were in imminent danger of being assaulted.

In those perilous times a Maltese delegation advised the grand master and his council to ask for an armistice. Eventually a Convention was signed on 12 June on board *L'Orient*. Its seventh article stated:

The inhabitants of the islands of Malta and Gozo shall continue to enjoy, as in the past, the free exercise of the Catholic, Apostolic, and Roman religion. They shall retain the property and the privileges which they possess; no extraordinary taxes shall be levied.

Napoleon came ashore that same day. But if he was welcomed by the Jacobins 'the mass of the people who actually constitute the nation feared the arrival of the French, seeing in them men without religion, enemies of the clergy'. A plot was laid to assassinate *l'eroe liberatore* and all his co-generals as they entered the Marina Gate to Valletta. The plan failed and Napoleon continued his way safely to the residence of Baron Paolo Parisio, where he stayed for the rest of his week's stay in Malta.

The next day a breath-taking series of laws started to be issued. The central government or Commission of government was composed of nine members, and the island was divided into twelve municipalities of 3000 inhabitants each. Political prisoners were set free; Muslim slaves gained their freedom in exchange for Maltese captives in North Africa. Jews were allowed to establish a synagogue and illegitimate children enjoyed all civil rights. The *Journal de Malte* signified that now that the Maltese were free they were to enjoy all the advantages of a nation which had broken its bonds. The administration of justice was reformed, and twelve Justices of the Peace were set up, one for each municipality. In civil proceedings they judged cases involving amounts up to 100 *livres*. In criminal cases they had the right to arrest malefactors for not more than fifteen days, and to inflict fines not exceeding the sum of 24 *livres*. Fifteen primary schools were to be set up and the university was replaced by a Central School which discarded such faculties as theology and the arts and emphasised utilitarian subjects like mathematics, science, navigation, and medicine. The right of sanctuary was abolished, and offenders could be apprehended also within church precincts.

These reforms by a brilliant man 'whose presence was enough to demoralise and put to flight your tyrants' would have ushered Malta into the modern world overnight, and were generally welcomed by the Maltese. Other orders, though, engendered much opposition. Men were pressed into service with the French expeditionary force to Egypt. Pensions formerly paid by the government of the Order were suspended, as well as the payment of interest on loans to the Treasury. Interest on loans advanced by the *Monte di Pietà* was increased to six percent. An order which resulted in much discontent was the granting of leases from three generations to a fixed term of one hundred years. Forced loans were exacted from wealthy families and sixty young men were to go and study in Paris at the expense of their parents.

The nobles were humiliated when on 14 July they burnt their patents at the Altar of Liberty. Heraldic arms were taken down and it was forbidden to wear any

Dun Mikiel Xerri (1738-99), one of the Maltese patriots executed by the French (Photo: Heritage Collection)

Vaubois, French Governor of the Maltese Islands (Photo: Heritage Collection)

The Battery on Jesuits Hill in action with British blockading vessels in the background (Photo: Ian Bouskill)

livery or mark denoting nobility. But the heavy hand of the lawgiver fell especially on the clergy. Napoleon's order that all foreign religious, with the exception of Bishop Labini, were to leave Malta was welcomed by the nationals as they got their benefices instead. All else however antagonised the church. No one could take religious vows before the age of thirty years. Appeals to the pope were prohibited, pious foundations suppressed, and cemeteries received all corpses, Catholics or not. Each religious order was allowed the retention of one convent only and churches were closed and despoiled. According to the inventory made by two French officers, the total value of the loot taken from St John's amounted to 420,438 *scudi*. At the Mdina cathedral only a few candlesticks and crucifixes were left for the main altar and the chapel of the Holy Sacrament. Village churches were not spared, either. At Qormi, St George's parish church was despoiled of various silver articles which were used for the religious celebrations of the feast of Corpus Christi.

Discontent rose to fever pitch, and the Maltese were only waiting for an opportunity to show their anger. The occasion came when the battle at Aboukir Bay on 2 August 1798 shattered French naval power in the Mediterranean and left the British fleet supreme in this inland sea. Fortified by this news they raised the flag of revolt exactly a month later. On Sunday 2 September it had been programmed that the gold and silver articles of the churches and convents of Rabat and Mdina which had been closed by the government were to be sold by auction. The old capital was soon captured, its defendants killed and then dragged to Mtarfa heights, where they were burnt. Soon each village raised its local battalion and a national assembly was formed to coordinate all future efforts against the enemy. Four different camps were set up to keep under constant watch the Valletta and Cottonera fortifications.

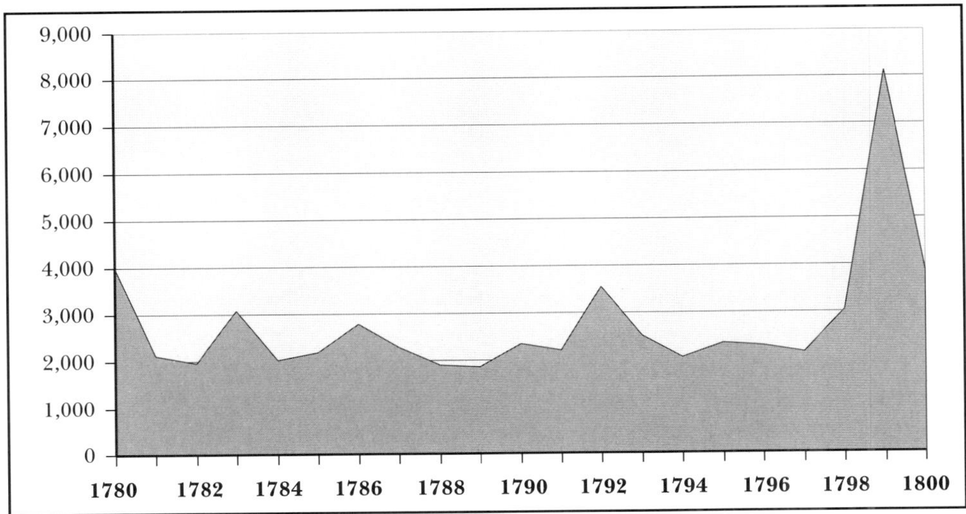

Table 1: Burials in Malta 1780-1800

Malta came to a standstill, trade completely ceased and all effort was concentrated on winning the war. The death rate rose to stunning heights (see Table 1). At the start of 1799 a great fever epidemic swept the island, and as the Maltese were living at a near-starvation level it wrought havoc on the population. So great was the number of the dead that they started to be buried outside the church in the outskirts of the villages. This desolation was accompanied by the displacement of people on a large scale from the towns into the villages. (Table 2). In 1799, for instance, there were 886 such refugees at Naxxar. The well-to-do returned to their summer residences; the others, like the 73-year-old widower Benigno Farrugia of Cospicua, found refuge with their relatives or with other families. Some however had nobody to turn to and when they died they were simply described as 'unknown paupers' and were buried *ex charitate*.

Burial of city dwellers in the villages					
	Valletta	Floriana	Vittoriosa	Senglea	Cospicua
Żejtun	20	4	23	29	121
Qormi	98	13	7	10	28
Birkirkara	68	10	–	8	7
Naxxar	33	5	8	17	30
Żebbuġ	37	3	1	9	6
Għaxaq	9	–	8	10	21

Table 2

There was a great scarcity of corn, money, arms and ammunition, since the greater part of the food supplies and money of the Maltese were inside the enemy-held cities. In these circumstances it was decided to send Luigi Briffa with a letter to the king of Naples. The Maltese informed Ferdinand that 'since they could no longer suffer the tyranny of the French they had rid by their own efforts the ... whole countryside of the French within 17 hours'. They requested permission to import food from Sicily on credit, and demanded as well arms and ammunition. A week later the Maltese leaders wrote to Nelson, asking him to blockade by sea the harbours of Valletta. The English admiral sent Nizza instead, who was in command of a Portuguese naval squadron.

To force the issue, in January 1799 some Maltese within Valletta, led by Guglielmo Lorenzi, hatched a plot to open the city gates and let in their compatriots. It failed and some 54 patriots were executed. The next month therefore they asked Great Britain for protection, and Alexander Ball was sent to Malta as supreme commander of all land forces. He assumed command of the

Maltese militias and brought peace among their leaders, often in disagreement with each other.

In November 1799 English troops were landed under General Graham and in July 1800 Major General Pigot arrived with the 35th regiment. The day of deliverance was nearer and the French capitulated on 5 September 1800 with all honours of war.

The Maltese who sacrificed their lives on the altar of liberty against the French did not die in vain. The revolt served first to cut Malta from the retrograde kingdom of Naples and attach it to the British Empire. The inhabitants looked forward to experience the advantages of being governed by Britain, earnestly hoping that their island would become the emporium of the Mediterranean and that the arts, sciences and manufactures would be protected. They might have been disappointed in their wishes but they did enjoy, among other advantages, the civilising benefits of a free press, primary education and the rule of law.

The revolt had a still more important result; it was an exercise in self-government. The high hopes of the Maltese that Britain was the harbinger of a democratic process by which they would be allowed to govern their home affairs proved illusory for one hundred and twenty one years. But during the insurrection against the French the Maltese had proved beyond any doubt that they could govern themselves and would not stop before their new masters allowed them to do so. And they had become so pregnant with nationhood that they dared to mention for the first time the word 'independence'. They were determined not to submit to any other Power than Great Britain, 'preferring otherwise to perish under the walls of their city if they cannot maintain their liberty and independence'.

References

Azopardi, V., *Giornale della Presa di Malta e Gozo* (Malta, 1836).

Blondy, A., *L'Ordre de Malte au XVIIIe Siècle. Des Dernières Splendeurs à la Ruine* (Paris, 2002).

Bosredon Ransijat, J. B., *Journal du Siege et Blocus de Malta* (Malta, 1837).

Ciappara, F., 'The Fear of the French Revolution in Malta', in *Proceedings of History Week, 1999* (Malta, 2002).

Denaro, V., *The French in Malta* (Malta, 1963).

Doublet, O., *Memoires Historiques de Malte* (Paris, 1883).

Hardman, W., *A History of Malta during the Period of the French and British Occupations, 1798-1815* (London, 1909).

Mifsud, A., *Origine della Sovranità Inglese su Malta* (Malta, 1907).

Testa, C., *The French in Malta, 1798-1800* (Malta, 1997).

Thompson, J. M., *The French Revolution* (Oxford, 1966).

Henry Frendo

LIFE DURING THE 'BRITISH' PERIOD:
STRAINS OF MALTESE EUROPEANITY

On the occasion of Malta's twenty-fifth independence anniversary in 1989, I had served as a consultant to the National Library of Malta in a commemorative exhibition, put up at the National Museum of Archaeology, Valletta, which was recorded in a set of publications.[1] How much more fitting is it that Malta's membership of the European Union on 1 May 2004 should be commemorated similarly by means of a tangible reality – an exhibition and a book – rather than it being solely or simply an occasion for one more fleeting spectacle, however luminous. Malta's membership of the EU in May 2004 deserves a discourse and a resonance: it has a lasting meaning and content for future generations, partly because it is also, historically and culturally, a fulfilment of past connections, sentiments and aspirations, not least during the last two centuries or so. It is for this reason that I accepted the invitation, albeit at short notice, to contribute some historical reflections on this occasion, and at the same time to take the opportunity to update, from a 'roots' perspective, the *exposé* already offered in an earlier volume: *Malta: Culture and Identity*.[2]

Various aspects of life in Malta from the coming of the French onwards - be they linguistic or literary, political or cultural, social, commercial or economic, religious or indeed diplomatic, even international – have been covered in a number of works since 1964, including several of my own. Here I can briefly indicate in what respects the present may be said to tie in and to be in some way rooted in that past. From insurrection in September 1798 to independence in September 1964 we had essentially, consciously or unconsciously, a 'nation-making' exercise, partly influenced or provoked by colonialism itself; but in addition the Maltese experienced many factors and went through various phases that changed and moulded them and their country, one of the smallest ethno-linguistic minorities in the world.

Already in 1802 the *Dichiarazione dei Diritti degli Abitanti di Malta e Gozo* showed a remarkable juridical and civic consciousness on the part of the leaders, such as the right to freedom of conscience under the rule of law, with a thinly veiled presumption of independence.[3] Like the Order before it, Britain, a naval power, was interested in harbours, docks, defences, militia and seamen, which meant that the pull from field to shore gathered momentum, radically altering demographic placement, occupational trends and production cycles. Wars, too, continued to affect the Maltese, wherever Britain was involved in the Mediterranean, as it increasingly was after taking Gibraltar from Spain in 1704, and more so after the opening of the Suez Canal in 1869. Some of these, such as, especially, the Crimean War in the mid-nineteenth century, and the two world wars in the twentieth, profoundly affected the Maltese, bringing work and in various ways, to some more than others, an accompanying prosperity, if only a temporary one. The last war literally changed the face of Malta, not necessarily for the better, wiping it out altogether in several places under intense, but ultimately unsuccessful, Axis bombardment. The war also wiped out what was left of *italianità* and *latinità* as a party political platform, although anglicization did not wipe out Malteseness, Maltese becoming increasingly the language of public debate. The '*Otto Settembre*', first recommended as a national day by nationalist leader Fortunato Mizzi in 1885, now came to commemorate two victories, the first over the Ottoman Empire, the second over the Nazi-Fascist Axis.

British influences may be traced in different spheres: they were administrative, military, constitutional and parliamentary, educational, even legal, although in this domain Malta's *corpus juris* was mainly non-English and remained so. To some extent, they were social and colloquial in more than linguistic terms, with plenty of mixed marriages over time. In education, after 1880, anglicization became a matter of policy, with attempts to push out Italian and introduce Maltese together with English continuing until 1934, after self-government had been revoked. At the same time, and partly for that reason, two main political parties had come about: although there was no very linear progression, both took root and evolved more or less in a continuum which in some respects remained recognisable and traceable.[4] The role of Roman Catholicism and of the Catholic Church in Malta and among her people remained steadfast throughout most of the period of British rule, which sought to garner the Church as an ally by generally respecting and honouring its status and privileges. At the same time, however, since Britain was a Protestant power, the firmly entrenched Maltese Catholicism was from the start a bulwark of in-group identity, devotion, piety and indeed festival. It was a buffer against 'the other', just as Italian remained for well over a century to those reared in it, brought up to regard it as Malta's language of education and public life, indeed of civilisation, a passport to the continent.

An industrial power in a pre-industrial society, Britain was a force for modernisation, as other expansionist European powers had been in their own ways. If one looks at infrastructural projects, from water to electricity to drainage, the nod came first from the British side, also because it was worried about infections or epidemics which could adversely affect the garrison, hence the traditional importance of quarantine restrictions. If one looks at communications – transport, for instance – a 'progressive' range of means may be sketched ranging from train to tram to bus to ferry and motor-car. Such technological advances, which might well have occurred irrespective of who was in power, mixed and matched with Maltese, Southern European and Mediterranean likes and traits, be that in fashion, food, housing, leisure, or indeed other more characteristic means of transport, such as the *karrozzin* or the *luzzu*. Apart from a new-found discipline, regimental practices left a mark on the local band clubs, which mushroomed after the second half of the nineteenth century, a lot of brass and marches, where Italian, Maltese, British and other composers featured prominently. In other respects, however, the British presence was telling: in sport, football started becoming popular by the beginning of the twentieth century, with plenty of teams from the fleet or the garrison to play against, while polo reached Malta from India before Britain. Other genres of folk entertainment and festivity were and remained purely Maltese, be that impromptu *għana* on the guitar or sea-side *ġostra* on the greasy pole, or the regatta boat-races, sailing and the popular seasonal fishing for *lampuki*, the rearing of pigeons, also hunting and trapping, or horse-racing in the street - before the Marsa *'ta' l-Inglizi'* finally provided a proper racing track which Maltese jockeys could use.[5]   There was the *festa*, and of course the *banda*.

In architecture, based on the Maltese stone, British influence was minimal compared to the earlier Baroque heritage, but one may trace in some detail what occurred in related fields over the last two centuries in the expert contributions made by some of our leading specialists: Dr Paul Cassar on medicine; Mr Justice Hugh Harding on law; Ġuże Cassar Pullicino on folklore; Antonio Espinosa on art; Professor Alexander Borg on the Maltese language; Professor Oliver Friggieri on Maltese literature; Professor Anthony Bonanno on archaeology; the late Leonard Mahoney on architecture; and so on.[6] To a greater or lesser extent, one will generally find, broadly, an Anglo-Italian mix with a variety of Maltese ingredients, some more distinct than others.

In Maltese poetry and literature, English inroads were limited, with Maltese largely taking over from the Italian, as in the law courts: English never managed to penetrate the inner sanctum of Malta's lawyer-politicians. In music too, Italian retained much influence, not only in opera, until the post-war populism of 'pop', where very slowly English had the better of Italian. A severe blow was dealt to theatrical, operatic and cultural productions of all kinds when their dearest repository, the Royal Opera House in Valletta, was razed to the ground by the Luftwaffe, and it has remained a ruin since. In the media, we find English chasing Italian, first on radio in the 1930s, then on television in the 1960s, with Maltese increasingly important. This was less so in the press, where World War II put paid to Italian, but English continued to be a preferred medium in several Maltese newspapers, as Italian had been before it, thereby underlining once again the

The British coat-of-arms at Palace Square, Valletta (Photo: Heritage Collection)

The British 100-ton gun at Fort Rinella (Photo: MTA)

bilingual, sometimes trilingual, nature of Maltese society, especially among the relatively large and growing middle classes. After 1964, Malta acquired an international persona, participating, sometimes seminally, in various fora, and not only through its diplomatic corps.[7]

In tourism, which picked up after independence (with industry and to a lesser extent agriculture becoming a pillar of Malta's now diversified economy), the British still lead as visitors, followed by the Germans, French and Italians. Meanwhile, holidaying abroad, not least in Britain and Italy, became widespread among the Maltese themselves. Having emigrated and settled right around the Mediterranean littoral in the nineteenth century, and in the far corners of the English-speaking world in the twentieth, of late the Maltese too have become more mobile and adventurous, thanks to airplanes and cruise-liners; as well as far better connected and less isolated, thanks to cable and internet. Such trends are likely to increase with Malta's membership of the EU.

Given the nature of this historic occasion on 1 May 2004, however, what I propose to do is rather more focussed and, as it were, tailor-made. I would like to search for, and to pinpoint, what I regard as a lingering aspiration interspersed through the past few centuries, on the part of Malta and of the Maltese (as they were a-becoming), for a greater affinity and belonging with Europe. I perceive Europe here not simply as a mainland but as a mainstream, not simply as a continental mass but as a matrix and milieu, in socio-economic as well as in politico-cultural terms. In EU discourse, that would be called a 'space'. For us, it certainly would comprise the sea together with the land. As times and situations changed, in ways which may at first sight even seem opposed or antagonistic, a tendency is nonetheless traceable, pointing towards a 'European' urge, latent or overt. For want of better words I shall call this syndrome 'being part of a larger whole'.

Neither linear nor constant, the yearning is recurring and decipherable. It is, in many ways, a need, geographical and circumstantial; but it has been a need conditioned by desires, qualities and preferences. This means that concerns of a socio-cultural nature repeatedly have weighed upon needs of a basic-survivalist kind, which in turn means that in modern times the sense of a self-respecting nationality vis-à-vis a wider, bigger community was increasingly present, in the forge, however imagined, however portrayed.

I have also put in inverted commas a defining chronological reference in the title to Malta's 'British' period. This was actually, more and more, a 'Maltese' period – and that precisely at a time when the islands were still ruled by the United Kingdom of Great Britain and Northern Ireland, part and parcel of a British Empire on which the sun never set (but set it did).

Britain, which greatly influenced what happened in the Maltese islands during the past two centuries, was not a mainland European power at all. It was an island in between the Atlantic Ocean, the North Sea and the British (or was it the French) Channel, with a great navy and merchant fleet. But cultural pedigree betrayed the physical geography no less than the mineral wealth. Some British newspaper's comment about the continent having been 'cut off' by a storm in the British Channel has been regarded as a joke for a long time, as indeed it should be. If David Hume, Adam Smith and John Locke were not Europeans, one might as well question the credentials of Montesquieu, Voltaire and Rousseau, or Lafayette for that matter. The jenny wheel and the steam engine were as 'European' as the railway and the shop floor, the consequences of which so impressed Dickens and Marx, among others, together with counter-parts throughout the continent, where speech and writing were not always as free as in Britain. Thus, the mainstream is more important than the mainland, even if, in Malta, still closer links to the neighbouring southern European countries and kingdoms (but also, in this case again, to the north African shores) had preceded the advent of the British in the Mediterranean region by a long stretch. These long-distilled 'Euro-Med' connections continued to leave their mark in spite of British rule, or because of it, as new conceptual, institutional and practical syntheses gradually emerged, with the ensuing symbioses coming to characterise life in the colony, itself increasingly a nascent nation-state, open to modernisation.

Without delving so far back as Malta's role within the Roman Empire (for a time as a *municpium*), or St Paul's shipwreck and the subsequent conversion of the islanders to Christianity (which in time took grip of the popular imagination unshakeably), by the first few centuries of the Rome-centred Christian European era Malta had already tasted or possessed, to some extent, arguably its two most outstanding formative features, in the complementary domains of law and religion, not to mention art and architecture. It was by virtue of such codes and ethics that Cicero would defend the Maltese in the forum against a Roman colonial official, one Caius Verres, who was a thief.

Even the Arab period, of which there is barely a surviving trace in Malta - other than in the slightly camouflaged Semitic roots of a vernacular language - was very largely an 'import' from Sicily until Norman times. Moreover, lest we forget, the Arab presence in the Middle Ages had assumed important mainland characteristics well beyond Sicilian shores, to which Andalusia's rich, eclectic heritage bears witness still.

Much more telling for Malta's 'European' moulding, according to this interpretation, was the fifteenth century. In a typically feudal situation, rendered at one time more remote and more particular by its insularity, rebellion against abuse and oppression does not simply take the form of a *jacquerie*, a slash and burn uprising by vassals against the lord or his overseers. No, in addition to an element of violence (including the holding of the Aragonese lord's dame in a castle) there is a difficult negotiation. A redemption from monies allegedly due is subjected to a pact. And that understanding, in 1428, presumes some acquired or re-acquired rights for the inhabitants of the land - not simply as serfs, indeed no longer as serfs, but as subjects with some rights, more or less as a distinct people. These rights, including the right not to be sold off as a private possession and a right of petition to the viceroy, are recognised by the throne in a kind of charter, a parchment preserved to this day. This miniature *magna carta* slots into the annals of European history, where a balancing of power between lords, kings and subjects could be hammered out, not infrequently on the battlefield. What it represents really is that in Malta too, there existed the wherewithal for a slow but sure transition from fiefdom or worse to nationality and nationhood, evident already in the organised mobilisation of effort, at very considerable sacrifice, in the face of sustained abuse by an avaricious foreign owner-overseer, Gonsalvo de Monroy, in a time of economic stress. Justice was sought in relation to an Aragonese oppressor just as it had been against a Roman pilferer. That presumes a commonality, a stamina and a leadership: the poor rural domains also had their citadel. No wonder, then, that as early as the fifteenth century the native idiom would be seen as a qualifier for position, and by the sixteenth century we find Malta described in different manuscripts as *'nostra patria'*, indeed as *'dulcissima'*, with aspects of its self-identity sometimes demonstrated in other ways.[8]

All this is not unrelated to what happened during the French and British occupations between 1798 and 1964 or so. Such a reading would be altogether unhistorical, for by the time these latest of rulers arrived they found what had been put in place and instilled earlier. That would include the physical as much as the social, the spiritual, and the cultural. Malta by the late eighteenth century may not have been plush but nor was it barren and neutral, generally bereft of a thinking mind, a throbbing heart and a sensitive soul.

Charles V's decision to find a home for a wandering Roman Catholic order of chivalry - the hospitallers - by giving them Malta, raised the Christian European colours more decisively than ever. But not only on the ramparts. Here, in Malta, was a well-endowed, multi-lingual aristocratic institution of alms and arms, Christian by mission, European by definition, holy and true, extending right across the borders of continental Europe and beyond them from Provence and Auvergne to France; from Italy to Aragon, Catalonia and Navarre; Germany, Castille, Leon, Portugal, and until Henry VIII's quarrel with the pope, to England. Elsewhere I have analysed at some length how the Knights 'of Malta' progressively changed the islands and their people in eight important ways.[9] Politically, Malta became a small European state, psychologically more secure and outward-looking, it moved from hinterland to harbour. Malta became more urbanised, administratively centralised in a baroque capital city, while economically new work practises, skills, crafts and opportunities arose in construction, the navy, trade, production and services, partly catering to a demanding market at close quarters. Religiously, Malta became almost a theocracy, a Catholic frontier, what later might be called 'Europe's Southern flank', the enemy being not fascism, nazism or communism but the Ottoman Empire and Islam, best exemplified by the (unsuccessful) 1565 siege, a full-scale fight to the finish against the turbaned infidel. Socially and culturally, the influences were widespread – mainly but not only in the towns, including folk feast and festival, as well as the more sophisticated recreations and pursuits of elites from theatre to fashion, cuisine to music. To all, Catholic Europe became an

Artist impression (above) and soldiers facing the crowd during the Sette Giugno riots (right) (Photo: Heritage Collection)

The crowd which gathered in front of the Governor's Palace on the occassion of the Self-Government constitution in 1921. Inset: British Governor Lord Plumer and Maltese leader Dr Filippo Sceberras (Photo: Heritage Collection)

ideological imperative, with Europe being rather more than just the Rome of popes and caesars. On the continent's southernmost edge and frontier, Malta came to have probably the biggest slave market in Europe. The ethnography and demography changed too, as did customs, manners, relations and aspirations, especially among the upwardly mobile. Knights were not as holy or removed as they seemed; to several, the harbour and the town became more attractive than the farm and the village (the more so as the Maltese cotton and tobacco industries declined in the nineteenth century). As the population increased fivefold or more, Italian remained throughout the main written language and means of formal communication, with Roman Catholicism the official religion, monitored by one inquisitor after another.

Into this stunned and betrayed old world did General Bonaparte's revolutionaries suddenly arrive, issuing edicts, burning titles of nobility, outlawing slavery, stopping the inquisition, fashioning out 'Parisian' education systems, restricting the numbers of ecclesiastics and monasteries, preaching liberty, equality and fraternity, frog-marching youngsters off to the Egyptian campaign, toying with agricultural tenure and land lease, auctioning church treasures, collecting monies, often looting, sometimes raping, occasionally shooting. Within three months, in a popular armed insurrection, the Maltese of all social classes quickly forced the French garrison to seek shelter behind the bastions of Valletta and its three surrounding harbour towns, taking control of the rest of the countryside, the citadels, towns and villages. With some Neapolitan, Portuguese and most importantly British naval help, the Maltese held out, with much difficulty, increasingly decimated, until finally the starving, blockaded French surrendered, not to themselves but to the British, in 1800. The British thus had come to stay in Malta for many decades and generations, at least until 1964.

In the French and British connections, however antagonistic they were at the point of first impact, Malta again had two major European fonts. The first, clearly, was its brush with the French Revolution and the (French) Enlightenment. However supine the revolutionary slogans may have appeared in practice, the fact is that they came to Malta with a bang, but come they did.[10] They were not easily forgotten, and would be applied against the British by the Maltese in their subsequent fight for freedom. Much the same happened elsewhere in Europe towards the final stages of the so-called Napoleonic era. In this too, therefore, the Maltese experience fits into a European typology – be it Portuguese or Spanish or Italian, where Bonapartist rule was overthrown in one popular uprising after another. Malta's was one of the first. The clash of the 'old' world with the 'new', if so it may be called, created a tension and a resonance, which would seep into the liberal psyche, catapulting in time beliefs about popular sovereignty wherein it was people not dynasties who mattered above all. In the late nineteenth century, when Nationalist crowds sang the Marseillaise beneath the (exclusively British) Union Club in Valletta's *Strada Rjali*, that was partly what they meant to say. The other part was a taunt, the more so at a time of renewed Anglo-French rivalry over colonial expansion.

British influences on the Maltese way of life were many and varied, although it is unfair to haul every influence to Britain's door. Much was going on elsewhere in Europe and in the European empires themselves, so that a unidimensional assumption as to 'reform' or 'progress' would be wrong. Moreover, in colonial situations, there are always problems with terminology, or rather discourse, and Malta is no exception. The reason is that what the ruler may choose to call 'reform' may be seen as a deformation by the would-be recipient, and similarly for 'progress', which could be resisted as an attack on tradition, or a misconceived interpretation or disruption of a value system. A classical case would be that provided by one Sir Penrose Julyan who once referred in a report to those (distinguished) Maltese members of the bar who did not know English as its more 'ignorant' members. Once again here, racial or linguistic superiority or immersion would posit 'intelligence' against 'ignorance' on the basis of prejudice or misconception. By the same token would policies based on Darwinian 'survival of the fittest' principles be advanced or applied. On the other hand, British liberalism (and Maltese agitation) made a free press possible in Malta as early as the late 1830s, while the elective principle for a crown colony legislature was introduced, cautiously, a decade later.[11] By such means, a public opinion could start being formed and sustained, at least among the literate classes.

A resounding confrontation during the British period in Malta was undoubtedly the so-called 'language question'. This was largely a struggle between resistance on one side and assimilation on the other; but as British influences grew, not least on the labour market, and emigration prospects, a knowledge of English came to assume a 'job' value which, to an average worker, had precious little that was political about it. In fact, however, British assimilationist drives in Malta, more than elsewhere, were propelled by the presence of yet another European power amidst the Maltese. That was Italy. Such pressures were not simply motivated by the need to create a class of intermediaries, mediators, employees and servants, as in Macaulay's India. More than that, they were meant to ensure loyalty through assimilation in a strategic fortress, where *italianità* and *latinità* had deep roots. And the more so after Italy became a unified state and began to flex its muscles with aspirations for a Mediterranean policy of its own. Thus it came to pass that anglicisation bred resentment and resistance rather than loyalty among those classes who were educated enough to have internalised Italian rather than English as their main life-line to the outside, or indeed the inside as well. In their conscious and unconscious efforts to create new classes more loyal to themselves, by means of the educational system, job recruitment and promotion policies, commercial or contractual preferences and suchlike, the British deepened and further crystallized the social divide, with repercussions on social cohesion. But at the same time they opened up society through opportunities made available by imperially-linked projects as in the dockyard, the navy and merchant marine, the army and later the air force, and any other occupations which they deemed to hold 'in their gift', as the saying went.

Major works such as the building of the breakwater and docks at the turn of the twentieth century, or the full employment at the naval dockyard during the first and second world wars, brought prosperity. But this was temporary, it was convenient, not structural, not organic, fostering an economy liable to booms and slumps depending largely on imperial interest and movement. Social cohesion was ruptured when, as imperial interests shifted and changed, thousands of already displaced workers would find themselves out of a job, in many cases having abandoned their rural lifestyles and moved to the inner suburbs crowding the harbour creeks and bays. Development plans for the Maltese islands only began in 1959.[12] In the language question, so too in the work ethic, colonialism was a double-edged sword. Citing the utility of English to emigrate was a last resort, basically signifying that Malta no longer offered scope for a worthwhile existence. Tens of thousands emigrated in the twentieth century mainly to the English-speaking world and, unlike many others before them who had lived and worked in neighbouring Mediterranean lands, most never returned. Their new homes were too far away and more different, if more promising. In the 1950s and 1960s others of Maltese stock found it difficult or impossible to 'repatriate' after generations spent in Algeria, Tunisia, or Egypt.

There can be no doubt that modernisation during the British period can be seen as an aspect of Europeanity – gas and then electricity; the telegraph and then the wireless; the omnibus, the tram, the railway and the ferry; the bicycle and then the motor-car; better roads and services from drainage to water to the telephone; all these were pace-setting changes which of course greatly changed Maltese ways, bringing about a more 'modern' infrastructure - from aqueducts to tap water, better hygiene and hospitals, and so on... Such improvements came about while Malta was a British 'possession', which is not to say that they necessarily would not have arrived differently, perhaps a little later, if it were not. The transition from sail to steam or from timber to steel, from manual to automated, did not bear an exclusive British copyright.

The tension in such 'modernisation' hid within it an internal contradiction, once again a product of the colonial system. In many cases, the British were keen to press changes because of their own priorities: Malta as a naval and garrison station could not afford to risk some epidemic for the troops, nor afford not to have good roads for moving military hardware, or harbour anchorage for the navy, let alone the 'native' Maltese trade and commerce. The argument that from such improvements the Maltese too would benefit, if only by default, naturally clashed with the views of elected members in the Council of Government between 1849 and 1903, the more so when the penny dropped. Partly as a result of the British and imperial obsession with Malta as a fortress, not just any other colony, political freedoms were granted on sufferance, and repeatedly withdrawn, so that constitutional history became, as it has been aptly said, like a game of snakes and ladders.[13] This undermined the very nature of a constitution, in the sense of a basic law, rendering it more akin to a piece of paper, depending on the direction in which a wind blew.

Prime Ministers George Borg Olivier (above) and Dom Mintoff (below) celebrating on the occasion of Malta's Independence in 1964 and Malta becoming a Republic in 1974 (Photo: Department of Information)

In the stunting or denting of a natural home-grown, self-reliant evolution, there are thus fundamental similarities in the disputes relating to language, education and nationality, as in those relating to investment, jobs and discharges, as in those relating to civil, constitutional rights and privileges under the Crown. During the inter-war period Malta obtained internal self-government, after a bloody clash in 1919 known as the *Sette Giugno*, but once again this did not last a decade. Even after the Second World War, in which Malta played so vital a role, self-government, once restituted, would again be revoked in the late 1950s.[14]

The repeated removal from Malta without charge or trial of Maltese critics of the colonial regime (as happened elsewhere, not only in the British empire) epitomises the worst aspect of civil life under British (or any other) occupation. In our case, one 'human rights' monument which stands out to such infamy must certainly be Sir Ugo Mifsud's spirited juridical rebuttal of and opposition to Britain's policy of deporting innocent Maltese subjects, so eloquently delivered on 9 February 1942 in the Council of Government, surrounded by an historic set of French tapestries (and another of spineless Maltese deputies) shortly before he collapsed and died.[15] But there are others.[16]

In the nineteenth century the Anglo-Italian tensions as reflected in Malta were best brought out first during the *Risorgimento*, when hundreds of mainly Mazzinian Italian exiles piled into Malta, many of them anticlericals, and then because of the jingoistic plan to eliminate Italian, which soured relations until it was somewhat revised. I need hardly say that the Italian *Risorgimento*, which Britain generally supported in principle, was once again a Europeanising strain in Maltese affairs, perhaps most evidently so in the journalistic activity of the time. The conservative Catholic Church, which generally opposed it, was itself a European strain, clearly a more 'papist' one. It would take a good half-century for Italians themselves to reconcile themselves to the fact that a unified secular state and a papacy in the Vatican City need not be at loggerheads for ever. Such strains in the secularising of tradition continued to embattle Maltese society and indeed party politics well into the 1960s, until in the post-colonial era the floodgates of permissiveness opened as cinema, television, tourism and later IT, cable and satellite saw globalising waves gushing in from every nook and cranny, not always so refreshingly.

In the twentieth century, we have two outstanding examples of culture and politics which bring out evocatively the Italian and the British strains in Maltese 'europeanity'. Highly antagonistic at first, leading to much contestation over a prolonged period, in time these may now be seen as complimentary, even formative of a more holistic Maltese Europeanity.

The first of these occurred in 1912, when an up-and-coming 'pro-Italian' Nationalist leader, Enrico Mizzi, proposed in a journal article that Britain could exchange Malta for Eritrea with Italy, on the understanding that Britain would be granted access to Maltese harbours and facilities. There would be an Italo-Maltese federation of sorts wherein Maltese would benefit as much as possible from all that Italy, a much bigger country, could offer them, such as job recruitment entitlements and university placements, while at the same time being exempted from unpalatable obligations, such as conscription. With her coat-of-arms in the *tricolor* and elected representatives in the Italian parliament, Malta would thus become an autonomous entity within a larger whole, with which it had strong historical, religious, linguistic, ethnic and cultural links, a return to the maternal fold. This was essentially a bold irredentist dream, given some realistic justification by the changing international politics of the time, as Britain, in the face of a growing German naval threat, sought to divest itself of direct responsibility in the Mediterranean by means of an *entente* with France, which anyway cared more for its North African ports. Ideally, it would settle cultural affinities (with Italy) without risking naval employment (through use of Maltese harbours by Britain, France, Italy and other powers).[17] Nerik Mizzi, the son of the Nationalist Party's founder Fortunato, remains to this day one of the more charismatic political figures in Maltese anti-colonial history: court-martialled for sedition in 1917, interned and deported without charge to Uganda in the early 1940s, prime minister in 1950, when he died in harness and had a state funeral, with the British military and naval top brass filing in after it. If ever there was a poetic justice, this was it.

The other twentieth century event which I wish to draw attention to is as strikingly different as it is strikingly similar. This came to a head in 1956 when the Labour Party leader Dominic Mintoff and his party went all out for Malta's integration with Britain and, in that year, held a referendum about the plan.[18] The British were tickled pink that in 1956, just as they were being thrown out of Egypt by Nasser, in another part of the empire somebody would wish to become part of the UK. But Mintoff's plan was not unlike Mizzi's in some ways. He wanted integration as well as autonomy, assistance as well as opportunity; just as the dockyard was becoming of less use to the Royal Navy, and even its possible closure was being contemplated, he wanted to have a safety net of some kind. Malta could become part of a larger whole, with the Maltese acquiring citizenship rights like the British, minimum wages at the same rates, security and pensions, health services, schooling and university openings, and some Maltese MPs elected to the House of Commons. The late Commissioner of Police Vivien De Gray told me in 1989 (and the late Dr Ġużè Cassar would later confirm this to me) that Mr Mintoff had long contemplated the prospect of Malta somehow slotting into a bigger entity from which it could draw advantage, it being really too small to go it alone. Other findings confirm that in addition to integrating with Britain, Mr Mintoff had also more than once, before and after that, toyed with the idea of coming to some special arrangement with Italy.[19] It was only later, when neither of these prospects materialised or seemed realisable, that Mintoff's party steered away to a policy of 'Mediterranean neutrality', with the seemingly original idea of Malta as a 'bridge' between North and South – one, however, already dear to Mizzi's own heart a generation earlier, expressed in the same metaphor, but at a time of course when there was an 'Italian' southern shore.

Mizzi was a child of the nineteenth century. Malta's perceived self-identity struggle was that of a Latin Mediterranean nation at odds with an Anglo-Saxon and Protestant empire; it would derive what economic benefits it could from the British connection but not sacrifice its linguistic, cultural and spiritual beliefs and heritage. Mizzi was a romantic, slightly out of touch with the times perhaps, but a man of great sincerity and dedication to the cause in which he believed, as Mintoff was the first publicly to admit on his death in the most glowing terms (*'l-ikbar fost il-Maltin'*). Mintoff was born into a different world, a different class as well, his father being not a lawyer like Mizzi's but a cook in the Royal Navy. His mother was not a pedigree continental European from the south of France, but a money lender *'taht il-bastjun'*. One was born in Valletta, not far from St John's co-cathedral, the other in Cospicua beside the docks. One read law in Urbino and in Rome. The other, an architect and civil engineer from a later generation, was awarded a Rhodes scholarship and went to Oxford, returning to Malta after the war. The British connection by accident or design undermined the traditional (italianite) middle class and created a new (anglicised) one: the younger Mizzi, like his father and that generation, epitomised the former traditional consensual ethic expressed in the slogan *'patria et religio'*. Mintoff, like Sigismondo Savona and others before him, was a 'product' of the latter, if not a very malleable one, at the other end.

Moreover, the second world war had transformed Malta irredeemably, killing off any *italianità* policy that had survived if only through fear, and pushing the Maltese and the British together closer than ever before in a total war for survival and democracy. To the extent that Mizzi's option for partnership had been Italy, for Mintoff and many of his generation it logically was Britain. Indeed, most of those who voted in the 1956 referendum (many did not) approved of the Integration plan. It was Archbishop Gonzi's Catholic Church and Dr Borg Olivier's Nationalist Party who opposed it.

As Malta joins the EU in May 2004, such harshly fought and seemingly opposed remedies for future generations clearly may be seen in a different light, as they should. Unconscious to the Maltese, who had been born and bred into a colonial situation of cultural and political dissonance, both Italy and Britain were European countries, sharing many readily intelligible and appreciable cultural traits as in literature, music, art, architecture, economic development and democratic evolution. They both were, at least nominally Christian, one Protestant, and the other Catholic. Britain had supported Italy's unification, and in the nineteenth century even the best British schooling continued greatly to admire the Italian renaissance, poetry, art. Until Mussolini's invasion of Abyssinia, and at Sir Anthony Eden's behest the imposition of economic sanctions on Italy by the League of Nations, which greatly boosted Mussolini's popularity in Italy, Anglo-Italian relations always had been very cordial. Except on two or three occasions, anglicisation policy in Malta was but a niggle, a ripple, a ruffle, although there was always space for it in Italian newspapers, and occasionally in parliament. By 1938, Mussolini at Munich was even posing as Europe's peace broker.

After the war, as a good chunk of the Italian fleet surrendered in St Paul's Bay, the Allies, with Badoglio's assistance, invaded Italy, using Malta *en route*, as the German-protected Mussolini fled northwards to Salò. Soon afterwards, not only were Britain and Italy together in NATO but ironically it was in Rome that the treaty founding the EEC was signed, with Britain only admitted as a member in 1973. Well before then, Malta had become independent, and in the 1960s Dr Borg Olivier, whose administration piloted independence from Britain in 1964, was already hinting strongly at the possibility of Malta's eventual membership of the Common Market, what became his party's policy in 1979, shortly before he himself passed away. An association agreement with the EEC was signed in 1970, which could have turned into a customs union a decade later, but it was not to be, not so soon.[20]

The rest is 'history', but the point is this. In past times, recent and not so recent, Malta has on a number of occasions felt the need or been led by circumstance to belong to a larger whole, that being in some form a European empire or bloc, be it Roman or Spanish, Italian or British. Antagonisms, which seemed so real and so profound at the time, were ultimately centred around preferences between one European country and another.

Countries which were cultural, imperial or ideological rivals before are no longer so now, united as they are in the same European Union which Malta, with their full support, is joining more or less at par. Malta's membership of the European Union can thus be seen historically as a fulfilment in time, not simply as a recent, isolated event, or as a financial or economic convenience. It is a woven sinew, not a fireworks display. As the founders of the European Cultural Foundation in Geneva stressed after the Second World War, a united Europe would not and could not survive if its sole or even its primary motivation were simply a financial or economic one - a greedy grab. Cultural affinities and achievements over the centuries were still more European, more valuable because more lasting and inspiring: these transcended occasional political or military squabbles or confrontations, they were the real gel of which Europe and Europeans were made.

Cultural sap is a root source in the making and understanding of nations, and in the forging of lasting friendships among those of a shared human experience in time. With the advantage of hindsight, I would say that it is no shame that so small a place as Malta should have produced the Mizzi-Mintoff paradigm, on which we usefully and meaningfully could draw today. In comparative regional contexts, it could be seen to resemble the Anglo-Spanish pulls in Gibraltar, an enclave which still covers itself in Union Jacks even as its inhabitants speak a colloquial Andalusian; in the meantime, both Britain and Spain had joined the EU. It may be seen too against the difficulties of another island and ex-colony, Cyprus; but, in synthesis, Malta's experience was neither *enosis* nor *taksim*. The internal ethnic-linguistic-religious tension in which Cyprus long has been caught is unknown to Malta in modern times, the Maltese being more homogenous and distinct as an entity, with a language paralleling their history, as Ġużè Aquilina has observed.[21]

Malta did not have a 'pied noir' army of *colons* from the 'mother country' as in Algeria or Tunisia, and to a lesser extent Libya; nor thousands of non-native settlers holding foreign passports, as the Maltese themselves were in Turkey until the 1920s and in Egypt until the 1950s. The dual option of integration or independence was by no means unique to Malta: it features, in different ways, in northern Africa, perhaps especially in Algeria between the Ferhat Abbas and Messali Hadj parties; nor did Malta have a 'khedive' or a 'bey' or a 'sultan' balancing out on a collaboration-resistance tight-rope between nationalist and imperialist pressures, with a price on his head either way. Governors did not depend for favour on natives or creditors: they reported straight to the imperial metropolis, by whom they were appointed and transferred, and that was not the Porte. As it turned out, Malta's nation-forming matured in the twentieth century without any of the bloodshed common to most other parts of the Mediterranean on all its borders in their quests for nationhood and statehood, starting with Greece and Italy, ending with Algeria and Cyprus, let alone Palestine since the formation of Israel in 1948, and indeed before that. In so far as political policies responded to cultural and/or economic pulls from seemingly antipodal founts, these were generally restrained and ultimately absorbed by a 'Malteseness' cushioned by homogeneity and size. Difficulties, disagreements and upsets notwithstanding, that is still evident today, and more so than earlier.

In the Spring of 2004 we have all Maltese political parties consenting to face, as best they can, the opportunities and challenges of Malta's membership of the EU, without any of the old rival fixations about Italy, Britain or France; or indeed about the pioneering multi-lingual, multi-cultural European prototype already prevalent in Malta between the sixteenth and the eighteenth century, despotic and elitist though its proponents and practitioners had been.

Notes

1   See H. Frendo, *Lejn Stat Sovran: Storja Kostituzzjonali tal-Gżejjer Maltin* (Malta, 1989).

2   H. Frendo and O. Friggieri (eds), *Malta: Culture and Identity* (Malta, 1994).

3   See H. Frendo, *Id-Dikjarazzjoni Maltija tad-Drittijiet, 1802-2002. Diskors fil-Palazz ta' Sant'Anton, H'Attard, 11 ta' Ġunju 2002* (Malta, 2002).

4   On the formation of political parties see H. Frendo, *Party Politics in a Fortress Colony: The Maltese Experience* (Malta, 1991); but see G. Hull, *The Malta Language Question: A Case Study in Cultural Imperialism* (Malta, 1993). See also H. Frendo, 'Language and Nationhood in the Maltese Experience: Some Comparative and Theoretical Perspectives', in R. Ellul-Micallef and S. Fiorini (eds), *Collegium Melitense Quatercentenary Celebrations: Collected Papers* (Malta, 1992), 439-72. A comprehensive, analytical history of the Maltese language is J. M. Brincat's *Il-Malti: Elf Sena ta' Storja* (Malta, 2001).

5   See T. Cortis (ed.), *L-Identità Kulturali ta' Malta* (Malta, 1989), including this author's own paper, chapter 2 in the volume, written shortly after repatriating from the emigration, asking who are the Maltese: 'Storja u Għarfien: Il-Maltin min huma?', 17-34.

6   See Frendo and Friggieri.

7   See, for example, G. Saliba (ed.), *A Council for all Seasons: 50th Anniversary of the Council of Europe* (Malta, 1999).

8   On the medieval period see researched writings by, among others, A. Luttrell, S. Fiorini, G. Wettinger, and most recently C. Dalli, *Iż-Żmien Nofsani Malti*, which also has an extensive bibliography (Malta, 2002); but for a quick general insight into the moulding of a 'national identity' over the ages, including the main influences of the Knights Hospitallers, see H. Frendo in Frendo and Friggieri, 1-25, and the accompanying bibliographies to all chapters in this pivotal reference work for Maltese studies. A recent general history of the period is J. F. Grima's *Żmien il-Kavallieri, 1530-1798* (Malta, 2001). On the early modern period, the most recent scholarly works are those by C. Cassar, *Society, Culture and Identity in Early Modern Malta* (Malta, 2000), mainly on the sixteenth and seventeenth century, and F. Ciappara, *Society and the Inquisition in Early Modern Malta* (Malta, 2001), concentrating more on the eighteenth century.

9   Frendo and Friggieri, 4-9.

10   The most extensive recent work on the French period is C. Testa's *The French in Malta* (Malta, 1998).

11   See H. Frendo, *Miċ-Ċensura ghall-Pluraliżmu: Il-Ġurnaliżmu f'Malta 1798-2002* (Malta, 2003), and for a general history of Malta during the nineteenth century, by the same author, see the first volume of *Żmien l-Ingliżi*, in the press, a continuation of the late A. Vella's *Storja ta' Malta*. Another volume will cover the twentieth century.

12   For socio-economic analyses and overviews see H. Bowen-Jones et al, *Malta: Background for Development* (Durham, 1961); M. M. Metwally, *Structure and Performance of the Maltese Economy* (Malta, 1977); L. Briguglio's entry in Frendo and Friggieri, 233-51; E. J. Spiteri, *An Island in Transition: Maltese Economic History, 1954-1974* (Malta, 1997).

13   Malta's leading constitutional historian is J. J. Cremona, a former chief justice, who has authored several monographs. See *The Maltese Constitution and Constitutional History since 1813* (Malta, 1997).

14   For an analytical overview see H. Frendo, *Maltese Political Development, 1798-1964* (Malta, 1993) and *Malta's Quest for Independence: Reflections on the Course of Maltese History* (Malta, 1989); but for a detailed and meticulous rendering of the post-war period up to 1961, see J. M. Pirotta's three volumes, *Fortress Colony: The Final Act* (Malta, starting in 1987).

15   See the text of the proceedings in H. Frendo, *Maltese Political Development*, Part 7, Doc. 70, 517-38. Only one Maltese elected member voted against deportation, Dr G. Borg Olivier; and see his tribute to the leader Mifsud, *Ibid.*, 538-43.

16   See for instance the first books about Dimech and his times, *Lejn Tnissil ta' Nazzjon: it-twemmin socjo-politiku ta' Manwel Dimech* (Malta, 1971), *Birth Pangs of a Nation: Manwel Dimech's Malta, 1860-1921* (Malta, 1972), which are out of print, and the second edition of *Party Politics in a Fortress Colony: The Maltese Experience*, especially 148-51. Writings about later internees and deportees, biographical and autobiographical, would include those by A. Mercieca, H. Ganado, E. Soler and R. Bondin, among others, the best known among the victims being of course Nerik Mizzi (1885-1950), who had already been court-martialled for alleged sedition in 1917.

17   See Frendo, *Party Politics*, 150-67.

18   On this see D. Austin, *Malta and the End of Empire* (London, 1971); see also Pirotta, *Fortress Colony*, II (1991); H. Frendo, *The Origins of Maltese Statehood: A Case Study of Decolonization in the Mediterranean* (Malta, 2000); and *Id., Ċensu Tabone: The Man and His Century* (Malta, 2001).

19   Frendo, *The Origins of Maltese Statehood*, chapter 12: 'Oltre Mare: The Italian Option', especially 333-34. See also *Id., Ċensu Tabone*, 155-57.

20   For an outline history of Malta's path to Europe since 1970 see the writings of C. Pollacco and R. Pace; see also my biography of Ċensu Tabone, especially chapter 14: 'Second Thoughts: Foreign Policy and the Stalled E.U. Application', 249-72. For relevant selected textual documents, see my *Maltese Political Development*, Part 8, 809-921.

21   See his contribution in Cortis, *L-Identità Kulturali ta' Malta*, 'L-Ilsien Malti: Dokument ta' l-Istorja', 225-34.

John A. Mizzi

A BULWARK OF FREE EUROPE:
MALTA DURING THE SECOND WORLD WAR

Free Europe owes a debt to Malta. During the dark days of the Second World War, the island stood a bastion against the totalitarian forces which enslaved the Continent. For three long years this beleaguered outpost of freedom withstood the fury of the Axis forces and contributed to their defeat in the Mediterranean. At daybreak on the morning of 10 July 1943 the Allied invasion forces sailed from Maltese waters to land in Sicily and return to Europe from where they had been evicted in the spring of 1940. It had been a long haul.

In the 1930s, as the Italian and German dictators bared their teeth, the Maltese people trained putting on gas masks, listening to the banshee wail of the air raid sirens during mock air attacks, groping their way in the dark during practice black-outs, taping window panes with strips of paper to stop flying glass in imaginary explosions, and to swim from beaches and rocky foreshores almost inaccessible because of row upon row of barbed wire and partly submerged spiked triangular blocks of cement.

The first months of the war following the outbreak of hostilities in 1939 and early 1940 did not affect life in Malta, although the black-out was enforced and air raid precaution exercises were the order of the day. The devastating blitzkriegs first over Poland, then on the Netherlands and Belgium were heralds of what was yet to come.

The newspapers carried lists of names of Maltese naval ratings who died when their ships were sunk, ships that had become part of the Malta scene during the decades the island was the premier naval base of the British Empire - the carriers *Courageous* and *Glorious*, the battleship *Royal Oak* and the smaller ships, some of which were lost at Dunkirk as the British Army was evacuated from France.

When Italy declared war on 10 June 1940 the warships of the Royal Navy no longer rode at anchor in Malta's harbours. The Mediterranean Fleet had moved

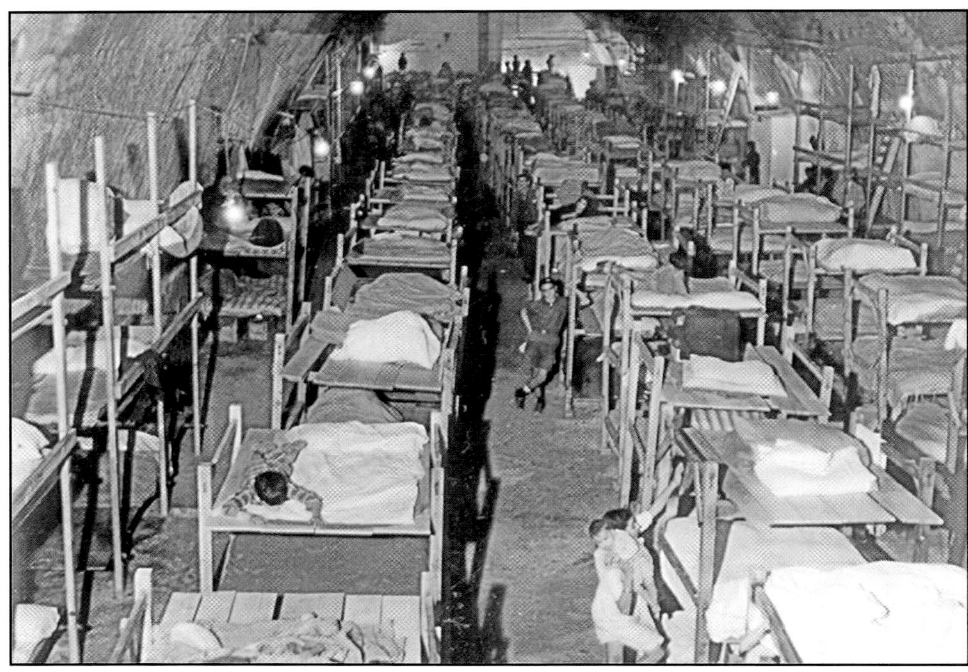

People sleeping in bunks in the Valletta railway tunnel shelter (Photo: 'Malta at War')

People queuing for rationed food outside a local branch of the Victory Kitchen (Photo: 'Malta at War')

some 815 miles eastward to Alexandria as the island was considered untenable, even had France and her North African empire remained in the war. When France signed an armistice with Germany, Britain and Malta were the two islands, disparate in size, which remained in the frontline of the conflict. Malta was defenceless.

The onslaught

Malta was a solitary rock, with an overall area of 95 square miles and an expanding population of just over 275,000; the most densely populated spot in the world. It was dependent on imports for its food and clothing and for almost all its daily requirements such as petrol, flour, tea and coffee, sugar, oil, soap and other needs. The towns and villages were situated close to each other and the buildings were constructed of local limestone - which was to prove providential in certain circumstances under air attack as they did not catch fire, even if few people rarely survived buried under rubble.

At the time of the Abyssinian crisis in 1935, when Britain had opposed Italy's attack on that kingdom, superficial preparations were made for civilian defence from enemy aircraft, and the decision was taken with foresight to dig tunnels, corridors and cubicles in the soft rock to serve as shelters. It was these underground quarters which kept the number of civilian casualties down to 1,580 during the long siege.

After the fall of France, the only friendly spot to the west was the rock of Gibraltar under the shadow of Falangist Spain 1,000 miles away. The Mediterranean basin appeared dominated by Italy with sea and air bases in Sardinia and Sicily. Mussolini spoke proudly of *Mare Nostrum*, even if Malta stood astride the sea route between Sicily, sixty miles to the north, and Libya, 190 miles to the south. In June 1940 there were only thirty-four heavy anti-aircraft guns and eight light Bofors guns and twenty-four searchlights. There were three rudimentary airfields in the eastern part of the island which were nothing more than fields with tarmac runways. Four naval Gladiator biplanes took on the Italian air force. The coastal defences were equipped mostly with old naval guns, manned by the Royal Malta Artillery. The King's Own Malta Regiment, made up of territorials, and five British regular battalions, formed the infantry. All the Army strength combined totalled about 4,500 men in the first months of war. This doubled when conscription was introduced early in 1941 and Malta's youth went on the frontline. By 1942 the ground forces numbered 30,000. Convoys with supplies and reinforcements had to fight their way to the island.

The first Italian raids provided a baptism of fire. There was a mass exodus from the bombed areas and there was panic in the first weeks of bombing. Families packed their belongings on cars or horse-drawn carts and sought refuge with strangers in the central parts of the island. A few crossed over to Gozo, the sister island. Life came to a halt - but not for long. The authorities moved the government offices from Valletta to safer zones inland. In time air-raids became spectator events with people on roof-tops or by the side of the street to watch the smoke puffs close to the attacking Italian aircraft flying in formation at great heights. Life took on a new routine. The government departments were now almost all operating regularly in their new localities. Shops were open. So were the schools and the cinemas. Public transport services were running restricted schedules, even though an incendiary bomb had set fire to a bus killing thirty-eight passengers.

The fury of the Luftwaffe was unleashed in January 1941 when the German air force started operating from bases in Sicily. The Cottonera area was devastated. At that time Greece and Yugoslavia to the east were still neutral, but not for long. German forces swarmed across their frontiers in April 1941, and within weeks had also occupied Crete. Malta had been regularly reinforced and naval aircraft and R.A.F. bombers were attacking enemy ports and convoys, while submarines were operating from a new base in Marsamxett Creek. Besieged Malta had begun to show her teeth despite the heavy and prolonged bombing.

The Germans were determined to put a stop to this offensive spirit and when in April 1941 a naval surface force began to operate from Malta with success against Axis convoys to Libya, threatening the German and Italian counter-advance against the British Eighth Army in North Africa, the Luftwaffe mounted intensive night raids which devastated a large part of the commercial high street and other quarters of Valletta, and other towns and villages. This was war with a vengeance, disrupting life and sowing death. Sleepless nights spent in shelters sapped the strength of the population and many saw their homes and businesses destroyed. Food was getting scarce and a limited system of rationing was introduced. Various items such as sugar, coffee, soap and matches could only be bought against coupons. Milk was restricted to babies and invalids. Frozen meat was sold twice a week and eggs came in powder form. Kerosene, which was a prime necessity as many still cooked on stoves, was in short supply, as was petrol for vehicles. Many were cooking on open fires using wood from bombed sites.

The general staff in Berlin sought to persuade Hitler to take Malta but he would not change his plan of capturing Crete in May 1941 with airborne troops. This mistake was to cost him the victory he sought in North Africa as Malta was strategically more valuable than Crete. Hitler was also bent on invading the Soviet Union, and the Luftwaffe squadrons were withdrawn from Sicily to prepare for this campaign. This interlude gave a breathing space to Malta, and with the Italian air force taking over the bombing the civilian population was spared the heavy ordeal of day and night raids. This lull was exploited by the Royal Navy and the Royal Air Force which intensified their attacks on Axis convoys with marked success.

The threat of a seaborne assault was a constant preoccupation so that the coastal defences manned by the Royal Malta Artillery were on watch round the clock. On the evening of 23 July 1941 various movements of surface craft were detected by radar to the north of Valletta soon after the arrival of a convoy of six merchant ships. A crack unit of the Italian Navy composed of E-boats and human torpedoes had been specially formed to operate against Malta from Sicily to penetrate into the Grand Harbour and sink merchantmen. This assaulting force was detected early, engaged by the guns, and annihilated.

The second half of 1941 was relatively free of heavy concentrated bombing. The Afrika Korps by now felt strong enough to launch its attack on the British forces defending Egypt, but the German offensive was restricted by the loss of supplies as the submarines, surface forces and aircraft from Malta operated with great success against Axis convoys. 49,000 tons were sent to the bottom in November, which was two-thirds of all supplies sent to Rommel by sea. Axis losses were so heavy that by December the Italians were cancelling convoy sailings. That month the Luftwaffe returned to Sicily with orders to eliminate Malta once and for all.

The Afrika Korps had been pushed back by the Eighth Army to El Agheila, almost half way between Benghazi and Tripoli, and the besieged garrison at Tobruk relieved. On the debit side, the Royal Navy had lost valuable ships in the Battle for Crete and elsewhere. On 25 November 1941, for instance, the battleship *HMS Barham* was lost with heavy loss of life, including twenty Maltese. All this boded ill for besieged Malta, which relied on convoys escorted by the Mediterranean Fleet.

Hitler withdrew Field Marshal Albert Kesserling and his entire staff from the Eastern Front, with orders to neutralise Malta at all costs. The opening weeks of 1942 saw mounting raids by the Luftwaffe in a bid to tire out the defenders and the population with round-the-clock attacks. The Germans suffered heavy losses and could never quite comprehend how such a tiny densely populated rock could effectively retaliate. They changed their pattern of bombing. From pin-point attacks on the airfields, the dockyard, the harbours and other military objectives, they started the first pattern bombing of the Second World War - concentrated assaults by day and night by massive formations on one specific target.

Various attempts were made to fight convoys to Malta from both ends of the Mediterranean. In February 1942 three merchant ships were sailed from Alexandria - two were sunk and the third turned back. Another attempt was made in March with four ships; all were sunk, two of them in the Grand Harbour after catching fire. They were scuttled before the ammunition they carried could explode with disastrous consequences to Valletta and the towns round the harbour. Malta was by now facing starvation, and the R.A.F. fighters were being shot out of the sky or destroyed on the ground. The submarines were withdrawn from their base at the Lazzaretto. Anti-aircraft shells were in short supply and ammunition was rationed.

The first Spitfire fighters, long overdue, arrived in March, having been flown off two carriers. The first batch did not survive for long against the 400 German and Italian fighters and bombers operating from Sicily. The soldiers, too, were fully occupied building safety pens for the aircraft from sand-bags, empty petrol cans

Walking over the rubble along the devastated Victory Street in Senglea (Photo: 'Malta at War')

The battleship HMS Barham disintegrates after being hit by torpedoes from U-331 on 25 November 1941. 861 lives were lost, including 20 Maltese (Photo: 'Malta at War')

and stones. They filled the bomb craters in the intervals between air-raids to keep the airfields operational. Mr Winston Churchill, the British prime minister, asked President Franklin Roosevelt of the United States to make available a US Navy aircraft-carrier to ferry Spitfires to Malta. On 20 April the *USS Wasp* flew off forty-seven Spitfires, joining the embattled fighter squadrons. At this stage the Axis were planning in detail the capture of Malta.

Operation Hercules was planned by the Italian High Command with 30,000 men in the initial airborne attack to match the strength of the defending forces, backed by a massive seaborne armada of 70,000 men. This was five times the force that took Crete. The Luftwaffe in Sicily in an Order of the Day recorded that 'during the period 20 March till 28 April 1942 the naval and air bases of Malta were put completely out of action. In the course of 5,807 sorties by bombers, 5,667 by fighters and 345 by reconnaissance aircraft, 6,557,231 kilograms of bombs were dropped'. That was more than on the whole of Britain at the height of the blitz in September 1940.

A few days previously, on 15 April, Malta had been awarded the George Cross. The hand-written citation by King George VI said: 'To honour her brave people I award the George Cross to the Island Fortress of Malta to bear witness to a heroism and devotion that will long be famous in history'.

By now strict food and petrol rationing was enforced. There was no longer any frozen meat available. The staple diet of bread was reduced to ten ounces per person. Tinned milk was only available whenever a rare convoy brought supplies. Other items could be had on staggered weeks marked on the ration books. Valletta was laid in ruins with people climbing over mounds of rubble to get from one part of the city to another. The three cities - Birgu, Isla and Bormla - were laid waste. Floriana, Sliema, Marsa and every other inhabited area had their fair share of destruction and death.

The government took the decision to open Victory Kitchens, run by volunteers, mostly untrained personnel, who came in for harsh criticism for their cooking. People registered for midday and afternoon meals and one had to hand in a percentage of one's coupon entitlements in exchange for the meagre food supplied and also paid 6d. The skinny goats and horses were slaughtered to provide meals. People were sold the fruit of the carob tree which grew wild and was normally fed to horses. Petrol was only available for a few public buses which maintained a semblance of service. These ran for two hours in the morning and three hours in the evening. There were times when there were no services. People walked or hitched lifts on military lorries or on the few donkey driven carts still remaining. Some rode bicycles - as did the troops to go from one place to another.

There was lack of sleep at night as the Luftwaffe kept up the pressure, dropping bombs, incendiaries and anti-personnel bombs. On one particular day, for example, the island was under attack for twenty continuous hours. There were heavy casualties when air raid shelters were hit. And yet the people endured.

The turning point

Lord Gort, who in the summer of 1940 had extricated the British Expeditionary Force from France, was appointed governor in May 1942. He was told that the island was not expected to hold out for more than six weeks. He arrived on the island by flying-boat on 7 May, bringing with him the George Cross. That very day, to the west of Malta, the *USS Wasp* and *HMS Eagle* were preparing to fly off another sixty-four Spitfires to Malta within 48 hours. These aircraft engaged the enemy formations within a short time of their arrival and the following day the defending fighters were airborne en mass, scoring a notable victory and inflicting heavy losses on the enemy formations. This was the turning point in the battle for Malta.

That same day the fast minelayer *HMS Manxman* dashed into the Grand Harbour and her precious cargo of anti-aircraft ammunition was unloaded in a few hours. She was hidden by a smoke-screen and the Germans missed her. That day Kesserling signalled optimistically to Hitler: 'Enemy naval and air bases at Malta eliminated'. In North Africa Rommel decided to take a gamble when on 26 May 1941 he attacked the British forces, taking Tobruk, and driving the Eighth Army back to a small village called El Alamein on the Egyptian frontier. This success persuaded Hitler that the capture of Malta was unnecessary and he postponed the assault on the island.

Still more Spitfires were ferried to Malta, and the Germans diminished the scale of their raids to take stock after suffering heavy losses. The Navy made a desperate attempt in mid-June to relieve Malta, now facing starvation. Two convoys sailed simultaneously, one from Alexandria, the other from Gibraltar. The eleven merchant ships from the east were forced to turn back after two ships were lost and escorting warships sunk or damaged. Of the six ships from Gibraltar only two reached the Grand Harbour with 25,000 tons of supplies, enough to sustain Malta for two months. Disease was now rife, with epidemics of typhoid, polio and scabies.

August 1942 was to prove a memorable month. The R.A.F. and Fleet Air Arm had revived their operations from Malta despite the constant bombing, the submarines were back hunting the Axis convoys and more and more enemy aircraft were being shot down over Malta. As the Axis shipping losses mounted, Rommel's hopes of continuing his advance into Egypt sank. Once again the Royal Navy mustered all its ships for Operation Pedestal, an all-out attempt to escort fourteen merchant ships to Malta from Gibraltar. The warships which had been escorting the convoys to Russia were sailed south to join the Mediterranean Fleet. A force of two battleship, three aircraft carriers, seven cruisers and thirty-two destroyers provided the convoy's defence. The ships were attacked by warships of the Italian Navy and by enemy submarines, by small fast surface craft, and by relays of German and Italian aircraft during the five-day passage. Only five damaged ships made it to Malta on 15 August, feast-day of *Santa Marija*. These included the gallant tanker *Ohio* which entered harbour lashed between two destroyers to prevent her from sinking and a Stuka dive-bomber crashed on her deck. The fleet suffered heavy losses. But the siege had been lifted.

In a final fling the Luftwaffe made a determined, prolonged assault on the airfields, but in the space of over a week, entire formations were shot down by the Spitfires and the guns. On 25 October the Eighth Army went on the initiative at El Alamein and the Axis' retreat from North Africa began. Within two weeks, Anglo-American forces landed in French North Africa.

Malta continued to play a front role as squadrons of long-range fighters shot down the German airborne reinforcements over the Sicilian Channel. When on 16 July 1943 the armada of ships which had assembled off Malta landed the invading Allied troops on Sicily, air cover was provided by R.A.F. and U.S.A.F. fighter squadrons operating from airfields in Malta and Gozo. The Allies were back on European soil. The tables, as far as the island was concerned, had been completely turned.

The climax came on 8 September 1943, Malta's national day, as the Italian fleet surrendered at Malta. Admiral Cunnigham signalled the Admiralty: 'Be pleased to inform Their Lordships that the Italian battle fleet now lays at anchor under the guns of the fortress of Malta'. The Italian Government signed the armistice with the Allies on the deck of the Royal Navy battleship *HMS Nelson* in the Grand Harbour on 29 September 1943.

Personal memories

Lucy Genovese was sixteen years old, living with her widowed mother and eight brothers and sisters when the Luftwaffe bombed Sliema at night on 11 March 1941. "My mother took my brothers and sisters to a shelter near our home. Three of us, however, decided to stay at home; my twenty-year-old brother Ninu, my sister Mary, aged seventeen, and myself. Even now I cannot remember clearly the events of that night except that I was sleeping in bed when it all happened. I woke up suddenly to find myself buried under the rubble. I heard my sister cry out: 'Mama!' and my brother screaming. After a few minutes silence I heard lots of voices, among them my mother's. I was hauled out by Fr Austin Born and I was made to stand but I collapsed. I heard someone say: 'Poor Lucy, she's broken her spine - it would have been better for her if she had died'. I was rushed to hospital in an ambulance. At about three in the morning my brothers and sisters came to see me. They told me Mary had been killed and Ninu had multiple fractures. I learned, too, my brother Alex, 14, was dead. He had gone down to the shelter barefoot and my mother had sent him back to get his shoes because he had a cold. The bomb had exploded just as he stepped into the house. I survived. My mother would afterwards wake up with a start at night and scream: 'They are killing my children!' Twenty-three people in our street died that night".

Cheers for s.s. Port Chalmers, one of the five ships out of fifteen, which relieved Malta in Operation Pedestal in August 1942 (Photo: 'Malta at War')

The official presentation of the George Cross in 1942 (Photo: Heritage Collection)

Ġuża Bondin had a nine-month-old daughter whom she took with her when she went to get her milk ration from the grocer at Żurrieq on 23 July 1941. "It was around 5.30 pm and as I turned a corner I heard a deafening explosion. In the morning a number of delayed action bombs had been dropped over the village and this must have been one of them. I squeezed myself against a door and covered my child with my body to protect her from the stones that were raining down. In spite of my efforts my child was struck in the head by a flying splinter. All I can remember is that some A.R.P. people came and took my baby from my arms. She was unconscious and she died just as we took her home. I was told later that she had died from the effects of the blast from the explosion. The bomb had lodged in a small garden near the church and began to tick away loudly. Two young girls went to peep to see where the ticking was coming from and at the moment they raised their heads above the wall the bomb exploded, killing them on the spot. Seven people lost their lives".

Doris Camilleri was nine on 21 March 1942 and her family was living at Mosta. Her eldest brother, Charlie, was 12, Ġużi, 10, she was the third child, and there were three younger children. "When the siren sounded that day we went to the nearby public shelter where we had a cubicle all to ourselves. At one stage my father decided to go out. Seconds later I heard my brother Charlie call my mother to go up with him to see the German bombers. My other brother Ġużi was about to follow Charlie and my mother grabbed him by the jumper but he escaped her. The next instant a deafening explosion plunged the whole place into darkness and sent us reeling against the wall. I began to grope around and felt the heads of the three young ones. The straw mattresses on the bunks caught fire and burst into flames. Our neighbour, Vitor, lay lifeless and her baby crawled from under her body. My mother lit a match and as she and I walked through the passageway my eyes fell on the lifeless body of my brother Ġużi. My mother did not see him and when our eyes had got accustomed to the dim light we saw dead bodies piled on top of each other. We walked in a state of shock to our house and saw carts carrying bodies. We learnt that three bombs had landed on the emergency exit of the shelter. My father had been killed as also my eldest brother, his body almost beyond recognition. For two days we did not know what had happened to our three youngest, until we traced them safe in the hospital. After a few months my mother gave birth to a healthy girl, her seventh child".

On 18 April 1942 eighteen-year-old Dr George Borg was with his father at Marsa, near the Civil Abattoir, when Stukas attacked the dockyard. "I was tethering the horse to the iron bars of the gate when I heard the whine of a falling bomb. I threw myself flat on the ground; my father instantly threw his body across mine to shield me. A split second later, an ear-splitting explosion ... splinters of rock flying around ... a cloud of dust and choking smoke ... and the sensation of being struck by flying stones. When the air cleared a bit I made an effort to rise and looked for my father; he was nowhere to be seen, nor was the horse. The buildings around had been reduced to rubble. I caught sight of the horse, dead some twenty yards away with the shattered cart nearby. Between me and the horse lay my father and as I staggered towards him, I realised that blood was flowing from my leg and my clothes were in tatters. I knelt beside my father and saw that he was still alive. I heard him mutter: 'Son, I'm dying'. He was bleeding profusely from a wound in the chest caused by a splinter. Minutes later another stick of bombs hit the ground and although there was nobody in sight I started calling for help. Six men emerged from a nearby shelter and looked shocked at the sight of me and my father. I was grabbed by the shoulders and dragged to the shelter. 'What about my father?' I screamed, and one of the men said: 'How do you expect us to carry him?' My father was a six-footer and well-built. After five minutes we crawled out of the shelter and I ran to where my father lay. When he saw me he said: 'I am dying George but I saved your life'. My father died later in hospital".

Inez Portelli was a refugee at Siġġiewi with her husband and four children. On 10 October 1942 she went to Rabat to see her daughter who was staying with her sister. "My daughter was not well so I took with me some sugar and some milk from the goat we kept in the house. There was an air-raid alert so I hurried with my son and brother-in-law to the nearest shelter. Before I had gone down two or three steps a terrific explosion sent us all reeling. Suddenly all was confusion. Panic stricken people were screaming and running aimlessly around and I saw people lying on the ground, motionless, while others were crawling away or writhing in agony and moaning. My arm had been torn away but I did not feel any pain. My brother-in-law looked at me and fainted. I was put on a stretcher and taken to the infirmary at *Santu Spirtu* Hospital at Rabat where my arm was bandaged. I was then carried into a van with some six other persons of whom two were dead and the others badly injured. My arm was amputated at Bugeja Hospital where I stayed for a month to convalesce. When I returned home I was greeted by my little daughter of four saying: 'It's better to be alive with one arm missing than to be dead'".

On the afternoon of 22 May 1941, German Stukas sank the Royal Navy cruiser *HMS Gloucester* patrolling off Crete during the German airborne invasion of the Greek island. Many of the crew were killed, hundreds perished in the twenty-four hour ordeal in the water before a small number of survivors were picked up by German caiques. Of the ship's company of 807, only eighty-five were saved. All nine Maltese cooks and stewards died. The only survivor on one of the rafts, Electrical Artificer Albert Revans, recalled his experiences: "By eight o'clock it was dark, very dark, with no moon and only a faint starlight. After a while the wind rose and raised an icy, choppy sea which made clean breaks right over us. In addition to chilling us to the bone, it made it most difficult to cling to the raft and we were capsized several times. At about 10pm Bill Hollett showed signs of weakening. His breath came in rattling, liquid gasps and there was white foam coming from his mouth and nose. After about an hour his head fell back, and quite peacefully, without a struggle, he died. Who next? I soon found out. The Maltese lad, Joe Simler, was already very weak but he clung on doggedly and kept on saying he was all right. At about an hour after midnight we were capsized again and when we got the raft righted, poor Joe was gone. Of the three of us left, the other two had gone blind with oil fuel in their eyes. We drifted all that following miserable morning. McCarthy's lungs were full of oil and water and he died at 11am. I put him over the side. At about midday the remaining boy, blind and very weak, could not last long and he died raving incoherently at two in the afternoon. By then I was too weak to take off his lifebelt, so he drifted away on the surface, his red hair resting on the water".

These personal recollections, taken from Laurence Mizzi's *The People's War*, are the most expressive aspect of the tragedies of war that beset Maltese individuals of all ages. Of the many war memorials to the civilians and the servicemen which have been erected in the towns and villages, two stand out. The Siege Bell Memorial overlooking the entrance to the Grand Harbour was unveiled by Queen Elizabeth II in May 1992, on the fiftieth anniversary of the award of the George Cross. It commemorates 7,000 servicemen and civilians killed in the defence of Malta - 4,000 sailors (including submariners) and 200 merchant seamen, 800 army personnel (including 300 Maltese) and 1,581 civilians. The Commonwealth Air Forces Memorial outside Valletta carries the names of 2,301 airmen from Britain, Australia, Canada, New Zealand, South Africa and New Foundland who perished over the Mediterranean and have no known grave. Commemorated in the various memorials round the world are 209 Maltese naval ratings, 215 merchant seamen and twenty-one N.A.A.F.I. managers, all lost at sea.

The cost to defend and supply Malta was immense - two aircraft-carriers, five cruisers, one fast minelayer, nineteen destroyers, and forty submarines were sunk, with many warships damaged, including battleships and aircraft-carriers. The R.A.F. lost 547 aircraft in the air and 160 on the ground (compared with some 2,000 Axis losses).

In Malta itself, over 29,000 buildings were destroyed or seriously damaged.

The cost was great, but the final prize was greater.

References

Boffa, C. J., *The Second Great Siege: Malta 1940-43* (Malta, 1992).
Cull, B. and Galea, F., *Hurricanes over Malta* (London, 2001).
Douglas-Hamilton, J., *The Air Battle for Malta* (Edinburgh, 2000).
Forty, G., *Battle for Malta* (Surrey, 2003).
Grech, C. B., *Raiders Passed* (Malta, 1998).
Holland, J., *Fortress Malta* (London, 2003).
Micallef, J., *When Malta Stood Alone* (Malta, 1981).
Mizzi, J. A., (ed.), *Malta at War* (currently being published in parts).
Mizzi, L., (ed.), *The People's War* (Malta, 1998).
Shores, C. and Cull, B., with Malizia, N., *Malta: The Spitfire Year 1942* (London, 2002).
Smith, P. C., *Pedestal* (Manchester, 1999).
Spooner, T., *Supreme Gallantry* (London, 1996).
Vella, P., *Malta: Blitzed but not Beaten* (Malta, 1988).
Woodward, R., *Malta Convoys 1940-43* (London, 2000).

Carmel Attard

THE LONG ROAD TO MALTA'S ACCESSION TO THE EU 1970-2004

1 May 2004 marks a new chapter in the chequered history of Malta. This sovereign island-state in the middle of the Mediterranean joins the European Union as a fully-fledged member state in a community of twenty-five European states. Indeed, the entry of Malta in the EU marks the culmination of the best relations that the island has had over the past three decades or so.

Upon gaining independence from the British on 21 September 1964, the Nationalist Government led by Prime Minister Dr George Borg Olivier immediately embarked to establish trade relations with the then European Economic Community (EEC). Malta already had good relations with the six founding members of the Community, namely Germany, Italy, France, Belgium, the Netherlands and Luxembourg. However, the Maltese Government wanted to establish relations also with the Community of the Six as a whole. The Community at the time had already achieved substantial success in integrating the economies of six European States, a process which started fourteen years earlier by the Declaration of the then French Foreign Minister Robert Schuman on 9 May 1950. A year later the Six formed the European Coal and Steel Community and six years on they founded the EEC.

Negotiations between Malta and the EEC started in earnest and on 5 December 1970 Prime Minister Borg Olivier signed an Association Agreement with the EEC. The signing was held in Valletta, Malta with Sigismund von Braun representing the Council of the European Communities and Italian Franco Maria Malfatti in his capacity as the President of the European Commission. The purpose of the Agreement was 'to bring about in two stages the progressive elimination of obstacles with respect to substantially all the trade between the Community and Malta, leading to the formation of a customs union'.[1]

Eighteen months after the signing of the Association Agreement, a new Labour Government led by Prime Minister Dom Mintoff was elected in June 1971. Mr Mintoff was more interested in obtaining the much needed funds towards Malta from various sources. He started first by negotiating a new defence agreement with the British Government whereby the British were to pay millions of liri for using military facilities in Malta until March 1979. Prime Minister Mintoff then turned towards the EEC and insisted that Malta should be given some form of financial assistance to help the island improve and diversify its economy based on economic and industrial development.

The first EEC-Malta financial protocol covered the years 1978-1983. Under this protocol the EEC gave Malta 26 million ECU, of which 16 million ECU were loans from the European Investment Bank (EIB), five million ECU were special loans, and the remaining five million ECU were in the form of non-payable aid. The aim of this first Malta-EEC financial protocol was to finance projects and schemes related to technical assistance and training, development of production in industry and agriculture, tourism, and scientific cooperation. Projects funded by the first financial protocol included the rehabilitation and expansion of the Maltese telecommunications system; improvements and re-development of wharves, jetties and cranes in the Grand Harbour; the setting up of a grain storage facility and new coastal station; the upgrading of Marsa Power Station and the X-ray Department at St Luke's Hospital; and the training of staff at the Civil Aviation Department and the Mechanical Engineering Department of the University of Malta.[2]

The Labour Government negotiated a second Malta-EEC financial protocol worth 29.5 million ECU and spanning the years 1983-1988. Sixteen million ECU were in the form of loans from the EIB to be used in the construction of the new air terminal at Luqa. The terminal was inaugurated in 1992. Three million ECU were special loans and were used for the construction of a plan to recycle domestic refuse, mixed with sewage sludge into compost for agriculture use. The grant of 10.5 million ECU was specifically utilised for the upgrading of the tourism sectors, including the setting up of the Institute for Hotel and Tourism Studies (ITS) as well as for projects improving Malta's infrastructure and educational standards.[3]

In May 1987 the Nationalist Party was voted back into power and the newly-formed government led by Prime Minister Dr Eddie Fenech Adami wanted to deepen the Malta-European Community (EC) relations. The EC had come a long way since the days of the late 1960s. The Community had witnessed three enlargements, the last two involving three Mediterranean countries, namely Greece (1981) and Portugal and Spain (1986). In 1987 Turkey applied to join the EC and the Maltese Government was also actively thinking of applying formally to join the Community. The Maltese Government made the bold step to apply only in 1990.

In the meantime, the Nationalist Government negotiated a third financial protocol with the EC covering the period 1988-1993. This third protocol, worth 38 million ECU, was mainly committed to further infrastructure projects such as the urban environment, upgrading of health facilities, Maltese standards and the telecommunications sector. Of the 38 million ECU, 23 million ECU were loans from the EIB, whereas 10.5 million ECU were grants. In order to prepare Malta for membership, the Maltese Government had set up an EC Directorate under the headship of Dr Joe Borg, who was to play a major and important role a decade or so later in Malta's accession process.

An interesting development took place on 15 September 1988 when the European Parliament approved a report prepared by its Political Affairs Committee (rapporteur Derek Prag) in which it was stated: 'Many perhaps a majority of the twelve member states would be anxious that Malta's policy of neutrality and non-alignment should not make agreement in European Political Cooperation (EPC) even more difficult than it is already. The Twelve might wish to examine entirely new possible solutions: one such solution, for example, could be full membership of the three communities for Malta but without the right of veto in EPC or in certain aspects of EPC such as security'.[4]

On 16 July 1990 Malta formally applied to join the EC. The then Maltese Foreign Minister Dr Guido de Marco presented the application to his Italian counterpart, Gianni De Michelis. Italy was at the time assuming the presidency of the EC. By then world events had taken a new course.

In November 1989 the Berlin Wall fell and with it the whole of the Warsaw Pact, including the dismantling of the Soviet Union. Malta served as the venue of a historic summit between the US President George Bush and Soviet President Mikhail Gorbachev in December 1989. This summit marked a new era in international and European relations. A few months before the fall of the Berlin Wall in 1989, neutral Austria applied to join the EC. Cyprus applied to join on 3 July 1990, thirteen days before Malta.

Following Malta's application to join, the EC officially inaugurated the offices of the Delegation of the European Commission of the European Communities to Malta at Ta' Xbiex on 29 November 1991. A year later, in September 1992 the EC-Malta Joint Parliamentary Committee was set up. The Edinburgh European Council of December 1992 urged the rapid examination of the European Commission's *avis* (opinion) on Malta's and Cyprus' applications by taking into account 'the particular situation of each of the two countries'.[5] Indeed, it took the European Commission three full years to present its *avis* on Malta's application. It must be said though, that the EC itself was undergoing major debates on its future and which culminated in the new Treaty on European Union signed at Maastricht on 7 February 1992. The fifteen EU leaders meeting at the Copenhagen European Council on 21-22 June 1993 welcomed the Commission's intention to publish its *avis* on Malta and Cyprus.[6]

In its opinion of 30 June 1993 the European Commission was generally positive. It pointed out that some economic and institutional reforms were needed to prepare the island for accession. The Commission concluded: 'Bearing in mind the democratic status and consistent respect for human rights, Malta is entirely justified in asserting its vocation of membership of the European Union, a right that should be confirmed by the Community'.[7]

In March 1994 the EU and Malta agreed on a programme and timetable for implementing economic reforms in order to prepare the country for EU accession. In the meantime, three other countries from the European Free Trade Agreement (EFTA) applied to join the EU: Finland (1992), Sweden (1991) and Norway (1992, for the second time). Along with Austria, these four countries were by far advanced in their preparation to join the EU because almost seventy percent of the EU *acquis* (laws) were already in place. Malta and Cyprus were put on the backburner. Eventually, Austria, Sweden and Finland joined the EU in 1995 while the Norwegians refused for the second time to ratify in a referendum their country's Accession Treaty.

Malta and Cyprus were however promised by the twelve member states during the summit of their heads of state and government at Corfu in June 1994, that the next enlargement will involve the two Mediterranean islands: 'The European Council notes that...the next phase of enlargement of the Union will involve Cyprus and Malta'.[8] Six months later the European Council (EU summit) at Essen in Germany confirmed the Corfù declaration.[9]

It must be said that within a few years from the historic dismantling of the Berlin Wall, the EU was all of a sudden inundated with new European democracies applying to join the Union. By 1996 the applications of Malta and Cyprus were joined by those from Poland (1994), Hungary (1994), Estonia (1995), Lithuania (1995), Bulgaria (1995), Romania (1995), Latvia (1995), Slovakia (1995), the Czech Republic (1996) and Slovenia (1996).

On its part the Maltese Nationalist Government, still led by Prime Minister Fenech Adami in its second legislature, continued with its programme to reform the country's economy. In June 1995 the Eighth EU-Malta Association Council adopted a resolution on the establishment of a structural dialogue and drew up the elements of a pre-accession strategy. Another important event took place later that month when upon being elected President of France, Jacques Chirac invited the Heads of Government and State of all applicant countries, including Malta, to attend the EU summit at Cannes. At this summit, the European Council reaffirmed that 'negotiations on the accession of Malta and Cyprus to the Union will begin on the basis of Commission proposals, six months after the conclusion of the 1996 Intergovernmental Conference and taking the outcome of that conference into account'.[10] The Cannes summit marked a new step towards the EU's enlargement because from then onwards it became a common practice for the fifteen EU leaders to invite their counterparts from the candidate countries to European Council meetings.

In July 1995 the European Parliament adopted a resolution in which it took a stance in favour of accession by Malta in the EU. At the time, the EU was debating on how best it could reform itself in order to allow more member states to join the bloc. An intergovernmental conference (IGC) was convened and eventually led to the drafting of the Treaty of Amsterdam which was signed in 1997. The treaty however failed to address the institutional reforms necessary to make the EU work effectively with twenty-five or more member states. The reforms were only agreed after another IGC which led to the Treaty of Nice of December 2000.

At the EU summit held in Madrid in December 1995, Malta was again promised 'that the accession negotiations with Malta and Cyprus will commence, on the basis of the Commission proposals, six months after the conclusion of the 1996 Intergovernmental Conference, and will take its results into account. It is pleased that structured dialogue with both countries began in July 1995 within the framework of the pre-accession strategy'.[11]

The same promise was again made in June 1996 at the Florence European Council, where the EU leaders recalled their Madrid conclusions and reiterated 'the need for the Commission's opinions and reports on enlargement as called for at Madrid to be available as soon as possible after the completion of the Intergovernmental Conference so that the initial phase of negotiations with countries of Central and Eastern Europe can coincide with the beginning of negotiations with Cyprus and Malta six months after the end of the IGC, taking its results into account'.[12]

Meantime, a fourth financial protocol was negotiated amounting to 45 million ECU. The aim of this protocol, covering initially 1995-1998, and then extended till 1999, was to promote the development of the Maltese economy and fulfil the objectives of the Association Agreement of 1970. It was also aimed to offer technical assistance and training to facilitate Malta's economic transition with a view of accession.[13]

The Nationalist Government called general elections in October 1996 and the Malta Labour Party was voted into Government, led by Prime Minister Dr Alfred Sant. The new Labour Government, having obtained the mandate from the people, decided to put Malta's application for EU membership on hold. Instead, Prime Minister Sant expressed his desire to establish the closest possible relations between Malta and the EU, short of membership. The Labour Government favoured an industrial free trade area with the EU that did not rule out membership in the future. On 23 November 1996 an *aide memoir* was sent to all EU member states in which the Maltese Government explained its intentions. On its part the Council mandated the Commission to prepare a communication on the nature and scope of relations in light of the Labour Government's new objectives regarding Malta-EU relations.

In May 1997 EU Commissioner Hans van den Broek paid an official visit to Malta to discuss further with the Maltese Government the definition of the new EU-Malta relations. During the discussions, a tentative timetable for further progress was laid down which foresaw the culmination of the process of reorientation at a meeting of the EC-Malta Association Council in 1998.

On 5 February 1998 the Council of Ministers adopted the European Commission's communication on future relations with Malta, based on the

Association Agreement of 1970.[14] The communication paved the way for the convening of the Council of Association. This council met in April 1998. It formalised the parameters within which EU-Malta relations were to be conducted in the years to come. The council was held at ministerial level in Luxembourg. The EC-Malta Association Council adopted a joint declaration that covered a wide range of areas including the establishment of a Free Trade Area. The Association Council took note of the intention of the Maltese Government to embark on an industrial restructuring programme planned to take between five to seven years.[15]

National events in Malta dictated otherwise and in a snap general election called by the Labour Government in September 1998, the Nationalist Party was returned to power, led again by Prime Minister Dr Eddie Fenech Adami. The new cabinet immediately reactivated Malta's application to join the EU. In October of that same year, the European Council, meeting in Austria, asked the Commission to prepare a report assessing Malta's progress of reforms at the time. The European Parliament once again approved a resolution for a positive stance to reactivate, as soon as possible, Malta's application for EU membership.[16]

In December 1998, the Vienna European Council welcomed 'Malta's decision to reactivate its application for European Union membership' and took note 'of the intention of the Commission to present at the beginning of next year an updating of its favourable opinion of 1993'.[17] Six months later the Cologne European Council welcomed that, 'on the basis of the Commission's updated opinion on Malta's accession application, it has now been possible to make a start on analytical examination of the Union *acquis* with Malta. The Commission will also submit a report, in good time for the Helsinki European Council meeting, on Malta's progress in preparation for accession, to form the basis, together with the corresponding reports on the other applicant countries, for any decisions to be taken by the Helsinki European Council'.[18]

In February 1999 the Commission published an updated opinion on Malta's application for EU membership.[19] A month later, on 22 March 1999 the General Affairs Council decided that screening with Malta should start as soon as possible and a specific strategy for pre-accession be prepared for Malta.[20] In October 1999 the Commission published the first in a series of annual regular reports in which it analysed Malta's progress towards accession. In its 1999 report the Commission recommended the opening of negotiations with Malta.[21] The report paved the way for the fifteen EU leaders to agree on opening accession negotiations with Malta. The Commission even adopted a draft resolution to finance the pre-accession phase for Malta by 38 million euros to be used in various projects.

It was only in December 1999, at the Helsinki European Council that Malta, along with other five candidate countries, was given the green light to start accession negotiations as from February 2000. The fifteen Heads of Government and State declared: 'Determined to lend a positive contribution to security and stability on the European continent and in the light of recent developments as well as the Commission's reports, the European Council has decided to convene bilateral intergovernmental conferences in February 2000 to begin negotiations with Romania, Slovakia, Latvia, Lithuania, Bulgaria and Malta on the conditions for their entry into the Union and the ensuing Treaty adjustments'.[22]

A negotiating team was set up by the Maltese Government led by Foreign Minister Dr Joe Borg and included Chief Negotiator Mr Richard Cachia Caruana, Mr Patrick Tabone, Mr Saviour Falzon and Ambassador Mr Victor Camilleri.[23] In order to involve fully civil society in the preparation of Malta's official positions regarding the various chapters and sectors to be negotiated, Foreign Minister Borg had set up the Malta-EU Steering and Action Committee, MEUSAC. Through MEUSAC Government ensured that all interested parties would be actively and directly involved throughout the negotiations.[24] Government had also set up the Malta-EU Information Centre (MIC) headed by Dr Simon Busuttil. MIC's task was to explain to the public in simple terms and in an objective way what the EU is all about as well as provide information on the outcome of accession negotiations.[25] Dr Busuttil participated fully in the Core Negotiating Team in order to have first-hand information on the process of negotiations.

Negotiations began in earnest in February 2000 under the Portuguese presidency. By the end of June 2000 Malta had already concluded accession talks on seven sectors: industrial policy, SMEs, science and research, education and training, telecommunications, external relations and common foreign and security policy.[26] The EU leaders, meeting at Santa Maria da Feira welcomed 'the launching of accession negotiations with Malta, Romania, Slovakia, Latvia, Lithuania and Bulgaria, and the first concrete results already achieved'.[27]

Talks continued under the French EU Presidency and by December 2000 Malta had provisionally closed a further five chapters: company law, economic and monetary union, statistics, culture and audiovisual policy, and consumers and health protection.

The French presidency marked a new page in the history of the EU since the fifteen Member States finally agreed on how to reform the Union's institutions in order to be able to work properly in an enlarged EU of twenty-seven member states. Under the new Treaty of Nice, Malta was given three votes in the Council of Ministers, five seats in the European Parliament, five members each in the Committee of the Regions and the European Economic and Social Committee, and one judge each in the European Court of Justice and the Court of First Instance. Malta was also given the right, like all the rest of the member states irrespective of size, to nominate one commissioner in the European Commission.[28]

During the first six months of 2001 accession negotiations continued and Malta obtained its first special arrangements. Under the six-month presidency of the Swedes which ended in June 2001, Malta had provisionally closed six chapters: free movement of goods, free movement of persons, free movement of services, energy, justice and home affairs, and financial control. Special arrangements included a safeguard measure in the event of a high influx of workers that could threaten the local labour market in the first seven years after accession and beyond;

Family photo at the EU Copenhagen Summit of December 2002 (Photo: Department of Information)

Prime Minister Dr Eddie Fenech Adami and Foreign Minister Dr Joe Borg signing the Accession Treaty on 16 April 2003 (Photo: Department of Information)

transitional periods for the registration of medicine and to increase oil storage to cover supply for ninety days.

At the Laeken EU summit in December 2001, the fifteen EU leaders gave a date for the conclusion of negotiations: 'The European Union is determined to bring the accession negotiations with the candidate countries that are ready to a successful conclusion by the end of 2002, so that those countries can take part in the European Parliament elections in 2004 as members. Candidacies will continue to be assessed on their own merits, in accordance with the principle of differentiation'. They also declared that if the present rate of progress of the negotiations and reforms in the candidate States is maintained, Cyprus, Estonia, Hungary, Latvia, Lithuania, Malta, Poland, the Slovak Republic, the Czech Republic and Slovenia could be ready.[29]

Hence the year 2002 was going to be crucial for Malta's accession process. Negotiations became tougher as the country began to deal with difficult sectors in which it was demanding a number of special arrangements to address the concerns of certain sectors of civil society in Malta.

Under the Belgian EU presidency Malta obtained more transitional periods to implement the EU *acquis* in the area of employment and social policy, and transport. An important breakthrough was the permanent arrangement in the field of free movement of capital. The EU member states recognised the negative impact that such a right would have on a small island like Malta, and have accepted a permanent arrangement controlling the purchasing of secondary residence in Malta by EU citizens.

When the Spaniards took over the EU presidency in January 2002 Malta had still ten chapters on which to conclude negotiations. By the end of June 2002 Malta had concluded talks on fisheries, obtaining a permanent arrangement to control fishing effort in a 25-mile zone. Negotiations were also provisionally closed on institutions. The Maltese language was also accepted as one of the EU's official languages.

At the Seville Summit in June 2002, the EU leaders expressed their optimism that accession negotiations could be ready by December 2002, and for the first time they even mentioned Spring 2003 as the possible date when the Treaty of Accession could be signed: 'Drafting of the Treaty of Accession should continue so that it can be completed as soon as possible after the conclusion of the accession negotiations. It would seem reasonable to expect it to be possible to sign the Treaty of Accession in spring 2003. The objective remains that these countries should participate in the European Parliament elections in 2004 as full members'.[30]

The last three months of 2002 under the Danish EU presidency were indeed very tough. The most difficult chapters were still open and it was only at the Copenhagen Summit in December that a deal was struck on the hottest issues including agriculture and structural funding for all new member states and also taxation in the case of Malta. Meantime, the commission published its regular report in October 2002 in which it stated 'that Malta will be able to assume the obligations of membership in accordance with the envisaged timeframe'.[31]

In agriculture the EU recognised the fragility of Maltese agriculture and accepted various special measures to safeguard this industry. The Maltese islands were also declared as a less favoured area, making them eligible to the highest amount of aid to make up for such a handicap. In taxation, Malta obtained a special arrangement whereby food and medicine will remain with zero VAT until 2010 and with the understanding that until then no other EU member state would have such exemption. Malta also managed to get a financial package worth 371 million euros (Lm155 million) during the first three years after accession. Malta will be contributing Lm73 million during the same period. The net benefit for Malta, Lm81 million was later increased to Lm90 million.

The Copenhagen summit of December 2002 concluded negotiations stating: 'Today marks an unprecedented and historic milestone in completing this process with the conclusion of accession negotiations with Cyprus, the Czech Republic, Estonia, Hungary, Latvia, Lithuania, Malta, Poland, the Slovak Republic and Slovenia. The Union now looks forward to welcoming these States as members from 1 May 2004. This achievement testifies to the common determination of the peoples of Europe to come together in a Union that has become the driving force for peace, democracy, stability and prosperity on our continent. As fully fledged members of a Union based on solidarity, these States will play a full role in shaping the further development of the European project'.[32]

At Copenhagen the fifteen EU leaders gave a timetable of how the EU's biggest enlargement in its whole history would unfold: 'All efforts should now be directed at completing the drafting of the Accession Treaty so that it can be submitted to the commission for its opinion and then to the European Parliament for its assent, and to the council with a view to signing in Athens on 16 April 2003.

'By successfully concluding the accession negotiations the Union has honoured its commitment that the ten acceding States will be able to participate in the 2004 European Parliament elections as members. The Accession Treaty will stipulate that commissioners from the new Member States will join the current commission as from the day of accession on 1 May 2004. After the nomination of a new president of the commission by the European Council, the newly elected European Parliament would approve a new commission that should take office on 1 November 2004. On the same date, the provisions contained in the Nice Treaty concerning the commission and voting in the council will enter into force. The necessary consultations with the European Parliament on these matters will be concluded by the end of January 2003. The above arrangements will guarantee the full participation of the new Member States in the institutional framework of the Union.

'Finally, the new Member States will participate fully in the next Intergovernmental Conference. Without reform the Union will not fully reap the benefits of enlargement. The new Treaty will be signed after accession. This calendar shall be without prejudice to the timing of the conclusion of the IGC'.[33]

Having obtained a negotiated package with some seventy-six special arrangements to suit the country's special circumstances, Prime Minister Fenech Adami, on 29 January 2003 called a referendum for 8 March 2003 on Malta's accession. Malta was to be the first applicant country to put accession to a popular vote. The electorate was asked: Do you agree that Malta should become a member of the European Union in the enlargement that is to take place on 1 May 2004?

The five-week campaign was really intensive. On one side the Nationalist Party in government was rallying in favour of EU accession while the Malta Labour Party spoke in favour of partnership with the EU instead of membership. Turnout at the polls was high, reaching 91 percent. The referendum was carried by the yes vote which polled 53.6 per cent with 46.4 percent voting against.[34]

Immediately after the referendum result was out, Prime Minister Fenech Adami called a general election for 12 April 2004. The Maltese electorate, in its majority confirmed the referendum result.

On 16 April 2003 Prime Minister Fenech Adami flew to Athens to sign the Treaty of Accession[35] in a ceremony held under the Acropolis. The treaty was ratified on 14 July 2003.

As a sign of welcome to the new acceding states, the European Parliament invited the ten new members to send members of the national parliament to serve as observers until the June 2004 elections. The number of observer MPs was to be according to the Treaty of Nice arrangements. Malta's five observer MPs were Dr Michael Frendo, Mr Tonio Fenech and Professor Josef Bonnici representing the Nationalist Party and Dr John Attard Montalto and Dr George Vella, on behalf of the Malta Labour Party.[36] On its part the MLP has accepted the new reality of Malta as an EU member state.

As the day of formal accession approached, the Maltese Government had to announce a number of nominations for posts at EU institutions. Foreign Minister Dr Joe Borg was nominated to be Malta's first EU commissioner. Until a new commission takes over in November 2004, Dr Borg will be 'twinned' with the Danish Poul Nielson, the Commissioner responsible for Development and Humanitarian Aid.[37] Mr Richard Cachia Caruana will serve as Malta's permanent representative in Brussels. Dr Anthony Borg Barthet was nominated as Judge at the European Court of Justice while Dr Ina Cremona will serve at the Court of First Instance. According to the Treaty of Nice each member state has the right to nominate one member in the European Commission and one Judge in each of the two EU courts.

The accession of Malta has also brought with it a number of employment opportunities in EU institutions for Maltese citizens. Several Maltese have already served as auxiliaries in these institutions and several others are in the process of joining the EU public service on permanent posts.

Government has restructured MEUSAC by setting up a number of sub-committees to shadow each of the various Council of Ministers formations. In this way, Government is ensuring that civil society is actively involved and consulted at national level on all legislative proposals coming out of the European Commission.

Joining such a strong economic bloc is in itself a big challenge for all the ten acceding countries, not least for Malta. EU accession will not only mean added rights and duties, better quality and standards; it will also provide the opportunity for new member states to participate fully in decision-making and in the construction of Our Europe, United in Diversity.

Notes

1   *Agreement establishing an association between the European Economic Community and Malta* in *Official Journal* No L 61, 14 March 1971, 2.

2   *The European Union and Malta*, Delegation of the European Commission, Malta (1998), 34.

3   Ibid. 35-36.

4   European Parliament Document A2-0128/88 of 29 June 1988 after R. Pace, *Microstate Security in the Global System: EU-Malta Relations* (Malta, 2001), 218.

5   Edinburgh European Council December 1992: Presidency Conclusions, *Bulletin of the European Communities* EC 12-92.

6   Copenhagen European Council 21-22 June 1993: Presidency Conclusions, Bulletin of the European Communities EC 6-93.

7   *Commission's Opinion on Malta's application for membership of the European Union*, COM (93) 312 final, http://www.mic.org.mt/Malta-EU/Avis93.doc

8   Corfu European Council 24-25 June 1994: Presidency Conclusions, http://ue.eu.int/newsroom/LoadDoc.asp?BID=76&DID=54738&from=&LANG=1

9   Essen European Council 9-10 December 1994: Presidency Conclusions, http://ue.eu.int/newsroom/LoadDoc.asp?BID=76&DID=54760&from=&LANG=1

10   Cannes European Council 26-27 June 1995: Presidency Conclusions, http://ue.eu.int/newsroom/LoadDoc.asp?BID=76&DID=54749&from=&LANG=1

11   Madrid European Council 15-16 December 1995: Presidency Conclusions, "http://ue.eu.int/newsroom/LoadDoc.asp?BID=76&DID=54768&from=&LANG=1" http://ue.eu.int/newsroom/LoadDoc.asp?BID=76&DID=54768&from=&LANG=1

12   Florence European Council 21-22 June 1996: Presidency Conclusions, http://ue.eu.int/newsroom/LoadDoc.asp?BID=76&DID=43679&from=&LANG=1

13   *The European Union and Malta*, 39.

14   Communication from the Commission to the Council on the Future Relations between the European Union and Malta, SEC (1998) 154 final, Brussels 5 February 1998.

15   Joint Declaration on the Future Relations between the Parties, EC-Malta Association Council, Brussels 28 April 1998, CE-M 602/98.

16   Text of Resolution, European Parliament, minutes of 8 October 1998, Provisional edition.

17   Vienna European Council 11-12 December 1998: Presidency Conclusions, http://ue.eu.int/newsroom/LoadDoc.asp?BID=76&DID=56427&from=&LANG=1

18   Cologne European Council 3-4 June 1999: Presidency Conclusions, http://ue.eu.int/newsroom/LoadDoc.asp?BID=76&DID=57886&from=&LANG=1

19   Report updating the Commission's Opinion on Malta's Application for Membership, COM (1999) 69 final, Brussels 17 February 1999, http://www.foreign.gov.mt/Malta-Eu/Avis/Avis99/default.htm

20   http://www.mic.org.mt/screen_process.htm

21   Regular Report from the Commission on Malta's Progress towards Accession, http://www.mic.org.mt/1999_reg_report.htm; for other regular reports see also http://www.mic.org.mt/MALTA-EU/mlteu_docs.htm

22   Helsinki European Council 10-11 December 1999: Presidency Conclusions, http://ue.eu.int/Newsroom/LoadDoc.asp?BID=76&DID=59750&from=&LANG=1

23   http://www.mic.org.mt/cng.htm
24   http://www.mic.org.mt/meusac.htm
25   http://www.mic.org.mt/MALTA-EU/mlteu8.htm and http://www.mic.org.mt/aboutmic/new/intro.htm
26   For Malta's negotiating position papers see http://www.mic.org.mt/Malta-EU/position_papers/mlteu_neg_pospaper.htm; for results of negotiations see http://www.mic.org.mt/Malta-EU/results/results.htm
27   Santa Maria da Feira European Council 19-20 June 2000: Presidency Conclusions, http://ue.eu.int/Newsroom/LoadDoc.asp?BID=76&DID=62050&from=&LANG=1
28   Treaty of Nice, http://www.mic.org.mt/EUINFO/nice.htm
29   Laeken European Council 14-15 December 2001: Presidency Conclusions, http://ue.eu.int/Newsroom/makeFrame.asp?MAX=&BID=76&DID=68827&LANG=2&File=/pressData/en/ec/68827.pdf&Picture=0
30   Seville European Council 21-22 June 2002: Presidency Conclusions, http://ue.eu.int/newsroom/makeFrame.asp?MAX=&BID=76&DID=72638&LANG=1&File=/pressData/en/ec/72638.pdf&Picture=0
31   2002 Regular Report on Malta's progress towards accession, http://www.mic.org.mt/MALTA-EU/Regular_Report_2002.pdf
32   Copenhagen European Council 12-13 December 2002: Presidency Conclusions, http://ue.eu.int/newsroom/makeFrame.asp?MAX=&BID=76&DID=73842&LANG=1&File=/pressData/en/ec/73842.pdf&Picture=0
33   Ibid.
34   http://www.doi.gov.mt/EN/elections/Referendum/03ref/default.asp
35   Accession Treaty, http://www.mic.org.mt/Malta-EU/treaty.htm
36   http://www2.europarl.eu.int/observateurs/srchres.jsp?ictry=220&lng=en
37   http://www.mic.org.mt/PR's/MIC%20Press/Official%20PRs/18022004_official.htm

PART THREE

CULTURAL PERSPECTIVES

George Mifsud-Chircop

MALTA'S *GHANA*:
THE FOLK MUSIC OF THE MALTESE

In this paper the author describes his involvement in the current situation of Maltese folk singing, better known as *ghana*. There are various types and sub-types, including the *Bormliża* or high-pitched singing. However, as the most popular live form nowadays, extemporised singing is the most highly developed ritualised form of singing revolving around values at the core of Maltese society, exposing its contradictions and tensions in contemporary Malta. Singers put the highest value on originality, self-expression, relevant, sententious content of the impromptu, and language manipulation at the expense of the opponent, rather than on the melodic line or rhythm. The theme during singing sessions in wine shops, restaurants, on the media or village/town celebrations is generally discovered and developed by the singers in the course of the introduction to their song duel, with each performer bent on outdoing his opponent in general knowledge, Maltese culture (especially semantics, including metaphors, many possible levels of nuance, double-entendres, implications, and diction), wit, and humour. Form is as important, especially the paramount basic need of the rhyme scheme.

Variety and change of innovative extemporising in *ghana* at surface level and deep level still remain to be discovered and analysed, thus constituting an open challenge to contemporary ethnographers, ethnologists and musicologists.

Studying and researching on the folk music culture of a small island like Malta is fascinating. Adopting a proactive perspective to various aspects of Maltese culture, transmitting the know-how and skills involved in the cultural aspect to present generations, and creating a healthy environment where, in spite of various difficulties and misgivings,[1] *ghana* has and is still receiving wider audiences locally and abroad, have constituted a rich experience for me involving field research, performances, and recordings.

The beginning

I had started my research on *għana* ['aːna] in the late 1970s. Male and female folk singers and folk musicians were repeatedly interviewed to the extent that they were eventually convinced that their sub-culture restricted to wine shops, should be projected in public through close collaboration and trust. Female and high-pitched performers proved a hard nut to crack, with the latter refusing to collaborate due to family pressure. This was the first phase of an arduous and slow though continuous cultural project, demanding perseverance, dedication and disregard of the various pecuniary interests which regarded my initiative as a threat. The result was reaped in 1998 when the First National Folk Singing Festival was held in Argotti Gardens through the support of parliamentary secretary Joe Cilia, and the then director of the Department of Culture, Joseph J. Mifsud. To date six editions of the festival have been held, with the participation of various local and foreign folk singers and musicians, mainly from the Mediterranean area. The seventh edition is being held on 21-23 May 2004. Whereas in 1998 high-pitched singers had to be physically pushed on the stage to perform and were practically ignored by a large section of the audience, today, through broadcasting and wider publicity of the previous editions and the installation of a monitor for simultaneous transcription and translations, we see the majority of our audiences enjoying these performances. A concurrent strategy of recording and broadcasting performers' life biographies and *għana* programmes on two local radio stations have helped me in gaining the trust of many singers and musicians. This led to the founding of *Kadenzi* in October 2002, followed by the official opening of its headquarters in Qormi on 14 March 2004. *Kadenzi* is the first society of Maltese folk singers and musicians.

As the originator and artistic director of the National Folk Singing Festival, it has always been my topmost priority to involve talented female performers and promising elements of the younger generation in *għana*. For the first edition (May 1998) only ten-year-old Jesmar Bezzina *l-Artist iż-żgħir* participated as an accompanying guitarist; for the second edition (April-May, 1999) one also finds twelve-year-old and seven-year-old sisters Melissa and Mirabelle Caruana *Tal-Mellieħa*, twenty-one-year-old Charmaine Catania *Tal-Ballu*, nine-year-old Jean-Vic Cutajar *Tal-Mellieħa*, eight-year-old Rebecca Dalli *Ta' Birżebbuġa*, thirteen-year-old Jean Paul Gauci *Ta' Seba' Rġiel*, ten-year-old Julia Grima *Tal-Mellieħa*, and nine-year-old Jean Claude Zahra *Ta' Gawdura* as new folk singers, and twelve-year-old Kevin Spagnol *iż-Żejtuni ż-żgħir* as a new accompanying guitarist. In 1998 there were only two practising female *għannejja* in Malta and Gozo, Fidiela Carabott *Ta' Ċikku tal-Madum* and Lordes Mifsud *Ta' Nazju*. In the seventh edition other female singers will be participating: Susann Agius *Ta' Ħat-Tarxien*, Rita Pace *Ta' H'Attard*, Katerina Saliba *Tar-Rabat*, and Marisa Sammut *Tal-Mellieħa*.

Types and sub-types

As already remarked in Mifsud-Chircop,[2] *ghana* is sung by folk singers from Malta and Gozo, and Maltese emigrants in Australia. Out of 400,000 inhabitants in Malta and Gozo there are circa 180 folk singers (*ghannejja*) and guitarists[3] including fifteen practising main guitarists (*prim kitarristi*) and some more accompanying guitarists (*daqqaqa sekond/akkompanjaturi*). Their age ranges between ten and 86. Performers include children, and young men and women who are constantly encouraged to perform in the various *ghana* programmes on the media and *seratas* organised by the *ghannejja* themselves or by the various local councils, at times with the collaboration of *Kadenzi* and/or the now defunct Department of Culture.

Paul Sant-Cassia[4] was the first scholar to define *ghana* as a trope. As it is performed today performance is the central stylised ritual of *ghana*, sung in wine shops and restaurants and village/town celebrations, as with the *Lejla Maltija* (Maltese Night). Maltese folk music is fully functional as a creative form, basically sung and played in octosyllabic quatrains to the accompaniment of guitar playing, generally a trio of illiterate and semi-literate musicians, or rather, in formal terms, self-taught, which means by ear and hand (rather than by score and teacher).[5] The trio consists of *il-prim* who improvises traditional motifs, and two *daqqaqa sekond* who play an accompaniment based on simple triads. During an *ghana* session the main guitarist has to join in with this same type of accompaniment during the singing, and only allows himself to improvise his motifs during the introduction and conclusion and during the *qalba* (interval between the *ghanjiet*). It was only in 1999 that unaccompanied *ghana* was introduced in the Second National Folk Singing Festival on the initiative of the adjudicating board of the previous year's Festival and on that of the present writer. The former suggested in their short report that unaccompanied singing should be introduced for high-pitched singing (*l-ghana la Bormliża*). As artistic director I dared take the opportunity to present all types of *ghana*, resulting in the best moments of the whole event.[6]

The folk singing and music of Malta is by and large the work of semi-literate or illiterate singers and musically untrained composers. Our primary instrument is the guitar, originally of the Spanish model, but produced locally, prominently by elder main guitarist Indrì Brincat *Il-Pupa*, and played with or without picks. As aptly defined by Herndon,[7]

> ... The Maltese guitar is a standard instrument, with metal frets and turning keys, metal strings, and traditional decorations on the front. It differs from the standard guitar only in that there are two sizes. The solo guitar is slightly smaller than the accompanying instruments. This, along with the method of tuning, indicates the presence in Malta of an older tradition of guitar playing which has almost died out elsewhere in the Mediterranean.

Indrì Brincat (**Il-Pupa**) *who constucts and plays the guitar (Photo: George Mifsud-Chircop)*

Children at the Fifth National Folk Singing Festival of 2002   (Photo: George Mifsud-Chircop)

There are four main types[8] of *ghana*:
1. *l-ghana tal-banju* (traditional *ghana* stanzas; lit. 'singing at the washing fountain')
2. *l-ghana spirtu pront* (extemporised singing)
3. *l-ghana tal-fatt* (ballad singing)
4. *l-ghana la Bormliża, l-ghana fil-gholi* (singing in high register), *l-ghana bit-tkaxkira* (dragged song), or *l-ghana tan-nisa* (women's song).

The four types of *ghana*

L-ghana tal-banju is still a strong living tradition in Malta and Gozo, but it needed quite a push to come to the fore. This actually happened in April/May 1999 during the second edition of the Singing Festival. The participation of no less than ten *banju* singers, including three top *ghannejja*, two women and four children, proved me right. Karmnu Debono *Il-Pikipakk*, one of the male singers, took the trouble to collect scores of these quatrains, mostly undocumented by any Maltese or foreign scholar or folklorist.[9] Here are three of his examples, the first two from Mosta Malta, and the third from Gharb Gozo.[10]

1. Ġib idejk ġewwa idejja,   *Place your hands in my hands,*
   Tistrinġini w nistrinġik.   *You hold me tight and I hold you.*
   Hemmx li tasal dik is-siegha   *I cannot see the hour*
   Li tgawdini w ingawdik!   *When you enjoy me and I you.*

***

2. Sinjorina ttradiet ruħha,   *A young lady mistook herself,*
   Ġuvni rat qieghed jixxemmex,   *She saw a young man sunbathing,*
   Minn wara hasbitu tfajla,   *From behind she thought he was a young girl,*
   Minn quddiem kemm kien imkemmex! *From in front how wrinkled he was!*

***

3. Il-ġuvintur kollha fraxketta,   *All young men are cads,*
   Flok namrata ghandhom tnejn.   *Instead of one girlfriend they would have two.*
   Namrat veru dak hanini   *My darling is a true lover*
   Ghax jew lili 'nkella xejn.   *Because he loves only me and no one else.*

***

It is generally accepted that popular poetry echoes the ideology from which it has sprung much more faithfully than that of an individual poetic creator. It is discourse in its own right. Today the *banju* quatrains have different semiotic implications and displaced performances. Traditionally they were the expression of pre-capitalist agricultural Maltese communities. For this reason they offer an especially rich field for the investigation of this interaction.

Spirtu pront (improvised singing): As the most popular live form of *ghana* nowadays and almost exclusively practised by men, *l-ghana spirtu pront* (extemporised singing, lit. quick/ready wit) or simply *ghana* is the most highly developed ritualised form of singing. It revolves around values at the core of Maltese society, exposing its contradictions and tensions in contemporary Malta. To be understood fully it must be taken in context; otherwise singing appears to be focusing on insignificant and banal facts.[11]

Maltese extemporised folk singing has five sub-types:[12]

1. *taqbil* or *l-ghana spirtu pront bil-qalba* (improvised *ghana* stanzas with music intervals);
2. *l-ghana spirtu pront bla qalba* (improvised *ghana* stanzas without music intervals) or simply *spirtu pront*;
3. *l-ghana bin-nofs ghanja/l-ghana maqsum/l-ghanja maqsuma/nofs u nofs* (improvised *ghana* in equally divided stanzas);
4. *l-ghana spirtu pront fuq il-kelma* (improvised *ghana* on words);
5. *l-ghana bid-denb* (improvised concatenated *ghana*).

The five sub-types of improvised *ghana*:

Taqbil: The first sub-type, *taqbil* (lit. rhyming) or *ghana normali* (lit. normal folk singing), is the standard form for any singer today.[13] In fact the word *ghana* generally refers specifically to this type of singing. *L-ghana spirtu pront bil-qalba* implies that singers normally sing in duos, with a separate subject for each pair.[14] It consists in two or more singers (minimum two, but generally four; occasionally one also has five, six, seven or eight). Each performance is a micro-universe in song duel, the ultimate aim being to establish the singing and mental prowess of the singer/s. Besides the form of each quatrain (*ghanja*), thematic control is also important. Normally a singer would first mentally compose his punch for the second part of his quatrain (lines 3-4), then after discovering a rhyme for the last word of the fourth line would compose the first half (lines 1-2) which may or may not fit with the other part, depending on his ability and mental versatility. Singers put the highest value on originality, self-expression, relevant, sententious content of the impromptu, and language manipulation at the expense of the opponent, rather than on the melodic line or rhythm – though in the second line of a verse it is possible for certain singers to use a descending melisma, known as *il-kisra* (lit. the breaking, the fracture).[15] At times the *kisra* is also used to take more time to find the proper rhyme or hide away the singer's incompetence to compose the proper octosyllabic line. The theme (*is-suġġett*)[16] during singing sessions in wine shops, restaurants, on the media or village/town celebrations, whether *serju* (lit. serious) or *tad-daħk* (lit. comic), is generally discovered and developed by the singers in the course of the introduction to their song duel, with each performer bent on outdoing his opponent in general knowledge, Maltese culture (especially semantics, including metaphors, many possible levels of nuance, double-entendres,[17] implication, and diction), wit, and humour.[18] Form is as important, especially the paramount basic need of the rhyme scheme. The music interlude or *il-qalba* offers some time for each singer to think while the main guitarist is improvising his motifs. As masterly described in summary form by Sant-Cassia,[19]

> in style, context, content, and contestation, *ghana* can vary from the informally amiable, egalitarian and exploratory singing between friends (the *serata*) emphasising commensality, to almost hostile, barely concealed antagonistic challenges (*sfida*) in wine bars which can develop into socially disapproved, but often vicariously enjoyed (by singers' followers), 'vendettas' between singers … In such a competitively egalitarian society, a bad performance can severely damage a singer's reputation and prestige. Some singers have a reputation for aggressivity and for personalising their songs, and risk permanently alienating their opponents. Many singers … learn informally … from accompanying their elders. In being exposed to subtle, complex, and exophoric references to the slipperiness of language and metaphors, children are socialised into the flexible and ambiguous world of Maltese adult society.

Following the exposition and development of the theme, a *kadenza/kadanza/gadenza* or cadence of eight lines for each singer sums at the end the theme evolved during the performance, thus ending the particular singing session. The *kadenza* may include a reminder that no insult was intended or that insults and jokes are not really meant to be taken seriously (*'konna qed niċċajtaw'* lit. we were joking).[20] It is an octave, though the singers themselves conceive of it as a pair of quatrains with a rhyme scheme a-b-c-b-d-b-e-b, or more commonly, a-b-c-b-d-e-f-e. The implications of the discourse are quite intricate and complex to discuss or condense here.[21]

The proper *spirtu pront*: The other four sub-types of *spirtu pront* are more demanding as they present additional restrictions on the creativity and ingenuity of the performers. Proud singers show their mental prowess when taking to these variations. In improvised singing without music intervals, properly called *spirtu pront*, singers must be quick and alert with no time at hand spent at creating the stanza. Elder performers contend that *l-ghana bil-qalba* is comparatively speaking a recent innovation, and, according to some singers, a

Traditional Maltese għannejja *from a lithograph by Brockdorff of 1838*

The Żavolin *a recently invented musical instrument (Photo: George Mifsud-Chircop)*

Old photo of musicians using tambourine and żaqq *(Photo: Department of Information)*

'deterioration' of *l-ghana bla qalba*, the proper *spirtu pront*, since here singers are given no advantage to prepare their song during the musical interval or *il-qalba*.

In *l-ghana maqsum* (the divided quatrain) only two singers sing at a given time, which is divided equally between them. Normally singer A improvises his first two lines of each quatrain in the first half of the allotted time, with singer B completing the remaining lines and rhyming his second line with the second line of the former; the order is reversed in the second half, with singer B being in command and introducing the first two lines of each quatrain.

The divided quatrain: If the divided quatrain sub-type is difficult for the average singer, *l-ghana fuq il-kelma* (improvised singing on words) is more demanding. The singer is restricted in content and form of one quatrain. The audience or the presenter would throw words at the singer/s to extemporise a concise stanza. In the 1999-edition of the Folk Festival I did successfully introduce this sub-type on a national level. Here are four quatrains from two different sessions in that festival. First we have Mabbli Camilleri *Il-Bohen* (MC) and Karmnu Debono *Il-Pikipakk* (KD), accompanied by John Saliba *Ta' Birzebbuga* (main), and Pullu Formosa *Ta' Karti* and Salvu Tanti *Il-Kanadiz*. The three words drawn by lot are: *mejkapp* (make-up), *likuri* (liquors) and *mandolina* (mandolin). Note the sharp creativity of Camilleri and the great attention he pays especially to audience and guitarists' participation – John Saliba is also a keen mandolin player.

MC:	U ghedtilkom li mohhi tajjeb,	*And I've told you I'm clever.*
	Inhoss illi ma jfallix,	*I feel I won't go wrong,*
	Ma nafx ghax il-'mejkap' tajtuni	*I don't know why you've given me 'make-up'*
	Meta jien tfajla m'iniex.	*When I'm not a young woman.*
KD:	U il-likuri xorb tan-nisa,	*And liquors are women's drink,*
	Ghax ix-xjuh jixorbu l-inbid,	*Because old people drink wine,*
	Jien ghalija hudu li tridu	*As for me drink what you wish*
	Ma nixrobx biex naghmel gid.	*I don't drink to keep fit.*
MC:	U t-taqbil illi jitqabbel	*And the improvised singing which is sung*
	Ghall-ghannejja, halluh ghalina,	*Is for singers, leave it to us,*
	Imma 'l Johnny Ta' Birzebbuga	*But to Johnny of Birzebbuga*
	Hallulu l-mandolina.	*Leave the mandolin.*

Another example of this sub-type of *spirtu pront* is the following: here audience participation is at its peak, singers are stout Karmnu Bonnici *Il-Bahri* and corpulent Fredu Abela *Il-Bamboccu*, engaged in a keen song duel inspired by the words. Here the latter's word is *minutiera* (the minute hand (of a clock/ watch)).

<table>
<tr><td>U kollox ċkejken qed naqlagħlek,</td><td>I am mentioning all the defects
pertaining to your stature,</td></tr>
<tr><td>U ħu ħsiebu ftit il-Bamboċċ.
Il-lejla beħsiebu jdawrek
Daqs minutiera ta' l-arloġġ.</td><td>And beware considerably of Il-Bamboċċ.
This evening he intends to twist you round
Like the minute hand of a clock.</td></tr>
</table>

Concatenated improvisation: Improvised concatenated singing, also introduced for the first time in the second Folk Singing Festival on a national level by the present author, has its own special merits: the last line of the stanza sung by singer A must introduce the first line of quatrain of singer B, *et sequitur*. This in itself seems simple repetition, but not for the keen Maltese singer who is proud of his knowledge of the language.

Ballads: The ballad (*l-għana tal-fatt*) is still popular in Malta and Gozo, though much less popular than *spirtu pront* in performance. It is usually written by the folk singer himself as with Ċikku Degiorgio *Tal-Fjuri*, Ġużeppi Spagnol *Iż-Żejtuni* and Karmnu Debono *Il-Pikipakk*, or by a schooled or semi-literate (popular) poet commissioned by the singer himself.[22] One also finds folk singers who are ready to pass on their written ballads to other singers. A case in point is Karmnu Debono. Contrary to the *spirtu pront* sub-types, the Maltese ballad is always polished to perfection by its author, performed in *ottava-rima* (written and sung in pairs of quatrains the rhyme and metric schemes of which correspond to the *spirtu pront* structures), each pair generally followed by the main guitarist's interlude (*il-qalba*). As with improvised singing, ballads also make use of *il-kadenza* (the octave or double quatrain) to round off the song. Thus, the *fatt* is westernised in style, its narrative to proceed logically and linearly, words are expected to be clearly expressed and understood, also providing particular social commentaries on moral crises or local issues. However, contrary to the pre-1960/70 texts, modern ballads today are not 'heavily influenced by Maltese popular poetry, and translations of, and elaborations on, well known Italian songs or poetry'.[23]

The Maltese ballad is either factual (*fatt mill-veru*) or not strictly factual (*fatt mill-fantasija* or *storja* or *poeżija*) in subject matter. The factual composition takes some unusual, sensational or gruesome event (e.g., '*Il-Qtil ta' Toni Aquilina*' (The Murder of Toni Aquilina, when a mother murdered her young son), a sad tale (generally a murder) in a particular period in Maltese history – contemporary history included - or dealing with well known stories or events, taken either from life or from Maltese or European literature. The major exponents of these sub-types are Ċikku Degiorgio *Tal-Fjuri* from Qormi, and Ġużeppi Spagnol *Iż-Żejtuni* from Żejtun.

Telling lies in improvisation: A sub-sub-type of the fantastic Maltese ballad is *l-għana bil-gideb* or *bil-maqlub* (lit. telling lies in improvised *għana* or upside-down song). It is a mini-ballad in one quatrain form. Each song generally includes a humorous topic which may be either prepared beforehand or improvised. The present author introduced this type for the first time in 1999 on a national level in the National Folk Singing Festival.[24] It proved all the more successful because singers developed their theme individually or collectively.

The *Bormliża* or high-pitched singing: *L-għana la Bormliża, l-għana fil-għoli* (singing in high register) or *l-għana bit-tkaxkira* (lit. dragged song) is impressive in performance. It is also called *l-għana tan-nisa* (lit. women's singing) implying that men either find it very hard to sing or must sing it in the female vocal register. This is contrary to the *spirtu pront* or *fatt* singer's great vocal and lung power, breath and vocal control, and a magnificent full voice to sustain the melismatic intricacies of the presentation of its long phrases which are imperative. In spite of its simple diction, the *Bormliża* singing demands a sound knowledge of its intricate rules.

La Bormliża[25] is performed solo or by two, in which case the singers must alternate phrases of music. A song is only one verse long, but it is divided in two parts: the first is generally one of many fixed or standard traditional texts thematically having much in common with the *banju* verses, the second is known as *kadenza* (cadenza), at times improvised by the singer. It is here in the improvised *kadenza* where the performer can comment concisely on a particular theme. The *Bormliża* may be sung in either of three forms, the first two applicable for a duo, the third for a solo.

In the first form singer A has the right to choose a traditional text. Then each of the two singers alternately perform twice his line of this first part with the poetic rhyme scheme a-b-a-b; in the *kadenza* each singer has his two lines of an improvised comment to sing, although there are times, as with the case of Mikiel Cumbo *L-Iżgej*, that his *kadenzi* have also become fixed for him with much repetition and use. The rhyme scheme of the form becomes a-b-a-b-c-d-e-d.

The second *Bormliża* type is simpler: as with the first form, singer A has the right to choose the traditional text, but each singer now sings the same two lines *en bloc* and not one, then repeats them. In all, these same two lines are heard four times, to be followed by the *kadenza* when each singer performs two lines of his own. The rhyme scheme of this form is: a-b-a-b-a-b-a-b-c-b-d-b.

The third *Bormliża* form is performed solo, and the singer may opt for either of the two forms mentioned above, where the scheme of the second would be a-b-a-b-c-b. Our singers Mikiel *L-Iżgej* and Ċikku Degiorgio *Tal-Fjuri* prefer singing according to the second rhyme scheme. A typical stanza by *L-Iżgej*, our foremost *Bormliża* singer, runs as follows:

<table>
<tr><td>Kemm ili għanja ma ngħanni</td><td>It has been such a long time since I last sang a stanza</td></tr>
<tr><td>Għax ilsieni rabba' s-sadid,</td><td>Because my tongue has grown rusty,</td></tr>
<tr><td>Kemm ili għanja ma ngħanni,</td><td>It has been such a long time since I last sang a stanza</td></tr>
<tr><td>Għax ilsieni rabba' s-sadid.</td><td>Because my tongue has grown rusty.</td></tr>
<tr><td>Ommi ħabbet lil missieri,</td><td>My mother has loved my father,</td></tr>
<tr><td>U jiena nħobb lil min irrid.</td><td>And I love whomever I want.</td></tr>
</table>

Paraphrasing Herndon,[26] but going a step further than she has done in 1971, I would conclude that the common characteristic of Maltese folk singing and music is innovative extemporising (even in the case of the ballad style, where the main guitarist does also improvise his *qalba* within the fixed musical and written structure of the text) constrained and perhaps even predicted by the underlying constant system. It is the challenge facing ethnographers, ethnologists and musicologists of *ghana* to discover and analyse more of this constant by studying variety and change at surface level and deep level.

Notes and References

1   The present author researches in other facets of Maltese culture, including narratology and material culture and through his initiative and support various live exhibitions have been organised in collaboration with the University of Malta Library, local councils, the National Folklore Commission, and the Superintendence of Cultural Heritage since 2000.

2   G. Mifsud-Chircop, 'Ghana: una tradizione maltese sempre viva', *Avidi Lumi*, III, 6 (1999), 36.

3   A. Ragonesi, 'Maltese Folksong "Ghana": A Bibliography and Resource Material/L-Ghana Malti: Bibljografija u Materjal Ieħor għar-Riċerka. Ġ. Mifsud-Chircop, ed., (Malta, 1999), 69-84, 91-98.

4   P. Sant-Cassia, 'Foreword', in Ibid., i.

5   M. A. Herndon, 'Singing and Politics. Maltese Folk music and Musicians', (Ph.D. thesis, Tulane University, USA, 1971), 180-81; P. Sant-Cassia, 'L-Ghana: Bejn il-Folkor u l-Ħabi', in T. Cortis, (ed.), *L-Identità Kulturali ta' Malta* (Malta, 1989), 89.

6   R. Fsadni, 'Second National *Ghana* Festival: A Success – But the Judges Risk Being Immortalised … in Pungent Song', *The Sunday Times* [of Malta], 30 May 1999.

7   Herndon, 97.

8   A recent off-shoot of *ghana* is the *makkjetta* (humorous song). It has developed since the 1960s due to the merits and persistence of young Fredu Spiteri *l-Everest* who died tragically in 1965. His worthy successor is the late Fredu Abela *Il-Bamboċċu* who has a good number of compact discs to his name.

9   The best collections are B. Ilg and H. Stumme, *Maltesische Volkslieder im Urtext mit Deutscher Übersetzung* (Leipzig, 1909), and B. Koessler-Ilg, 'Maltese folk songs. Collected in 1909-1912, ed. with translation and introduction by J. Cassar-Pullicino, *Maltese Folklore Review*, I, 1 (1962), 8-39. However, Ilg's quatrains collected from Mdina and Valletta must be urgently complemented with others still to be recorded from the many other towns and villages in Malta and Gozo, and the Maltese communities in Australia.

10   All transcriptions and translations by the author.

11   Sant-Cassia, 'L-Ghana: Bejn il-Folkor u l-Ħabi', 89-91.

12   Herndon, 30, mentions 'a special form of singing... called simply ... 'Tra la li la tra la le', which, she explains, 'is not, strictly speaking, a substyle of *spirtu pront*. Although a related melody-type is used, the tempo is at least double that of the normal *spirtu pront*, and a refrain of 'tra la li la tra la le' is added at the end of each verse. Use of this special form is almost completely restricted to Christmas Eve, when everyone wishes to sing, and numerical pressures rule against continuity of *taqbil*.' This comment is too simplistic. I would define the whole performance as an extended variation of *spirtu pront bil-qalba*, the refrain 'tralalilalalalula-tralalilalalale' x 2 (and variants) functioning as a technical manoeuvre by the popular singer to keep his audience constantly alert and participate by accompanying him during the whole performance. No mention is made by the author of the place of origin of her ethnography. In various villages in Malta and Gozo, including Mellieħa (under the direct influence of the prominent local singer Gejtu Sultana *Tal-Qargħa*) and Qormi, this singing is not restricted to a particular occasion but is open to wide use by any competent singer.

13   See G. Mifsud-Chircop, 'Ghana: A living culture in Malta', in *Proceedings of an International Conference on Middle Eastern Popular Culture* (Oxford, 2000), 107-09, for transcription and comments on the discourse of a short session of *taqbil* from the First National Folk Singing Festival (1998).

14   P. Ciantar, 'From the Bar to the Stage: Socio-musical Processes in the Maltese *Spirtu* Pront', *Music and Anthropology*, 5 (2000).

15   Singers renowned for this optional characteristic include Salvu Cassar *Il-Ħamra* of Tarxien, Frans Mifsud *Ta' Żaren ta' Vestru* of Żejtun, Kalċidon Vella *d-Danny* of Marsa, and young Jean-Claude Zahra *Ta' Gawdura* of Siġġewi. The latter proved to be the revelation of Category B of singers participating in the Second National Folk Singing Festival (1999).

16   Sant-Cassia, 'The different types of *Ghana*', is highly critical of the chosen theme by lot introduced in the 1953 Imnarja Folk Singing Competition on the initiative of Ġ. Cassar-Pullicino: '... By determining the themes of the songs, which they wrote down on slips of paper which the singers had to draw, they depersonalised the songs, and turned singers into potential comedians of themselves. The subjects of the songs were influenced by images the elite themselves had of the *poplu* (e.g. spendthrifts, henpecked husbands) according to an agenda unconsciously influenced by their perception of what would amuse the *poplu* as public spectacle'.

As artistic director for the first two editions of the National Folk Singing Festival, I asked the participating singers and guitarists to do away with this system, but they insisted with an overwhelming majority (during our informal meetings in preparation for the event) on its retention. They prefer this system. The decision of the majority had to be respected, but I was keen to counter-balance somewhat the repercussion mentioned by Sant-Cassia by presenting universal and local themes, including 'L-imħabba kbira ta' l-omm' [A mother's great love], 'Karozzi u muturi – diżgrazzji u duluri' [Cars and motorbikes – accidents and sorrow], 'Il-ġmiel ta' madwarna' [Beauty around us], 'L-annimali l-id il-leminija tal-bniedem' [Animals are man's right hand], 'Il-bini ta' l-imgħoddi u l-bini tal-lum' [Old and new buildings], 'Ix-xogħol salmura tal-ġisem' [Work strengthens the body], 'Il-flus triq fil-baħar' [Money makes a path in the sea], 'Bla karozza ma nimxix' [I don't manage without a car], 'Għala nħobb l-għana' [Why I love folk singing], 'Fid-dinja ħadd m'hu kuntent' [Nobody is happy in the world], and 'L-ixkubetta fiha l-grillu' [The gun has got its trigger (implying everyone does what he likes or suits him best)].

17   It is an open secret among the older singers that circa thirty years ago a radio censor did have his say in *ghana* programmes. Herndon's remark, 302, 'the watchful but ignorant eye of the radio censor' was confirmed to me by one of the censors concerned, the late Dr George Zammit (1908-90) who confided with me that though born and brought up in Qormi, one of former rural *ghana* centres, he could hardly understand their innuendoes during their singing. (Personal communication, October 1988).

18   During my ethnographic research I have come across various instances when singers agreed beforehand on a particular theme. This was due either to insecurity of a young budding singer having a (first) try with an older singer, the touchy character of one/both singers or because the organiser of the event dictates his own theme for the occasion.

19   Sant-Cassia, 'The Different Types of Ghana'.

20   I do not agree with Sant-Cassia, 'L-Ghana: Bejn il-Folklor u l-Ħabi', 83-84, that in *ghana* '... tiġi

eskluża kull tema li taffordja xi gideb dwar individwi jew dwar għannejja oħra; kif qal wieħed minnhom stess: 'Fuq il-gideb ma tgħannix.' ... ċertu għajdut falz u ċertu kliem li jweġġa' huma espliċitament eskluzi mill-għana, u b'dak [sic] *il-mod l-għana jsir eżattament il-maqlub taċ-ċaċrar u t-tpaċpiċ fuq dak u l-iehor u li spiss ikun espliċitu, privat u jsir fil-moħbi.'* [... Every theme which consists of untruths about persons or about other singers, as one of the latter said, is excluded! 'You don't sing on lies.' ... Certain false rumours and certain offensive words are explicitly excluded from *għana* and thus *għana* becomes exactly the opposite of the denigration of other persons spreading rumours and gossip which is very often explicit, private and behind closed doors.] One would have only to attend an *għana* session in one of the most frequented wine shops to discover the intricacies of one-to-one, one-to-group, group-to-one, insider-outsider relationships, etc. Singers have confided with me in private their disgust at certain outspoken performers who unashamedly offend other singers, topics ranging from sexual to family matters, extra-marital relationships, (il)legitimate children, etc. Recorded sessions of offensive *għana* do exist: these prove Sant-Cassia wrong when he reiterates in Ibid., 84, that: *'Hemm żewġ temi oħra li jiġu mwarrba mill-għana: mankamenti u nuqqasijiet personali, u l-politika.'* [There are two other themes which are avoided in folk singing: *physical defects and personal drawbacks*, and politics.] (my emphasis). G. P. Badger, in his *Description of Malta and Gozo* (Malta, 1838), had already mentioned Maltese singing 'satire upon the faults or character of each'.

21 Ciantar; Herndon, 77.

22 J. Vella, 'L-Identità kulturali Maltija – Il-Mużika', in T. Cortis, (ed.), *L-Identità Kulturali ta' Malta*, (Malta, 1989), 38, fails to distinguish between oral and (semi-) literary ballads: '... *L-għannej ... jirrakkonta f'taqbila storja diġà eżistenti (għana tal-fatt)'.* [The singer narrates in rhymes an already existing story (ballads)]. With very few exceptions all Maltese ballads are (semi-)literary. See, J. Cassar-Pullicino and M. Galley, 'Maltese *Għana*: Some remarks on the progress of invention', *Journal of Maltese Studies*, VI, 1 (1996), 99-127.

23 Sant-Cassia, 'The Different Types of *Għana*'.

24 I recorded *l-għana bil-gideb* in two areas, i.e. Birkirkara and Żejtun. The existence of this sub-type is also confirmed by Herndon, 90, where she refers to *l-għanja bil-maqlub* (upside-down song).

25 For a study on the various theories on the origin of *La Bormliża* with special reference to a unique symbiosis of Arabic and European characteristics, see G. Mifsud-Chircop, 'Musica folklorica Maltese: *la Bormliża'*, *Avidi Lumi*, IV, 11 (2001), 44-47.

26 Herndon, 165.

Besides the basic works referred to in the notes, the reader who wants to delve further into the subject of Maltese *għana* is referred to the following titles:

Camilleri, C., 'The Growing Awareness by Mediterranean Countries of their Musical Homogeneity', in *Proceedings of the First Congress on Mediterranean Music* (Alger, 1973).

Cassar-Pullicino, G., *Studi di tradizioni popolari maltesi* (Malta, 1989).

Cassar-Pullicino, J. and Camilleri, C., *Maltese Oral Poetry and Folk Music* (Malta, 1998).

Cassar-Pullicino, J. and Galley, M., 'Maltese *Għana*: Some Remarks on the Progress of Invention', *Journal of Maltese Studies*, VI, 1 (1996), 70-81.

Ciantar, P., 'The Maltese *Għana*. The Linear versus the Vertical', (BA Dissertation, University of Malta, 1994).

Ciantar, P., 'Styles of Transcription in Ethnomusicology', (MA thesis, University of Durham, 1996).

Fsadni, R., 'The Modernity of Maltese *Għana'*, *The Sunday Times* [of Malta], 3 August 1992.

Fsadni, R., 'The Wounding Song. Honour, Politics and Rhetoric in the Maltese *Għana'*, *Journal of Mediterranean Studies*, III, 2 (1993), 335-53.

McLeod, N., 'The *Bormliża*, Maltese Folksong Style and Women', *Journal of American Folklore*, 88 (1975), 82-100.

McLeod, N., and Herndon, M., 'The Interrelationship of Style and Occasion in the Maltese *Spirtu Pront'*, in *The Ethnography of Musical Performance* (Norwood, Pa., 1980), 147-66.

Scarnecchia, P., 'L'*Għana*, il canto a chiterra a Malta', in *Ittiritmi '99. Il canti delle isole, la voce del mare*. Ittiri 4, 5, 6, 7, agosto 1999, P. Scarnecchia, ed. (1999), 19-22.

Joseph Vella Bondin

MALTA'S MUSCIAL HERITAGE:
A HISTORICAL OVERVIEW

Even if it has become a cliché to state that any branch of a country's creative arts reflects its history, it is nonetheless true. Malta's historical vicissitudes explain not only the form and structure of its musical heritage[1] but also the dichotomy between its traditional music and its art music.

Traditional Music

The forces that shaped Maltese folk music and its origins are still a matter of conjecture, as is the extent of its dispersion over time.[2] However it is safe to assume that in its most characteristic form, known as *ghana*, it knows its origins in the Middle Ages when the Arabs occupied Malta. There are clear signs that the rich and the men of learning and power anticipated the capture and had time to flee to Calabria and Puglia in Italy, leaving only peasants, herdsmen and fishermen to face the conquering Arab invaders in 870.[3] The total destruction of the previous flourishing Byzantine-Christian culture and the gradual thorough adoption of Muslim ways and manners, including religion, architecture, dress and language is now well known and accepted. It also signified the obliteration of whatever musical usages had existed and their natural substitution by North African song, tones, rhythms and cadences. These became the basis of what today is designated Malta's folk music,[4] zealously guarded and utilised over the centuries by the descendants of those peasant Maltese who remained in their native land but frowned upon by the later incoming upper classes as a relic of what they considered were shameful times.[5]

Ghana allows plenty of scope for tonal extemporisations, elaborate melismas, and harmonic inflections and as a consequence sounds off-key and rather primitive.

Interior of the Manoel Theatre, completed in 1732 (Photo: Heritage Collection)

The Royal Opera House constructed in 1866 and destroyed in 1942 (Photo: Heritage Collection)

Indeed the glissandi, the micro-tones, the high-pitched singing, the narrow range of the melodic motifs and the variations in the tempi show clearly the North African influence. It is a pity that under the stimulus of western modalities and tonalities, some contemporary folk singers are trying to 'tame' the North African genealogy.

The European Christian tradition was reintroduced after 1127 when the Normans, under Roger II of Sicily took concrete steps to reinforce the offensive his father Count Roger of Normandy had begun in 1091 and colonise the islands, leaving a contingent of Christian soldiers to consolidate the dominion. These Christian ranks were swelled by incoming merchants and sailors from Italian towns and ports and, later, even from Barcelona. With them came monks to look after their spiritual needs.

But Malta remained mainly Muslim and a *c.* 1240 census[7] found that of the 1,119 existing families, 836 (681 in Malta, 155 in Gozo), or 75 percent of them, confessed the Islamic faith. A few decades later, Muslims were exiled to the Italian city of Lucera. Apart from some thirty-three families professing the Jewish faith,[7] Malta was now entirely Christian. However, the reintegration of Malta within the European Christian tradition through the Kingdom of Sicily did not mean that the country people renounced the traditions, customs and language they had become accustomed to during the Maghrebi colonisation.

Establishment of Plainchant

However a new emerging elite, most of it based in Mdina, the island's capital, desirous of closer links with the Royal Court, began to look towards Italy for its cultural inspiration. Moreover the traditionally influential see of Catholic Malta always turned to the Vatican for its spiritual inspiration and, after 1443, the Kingdoms of Sicily, to which Malta belonged, and of Naples were united under King Alfonso of Aragon, giving Maltese easy access to the institutions of both Sicily and Naples. As a result the emerging art music could not but be closely influenced by developments in Italy.[8]

By the end of the thirteenth century a new Cathedral was erected in Mdina and its organisation, with dignitaries and prebends, quickly evolved. The earliest evidence on the use of plainchant goes back to this era.[9] A document of 1244 names Johannes Zafarana as *Maltensis canonicus* and another of 1274 refers to Alexander *Malte ecclesie cantor.* If the cathedral had its canons and its precentor, then the Divine Office must have been chanted. The earliest unearthed reference to a Cathedral organist is dated 1494 when *Venerabili Frati* Joanni Rapi is identified as the cleric holding that position, performing on what documents imply to have been a fairly large instrument. Besides some beautifully illuminated, locally-produced psalters, the Mdina Cathedral Museum possesses two provenance-unknown antiphonaries, one dating from the first half of the twelfth century and the other from the middle of the thirteenth, written in an unusual type of Aquitanian notation.[10] Mdina could also boast of a school going back to the late Middle Ages but documented from 1461 onwards.[11] Most of its known masters, many of them clergymen, hailed from Sicily. Since the majority of students were clerics and the Cathedral provided an important segment of the expenditure involved, it is very likely that liturgical music was taught.[12]

The Cathedral's *Cappella di Musica*

Musica figurata was introduced in the mid-sixteenth century when two *cappelle di musica* were created. In October 1573 payments were made by the Cathedral Chapter to Giulio Scala, designated *maestro di canto fermo et figurato*, a terminology used in contemporary literature to indicate plainchant (*canto fermo*) and polyphony (*canto figurato*). The practice of polyphony implies the existence of a *cappella di musica* of some sort.[13] Scala, a Sienese,[14] the first of a long list of Italian *maestri* brought by the Cathedral Chapter to Malta at great cost and sacrifice, remained in Malta until June 1574 when he left for Messina.

A reform of the Cathedral's *cappella di musica* with the aim of introducing musical instruments to complement the voices and organ was proposed by bishop Baldassere Cagliares in 1619. The Sicilian Don Francesco Fontana, *maestro* between 1616-23, purchased musical works from Venice in April 1622 and later that same year *un controbasso grande, due violini, due tenori di contralto,*[15] *cinque archetti e tre scudi di corde con il loro cassone.* Subsequent important *maestri* included the Sicilians Antonio Campochiaro (between 1626-7 and 1635-8) and Andrea Rinaldi (1627-31).

Whenever a suitable Italian candidate was not available, a Maltese musician was temporary nominated. Such was Don Michele Zahra (1574-1646) who, in 1589, on the initiative of the Chapter, went to study the organ in Palermo. On his return to Malta he was appointed organist of the Cathedral and filled in as *maestro di canto fermo et figurato et musica* whenever needed.[16] Another important Maltese musician, the Cathedral's *maestro* for most of the years between 1661-97, was Giuseppe Balzano (1616-1700),[17] whose intricate motet *Beatus Vir*[18] (1652), is the oldest extant work by an identified Maltese composer[19] and is preserved in the Mdina Cathedral Museum Music Archives.[20] Scored for two tenors, bass and *basso continuo*, it is in two sections and is not only a noble work but also an extremely exciting example of early Italian baroque.

After 1711 the Cathedral Chapter employed only Maltese *maestri*, encouraging potential candidates to advance their musical capability abroad. Pietro Gristi, by attending the *Conservatorio dei Poveri di Gesù Cristo*, started the tradition of Maltese musicians[21] studying in the conservatories of Naples. These included the two outstanding composers and *maestri* of this era: Benigno Zerafa (1726-1804), a student like Gristi of the *Conservatorio dei Poveri di Gesù Cristo*,[22] and Francesco Azopardi (1748-1809), a student of the *Conservatorio di Sant'Onofrio a Capuana*.[23]

Zerafa[24] and Azopardi, together with other eighteenth century Maltese church composers could, as a result, manipulate a spectrum of ecclesiastical styles then fashionable in Italy, synthesised as *stile antico*, *stile moderno* and the simple *stile breve*, with the distinct flavour of the Neapolitan school in which they trained.[25] Naturally, such regional nuances are very difficult to detach. However they may be detected in the 'Neapolitan' mass[26] with its alternate choral and solo passages in the aria form and in which generally only the *Kyrie* and the *Gloria* are set to music;[27] solos in the *bel canto* vocal idiom of the emerging *galant* style adopted from the opera houses;[28] the use of double choir writing to create a specifically *stile antico* effect[29] including a fugue usually in the final section of the *Gloria*.[30]

The *Cappela di Musica* of the Order of St John

The other *cappella di musica* was that created by the Knights of St John for their Conventual Church in Valletta. The advent in 1530[31] of the Hospitaller Order made up of knight-monks hailing from the noblest European families was to push Malta, musically and in many other fields, closer to European thought and trends. The Order's greatest internal achievement was the building after 1565 of Valletta, a fortified town that was to act as the Order's convent, with its nucleus being the majestic conventual church dedicated to St John the Baptist. The Order's intentions about a *cappella* for their conventual church were made clear in their 1574 Chapter General: *Si è ordinato che si trattenga una buona musica figurata per le feste principali governata da un valente Maestro di Cappella.*[32]

The Order's *cappella*[33] attained exceptional levels of excellence by employing the best available foreign and local talent. Its *maestri*, on existing evidence all Italians and all trained in Neapolitan conservatories, included the long-serving Giuseppe Sammartini (between 1724-65) and his nephew Melchior (between 1765-98), whose probable relationship to the more famous Sammartini brothers has yet to be investigated.[34]

In a way, it is remarkable that the three leading Maltese musicians associated with the Order, Giuseppe Arena (1709-84), Girolamo Abos (1715-60) and Nicolò Isouard (1773-1818) never reached this prestigious position. Both Arena, son of Matteo, organist of St John's for thirty-six years (1687-1723) and Abos, cousin of Carlo Farrugia, *uditore* to a number of grandmasters,[35] left Malta to study in Naples when still young and never returned, achieving widespread fame in Italy as composers of operas and liturgical music. Arena's appointments included that of organist to the *Chiesa dei Filippini* and as *virtuoso* to the Prince of Bisignano.[36] Abos was *maestro di cappella* of the Archiepiscopal Cathedral of Naples and of other eminent Neapolitan churches for which he wrote liturgical works of the highest inspiration, including his masterpiece, *Stabat Mater* (1750).[37] The closest to achieve the post of *maestro* of the conventual church was Isouard[38] who, on the death in 1796 of Vincenzo Anfossi,[39] became its organist with the right of succession to

Melchior Sammartini. But when the French expelled the Order from Malta on 12 June 1798, Melchior Sammartini was still *maestro*! Regrettably, with the exception of Isouard's sacred works,[40] the Order's rich music archives remain untracked.

The expulsion of the French from Malta in September 1800 and its colonisation by the English brought about the disbandment of the Order's *cappella* and, later, St John's was nominated co-cathedral with that of Mdina whose *maestro di cappella* now began serving both temples.[41]

The Operatic Theatre

The Knights of St John were also outstanding patrons of secular music, a typical initiative being the *Calendimaggio* cantatas[42] performed annually on the eve of Mayday. The finest contemporary composers, among them the Italians Matteo Capranica and Gianbattista Lampugnani, and the Maltese Filippo Pizzuto and Michel'Angelo Vella,[43] were commissioned to set to music the specially written Arcadian texts. It was also the Knights who in 1732 built the enchanting Manoel Theatre, the oldest European theatre still functioning within its original structure.

In many ways, the Manoel Theatre,[44] constructed *ad honestam populi oblectationem*[45] and up to 1866 the only regular theatre in Malta, reinforced Italian, particularly Neapolitan, musical traditions, this time in the operatic field. Known operas performed[46] during the first decades of the Manoel Theatre's existence were either by the leading Neapolitan composers or composers closely associated with the Neapolitan tradition, including Pergolesi, Leo, Piccinni, Prota, Cimarosa and Paisiello. The operas were performed by visiting professionals from Italy, introducing a custom that was to dominate all subsequent opera productions in Malta.

The handful of operas written by Maltese composers[47] during the eighteenth century also followed the Neapolitan pattern. The Manoel Theatre saw the performance of six operas by Isouard - an *opera seria*, *Ginevra di Scozia* (1798), and five *opere buffe*, *Rinaldo d'Asti* (1796), *L'improvisata in campagna* (1796), *Il barbiere di Siviglia* (1796), *I due avari* (1797), and *Il barone di Alba Chiara* (1798). Isouard continued to exploit his marked comedy flair in Paris where he settled in 1800 and where he composed about thirty *operas comique* to an impressive success.

The popularity of Italian opera continued unabated during the nineteenth century. The demand outgrew the potentialities of the Manoel Theatre and the need for a bigger, technically improved theatre arose. On a design by Edward Middleton Barry,[48] the magnificently proportioned Royal Opera House,[49] sited at Valletta's entrance, opened its door on 9 October 1866, with Bellini's *I Puritani*. The production emphasis in the new theatre remained basically that of the Manoel Theatre - the predominant presentation of Italian opera, with those of Verdi, Rossini, Donizetti, Bellini, Petrella, Pacini, and Puccini dominating the entire menu.[50] The few non-Italian operas produced[51] were produced in the Italian versions performed in Italy. Operas continued to be staged by visiting professionals principally from Italy. The rigorous standards of the House made it an indispensable step for aspiring singers and many celebrities[52] graced its stage at some point of their impressive international career.

As in the case of the Manoel Theatre, the Royal Opera House saw the performance of few operas by Maltese composers. Those produced were Vincenzo Bugeja's *Lodoiska* (1832), Alessandro Curmi's *Rob Roy* (1832) and *Il Proscritto di Messina* (1843), Paolo Nani's *La Mezza Notte* (1844), Giuseppe Malfiggiani's *I Due Dottori* (1848), Anton Nani's *Zorilla* (1874), *I Cavalieri di Malta* (1880) and *Agnese Visconti* (1889), Giuseppe Emmanuele Bonavia's *Ginevra di Monreale* (1890), Paolino Vassallo's *Amor fatal* (1898), *Frazir* (1905) and *Edith Cavell* (1927), Carlo Fiamingo's *Redenta* (1912), and Carlo Diacono's *L'Alpino* (1918).[53] It was not that Maltese composers were not willing to compose operas; it was rather that the impresarios were seldom willing to produce them. The Maltese composer found that he was not welcome in his own country's operatic theatre.[54]

But, in spite of this, the Royal Opera House's destruction by enemy action on 7 April 1942, was a massive setback to Malta's cultural traditions. It is yet to be rebuilt and many Maltese feel that the Manoel Theatre, which following major refurbishments reopened as Malta's National Theatre on 27 December 1960, with the Ballet Rambert's performance of Delibes's *Coppélia*, has only partially filled the gap created.

Liturgical Music during the Nineteenth Century

The only valid patron of the Maltese musician continued to be the Church and most of the foremost Maltese composers up to the beginning of the Second World War were able to verbalise their talent primarily as a result of their employment as *maestri di capella*. However in the nineteenth century the focus of liturgical music was no longer the two cathedrals but the parish churches. This change was the result of the birth of two illustrious *cappelle*[55] that were to dominate Maltese church music during that century. These were instituted and managed not by a church but by a *maestro*, whose aim was to provide liturgical services based on his or his family's compositions in any church that commissioned his services.

The older of the two was the Bugeja *cappella* whose organiser and first *maestro* was Pietro Paolo Bugeja. Head of the Bugeja family of *maestri*,[56] he studied with Azopardi before leaving for Naples to spend six years in the *Conservatorio San Onofrio*. He returned to Malta in 1797 and in 1809 succeeded Azopardi as the two Cathedrals' *maestro di cappella*. An admired composer, parish priests and *festa* procurators began to commission him to perform his music in their own churches and to be able to do that he set up his own *cappella*, which became known as the *cappella* Bugeja. On his death, his son Vincenzo,[57] a student of his father and of the *Conservatorio San Pietro a Majella* in Naples, where he went to perfect his musical studies after being appointed, on 15 June 1828, to succeed his father as *maestro* of the two Cathedrals,[58] inherited the rapidly expanding Bugeja *cappella*. New ecclesiastical commissions took more and more of his time not only in the composition of appropriate works but also in the *cappella*'s management. But he was now facing tough competition from the newly instituted Nani family *cappella*, a rivalry that spilled over into several directions, not least being the formation of two powerful popular parties that filled to overflowing any church in which the favoured *cappella* performed.

The Nani *cappella* was formed by Paolo Nani, grandson of the Venetian violinist Angelo who came to Malta in 1766 and was appointed chamber musician to Grand Master Manoel Pinto. He begun the Nani dynasty of musicians[59] when he married Ninfa Schembri on 11 April 1768. After graduating as a lawyer in December 1832, Paolo left for Naples to study at the *Conservatorio San Pietro a Majella*. On his return to Malta in August 1838 he formed his own independent *cappella*. His very first commissions included the *festa* of St Paul Shipwreck celebrated in Valletta. Among his new works for this feast was the antiphon *Sancte Paole*, the famous, luminous antiphon that introduced the tradition marking the composed antiphon as the single piece of sacred music identifying a particular Maltese *festa*. The boldness and audacity of this and his other compositions, which used very evident operatic techniques and *forte* orchestration highlighting brass instruments, caused literally, a sensation.[60] It was music the like of which had never been heard in Maltese churches. Pure opera had entered the church in the guise of liturgical music. Paolo's son, Anton, continued composing works in this manner, among them the famous *Requiem* (1879) written on his mother's death, the single work that best represents Maltese Romanticism.[61]

But, generally, the last decades of the nineteenth century were an era of stagnation in liturgical music, traditionally the main field of Maltese musical expression. The predominant reason was not lack of talent - gifted composers like Giuseppe Spiteri Fremond (1804-78),[62] Giuseppe Vella (1827-1912) and his son Luigi (1868-1950),[63] Giuseppe W. Malfiggiani (1828-93), Luigi Fenech (1837-1905), Emanuele Bartoli (1852-1933),[64] Gaetano Grech (1855-1933), and others should have then been at the height of their potential creative talent. But the almost complete monopolising hold the Nani and Bugeja *cappelle* had on available ecclesiastical assignments staved off almost totally any potential introduction of innovative ideas by new *maestri*.

The *Motu Proprio* and its Aftermath

The status quo was at last thoroughly shaken by an external ecclesiastical development – the promulgation of Pope Pius X's *Motu Proprio* of 1903. This famous papal bull was of the nature of an instruction upon the music that was appropriate for sacred rites. It emphasised the prime values of plainsong and Palestrina period polyphony, strongly condemned and proscribed music of a theatrical style, and the fortuitous division of liturgical texts into separate, self-contained movements. Instruments other than the organ were not to be employed without the bishop's special permission, and long instrumental preludes or interludes were reprehended.

The *Motu Proprio* signified that the liturgical music then being executed in Malta's churches had to be replaced. The heated ferment[65] that arose when the local bishops started applying the pope's instructions is now a matter of history. The greatest opposition came from the two traditional *cappelle*. Very indicative is the sentence that concluded a newspaper notification of Paolo Nani's demise on 22 March 1904: 'Mro. Nani realised that music in Malta has died and wanted to die as well'.[66]

Anton Nani and Riccardo Bugeja refrained from taking immediate steps to introduce music in their *cappelle* that conformed - Riccardo Bugeja only did so five years later when he composed *Messa a 3 voci in omaggio alla Immacolata Maria* which gained the Roman Curia's approval on 6 January 1908, while Anton Nani waited another six months to present and win approval for his *Messa in fa*.

The long-drawn out hesitation gave the chance to a promising new crop of musicians to enter an arena that the Bugeja and Nani families had, for over a century, made their virtual province.

The initiator was Paolino Vassallo, the first Maltese to move away consciously from the dominating Italian influence on Maltese music. After local studies with Domenico Amore,[67] Luigi Fenech and Giuseppe Spiteri Fremond, he went to Paris in 1875, where he remained for ten years and studied with Ernest Guiraud and Jules Massenet. His later work, as a result, especially his three operas where Massenet's example is quite evident, exhibits the Gallic line of elegance and verbalisation in its harmonic structure.[68] On his return to Malta, he founded his extremely successful Music Institute. The vast majority of composers who dominated Maltese music for practically the first half of this century - including Domenico Anastasi (1886-1938),[69] Giuseppe Abdilla (1886-1944), Pietro Paolo Galea (1873-1929), Lorenzo Gonzi (1887-1934),[70] and, more importantly, Carlo Diacono (1876-1942), Giuseppe Caruana (1880-1931),[71] and Josie Mallia Pulvirenti (1896-1964)[72] - were his students. Vassallo was one of the most influential figures in modern Maltese musical history and his reputation was confirmed with his appointment as *maestro di cappella* of the two cathedrals in 1902, following Giuseppe Vella's resignation.

After the issue of Pius X's *Motu Proprio*, Vassallo immediately started producing effective liturgical music in line with these instructions and was engaged as *maestro di cappella* in a number of churches mainly in the Cottonera area. New composers, writing in the *Motu Proprio* style learnt from Vassallo, also infiltrated into a good number of those churches which up to then had formed part of either the Bugeja or Nani *cappelle*. This development brought in new energy and a wealth of talent that made this major field of Maltese creativity as exciting and fruitful as it had been in the eighteenth and first half of the nineteenth century.

Nicolò Isouard (1773-1818)

Vincenzo Bugeja (1806-60)

Paolo Nani (1814-1904)

Carmelo Pace (1906-93)

From this point of view, the most successful were Carlo Diacono, Giuseppe Caruana and Giuseppe Camilleri (1903-66) who expanded the groundwork of his father Ferdinando (1859-1942). These three musicians succeeded in establishing very popular *cappelle*. Of great importance are the sacred works[73] of Diacono, exhibiting a splendid natural talent, a musically inventive dramatic scheme and a delicate sensibility in orchestral and vocal colouring that triumph over the musical limitations imposed by the *Motu Proprio*. In them Vassallo's Gallic influence is very apparent, as it is in his secular compositions, such as his opera *L'Alpino*.[74]

Though no longer in family hands, three of the *cappelle* still function and are still known by their traditional name: the *Cappella* Nani, the *Cappella* Bugeja and the *Cappella* Diacono. But the changed post-Second World War environment leading to the marked decrease in church attendance and the faithful-orientated promulgations of Vatican Council II have narrowed their activities considerably. The services of the church musician became less and less solicited; the unfortunate corollary being that substantially less liturgical music, the major contributor to Malta's musical heritage, is now being composed.

Post Second World War Developments

These currents have meant that the forces that influenced the resident Maltese composer in the past have shifted from a church-centred, Italian-orientated direction to one that is more theatre-centred and musically cosmopolitan. Typical of this new attitude is Pawlu Grech (b. 1938) who in 1954 left Malta for musical studies in Italy. In 1964 he left for London and continued working with Hans Keller with whom he consolidated his ample knowledge of the twentieth compositional techniques that he uses in his splendid works. In style, consequently, he is decisively a modernist and expounds the theoretical aspects of his approach with consummate skill. He has influenced greatly, especially by his teaching, the local development of the philosophy and mechanism of contemporary composition and the methodology of teaching it.

But the three most frequently performed post Second World War composers are Carmelo Pace (1906-93),[75] Charles Camilleri (b. 1931) and Joseph Vella (b. 1942).

Pace was the first major Maltese composer to explore comprehensively, and in various styles, a wide range of orchestral and instrumental forms never attempted by antecedent Maltese composers, thereby considerably extending Maltese musical development.[76] Thus he can be credited with composing the first symphonies, concertos, ballets, rhapsodies, tone poems, variations and *scherzi* in Maltese musical history. His area of influence was extended through his teaching for he was one of the most competent and charismatic teachers in Maltese history.

Camilleri[77] is the most cosmopolitan of contemporary Maltese composers. Having lived, studied and worked in the 'new' countries, first in Australia and later Canada and the USA,[78] he has been emotionally freed from European traditions. Perhaps because of the melting pot of styles to which he was subjected, he eventually returned to Malta to discover the roots of the authentic musical heritage of his native land. He found this in its folk-tunes and abstract sound-scape and these now illuminate many of his recent outstanding compositions.[79] In 1992 he was appointed first Professor of Music at the University of Malta, a position that he held till 1996. A detailed catalogue of his numerous, brilliant, and wide-ranging works has still to be written.

Joseph Vella,[80] composer, conductor, editor and teacher, studied with his father, with Franco Donatoni and Franco Ferrara, and is a music graduate of the University of Durham. In 1994 he was appointed Associate Professor of Music at the University of Malta. A composer with a self-confessed allegiance to contrapuntal music, his works are all ingrained in a personal idiom that stems mainly from a neo-classicist indication. His impressive *oeuvre*, in various forms and designs, now counts over a hundred major works and his deep interest in old Maltese music that he continues to edit has been instrumental in enabling the Maltese nation to discover its impressive musical past.

Liturgical Music in Gozo

Joseph Vella was born in Gozo. The *Matrice*, the mother church,[81] in this island is that found in the *cittadella*, dedicated to the Assumption of the Blessed Virgin Mary. Music[82] in the *Matrice* has a long history, and musicians brought over from Malta often reinforced its execution. When in September 1864 Gozo was erected a diocese independent from that of Malta and the *Matrice* was elevated to the dignity of a cathedral, steps were taken to strengthen its *cappella di musica*. *Maestri* included Vincenzo Bondì, Canon Giorgio Mercieca, Paolo Lanzon, Mgr Giuseppe Debrincat and Canon Martin Portelli. Most of the *maestri* were also composers and manuscripts of their works are to be found in the Cathedral's music archives.[83]

But probably, besides Joseph Vella, the other most important composer born in Gozo is Mgr Giuseppe Farrugia (1852-1925). Born in Victoria, he had his main schooling in the Gozitan seminary where he studied music under the Jesuit Enrico Scio and developed into one of the most interesting and gifted composers in Malta's musical history. Illustrations would be the marvellously melodious and harmonically inventive fifth, *O dulcis Christi caritas*, and eighth, *O heros invictissime*, strophes of the triduum hymn *Georgi miles inclyti* (1878) executed annually during the titular *festa* of St George's Basilica in Gozo.

Other Forms of Art Music

Although this article has concentrated on classical (mainly liturgical) music and opera, the musical interest of the nation also includes other forms of art music. Chief among them is civil bands and pop music. Bands[84] evolved in the mid-nineteenth century and now number eighty-two - surely the highest comparative concentration of bands in any European country. The post-1964 tourist expansion boosted 'pop' music, the annual highlight being the Malta Song Festival, which selects the Maltese entry for the European Song Contest. Doubtless, this type of art music, heavily influenced by the American and European example, is currently the most dynamic.

Maltese Contribution to European Music Development

The overall impression of this article may have been that of a very small nation in the centre of the Mediterranean receiving and adapting the European musical heritage to suit its national proclivities. Given Malta's socio-economic constraints, this is mostly true. But Maltese musicians have also contributed to European musical development. The contribution has come from at least four musicians: Abos, Isouard, Arena and Azopardi.

Azopardi's contribution is not to be found in his excellent and inventive compositions but rather in his theoretical opus, *Il Musico Prattico*, on the art of the counterpoint.[85] Published in the form of a French translation by Framery in 1786, re-edited and published by Choron in 1816, (2/1824), and introduced as a textbook in Paris by Grétry, it influenced not only generations of French students but also paramount composers like Cherubini. The latter found Azopardi's discussion on 'imitation' so valid that it became the basis of Chapter XIX of his own treatise, *Cours de contrepoint et de fugue* (1835).

Isouard's place in the development of *opéra comique* is widely recognised. Endowed with a remarkable flair for writing effective and melodic theatre music of popular appeal and outstanding ensemble construction, his style developed from the sheen of such early works as *La statue* (1802) and *Michel-Ange* (1802) along musically more serious lines to reach a peak in works like *Joconde* (1814) and *Jeannot et Colin* (1814). He helped to give the *opéra-comique* its essentially final form and influenced the development of other composers, including Rossini, whose *Cenerentola* (1817) is founded on Etienne's libretto for Isouard's *Cendrillon* (1810). The development of Rossini's ensemble writing also seems to owe a lot to Isouard.

As a composer of *opere buffe* and *opere serie*, of cantatas, arias and instrumental works and of sacred music, Abos earned the admiration of important musicians, including the mezzo-soprano castrato Caffarelli for whom he wrote the operas *Arianno e Teseo* (1748) and *Tito Manlio* (1751) and the cantata *L'arca del testamento* (1747), the composer Johann Simon Mayr who kept a copy of Abos's *Benedictus Dominus* for his own use, and the librarian and historian Giuseppe Sigismondo, who did much to preserve Abos's extant *oeuvre*. But it was as a teacher that Abos produced his most valid contribution to European music. His acknowledged ability in this critical field was so much in demand that he held appointments in three of the four Neapolitan conservatories - that of *dei Poveri di Gesu Cristo* (between 1742-

43), *San Onofrio a Capuana* (between 1742-60) and *della Pieta dei Turchini* (between 1754-59). His students included composers Boroni, Tritto, Paisiello, Piccinni, Insanguine, Zerafa and Brunetti.

Like Abos, Giuseppe Arena became one of the most important and distinguished composers of eighteenth-century Naples, designated *celebre maestro* in the libretto of *Il vecchio deluso*, his most admired opera and a prime example of his ingenious creativity, solid craftsmanship and dynamic melodic direction. His most important claim to fame was his introduction, for the first time in its history, of more than four roles in the finale of the *opera buffa*.

An ending consideration may be given to Francesco Schira, born in Valletta in 1809, and died London in 1883, perhaps the most European of Maltese composers. In the 1820s he was at the Milan Conservatory and his first opera, *Elena e Malvina* (1832) was premiered to great acclaim in La Scala. He soon left for Lisbon where he presented his next two operas, *Il fanatico per la musica* (1835) and *I cavalieri di Valenzia* (1837). In early 1842 he moved to Paris but on 26 December of the same year he conducted *La sonnanbula* in Princess Theatre in London, where he settled. He also conducted regularly at Drury Lane and Covent Garden. After 1852 he decided to concentrate on composing and the teaching of singing. His most successful operas were his last two, *Selvaggia* (1875) and *Lia* (1876), premiered not in London but in Venice's Teatro La Fenice.

A paragraph in Frank Walker's famous book, *The Man Verdi*,[86] is well worth quoting:

> It is fair to remember that Lavigna (Verdi's teacher) made Verdi hire scores ... and advised him to take a season ticket for the opera house where he would hear 'how to treat dramatic music' by practical example. The operas performed at La Scala in this winter season, 1832-3, were *Donna Caritea*, *Ismalia* and *Il conte d'Essex* - all by Mercadante; *Chiara di Rosemberg*, *Fernando Cortez* and *Il nuovo Figaro* - all by Luigi Ricci; *Fausta* by Donizetti; *Caterina di Guisa* by Carlo Coccia and *Elena e Malvina* by the Maltese composer Francesco Schira. It was on operas like these, totally unfamiliar today, that Verdi was brought up.

Notes

1   For a more detailed account of the issues raised in this paper, vide the same author's two books on the history of music in Malta: *Il-Mużika ta' Malta sa l-Aħħar tas-Seklu Tmintax* and *Il-Mużika ta' Malta fis-Sekli Dsatax u Ghoxrin* (Malta, 2000). *The New Grove Dictionary of Music and Musicians*, Second Edition, ed S. Sadie, (London, 2001) carries a general article on Malta (Art & Traditional Music) and biographical articles on Girolamo Abos, Giuseppe Arena, Francesco Azopardi, Giuseppe Balzano, the Bugeja family of composers (Pietro Paolo, Vincenzo, Filippo, Riccardo, Censinu), Charles Camilleri, Alessandro Curmi, Carlo Diacono, Nicolò Isouard, the Nani family of composers (Angelo, Emmanuele, Paolo, Anton, Paul), Carmelo Pace, Francesco Schira, Filippo Pizzuto, Paolino Vassallo, Joseph Vella, Michel'Angelo Vella and Benigno Zerafa.

2   The book by G. Cassar Pullicino and C. Camilleri, *Maltese Oral Poetry and Folk Music* (Malta, 1998) examines in depth the subject. See also G. Cassar Pullicino, 'Folk Bards and Folk Music in Malta',

The Sundial, V, 5 (1945), 23-26; M. Fsadni, 'Ġrajja ta' Erba' Daqqaqa fil-Milied tas-Sena 1643', *Riflessi*, January 1972, 179-80.

3   G. Wettinger, 'Malta fiż-Żmien Nofsani', in T. Cortis (ed.), *L-Identità Kulturali ta' Malta* (Malta, 1989), 207-23.

4   The relationship between Malta's 'Arabic' language and its folkmusic is examined by P. Ciantar, 'Music, language and style of Maltese folk music', *The Sunday Times* (Malta), 16 November 2001, 34-35.

5   P. Sant Cassia, 'L-Għana: Bejn il-Folklor u l-Ħabi', in T. Cortis (ed.), *L-Identità Kulturali ta' Malta* (Malta, 1989), 81-91.

6   This is Abate Giliberto's *c*.1240 census. It is quoted in Andrew P. Vella *Storja ta' Malta*, I (Malta, 1984), 78. This important document may have suffered at the hands of copyists and a number of historians consequently dispute the figures. A. Luttrell, quoted in S. Fiorini, 'Malta in 1530', in *Hospitaller Malta 1530-1798*, ed. V. Mallia-Milanes (Malta, 1993), 113, suggests that the original number of Christian families in Malta in the census could have been 1047 and not 47. This would mean a total of 2119 families, or a total population of *c*. 10,000 living in the Maltese islands at that time. If Luttrell is correct, the Christian percentage would have been 59 percent of the inhabitants.

7   According to Abate Giliberto's *c*. 1240 census.

8   J. Vella Bondin, 'Malta's musical heritage - form and influences', *The Sunday Times* (Malta), 2 April 1989, 22-23.

9   S. Fiorini, *The 'Mandati' Documents at the Archives of the Mdina Cathedral, Malta, 1473-1539* (Malta, 1992), li-lvi.

10 J. Azzopardi and M. Sansone, *Italian and Maltese Music in the Archives of the Cathedral Museum of Malta* (Malta, 2001), 20-22. Attention can also be drawn to a number of Choral Books belonging to the Conventual Church of St John. See M. Caruana, *The L'Isle Adam Illuminated Manuscripts and other Illuminated Choral Books in Malta* (Malta, 1991).

11 S. Fiorini, *Mandati*, xxvi-xxviii. See also E. R. Leopardi, 'Appointment of a School Master in 1470', *Melita Historica*, III, 2 (1961), 55-58.

12 J. Azzopardi, 'L'insegnamento del canto fermo e del canto figurato nella cattedrale di Malta nel Cinquecento e agli inizi del Seicento', in *Tra Scilla e Cariddi, Atti del convegnio internazionale di studi Reggio Calabria-Messina 28-30 maggio 2001* (Reggio Calabria, 2003), 363-80.

13 J. Azzopardi, 'La cappella musicale della cattedrale di Malta e i suoi rapporti con la Sicilia', in D. Ficola (ed.), *Musica sacra in Sicilia tra rinascimento e barocco* (Palermo, 1988), 47-67. See also Azzopardi and Sansone, ch. 2. F. Bruni, *Musica e musicisti alla Cattedrale di Malta nei secoli XVI-XVIII* (Malta, 2001), chs. 1-2.

14 Author of six published books of madrigals.

15 A term for a string instrument, most often denoting a type of viola or a small cello.

16 Information in J. Azzopardi, 'Il-Kattidral ta' l-Imdina: Kappella Mużikali u Arkivju Mużikali', in T. Cortis (ed.), *Oqsma tal-Kultura Maltija* (Malta, 1991), 104.

17 N. Chircop, 'Scores Attributable to Giuseppe Balzano: A Critical Analysis' (B.Ed. dissertation, University of Malta, 1989).

18 J. Vella, 'A Tale of Two Motets', *The Sunday Times of Malta Supplement*, 4 December 1977, 4-5.

19 The Mdina Cathedral Museum Music Archives include a number of anonymous compositions of earlier periods. Among them may be the earliest extant work by a Maltese composer.

20 For details of the contents of these priceless archives, in which are also preserved unique works by important Italian composers such as Giacomo Carissimi, Andrea Rinaldi, Vincenzo Amato, and Bonaventura Rubino, see Azzopardi and Sansone, 24-37. The core of the archives, however, is works by the Cathedral's Maltese *maestri*, noteworthy among which are the *oeuvres* of Benigno Zerafa, Francesco Azopardi, and Giuseppe Vella. See also F. Bruni, *Musica e musicisti*, ch. 3. Other important but smaller (classical) music libraries, in addition to those mentioned elsewhere in these notes, include the Gozo Cathedral Music Archives; the Wignacourt Museum Archives in Rabat; Archives of the Commissariat of the Holy Land, Valletta; Archives of the Franciscan Conventuals, Victoria, Gozo; the Music Archives of the St Lawrence Band Club, Vittoriosa; and the Music Archives of the Collegiate Church of Cospicua. Music by Maltese composers, mainly by those who worked overseas (e.g. Arena, Abos, Isouard, Schira, Camilleri) is also preserved in many European libraries including the Biblioteca del Conservatorio di Musica San Pietro a Majella in Naples; the British Library Music Collections; the Musiksammlung der Österreichischen Nationalbibliothek; the Diözesanbibliothek

Münster Santini-Sammlung; Bibliothèque Nationale de France, Département de la Musique.

21 See J. Vella Bondin, 'Five Maltese Composers of the 18th Century', *The Sunday Times of Malta*, 25 July 1976, 15; *Id.* 'Pietro Paolo Pullicino (1725-1786) Mużicista Kompożitur Żebbuġi', *Programm tal-Festa ta' San Ġużepp f'Ħaż-Żebbuġ* (Malta, 1996).

22 J. Azzopardi, 'Benigno Zerafa (1726-1804): a biography' in S. Fiorini and A. Borg (ed.) *Programme Notes for a Concert of Maltese Baroque Music by Benigno Zerafa held at St John's Co-Cathedral on January 30, 1987* (Malta, 1987), 6-10. J. Vella Bondin, 'Benigno Zerafa (1726-1804): An unsuitable *maestro?*', *The Sunday Times* (Malta), 28 March 2004, 42.

23 P. Pullicino, *Notizia biografica di Francesco Azopardi* (Malta, 1876); D. Buhagiar, 'Il musico prattico' by Francesco Azopardi' (M.A. thesis, University of Western Ontario, 1988), ch. 1.

24 S. Heighes, 'The Music of Benigno Zerafa: a preliminary study', in Fiorini and Borg (eds), *Programme Notes*, (Malta, 1987), 12-17.

25 See G. Galea (ed.), *Masters of Maltese Baroque Music* (Malta, 2002).

26 Azzopardi and Sansone, ch. 5. Setting to music the text of the Mass was as popular with the Neapolitan composers as the setting of an opera libretto. Jomelli set it at least eighteen times; Feo eighteen; Leo six and, additionally, also set miscellaneous mass movements, including the *Credo* five times. Azopardi's *oeuvre* includes thirty masses, Zerafa's eighteen.

27 But nine of Zerafa's settings utilise a three-section (*Kyrie, Gloria, Credo*) form.

28 Such as the beautiful aria for bass, *Domine Deus Agnus Dei*, in Azopardi's *Mass in F Major* (1776); *Te Gloriosus* in Zerafa's *Te Deum* (1746).

29 For example the *Sicut Erat* from Zerafa's *Dixit Dominus* (1756). This very effective double chorus is based on a psalm tone *cantus firmus* placed in the two alto parts.

30 For instance the majestic *Cum Sancto Spiritus* concluding Azopardi's *Mass in F Major* (1776), which begins homophonically and develops into a powerful double fugue.

31 For an overview of the colonisation of Malta by this military Order see V. Mallia-Milanes, 'Introduction to Hospitaller Malta', in V. Mallia Milanes (ed.), *Hospitaller Malta 1530-1798* (Malta, 1993), ch. 1.

32 NLM, AOM 290, f. 28v.

33 J. Vella Bondin, 'The *Cappella di Musica* of the Order of St John', *The Sunday Times* (Malta), 24 January 1993, 28-29; 31 January 1993, 30-31; 7 February 1993, 20-21.

34 Many of the musicians and singers engaged were also trained in Naples, among them tenor Fra Giovanni Pace and bass Don Saverio Farrugia. See J. Vella Bondin, 'Żewġ Kantanti Maltin tas-Seklu Tmintax', *Pronostku Malti għas-sena 1995*, 181-202.

35 *Id.*, 'Who was Girolamo Abos?', *The Sunday Times*, (Malta), 17 March 1996, 40-41.

36 *Id.*, 'Giuseppe Arena (1709-84), in T. Cortis, T. Freller and L. Bugeja (eds), *Melitensium Amor, Festschrift in honour of Dun Gwann Azzopardi* (Malta, 2002), 391-96.

37 *Id.*, *Girolamo Abos: Stabat Mater* (Wisconsin, USA, 2003). This work also contains an up-to-date biography of the composer.

38 *Id.*, 'Nicolò Isouard: His Years in Malta', in J. Azzopardi (ed.), *Nicolò Isouard de Malte* (Malta, 1991), 21-30. *Id.*, 'Commemorating Nicolo Isouard', *The Sunday Times* (Malta), 16 February 2003, 56-57.

39 Brother of the celebrated opera composer Pasquale (1727-97).

40 Preserved in Paris's Bibliothèque Nationale de France, Département de la Musique - Mss. 9113 A & B, 8039 B, 8910.

41 The first to do so was Francesco Azopardi.

42 The classical study on these is V. Laurenza, 'Calendimaggio settecentesco a Malta', *Archivum Melitense*, II (1913-1914), 18-20, 187-203.

43 J. Vella Bondin, 'Maltese Composers of *Calendimaggio* Cantatas - Fra Filippo Pizzuto and Don Michel'Angelo Vella', *The Sunday Times* (Malta), 15 May 1994, 28-29; 29 May 1994, 28-29.

44 Known as *Teatro Pubblico* during the Knights of St John's era, as *Teatro Reale* after 1810 and as *Teatro Manoel* after 1866. It was built and paid for by Grand Master Antonio Manoel di Vilhena on an elegant design based on that of the Teatro di Palermo. See P. Xuereb, *The Manoel Theatre, a short history* (Malta, 1994).

45 Inscription above the main entrance to theatre.

46 A. G. Miceli, *L-Istorja ta' l-Opra f'Malta (1631-1866)* (Malta, 1999). This book gives details about the operas performed in the Manoel Theatre before the opening of the Royal Opera House (Malta).

47 J. Vella Bondin, 'Maltese Composers and Opera Composition', in C. Xuereb (ed.), *The Theatre in Malta* (Malta, 1997), 63-79. The appendix to this article is a catalogue of operas written by Maltese composers

up to the end of the twentieth century, whether performed or not, with the exception of those composed by Giuseppe Arena. These are listed in the same author's article on Arena, 'Giuseppe Arena (1709-84)', in *Melitensium Amor.*

48   The architect of London's Covent Garden.

49   M. Ellul, 'The Building of the Royal Opera House (1861-1866), in C. Xuereb (ed.), *The Theatre in Malta* (Malta, 1997), 47-61. J. Bonnici and M. Cassar, *The Royal Opera House, Malta* (Malta, 1990).

50   A. G. Miceli, *L-Istorja ta' l-Opra f'Malta (1866-2000)* (Malta, 2001). This book contains details about the operas performed in Malta after the opening of the Royal Opera House.

51   E.g. Gounod's *Faust*, Massenet's *Manon, Thaïs* and *Werther*, Bizet's *Carmen* and *I pescatori di perle*, Mussorgsky's *Boris Godunow*, Saint-Saëns's *Sansone e Dalila*, Wagner's *Lohengrin, Tannhäuser, La Walkira* and *Tristan e Isolde.*

52   Such as Emma Albani, Gemma Bellincioni, Romilda Pantaleoni, Adelaide Saraceni, Licia Albanese, Pia Tassarini, Antonio Scotto, Mario Basiola, Francesco Navarrini, Adriano Pantaleoni, Giovanni Zenatello and many others of equal calibre.

53   J. Vella Bondin, 'Carlo Diacono - opera composer', *The Sunday Times* (Malta), 14 June 1992, 41.

54   *Id.*, 'A Struggle for Recognition', *The Sunday Times* (Malta), 26 February 1995, 30-31.

55   *Id.*, 'Il-Kappella Nani fis-Seklu Dsatax', *Programm Filarmonika Santa Marija Mosta*, ed. J. J. Camilleri (Malta, 1994), 71-75.

56   R. Micallef, 'The Bugeja Musicians' (B.Ed dissertation, University of Malta, 1989), includes a catalogue of extant works by the Bugeja composers. The musical dynasty of the Bugeja family of composers consists of four generations and five members: Pietro Paolo (1772-1828), his sons Vincenzo (1805-60) and Filippo (1808-91), Vincenzo's son Riccardo (1844-1926), Riccardo's son Censinu (1910-67). The Bugeja music is archived in the Jesus of Nazareth Priory, Sliema, of the Dominican Friars of Malta.

57   Anon., *Cenni storici sulla Vita del Maestro di Cappella Vincenzo Bugeja Maltese* (Malta, 1861).

58   F. Bruni, *Musica Sacra a Malta* (Malta, 1993).

59   C. Attard, 'Five Generation of Nani Musicians' (B.Ed dissertation, University of Malta, 1986), includes a catalogue of extant works by the Nani composers preserved in the Mdina Cathedral Music Archives. The musical dynasty of the Nani family of composers consists of five generations: Angelo (1751-1844), his son Emanuele (1769-1860) Emanuele's nephew Paolo (1814-1904), Paolo's son Anton (1842-1929), Anton's son Paul (1906-86). On Paul, see J. Vella Bondin, 'Paul Nani - The Closing of an Era', *The Sunday Times* (Malta), 9 November 1986, 38.

60   Paolo Nani's compositions have been said to possess *il brio di Rossini ed il sentimento di Bellini*. See G. Muscat-Azzopardi, 'Paolo Nani', *Malta Letteraria* I, 2 (Malta, 1904), 50-52.

61   J. Vella Bondin, 'Anton Nani and his *Requiem*', *The Sunday Times* (Malta), 29 October 1989, 24. *Id.*, 'Anton Nani - A Musical Legacy', *The Sunday Times* (Malta), 18 October 1992, 43. Since 1975 this *Requiem* has been revived in concert performances many times, each time with astounding popular success and critical acclaim.

62   Anon., *Di P. Giuseppe Spiteri Fremond, Cenni Biografici* (Malta, 1878).

63   F. Bruni, *The Vella Composers* (Malta, 1997). The book includes a complete catalogue of the works archived at the Cathedral Museum of Giuseppe and Luigi as well as of the other two sons of Giuseppe: Alberto (1866-1931) and Paolo (1873-1948). Giuseppe was *maestro di cappella* of the two cathedrals between 1860 and 1902.

64   N. D'Anastas, 'Emmanuele Bartoli (1852-1933), il-Bniedem li għex fil-Mużika' *Banda Cittadina Leone Programm ta' Santa Marija, Rabat, Għawdex*, No. 14, August 1993, 53-59; No. 15, August 1994, 49-58. Also contains a catalogue of known Bartoli compositions.

65   J. Vella Bondin, 'Carlo Diacono (1876-1942)', *Għaqda Mużikali Beland Programm Festa Santa Katerina*, Żejtun, June 1992, 37-67. The first part of this article gives a graphic description of the *Motu Proprio* aftermath.

66   Paolo Nani's obituary in *Malta Taghna*, 26 March 1904, 4.

67   Amore (1808-94) is an example of a number of Italians who came to work as musicians in Malta and decided to settle here. He was a violinist and later conductor and impresario at the Manoel Theatre and the Royal Opera House. He was especially noted as a teacher of the violin, among his pupils being Paolino Vassallo. An interesting side to his achievements as a composer was his ability to set to music comic texts in the Maltese language.

68   The Vassallo compositions form part of the Music Archives preserved in the St Augustine's Priory, Valletta, of the Augustinian Friars of Malta. These archives also include the works of Padre Domenico

Anastasi and Padre Albert Borg who was *maestro di cappella* of the two Cathedrals between 1945 and 1993.

69 J. Vella Bondin, 'Dumink Anastasi, O.S.A. – composer and conductor', *The Times* (Malta), 27 January 1989, 4-5.

70 V. Battistino, *Lorenzo Gonzi (1887-1934)* (Malta, 1994). Also contains a list of Gonzi compositions.

71 G. Mifsud, *Mill-Kompożizzjonijiet ta' Gużeppi Caruana (1880-1931)* (Malta, 1981). Includes a list of known Caruana compositions. These now form part of the Mdina Cathedral Museum Music Archives.

72 Josie Mallia Pulvirenti was the only major Maltese composer up to this era who was not interested in composing opera or church music. After finishing his studies with Vassallo, he went to Italy to work with Giulio Bas, professor at the Milan Conservatory. His abiding interest in impressionism, the only Maltese to have systematically shown a constant preoccupation with this mode of musical expression, resulted in notable works like *Ballata romantica* for two sopranos, tenor and orchestra; *Elegia della giovinezza perduta,* cantata for soprano, choir and orchestra and the orchestral *Impressione sinfonica* and *Espressionismo*. Salvatore Enrico Failla, 'Di Josie Mallia Pulvirenti, compositore 'impressionista' maltese, e di talune altre cose a questi più o meno riferibili', *Note su Note, Rassegna di contributi musicologici* (Catania) I, 1 (June 1993), 136-77.

73 J. Vella Bondin, 'Carlo Diacono - foremost composer of church music', *The Sunday Times,* (Malta), 22 November 1987, 37; G. de Domenico, *La Messa Funebre del Maestro Carlo Diacono* (Malta, 1918). The Diacono music is mainly kept in the Diacono Family Private Archives.

74 J. Vella Bondin, 'Carlo Diacono - opera composer', *The Sunday Times* (Malta), 14 June 1992, 41.

75 *Id.*, 'Carmelo Pace: A life in music', *The Sunday Times* (Malta), 22 May 1994, 33; *Id.*, 'A life devoted to music - Carmelo Pace (1905-1993)', *The Sunday Times* (Malta), 11 May 2003, 39.

76 M. De Gabriele and G. Caffari, *Carmelo Pace: Thematic, Annotated and Illustrated Catalogue of Works* (Minnesota and Malta, 1991). This catalogue, which gives detail about his approximate 500 works, shows the wide range of Pace's compositional interests. The Pace compositions in autograph manuscript score, with the exception of the operas, form part of the Mdina Cathedral Museum Music Archives. The opera scores are deposited with the Manoel Theatre but photocopies are available at the Cathedral Museum.

77 Many books and articles have been written about this composer and his music. These include C. Palmer, *The Music of Charles Camilleri - an Introduction* (Malta, 1975); J. Walbank, 'Charles Camilleri: the Organ Music', *Organist's Review,* (London, 1987) *Charles Camilleri, Portrait of a Composer* ed. E. Sapienza and J. Attard, (Malta, 1988); *The Piano Music of Charles Camilleri*, ed. M. Bonello (Malta, 1990); G. Protheroe, 'Soundscapes, the Music of Maltese Composer Charles Camilleri', *Musical Times*, CXXXIII, No.1790 (April 1992), 166-69; B. Ramsey, 'Charles Camilleri', *Classical Music*, 22 June 1996, 39.

78 Although he studied with his father, Joseph Abela Scolaro, Paul Nani, Carmelo Pace and with John Weinzweig at Canada's Toronto University, his ample compositional skills are mostly self-discovered which may be the reason why his continuing work reveals an ever-present sense of creative excitement and a relish for fresh challenges and original solutions.

79 Camilleri has expressed his thoughts about this in his seminal treatise *Mediterranean Music* [interviewed by Peter Serracino Inglott] (Malta, 1988).

80 J. Aquilina, 'Mro. Joseph Vella', *The Sunday Times* (Malta), 18 October 1987, 20-21; C. Violetti, 'The Music of Joseph Vella', *Studi e Documentazioni - Rivista Umbria di Musicologia* (June 1993), 71; 'Interview: First among Maestros', *The Times Arts Supplement*, 5 March 2004, 10.

81 See J. Bezzina, *Religion and Politics in a Crown Colony* (Malta, 1985). This book relates the story of how Gozo became a separate diocese.

82 G. A. Grech, *Mill-Istorja Mużikali ta' Għawdex* (Gozo, 2002), especially ch. 1.

83 J. Vella Bondin, 'L-Arkivju tal-Mużika tal-Katidral t'Għawdex', *Banda Cittadina Leone Programm ta' Santa Marija Għawdex 1992*, No. 13, 19-25.

84 M. Schiavone (ed.), *L-istorja tal-Każini tal-Baned f'Malta u Għawdex*, I-III (Malta, 1997-8); G. A. Grech, *Erbatax-il Profil ta' Mużicisti Għawdxin, Maltin u Barranin.* (Malta, 1998) includes a number of profiles of musicians who conducted bands in Malta and Gozo.

85 M. Sansone, 'Il Musico Pratico di Francesco Azopardi tra Malta e Parigi', *Tra Scilla e Cariddi* (Reggio Calabria, 2003), 381-408.

86 Published by J. M. Dent & Sons, London, 1962. The quotation is found on page 13.

Antonio Espinosa Rodriguez

ART IN MALTA: AN OVERVIEW

Art in Malta harks back to prehistoric times. Beautifully crafted clay and stone artefacts and a series of impressive megalithic structures mark the extraordinary ethos of early Maltese civilisations. The potter's craft evolved into a manifestation of cultural vitality through forms and patterns applied to utilitarian artefacts. Meanwhile man discovered the art of modelling and carving anthropomorphic figures. Sinewy organic spiral motifs, sometimes against a pitted ground, add a touch of magic to the massive stones that constitute the complex womb-like forms of Malta's prehistoric temples. The generous contours of the Hypogeum 'Sleeping Lady' and the so-called Maltese Fat Ladies were offset by abstract arrangements derivative from the vegetal and animal kingdoms. In this respect Maltese prehistoric art exudes an air of solemn monumentality that transcends spiritual and physical dimensions.[1]

The Phoenicians made their appearance in Malta around 700 BC.[2] They brought in a new architecture, charming amulets, ornamental trinkets and jewellery that betray egyptianizing forms. The fifth century BC baked clay anthropomorphic sarcophagus from Għar Barka near Rabat is illustrative of Egyptian influences. Imported wares, the typology of certain locally manufactured pottery and a pair of marble candelabra[3] bearing Punic and Greek inscriptions indicate contacts with the Greek world.

As time went by Malta's link with the Punic world, especially Carthage grew closer. However, the Carthaginians clashed with the emerging power of Rome and in 218 BC Malta fell to the Romans. Roman rule lasted some six hundred years. Notwithstanding its location in the periphery of the empire the Maltese islands experienced a flowering of the arts. Dating to the first century AD are fragments of mosaic pavements in the refined *opus tessellatum* and *opus vermiculatum* found at the Roman Domus in Rabat. Architectural fragments confirm the existence of lavish buildings, while a tombstone of a musician and comedian indicate that Malta had a theatre. The bust of Antonia the Younger and the head of the Emperor Claudius are high points of Roman statuary in Malta.[4]

Christianity made its debut in Malta during the Roman domination. Early Christian art in Malta is mostly found in underground cemeteries called catacombs. Fragments of mural paintings, graffiti and carvings gave visual meaning to the aspirations of the faithful and the Christian message of eternal life. Although mostly dilapidated and their artistic evaluation difficult, paleo-christian art range from the naïve carving at Ħal Resqun to the elaborate forms at the Abbatija tad-Dejr and the Salina catacombs. The best surviving traces of early Christian paintings are those in the St Agatha complex in Rabat. While vestiges of an early Christian basilica and a baptistery have been uncovered at Tas-Silġ, only a few tombstones, a silver ring and some pottery remains of Muslim arts and crafts.[5]

No painting in Malta, excluding fragments extant in Christian catacombs, can be dated before the Middle Ages.[6] The use of underground cavities as churches and dwellings was a common practice in medieval Malta. One of the earliest surviving paintings is the late thirteenth century image of Our Lady and Child in the rock-cut sanctuary at Mellieħa. Probably dating to the early fourteenth century is the Crucifixion and Annunciation from the Abbatija tad-Dejr, now in the National Museum of Fine Arts. Dating to the fifteenth century are the murals in the crypt of St Agatha in Rabat. This and other troglodyte paintings follow the iconography and hieratic formality of the Sicilian-Byzantine school. The late fifteenth century frescos in the chapel of Ħal Millieri are in the same tradition.

Besides murals, panels were now commissioned as altarpieces and devotional icons. By the mid fifteenth century works of outstanding artistic qualities made their appearance. The so-called St Luke Madonna in the Cathedral church is a refined Byzantinesque panel with marked Sienese and International Gothic traits. Similarly is the splendid Virgin of Mercy with Saints Paul and Augustine in the sacristy of the Augustinian church at Rabat. The altarpiece of the Lamentation in the parish church of St George in Qormi expresses strong emotional piety and pathos through the emaciated body of Christ and a doleful Madonna and her companions. The entire pictorial complex was flanked by panels depicting St George and St Gregory and was surmounted by a Crucifix encompassing Byzantine spirituality with International Gothic narrative zest.

The great St Paul polyptych, now in the Cathedral Museum, was the main altarpiece of the Cathedral in Mdina. It is a work of resplendent beauty attributable to the circle of the Catalan painter Luis Borassa (1360-1426). Given the subject and iconography it must have been purposely commissioned for Malta. The polyptych represents St Paul in Majesty surrounded by ten other smaller panels. Significantly two of the scenes refer to St Paul's shipwreck and stay in Malta. Notwithstanding the passage of time and the loss of its original gothic framework, it has retained the power to arrest and impress the beholder.

Malta received its artistic motive force through Sicily. Antonio de Saliba (1466-1535) and Salvo d'Antonio (active 1493-1526) were related to Antonello da Messina (c.1430-1479). In 1517 de Saliba painted an altarpiece for the church of Santa Maria del Gesù in Rabat, while in 1504 d'Antonio completed a polyptych for the Benedictine Nuns of Mdina. The painter from Syracuse Alessandro Padovano was engaged from 1520 to 1521 in decorating the ceiling of the old Mdina Cathedral. In 1529 Padovano was still receiving commissions from the Cathedral Chapter.

In 1530 Emperor Charles V ceded the Maltese islands to the cosmopolitan Order of St John. The knights were great patrons of the art. They brought with them from Rhodes their archives and many artistic treasures. These included the precious twelfth century Byzantine icon of Our Lady of Damascus and a set of French illuminated choral books commissioned by Grand Master Philip Villiers de L'Isle Adam in 1521.[7] With the knights came a large group of retainers that also included craftsmen. One of them was Nicola Caccialepre who in 1535 carved a marble stoup for the chapel of the Hospital of Santo Spirito. In 1504 the Sicilian sculptor Antonello Gagini (1478/79-1536) carved in marble a beautiful Madonna and Child for the Franciscan Friars in Rabat. When in 1535 Grand Master L'Isle Adam died, the same sculptor was commissioned to produce his effigy on his funeral monument.

Sicilian influences impregnated Malta during the first decades of the Order's rule. In 1551 Can. Giuseppe Manduca commissioned an altarpiece for the chapel of St Agatha in Mdina from an artist of Sicilian extraction or training. Renaissance models percolated into Malta resulting into an admixture of retardataire and innovative features exemplified by remaining fragments of the whimsical Last Judgment fresco in the church of Bir Miftuħ at Gudja.

Giovanni Maria Abela is one of the first Maltese painters we know by name. In 1591 he signed the painting of the Virgin of the Roses formerly in the parish of Siġġiewi and now exhibited in the Cathedral Museum. In Naxxar there is a similar composition, unsigned but dated 1595, which has been ascribed on stylistic considerations to Abela. Both works mark the charms and limitations of art in Malta at the time.

The founding of Valletta in 1566 marked a new era in the development of art in Malta. The Italian military engineer Francesco Laparelli designed the new fortified city. However, it was the Maltese Gerolamo Cassar who supervised its construction and designed its principal buildings. The Palace of the Grand Masters was one of the first edifices to be erected in Valletta. It was lavishly decorated with murals recounting episodes from the history of the Order. The Italian Matteo Perez D'Aleccio decorated the Sala del Gran Consiglio with impressive scenes recounting the Great Siege of 1565. He also produced the main altarpieces for the then new Conventual Church of St John and the church of St Paul's Shipwreck. Other late mannerist painters working in Malta included Antonio Catalano il Vecchio (1560-1606), Francesco Potenzano (c.1540-1599), Giovanni Battista Riccio (1537-1627), Daniele Monteleone (active 1600-1622) and Filippo Palladini (c.1544-1616).

'Baptism of Christ' by Mattia Preti (1613-99)

'Maltese lady visiting a friend' by Antoine de Favray (1706-98)

'Self portrait' by Francesco Zahra (1710-73)

Palladini reached Malta as a convict rowing aboard a Tuscan galley in 1588. He had been condemned to the galleys for his part in a violent quarrel. However, Grand Master Hughes Loubenx de Verdalle had him released and secured his services. Palladini worked on the decoration of the Verdala Castle and in the Magisterial Palace where he produced the splendid frescoes in the chapel. He also painted a number of fine canvases, including altarpieces like the memorable St James for the church dedicated to that saint and the Circumcision in the Jesuit church of Valletta.

The influence of Palladini's superb mannerist art continued to linger in Malta long after his departure. The nationality of Vincenzo Baiata is uncertain and we know next to nothing about him. Still his Madonna and Child from the chapel at Tal-Virtù is signed and dated 1611. Clearly influenced by Palladini, it is a handsome work whose execution and chromatic qualities are in the best tradition of late Italian mannerist tradition. Filippo Dingli was the brother of the well-known architect Tommaso Dingli (1591-1666). His attractive canvas of the Magdalene at Madliena, dated 1660, harks back to the style introduced by Palladini at the start of the century.

The Conventual Church of St John, built by Gerolamo Cassar in 1570, became a focal point of art in Malta. Michelangelo Merisi da Caravaggio painted, around 1608, the momentous Beheading of St John for the oratory and a magnificent St Jerome and for the Italian chapel. He also painted other canvases, including two portraits of Grand Master Alof de Wignacourt; one in armour, now at the Louvre, the other wearing his monastic habit. The whereabouts of this second portrait alas is not known. Unfortunately his pesky spirit soon landed him in prison from where he escaped leaving Malta in disgrace. Caravaggio's revolutionary dramatic realism, tonal values and interplay of light and shade turned him into one of the most influential and important European painters of the age.[8]

The enigmatic painter Cassarino particularly felt the influence of Caravaggio. Dr John A. Cauchi first identified him when his signature was uncovered during the cleaning of a St Sebastian belonging to the church of St John. A corpus of generally mediocre paintings has been ascribed to Cassarino on stylistic grounds. His figures emerge from a sombre and dark ground with tonalities highlighted by flashes of warm light. However Cassarino's rigid executions fall short of respectable artistic standards. Bartolomeo Garanona's (1584-1641) Deposition in the Cathedral sacristy, dated 1627, is saturated by Caravaggesque tonal values, but its expressive religious intensity recalls late Spanish Gothic models.

Fra Lucas Garnier (active 1650-1700) and Gaspare Formica (d.1647) were foreign painters active in Malta. Fra Lucas was a French member of the Order of St John. Although a competent painter, his works lack lustre. His huge altarpiece of St Theresa in Cospicua transmits the feeling it is the work of a well-exercised dilettante. Formica is said to have hailed from Piacenza, Italy. His works are monumental but charged with queer unreal light and chromatic values. However he defaults through a dearth in originality and his compositions are brazen plagiarisms like the Holy Family of 1626, in the convent of the Friar Minors of Valletta, directly lifted from Luca Cambiaso.

Mario Minniti (1577-1640), Pietro Novelli (1603-47) and Jusepe Ribera (1591-1652) probably never came to Malta. Still they received Maltese commissions which they must have executed abroad. A constant flow of fine paintings flowed into Malta from overseas. Guido Reni (1575-1642) is not known to have visited Malta yet his Christ holding the Cross, now in the National Museum of Fine Arts, probably reached Valletta during the master's lifetime. In 1653 Fra Jacques de Cordon d'Evieu, ambassador of the Order of St John to the Holy See, commissioned the Frenchman Pierre Mignard (1612-95) to paint his portrait in Rome.

The second half of the seventeenth century was dominated by the presence of Mattia Preti (1613-99). His splendid brand of Baroque resulted from the interpolation of Neapolitan and Caravaggesque modes with the brilliant chromatic qualities of Venetian painting. He was a fine draughtsman whose productions reflect an overpowering artistic personality. Preti commenced work on the ceiling decorations of the church of St John in 1661 converting an erstwhile unassuming interior into a dazzling Baroque scenario. He continued to work in Malta until his death, producing countless works of art for local and foreign patrons. He had several followers, assistants and imitators but none could match his bravura.

The painters Giuseppe D'Arena (1633-1719) and Stefano Erardi (1630-1716) managed to cut a niche for themselves and enjoyed a certain amount of prestige and success. They stirred a course parallel to that of Preti, avoiding to be overwhelmed by the latter's personality. D'Arena's compositions tend to be schematic and derivative but had the ability to rise above the average provincial painters. Erardi would not shy to emulate other artists but his fine compositions are articulate, fluid and grand. His son Alessio Erardi (1617-1727) was a worthy painter. His Virgin of the Rosary in the parish church of Lija is truly impressive.

Following the earthquake of 1693, the old Cathedral of Mdina was severely damaged. This gave the excuse to the Cathedral Chapter to pursue their plan to erect a new Cathedral. Its design and building was entrusted to the architect Lorenzo Gafà (1630-1704). The resulting building is an epitome of Maltese Baroque architecture. The skyline and character of the country is still governed by the baroque imprint of ingenious Maltese architects and stonemasons whose clever use of local stone is truly admirable. Romano Carapecchia hailed from Rome and came to Malta in 1706. However his ingratiating and elegant baroque forms transformed the face of Valletta, giving it much of its present urban character.

Melchiorre Gafà (1635-67) stands at a par with the greatest Italian sculptors of his age. Unfortunately he died an untimely death in Rome and his works in Malta are few. The Italian Giuseppe Mazzuoli followed Melchiorre's design in his remarkable Baptism of Christ. Maltese ecclesiastic and domestic architecture were enriched with refined sculptural motifs, the product of skilled carvers like Pietro Felici (1669-1743), Paolo Zahra (1685-1747) and members of the Durante family.

A taste for grand interiors evolved in concomitance with baroque tastes. Niccolo Nasoni (1691-1773) was invited to Malta to paint complex *tromp-l'oeil* architectural compositions in the grand master's palace, Verdala Castle, the chancery, the grand master's crypt and possibly the entrance hall to the Auberge de Provence and private residences such as Palazzo Spinola in Valletta. The Messinese Antonio Manoel produced the 'fake' dome in the Cathedral of Gozo around 1793. Artists such as Antonio Grech carried on this love for painted architectural fantasies into the nineteenth century.

The painters Gian Nicola Buħaġiar (1698-1752) and Francesco Vincenzo Zahra (1710-73) were the sons of gifted stone carvers. Buħaġiar and Zahra were two outstanding painters of the eighteenth century. They worked mostly for ecclesiastical establishments, with their grand compositions full of movements and articulated figures. Although they kept separate workshops and competed for the same commissions, their personal relations appear to have been cordial. At Żejtun they engaged in a sort of friendly competition, each taking the corresponding transept apses in the parish church of St Catherine. Of the two, Zahra emerges as the more dynamic and forceful.

Antoine Favray (1706-98) was a French painter who settled in Malta during the second half of the eighteenth century. He was a member of the Order of St John and became a sort of 'official' artist. Through his art Favray presided over the decadence of the Order and died shortly before its expulsion from Malta by Napoleon Bonaparte. His portraits of grand masters, members of the Order and the local nobility and gentry reflect the flamboyant elegance of his sitters. In addition he painted attractive altarpieces such as the Annunciation in the chapel of the Old Seminary and charming genre subjects recording the last vestiges of a vanishing era.

Giuseppe Grech (1757-87) was an artist of great promise. His untimely death in Rome robbed Malta of a brilliant painter. Michele Busuttil (1762-1831) was his fellow student at the *Accadenia di San Luca*. When Can. Francesco Saverio Caruana, the Rector of the University, incorporated an art class in the faculty of architecture, Busuttil was appointed Professor of Drawing. It fell on him to form the next generation of Maltese artists. Michele Busuttil was a competent painter of religious subjects whose late popular Baroque modes, however, made him look somewhat out of fashion. The painters Gaetano Calleja, who produced the official portrait of King George III, and Antonio Grech, who supplemented his income by painting watercolours, also deserve attention.

The nineteenth century saw a change of political regime in Malta. After the turmoil of the French interlude Malta became a British possession. Neo-classicism made its entry in sculpture and architecture while a reaction against Baroque was initiated by a group of painters inspired by the German Nazareners and led by the influential Giuseppe Hyzler (1794-1852). The Purist and Nazarene movements promoted a form of Christian art purified from what were considered to be pagan encrustations. The movement found fertile ground in Malta with dire

'Benedizione' by Willie Apap (1918-70)

One of the studies that Antonio Sciortino (1879-1947) left to the National Museum of Fine Arts

consequences to some of the island's Baroque churches. Pietro Paolo Caruana (1793-1858) was less dogmatic and restrained than Hyzler and did sometimes give reign to an uncommon expressive verve in the handling of his brush. His son Raffaele Caruana (1820-86) was also a talented though less successful painter than his father.

Giuseppe Calleja (1828-1915) was Hyzler's most assiduous and faithful disciple. He continued advocating Nazarene and Purist ideals to the end of his life. He was a prolific painter who delved in various media but who is best remembered for his altarpieces and as a pioneer art historian and critic. Other followers of the Nazarene and Purists movements were the painters Tommaso Madiona (1803-64) and Salvatore Micallef (1810-91). Michele Bellanti (1807-83) also deserves to be singled out for his outstanding altarpieces in the Carmelite church at Mdina and his refined views of Malta.

Topographical views of Malta enjoyed a certain amount of favour. In 1749 Alberto Pullicino painted a series of views for the Chevalier de Turgot. In the course of the nineteenth century the genre became increasingly popular. Luis Taffien (1811-66), the various members of the Schranz and Brocktorff families, Giorgio Pullicino (1779-1851) and the Italian Girolamo Gianni were specialists in the genre. Others like Nicolas Cammillieri (c.1773-1860) and the elusive G. D'Esposito concentrated on ship portraiture.

At the close of the nineteenth century and the start of the twentieth century several Italian artists dominated Malta's artistic scene. Domenico Bruschi (1840-1910) was active in Malta in the 1880s. His works can be admired in several churches, but his most impressive canvas is the large Annunciation altarpiece in the Mdina Cathedral. Giovanni Gallucci (b.1815), Francesco Grandi (1831-1891) and above all Pietro Gagliardi (1809-90), Attilio Palombi (c.1860-1912), Eliodoro Coccoli (1880-1974), Virgilio Monti (1860-1940), Giovanni Battista Conti (1880-1972) and Mario Caffaro Rore (1910-2001) have all left an incredible wealth of art in Malta.

Giuseppe Calì (1846-1930) was the most forceful Maltese artist of his age. He could not stomach what he considered to be the unfair competition from Italian artists working in Malta. Calì studied in Naples under Giuseppe Mancinelli (1813-75) but was greatly attracted to the art of Domenico Morelli (1826-1901). His strong personality and great facility with the brush saw no rivals. Avid for work, he had no qualms in undercutting prices to ensure he got commissions that would otherwise go to his Italian competitors. He was a prolific painter and his enormous productions encompass a very wide spectrum of subjects and genre. His son Ramiro Calì (1882-1945), although less able than his father, was a successful painter as were other members of his family.

Lazzaro Pisani (1854-1932) was a gifted painter who has left us some very fine paintings. Less forceful than Calì, he nonetheless managed to create a niche for himself and received a good number of important commissions, which he carried out with competence. Although aware of the various modern trends affecting the arts abroad, he remained the last of a breed of painters who owed their allegiance to bourgeois academism. Ġużè Duca (1871-1948) was a copious painter whose numerous altarpieces seldom rose above mediocrity.

After the death of Giuseppe Calì the sculptor Antonio Sciortino (1879-1947) took the limelight. Sciortino spent much of his active life in Rome, where he was director of the British Academy of Arts. His art was abreast with the times and his works show clear modernistic trends inspired by the sleek writhing forms of Art Nouveau and the Futuristic obsession with movement and speed. His impressionistic bronze Le Gavroches of 1907 and his Christ the King rate among the finest public monuments in Malta. His successes abroad earned him esteem and respect and turned him into a national celebrity. Francis Xavier Sciortino (1875-1958) was Antonio's brother. His talents as a sculptor were considerable but he preferred to exercise his art in Canada, where he died. Edward Galea (1893-1971) was another gifted sculptor who migrated to Canada. Abram Gatt (1863-1944) cultivated the art of *papier mâché* devotional statues and provided designs for church silver and furnishing. The remarkable Carlo Darmanin (1825-1905) had popularised this form of devout sacred imagery. The Gozitan Agostino Camilleri (1895-1979) carried on the tradition well into the twentieth century, passing it on to others, including his son Alfred Camilleri Cauchi.

Edward Caruana Dingli (1876-1950) was Malta's premier society painter. He excelled in portraiture, landscape and genre subjects. Caruana Dingli distinguished himself for his brilliant palette and great technical abilities. Obfuscated by his brother's shadow, Robert Caruana Dingli (1882-1940) merits better recognition. He was a first class illustrator and engraver and his paintings often vibrate with life. On a lower artistic key stood the painter of religious subjects Gianni Vella (1885-1977). Still, Vella could surprise the beholder with some of his almost impressionistic easel paintings. Joseph Briffa (1901-87) deserves to be remembered as one of Malta's outstanding twentieth century masters. His command of the paint medium was complete and his handling of the brush superb.

The years preceding the Second World War saw the formation of a remarkable new generation of artists. Most of them had received their training at the Government School of Art under the Caruana Dingli brothers, and had furthered their studies at the *Regia Accademia di Belle Arti* in Rome. However a few did go to England, while the remarkable Carmel Mangion (1905-97) travelled to Paris and New York. The Crucifixion by George Preca (1909-84) broke with local conservative taste and paved the way to a new form of religious artistic sensibility. Disappointed and little understood by his Maltese contemporaries, he opted to settle in Rome.

The intensely spiritual Anton Inglott (1915-45) seemed destined to dominate Maltese painting but his untimely death cut short a promising career. His moving Death of St Joseph in the parish church of Msida is rightly considered an epitome of Maltese sacred art. Willie Apap (1918-70) was a remarkable and versatile painter with a strong and original artistic personality. His Woman taken in Adultery in the National Museum of Fine Arts is a moving and powerful work that attests his superlative mastery. Emvin Cremona (1891-1987) was a great decorator and designer and his artistic productions bear a strong personal imprint. He embellished several churches with vast decorative schemes but applied himself, with equal élan, to non-sacred art. His innovative verve led him to experiment with new and unusual materials leading him to produce splendid abstract and semi abstract paintings.

The introvert George Borg (1906-83) was a perfectionist and in a sense he was a successor of Antonio Sciortino. His command of sculpture, especially modelling, was complete. His slow and fastidious manner of execution prolonged the completion of his works but the end result can only be described in superlative terms. Vincent Apap (1909-2003) was an extrovert and a fast worker. His personal charm and great facility coupled with his refined artistic sensibility earned him many important commissions. Joseph Kalleja (1898-1998) experimented with the tortured forms of expressionism, and his works are marked by great individuality and idiosyncrasy. The polished sensual figures by Ignazio Cefai (1894-1981) have a distinct Art Deco accent. Emmanuel Borg Gauci (1911-91) was not much of a painter but in comparison could stand his ground as a sculptor. Victor Diacono (b.1915), Joseph Galea (1924-93) and John Spiteri Sacco (1907-96) were all valid artists kissed by the muse of sculpture. Pertaining to a younger generation was the sculptor Edward Pirotta (1938-68) whose rising star was smashed in a traffic accident. His works are not numerous but what we have attested to his uncanny talents.

The post war period saw a remarkable artistic upsurge. The innovative spirit of modern and contemporary art inspired a new generation of painters. Antoine Camilleri (b.1922) engaged into a continuous process of introspection and experimentation. Esprit Barthet (1919-99) painted poignant portraits but his female nudes and his studies of rooftops are landmarks in Maltese contemporary art. Alfred Chircop (b.1933) ventured into a symphony of ever-changing ever-fresh abstract forms whose texture and chromatic values are delineated with the consummate skill and sensitivity of an old master. Harry Alden (b.1929) expressed himself through the hard-edged technique and clean facets of pure colour. Memorable works of arts have been produced by the sculptors Anton Agius (b.1933), Gianni Bonnici (b.1932), Samuel Bugeja (1920-2004), Frans Galea (1945-94), the ceramist Gabriel Caruana (b.1929) and the watercolourists Giuseppe Archidiacono (1908-97), Joseph Galea (1905-85) and his son Edwin Galea (b.1934), and Giuseppe Cassar (1917-2002), and the painters George Fenech (b.1926), Joseph Mallia (b.1937) and Frank Portelli (b.1922). Other more recent artists are Lino Borg, Raymond Pitre, Paul Carbonaro, Caesar Attard, Norbert Attard, Marco Cremona, Eman Grima, and Salvu Mallia. Among those of a younger generation are Luciano Micallef, Josette Caruana, Isabel Borg and many others worthy of repute.

As the older generations pass away, fledging new talents take their place. The test of time selects the chaff from the grain and the deserving receive lasting recognition and glory.

Notes

1   For an overview of Malta's prehistoric cultures see D. Trump, *Malta - Prehistory and Temples* (Malta, 2002).
2   S. Moscati, *The World of the Phoenicians* (London, 1973).
3   Only one candelabrum remains in Malta. The other was sent by Grand Master de Rohan as a gift to the King of France.
4   A. Bonanno, *Malta an Archaeological Paradise* (Malta, 1987).
5   M. Buhagiar, *Late Roman and Byzantine Catacombs and Related Burial Places in the Maltese Islands* (Oxford, 1986) .
6   M. Buhagiar, *The Iconography of the Maltese Islands* (Malta, 1988), 10.
7   J. Azzopardi (ed.), *The Order's Early Legacy in Malta* (Malta, 1989).
8   P. Farrugia Randon (ed.), *Caravaggio in Malta* (Malta, 1989).

Denis De Lucca

ARCHITECTURE IN MALTA

The architectural history of the Maltese islands before the arrival of the Hospitaller Knights of St John in 1530, was focused on four principal manifestations. The fourth millennium BC produced the earliest free standing monuments in the universal history of mankind in the form of several ritual shrines created by unknown architects. The latter, despite their association with a Stone Age level of culture, had mysteriously already understood the architectural merits of large scale, axiality, symmetry, curvature and careful detailing to create shadows and decorative effects. All this and much more is evident in the rich prehistoric heritage of Ġgantija, Ħaġar Qim, Tarxien and other monuments of remote antiquity which seem to antedate other megalithic buildings in Spain, France, Sardinia and other parts of Europe[1]. The second millennium BC produced a series of fortified settlements of the Borġ in-Nadur type which were sited on elevated territory and well equipped to resist armed invaders, all forming part of a widespread Mediterranean phenomenon culminating in the superb citadels of Mycenae and Tiryns in mainland Greece. Although vastly inferior in build to the megalithic ritual structures of Malta's first 'golden age', these walled settlements of Bronze Age Malta almost certainly inspired the hundreds of man-made rubble walls and corbelled huts called *giren* that over the centuries became an integral part of the Maltese landscape. The first millennium BC produced the fine Roman city of *Melite* which must have introduced the islanders to that taste of foreign luxury associated with the expansion of a victorious Rome. This fortified settlement of Punic origins[2] was large since the archaeological evidence shows that it incorporated the present towns of Mdina and Rabat. The centuries after the arrival of Paul the apostle in 60 AD produced a shrinkage of this fine city to the site of the present Mdina; this small enclave eventually became the citadel of successive Byzantine, Muslim, Norman,

Hohenstaufen and Spanish rulers who left little architecture beyond a now destroyed Romanesque cathedral, a few churches and some small palaces displaying fifteenth century Gothic-Chiaramonte and Gothic-Catalan facade ornaments[3] inspired by contemporary buildings in nearby Syracuse. The precarious situation of Malta as a land 'far away from help and comfort' as one medieval chronicler put it, explains this obvious lack of interest in architecture before the arrival in 1530 of Grand Master Philippe Villiers de L'Isle Adam. The coming of the heroes of Rhodes was the one factor that within a few decades unleashed the second 'golden age' of architecture in Malta. Eminently European and of noble lineage, the Hospitaller Knights of St John soon wanted to create a microcosm of a larger Europe in the Grand Harbour area, just as they had succeeded in doing in far off Rhodes, before Suleiman captured that island in 1522. Their arrival here ensured that isolated Malta became urban, cosmopolitan and Baroque, renowned throughout the European continent as a superb bulwark against the Turkish menace.

The Baroque age is generally considered to have begun in the last third of the sixteenth century and to have ended in the mid-eighteenth, covering the period of time between the Italian Renaissance and neo-Classicism. In Europe, the Baroque expression formed an integral and essential part of the fabric of a distinctive culture incorporating such different fields as art and architecture, religious and philosophical attitudes, social and political structures, literary endeavour and scientific discoveries. All these spheres of learning were soon forged together in a remarkably cohesive whole to form the basis of a unified European Baroque lifestyle. Essentially, this was Roman Catholic Europe's response to the Protestant rebellion of Martin Luther, described by Fisher as a 'revolt against papal theocracy, clerical privilege and the hereditary paganism of the Mediterranean races'.[4]

The origin of Baroque architecture in Europe is therefore to be found in the turbulence of the sixteenth century. A troubled century when human values, it was then said, had gone astray and when people had lost their ideological references. Luther's revolt of 1517 had started the trouble. Emperor Charles V's failure to control it at the Diet of Worms had compounded it and the terrible sack of Rome by Spanish troops and German mercenaries in 1527 had brought matters to a head. In a desperate attempt to stabilise matters, the pope in Rome first established the Society of Jesus and then convened the Council of Trent in 1545 to formulate the policy of the Counter Reformation, all this happening at a critical time when Europe was being threatened from within by endless rivalries and wars and, from without by the threat of an invasion of Turkish armies, this in itself leading to another great revolution in the field of military architecture and city planning, when the bastion and the straight avenue replaced the medieval tower and the curved way. Tiny Malta, precariously positioned between Catholic Europe and Muslim Africa, was not spared the turbulences that were shaking Europe. The small band of Knights and their Rhodian followers who arrived here in 1530 were soon faced by two terrible Turkish attacks in 1551 and 1565. Pestilence, desolation of the countryside, water supply problems and the unexpected infiltration of Protestant 'heresy' added to the woes of Malta in that unhappy century. In such threatening circumstances the response of the Maltese Catholic Church was swift and decisive. Eager to apply the principles of the Counter Reformation, it was by no accident that the Latin Cross Plan of the first parish churches built in Malta in the first years of the seventeenth century followed very carefully San Carlo Borromeo's *Instructiones fabricae* formulated at the Council of Trent.[5] It was also by no accident that the building of the magnificent city of Valletta was undertaken by Grand Master De Valette in 1566 to create a heavily fortified focal point in the legendary *Grande Porto di Malta*, which contained the precious war galleys and arsenal of the Knights. Valletta was indeed the response of the Baroque aristocracy of Europe to the dark labyrinthine streets of Maltese Mdina, then associated with an unacceptable local government known as the *Università* and with equally unacceptable ancient customs of a decisively medieval character. Despite the building of the new churches inspired by San Carlo Borromeo and the creation of Valletta however, it was not until the middle of the seventeenth century that Malta managed to finally emerge from this dramatic period of change, this state of crisis caused by Turkish raids, disease and religious dissent. The arrival of the Baroque expression in Malta at this time conveniently coincided with the aspirations of Grand Master Jean Paul Lascaris to introduce the new Catholic architectural expression that was now triumphant in Europe. Like their grand master, many Knights welcomed the arrival of the new architecture to their island home and 'new city' seeing it as a movement of exaltation and discovery, of hope, of great artistic achievements, of celestial inspiration ablaze with a blind faith in a triumphant Europe and in an infallible papacy.

Malta in 1650, when buildings that can stylistically be associated with European Baroque were first built, was a victorious island having a population of some 60,000 people. Human settlement was focused on two major nodes, these being the stronghold of Mdina and the Grand Harbour towns hinged on Valletta. Mdina was still fulfilling its ancient role of a place of refuge in times of war this explaining why the Knights, soon after their arrival in Malta, had taken great pains to re-fortify the *città vecchia* by providing it with new artillery defences following the much-praised Italian bastioned system of defence, already tested by the famous military engineer Gabriele Tadino de Martinengo in Rhodes. The old medieval bent entrance, containing a market place overshadowed by the ruins of a Chiaramonte castle, and the old Romanesque cathedral had however been left intact, probably because of great uncertainty concerning the future of the town. A plan drawn up by the famous military engineer Gabrio Serbelloni soon after the great siege of 1565 had even recommended the destruction of Mdina. It was only a riot of the womenfolk of the town that had prevented Grand Master Martino de Redin from demolishing the place so that Mdina in 1650 was still functioning as Malta's venerable old town, the seat of a proud nobility of Spanish extraction, of a recluse

The new baroque city of Valletta was planned as a strong fortress and an elegant city (Photo: MTA)

The impressive fortifications made Malta famous as a superb bulwark against the Turks (Photo: MTA)

bishop and of a rebellious *Università* headed by a *Capitano della Verga* who took great care to ensure that it was the Spanish flag and not the red and white ensign of the Order that was raised every morning above the walls of the town.

The *città nova* of Valletta, on the other hand, provided everything that Mdina was not. Built in the last third of the sixteenth century soon after the great siege, the orderly gridiron plan of Valletta was very much that of a fortress city, conceived in the same spirit of Savorgnan's outpost of Palmanova in the Friuli region of Italy, of Ferramolino's Carlentini in nearby Sicily and of several Spanish towns being then built in the recently discovered new world across the ocean. It would seem that the Italian military engineers Gerolamo Genga and Baldassare Lanci had originally intended Valletta to have a radio-concentric plan hinged on a large central plaza or *place d'armes* containing a magisterial palace and a conventual church dedicated to St John the Baptist. But captain Francesco Laparelli, sent out by Pope Puis IV in 1565 and the Spanish viceroy of Sicily, Don Garcia de Toledo, had charged all this, with the result that Valletta grew up as a city of gridiron streets built according to purposely drawn up regulations[6] and very reminiscent of those Spanish towns having a design that was based on the famous *Real Ordenanzas para Nuevos Poblaciones* issued by the King of Spain on 3 July 1573. By 1650, most of Grand Master De Vallette's new city had been built up. A rare view of Valletta at this time was that provided in a 1633 plan annotated by the military engineer count Giovanni Battista Vertova. This plan, forming part of a private collection in Bergamo,[7] gives us a fairly clear idea of contemporary street names and the disposition of the main buildings which then included a large magisterial palace, a conventual church, eight auberges belonging to the different Langues of Knights, a large slave prison, a munitions factory, a huge hospital, a projected arsenal and, finally, fortifications of an impressive scale that had been designed by Laparelli and approved by the famous Serbelloni. Compared to Mdina and to Birgu, the medieval fishing village which, as the first abode of the Knights in Malta had been fitted with a greatly modified fortress of St Angelo, new artillery fortifications and several auberges, Valletta was a 'new city' in the real sense of the word. It was planned to serve both as a strong fortress and as an elegant city, together forming a very European urban experience that was unprecedented in Malta. Needless to say, Valletta soon became a fitting receptacle for the first incursions of Baroque architecture which happened here after 1650 to eventually transform the military austerity of the architecture of the 'first' city into a sophisticated scenario that would have made anyone accustomed to living in any Baroque town in Europe feel very much at home. This of course perfectly suited the policy of later grand masters of the Order of St John, who saw in Baroque architecture a valuable tool to create a little Europe on the fringe of the African coast, very appropriately described by Albert Jouvin de Rochefort in 1672 as the *fior del mundo*.[8]

The way that all this came about is interesting. The military engineers Pietro Paolo Floriani and Galileo Galilei's prosecutor, Father Vincenzo Maculano da Firenzuola had towards the middle of the seventeenth century, optimised the security of Valletta and the other harbour installations by designing two new sets of outworks of impressive scale and strength know as the Floriana and Margherita lines, all this happening while Giovanni Battista Vertova and his friend the marquis of St Angelo focused their attention on the Valletta fortifications, which they very considerably strengthened. Their efforts were soon followed in the 1680s by count Maurizio Valperga's Fort Ricasoli and the Cottonera lines while the Spanish military engineer in charge of Sicily, Don Carlos de Grunenburgh, drew up ambitious projects for Manoel Island, St Elmo and St Angelo. All these impressive fortifications, unmatched elsewhere in Europe, created an indeed remarkable Baroque landscape where vast arrays of barren limestone walls enhanced the contrast between an improved rural life-style of medieval origins and the new Baroque city life associated with Valletta. These were unforgettable scenarios that soon became famous all over Europe so much so that many architects and artists ardently desired to serve the famous 'Religion' of Malta. In such favourable circumstances it comes as no surprise that three renowned architects, well versed in the fashionable Baroque idiom, rapidly responded to the new winds of change. These were Francesco Buonamici, Mattia Preti and Mederico Blondel des Croisettes.

A citizen of the Tuscan town of Lucca where he was born in 1596, Francesco Buonamici arrived in Malta in September 1635.[9] It is documented that he had served as an assistant to the military engineer Pietro Paolo Floriani. Well connected to Cardinal Francesco Barberini in Rome, Buonamici had originally planned to stay here for only a few months but he ended staying on for over twenty years as the Order's resident engineer. As such, Francesco was largely responsible for introducing Baroque architecture into Valletta and disseminating its magic through a number of Maltese apprentices employed in his Valletta office. He also seems to have had some exposure to early Baroque work in neighbouring Sicily, having visited that island in the 1650s to design the facade of the church of Santa Maria delle Monache in Siracusa. In that town he must surely have had the opportunity to admire Giovanni Vermexio's work on the magnificent Palazzo del Senato situated in the main square of Ortigia.

Back in Malta, Buonamici soon got involved in a large building operation involving the church and the adjacent Jesuit college in Valletta. Before being extensively damaged by an explosion of the Order's *polverista* in 1634, the original Jesuit church had been designed by Padre Giuseppe Valeriano on the model of Giacomo delle Porta's Jesuit headquarters in Rome. By the beginning of 1637 Buonamici had already been placed in full charge of the rebuilding operation so that the dark and austere spaces of Valeriano's church were soon transformed into illuminated and lighter spaces betraying the opulence of the new Baroque style. The altar chancel was deeply recessed to accommodate a beautifully designed altarpiece, a deep dome was introduced to admit light and a splendid facade was provided to define the interface with Merchant's Street. Compared to the earlier very Spanish flavour of church architecture in Malta before 1650 – one here recalls the Laparelli-Geronimo Cassar conventual church and the several village churches of Attard, Balzan, Għargħur, Mosta and Żebbuġ – Buonamici's facade had a very Italian Baroque flavour, displaying richly carved decoration introduced by the architect at pre-determined points to highlight the compositional qualities of the facade, not least its rich *chairoscuro* effect.

Before leaving the island in 1659 to take up a new appointment as *architetto primario* of Lucca, Buonamici managed to design at least two other major buildings in Malta, besides some palaces in Valletta and a new dream city at Marsalforn in Gozo which, however, was never built. One of these major projects was for the church of St Nicholas in Valletta where the architect employed a Greek Cross Plan, perhaps inspired by San Carlo ai Catinari which had been just completed in Rome in 1612. The other project was for the large church of St Paul in Rabat and the adjacent Wignacourt college. This was really an enlargement exercise, there having been already a parish church on the site. It is said that Francesco was commissioned to do this job by the devout noblewoman Guzmanna Navarra, the result being a large church, the largest that the architect ever designed. The foundation stone was laid in 1653.

After the architect's departure from Malta, Lorenzo Gafà and Pawlinu Formosa, two who had been earlier on working on the building, were commissioned to finish off the building by meticulously following Buonamici's designs. During his stay in Malta, Buonamici had achieved much. True to the spirit of Baroque, the vaulted interior spaces of his churches were admirably orchestrated into a holistic spatial experience which, when combined with sculpture and painting, very much reminds us of San Carlo Borromeo's instructions. It was however the *Calabrese* Mattia Preti who first introduced the Maltese to the real spirit of European baroque. Preti did this by painting the truly wonderful fresco cycle which in the 1660s transformed the barren vault of Grand Master De Vallette's conventual church into an animated fantasia of form and colour which must surely be regarded as one of the main contributions of Malta to European Baroque culture in the seventeenth century.

The arrival of Preti in Malta[10] was a classic example of how different members of the prestigious Order of Malta originating from different parts of Baroque Europe at its highest social levels, could not only facilitate a continuous inflow of new and refined ideas, but also afford to attract and employ the best architects and artists from their countries of origin. Thus Mattia Preti was seduced to come to Malta by the hope of bettering his position within the Order. With this aim in mind, he gladly accepted the commission to transform the bland stone interior of St John's into a masterpiece of Baroque integrated design. Preti lost no time to start working on the job which he managed to complete within five years between 1661 and 1666. His direct contribution was the great cycle of John the Baptist's life which he painted on the semicircular vault of the church. In the meantime he also found time to supervise an army of artists and artisans who were simultaneously engaged to apply marble claddings, gilding and relief decoration which soon transformed

Interior of Sta Marija del Pilar and entrance to the Armoury at the Grand Master's Palace by Romano Carapecchia (1666-1738) (Photo: International Institute for Baroque Studies)

Mattia Preti (1613-99) transformed the barren vaults of St John's into a spledid baroque theatre (Photo: MTA)

the walls of the church into a matching fantasia of polychromatic design, completed when the renowned *principe* of the *Accademia di San Luca* in Rome, Gian Battista Contini, was in the 1680s asked to design the magnificent main altar. Marble intarsia tombstones marking the resting place of the flower of Europe's nobility, magnificent altarpieces placed in the chapels of the Langues, majestic mausolea of the grand masters, priceless works by Bernini and Algardi, paintings by Caravaggio, precious relics from Rhodes and beautiful Flemish tapestries were among the numerous trappings that changed the bland interior of the conventual church into a splendid Baroque theatre, an indeed worthy stage setting for the very evident combination of temporal power and Catholic ritual symbolised by the Order of St John. The powerful Baroque scenography that was here suddenly presented to an awe-inspired Maltese audience was certainly intended to express the intense religious emotions that inevitably accompanied the Catholic liturgical functions of the Counter-Reformation – emotions that were unleashed by the celestial sounds of choir and organs; emotions that were intensified by the recital of the rosary, by incense, by impressive scenarios; emotions that were climaxed by the deep voices of the warrior monks singing the *Hosannah*, the *Te Deum* and the *De profundis*. It was in this church and in the other Baroque churches designed in Malta after 1650 that the joys, the anxieties, the hopes, the laments, the confessions, the contritions and the benedictions that formed such a central part in the life cycle of this typical Baroque Catholic community, flowed through the ponderous vaulted spaces of these same churches which, understandably, soon became a model and a goad for the emergence of a second 'golden age' of Maltese architecture.

The third important foreign architect practising in Malta in the seventeenth century was Mederico Blondel des Croisettes.[11] Brother to the famous French military engineer Francois Blondel, whose *cours d'architecture* had a profound influence on the development of French Baroque, Blondel's controversial stay in Malta was marked by his involvement in the design of a number of churches in Valletta which included those of St Francis, St Roque and St Mary of Jesus. Blondel also seems to have had a hand in the design of the new Carmelite church which was built in Mdina in the 1660s, this being the first Baroque building to grace the main ceremonial street of that ancient town.

Mederico's very classical version of the Baroque expression contrasted with the relative liberties that had characterised the work of Buonamici and Preti. He did however manage to influence a large number of local architects who, towards the close of the century, started producing a truly Maltese version of the imported Baroque idiom. Foremost among these young men was Lorenzo Gafà whose principal contributions to Maltese Baroque were his churches of Mdina, Gozo, Żejtun and Vittoriosa, all built after the devastation of a great earthquake that struck Malta and Sicily in 1693. Another student of Blondel, one Giovanni Barbara, designed in 1694 the parish church of Lija. Some promising Maltese architects even emigrated and started practising on the European mainland. Carlo Gimach, who designed the basilica of Sant' Anastasia ai Cerchi in Rome, the manor house of

Cannaverzes near Oporto and the church of Arouca in Portugal, was one of these emigrants. Carlo de Domenicis, who designed several churches in Rome, was another. Baroque architecture in Malta towards the close of the seventeenth century was also blessed by the presence of several capable Maltese mastermasons such as Salvatore Borg, Francesco Sammut, Antonio and Agostino Gassin, Giuseppe Azzopardo, Michele Aguis and the popular Capuchin friar architect Giuseppe Grech. Despite the obvious lack of finesse of their achievements, these Maltese *periti,* as they were known, deserve considerable credit because, interposed as they were between the 'high' architecture of Buonamici, Preti and Blondel on one side and, the vernacular expression of old Malta on the other side, they successfully managed to contribute to both. Their expertise in local materials and building methods made it possible for the European masters to execute their grand paper designs while they, in return, channelled the 'imported' Baroque compositional elements and ornamental motifs of Valletta back to the vernacular tradition. It is therefore to the credit of these Maltese *periti* that the vernacular architecture of the humblest village in seventeenth century Malta absorbed several 'high' motifs and developed accordingly, contrary to the situation in Europe where a great gap existed between the sophisticated urban architecture and the folk rural expression. The obvious implication of this situation was that Baroque in Malta, soon after its arrival from Italy, was rapidly transformed into a popular style eminently suited, because of its communicative and decorative potential, to serve the political purposes of both church and state at a time when both institutions were becoming increasingly unpopular. This 'popularisation' of the imported Baroque expression becomes clear when one discovers in the documented sources that Salvatore Borg, *egregius architector*, designed the facade of the Dominican church and the interior of the church of St Publuis, both in Rabat; that Francesco Sammut made a beautiful model of the Mdina Carmelite church; that Giuseppe Azzopardi nicknamed *iż-żgħir* designed the old Xewkija and Għarb churches in Gozo; that Michele Agius designed the church of Żebbuġ in Gozo; and that Fra Giuseppe Grech designed not only the capuchin monasteries of Santa Liberata in Kalkara and Gozo, but also found time to design the magnificent Baroque parish church of Nadur in Gozo. In so far as their role in the diffusion of Baroque architecture in the Maltese islands was concerned, the contribution of these Maltese architects[12] was indeed outstanding and voluminous.

One important factor concerning Malta's response to the intMûnational Baroque movement after 1650 involved the issue of patronage. In Malta, the main source of patronage was undoubtedly the rich Order of St John; the members of which enjoyed a wide range of international high level contacts and substantial revenues from their European estates. There was also the local church headed by rich prelates having close cultural links with Italy. On a lesser scale, there was the papal inquisitor in Vittoriosa and the local nobility of Spanish origins who had both lands and powerful connections in Sicily. Many grand masters also started setting up foundations, the income from which was meant to be applied in perpetuity to the strengthening of some aspect of the Order's organisational machinery, one case in point being the foundation of Grand Master Cotoner which was substantial enough to develop around 1664, a whole block near Palace Square in Valletta as dwellings, warehouses and shops. It was not only architecture, however, that benefited from such types of patronage. Several important painters of Baroque Malta like Stefano Erardi, Pedro Nunez de Villavicencio, Giuseppe d'Arena, Gian Nicola Buhagiar, Francesco Vincenzo Zahra and Antoine de Favray benefited greatly from the Order's patronage.

The eighteenth century also saw the consolidation of the academic influences that could be detected in the seventeenth century Baroque buildings of Buonamici, Preti, Blondel and others. Two important key players now entered the scene. Although Romano Carapecchia arrived from Rome in 1707[13] while Charles Francois de Mondion arrived from Paris in 1715,[14] both architects only managed to fully express themselves when the Portuguese Antonio Manoel de Vilhena became Grand Master in 1722.

Chronologically, the development of Baroque architecture in Malta during the Vilhena period can be neatly classified into three phases. The first phase, between 1722 and 1725, was mainly concerned with upgrading the defences of Malta in view of a Turkish war scare, this implying that most building operations involved the completion and amplification of the vast arrays of Baroque fortifications created in the previous century. Major building developments consisted in a number of military gateways at Vittoriosa and Mdina, in the creation of an impressive Baroque military setting at Fort Manoel, in the planning of a new city fortress in Gozo and in the laying out of two suburbs at Cospicua and Floriana. The second phase of architectural development during Vilhena's magistracy, between 1726 and 1733, was marked by a rich flowering of Baroque ornamentation designed to shift priorities from military matters to considerations of adornment, amusement and social services. The highlights of the considerable achievements of Carapecchia and Mondion during this phase included firstly, the rebuilding of large sections of Mdina incorporating a new magisterial palace and Law Courts building, a Banca Giuratale, a church dedicated to San Rocco, an enlarged St Peter's monastery, a bishop's residence, a seminary, an armoury building and several palatial residences in Villegaigon Street. Secondly, extensive housing developments within the new suburb of Floriana; thirdly, a typically late Baroque 'secularisation' of Valletta by the building in 1731 of the fine playhouse that is the Manoel Theatre and, of course, the rebuilding of several housing blocks and palaces within the city; fourthly, intensive work on at least seven hospitals and charitable institutions including those of San Giovanni Battista in Gozo, the women's hospital in Valletta, the Santo Spirito and Saura hospitals in Rabat, the *Ospizio Invalidi*, the *Conservatorio di Vergini* in Floriana and the extensive restoration works that were in 1732 carried out at the old San Giuliano hospital in Gozo. Fifthly, the 1726-1733 phase of Vilhena's building programme saw the building of no less than fourteen churches and chapels, including the magnificent parish church of St Helen in Birkirkara,

The Church of St Catherine of Italy designed by Romano Carapecchia (1666-1738) (Photo: International Institute for Baroque Studies)

Main entrance to the Auberge de Castille (1741) (Photo: International Institute for Baroque Studies)

The baroque Cathedral of Mdina by Lorenzo Gafà (Photo: International Institute for Baroque Studies)

the parish church of Safi and Żabbar, the round church of Tal-Virtù and the parish church of Floriana. A highlight of this very fertile period of building activity was Carapecchia's magnificent sacristy of St Paul's church in Valletta and the charming country palaces at Spinola and Ħamrun. The third phase of the building programme of Grand Master Vilhena was marked by several projects drawn by Carapecchia for the Conventual church. These projects included the beautiful altarpiece of the chapel of the langue of Italy and the two annexes which were now added to the church to mask the unsightly appearance of its bland side walls. In St John's church, Romano also designed three tombstones and a magnificent *chapelle ardente* which together with Pietro Paolo Troisi's altar of repose in the cathedral of Mdina, must surely stand out as two magnificent examples of the Baroque *effimero*, south of Rome.[15] Carapecchia and Troisi also designed several artefacts for festive and liturgical uses.

The Baroque architecture of the first third of the eighteenth century, dominated by the titanic presence of Mondion and Carapecchia, tends to show a clearly differentiated approach derived from the very different backgrounds of the two protagonists. Mondion stood for a military, disciplined, orderly and politically orientated architectural expression, a clear reflection of his earlier training in France as a military engineer apprenticed to the great marshal Vauban. Carapecchia, on the other hand, stood for an infinitely more imaginative and refined interpretation of late Roman Baroque architecture as it was associated with the very Roman *festa barocca* and taught at the Sunday lectures of the famous *Accademia di San Luca*, then under the spell of the great Carlo Fontana. All this was primarily aimed at upgrading the embellishment process of the austere fabric of the new urban Malta that had started in the previous century. Some excellent examples of Mondion's approach, where large open spaces rather than buildings tended to assume unprecedented importance, included the splendid parade ground of Fort Manoel hinged on a magnificent bronze statue of Grand Master Vilhena and, of course, the equally magnificent entrance area with its magisterial palace and decorated main gate at Mdina, again sporting the coat-of-arms and bronze bust of Grand Master Vilhena. The axial layouts of Cospicua and Floriana, the city fortress project in Gozo and the planned garden of Leone Palace at Santa Venera are other examples where Mondion and his assistants demonstrate a clear understanding of the vista effects, the theatricality, the concern for collective values and the communicative force of this Baroque architecture, where a marvellous interwoven relationship of large scale buildings, open spaces and fortifications predominated in a manner as yet unknown in Malta, indeed remarkable for Mondion's application of an elegant architectural geometry inspired by the best work of Vauban and others in France. One can even see that in certain buildings Mondion manages to employ some well known practices of Parisian baroque, one case occurring in the courtyard of the Mdina Palace which is based on the plan of a typical French hotel and where exciting theatrical effects are created by masking a relatively unpretentious building interior by means of a monumental facade treatment based on Manoel theatre type elliptical arches and ornamental motifs. This recalls the best Baroque overseas practice where, with the event of inadequate finances to perform that typical Baroque love of grandiose feats that would impress, then the appearance would be counterfeited by using monumental screen facades which, like theatrical stage sets, would be fixed to the front of an insignificant building. This all happens at the magisterial palace at Mdina. The Baroque architecture of the 'Mondion school' in Malta is also remarkable for its careful consideration of stereotomy and carved details, not to mention a bulldozing habit of mind that, as happened at Mdina, sought to clear the ground of all relics and encumbrances of the past so as to effect a clean beginning on the inflexible mathematical lines required by a military man. Had it not been for a priest who took care to record the plan of the medieval entrance to Mdina, Mondion would have succeeded in obliterating every trace of the superb bent entrance to that venerable old town, before Baroque took over.

The considerable output of the Italian Romano Carapecchia after 1707 poses an entirely different approach to the design problems of late Baroque Malta. Born in 1666 to poor parents residing in the spiritual capital of Catholic Europe, Romano was a self-made man. Having received his architectural education in the studio of the great Carlo Fontana, he soon started practising his profession in Rome where he is credited with the designs of the church and nearby hospital of San Giovanni Calibita, the Palazzino Vaini and the Tordinona and other theatres. In Rome, Romano also drew up projects for several large urban schemes, fountains and even designed a catafalque for Pope Alexander VIII. All these works collectively reflected to academic discipline and classicizing influences of the famous *Accademia di San Luca*, once described by King Louis XIV of France, *Le Roi Soleil* himself, as 'the focus and teacher of the many famous artists who have appeared during this century'. Disappointed with the limited opportunities available in Rome at the turn of the century, Carapecchia left the city in 1707 to eventually settle in Malta, where he managed as a result of Pope Clement XI's intervention, to find favour with Grand Master Ramon Perellos. Within the context of the ancient fortress situated on what was still considered to be the very edge of European Catholicism, the newly arrived architect soon drew up several brilliant projects which all reflected a total commitment to his profession to the extent that rarely has the spirit of the Baroque been more powerfully evoked here than it is in the work of this architect. A firm command of a wide architectural vocabulary, an exceedingly pronounced integrative approach, flexibility and a rare control of the design process presupposing the architect's ability to think out every detail on the drawing board, represent the hallmarks of Carapecchia's work in Valletta. All this can be seen in the church of St James, the church of St Catherine of the Langue of Italy, the church and convent of St Catherine in lower Republic Street, the beautiful Pilar church close to the Auberge d'Aragon and the church of Santa Barbara in Republic Street which was built after Romano's death in 1738. In all these buildings one can admire the architect's skill in employing the centralised type of planning which was so popular with Italian Baroque architects, here as in Rome roofed over with cavernous limestone domes shedding the right type of overhead light which was needed to illuminate the ornamented walls, the marbles and impressive altarpieces of all these buildings. In Valletta, Carapecchia also designed the municipal palace in Strada San Gaicomo, the facade of Palazzo Spinola, the annexes of the conventual church, the armoury door of the magisterial palace and the Perellos fountain which graces its courtyard. Very important from Grand Master Vilhena's point of view was the charming playhouse that is the Manoel Theatre, this reflecting the architect's experience in Rome where he had designed at least five theatres. For Valletta's waterfront, Carpecchia designed and built the so called Barriera stores which, although now destroyed, can still be admired in a 1707 drawing to be found in an album of drawings now kept in the Conway Library of the Courtauld Institute of Art in London. The architect's project here was perhaps one of the earliest attempts of the Knights to transform the shabby waterfront of Valletta facing the Grand Harbour into an impressive Baroque scenario which towards the middle of the eighteenth century culminated in the building of the impressive Pinto warehouses and in the two churches of Notre Dame de Liesse, designed by Andrea Belli, and the Flight from Egypt, designed by an unknown architect. The building of Giuseppe Bonici's customs house in 1774 completed the grand waterfront project of the grand masters of the eighteenth century.

The last flowering of Baroque architecture in Malta occurred in the second half of the eighteenth century. One now finds Grand Masters Pinto de Fonseca, Ximenes de Texada and Emmanuel de Rohan patronising a full-blooded mature Baroque architecture that added the final touches to Carapecchia's transformation of Valletta into a Baroque city. Among the principal large scale replacement buildings that were erected one can mention the Auberge de Castille in 1741, the Castellania in 1748, Palazzo Parisio in 1750 and the beautiful small palace with its superb staircase which now houses the museum of Fine Arts in South Street, built in 1761. Stefano Ittar's fine composition of the *Bibliotheca* building, evoking the post-earthquake architecture of nearby Catania and built close to the magisterial palace which was now fitted with two magnificent portals, closes the history of Baroque design in the Maltese islands. The architectural achievement which perhaps came closest to fulfilling the Baroque ideal was undoubtedly the Auberge de Castille, attributed by some to Andrea Belli, by others to Domenico Cachia. More than any other building, Castille symbolised the ultimate expression of Baroque spatial dominance, ornamental magnificence and, above all, Grand Master Pinto's considerable temporal power, greatly enhanced after his brutal suppression of a slave uprising. This grand palace certainly reflects the work of an architect who was well skilled in the use of compositional principles, shadow play, perspective artifices and a wide ornamental vocabulary all calculated to create the dramatic vista effects so much loved by all those Italian Baroque architects who mattered.

Charles Francois de Mondion's Calcara Magazines in Floriana (Photo: National Library)

Coat-of-arms of Grand Master Vilhena (1722-36) by Mondion (Photo: International Institute for Baroque Studies)

Here, an important interior design element now appears on the Maltese scene – a monumental staircase of the Palazzo Barberini tradition which one encounters not only in the Auberge de Castille but, also in the Fine Arts Museum. The aim of the still unidentified architect, who designed this magnificent palazzo, was to create an impressive interior effect based on subtle curvature, directional changes and spectacular light situations. With such models to inspire and to goad, it is little wonder that Baroque architecture became very popular with the residents of Valletta. This can be seen in several facades in the main streets of the town which mushroomed in quick succession in the eighteenth century, two very obvious examples being the Hotel de Verdelin and the magnificent facade of a refurbished Auberge de Provence with its elaborate portal and splendid frescoed hall having a trussed roof. There was then Ittar's *Bibliotheca* building. Just us the Baroque expression in Malta had been inaugurated by adopting a very academic approach, the last public building by the Knights in Valletta is restrained, orderly and intensely formal, presenting the onlooker with an academic composition on two floors with its centre marked with a raking cornice and clearly defined pediment. This was really a superb drawing board exercise inspired by the *L'Architetto Prattico* manual[16] used in the rebuilding of Baroque Catania.

The Knights were removed from Malta by Napoleon Bonaparte in 1798. The coming of the English in 1800 marked the official end of the Baroque expression that had characterised the previous century and its replacement by the then fashionable neo-gothic and neo-classical romanticist styles respectively inspired by British nationalism and by the re-discovered classical ruins of ancient Greece. The British colonial government also introduced a powerful new type of military architecture based on isolated forts well concealed in the landscape and on a distinctive type of barracks design. The Maltese however continued to cherish Baroque architecture as an expression of a perceived European affluence and as a symbol of Catholic Rome, also as a reminder of all that was admired and considered beautiful in mother Italy. Such social, religious and political overtones ensured that Baroque architecture in Malta lived on. It still survives in several twentieth century buildings and it is still acclaimed as an architectural movement associated with opulence and beauty. After all, Corrado Rizza[17] says that *Il Barocco è un inno all'occhio e alla teoria della visione* - Baroque feasts the human eye and pays homage to the theory of human vision.

Notes

1   D. Trump, *Malta Prehistory and Temples* (Malta, 2000), 55.

2   M. Buhagiar and S. Fiorini (eds), *Mdina, The Cathedral City of Malta* (Malta, 1996), 1-42. See also Diodorus Siculus, V, 12, 1-4 who remarks that the buildings of *Melite* were 'fine and decorated with carved cornices and stucco work'.

3   D. De Lucca, *Mdina - A History of its Urban Space and Architecture* (Malta, 1995), 41-47.

4   H. A. L. Fisher, *A History of Europe*, I (London and Glasgow, 1935), 501.

5   D. De Lucca, 'Baroque Architecture in Malta', in S. Fiorini and R. Ellul Micallef (eds), *Collected Papers* (University of Malta, 1992), 246-47.

6   R. De Giorgio, *A City by an Order* (Malta, 1985), 115-17.

7   D. De Lucca, *Giovanni Battista Vertova - Diplomacy, Warfare and Military Engineering Practice in early seventeenth century Malta* (Malta, 2001), 51-67.

8   A. Jouvin de Rochefort, *Le Voyageur d'Europe ou sont les voyages de France, d'Italie et de Malthe, d'Espagne et de Portugal, des Pays Bas, d'Allemagne et de Pologne, d'Angleterre, de Danemark et de Suede*, I-VI (Paris, 1672), 667.

9   D. De Lucca and C. Thake, *The Genesis of Maltese Baroque Architecture: Francesco Buonamici* (Malta, 1994), 1-2.

10 L. Mahoney, *5000 years of Architecture in Malta* (Malta, 1996), 323.

11 A. Hoppen, *The fortifications of Malta by the Order of St John 1530-1798* (Malta, 1999), 91. See also S. Spiteri, *Fortresses of the Knights* (Malta, 2001).

12 De Lucca, 'Baroque architecture', 266.

13 *Id., Carapecchia - Master of Baroque Architecture in early eighteenth century Malta* (Malta, 1999).

14 *Id., Mondion - The achievement of a French military engineer working in Malta in the early eighteenth century* (Malta, 2003), 2.

15 *Id., Mdina*, 84-85.

16 G. Amico, *L' Architetto Prattico* (Palermo, 1726).

17 C. Rizza, *Verso una Teoria del Barocco* (Milan, 1985), 8.

PART FOUR

THE MALTESE LANGUAGE

Joseph M. Brincat

LANGUAGES IN MALTA AND THE MALTESE LANGUAGE

Foreigners are often intrigued by the linguistic situation prevailing in Malta. When they hear Maltese being spoken they are invariably struck by some sounds that recall Arabic, when they read it they recognise a number of Italian words and when they follow the locals' conversation they wonder at the weaving of Maltese and English phrases. These impressions are not mistaken because the Maltese language we use now faithfully reflects the historical experiences of the community and the speaker's own use of at least three languages.

Unfortunately it is not possible to determine what language was spoken by the builders of our magnificent prehistoric temples because the graphic messages they left us are only pictorial. It might have been what the traditional theory called a 'Mediterranean' language or, according to the latest theories, an Indo-European language, because the coming of this linguistic family in Europe has been linked by Colin Renfrew with the spread of agriculture. We do know, however, that the first inscriptions in Malta were in Punic and that they cover a long period from the sixth to the second century BC. Bilingualism was already practised in Malta when the Phoenicians settled here side by side with the last Bronze age community which was later absorbed culturally and linguistically. The Romans introduced Latin in 218 BC but for at least two hundred years three languages were in formal use, a fact witnessed by inscriptions in stone and legends on coins in Punic, Greek and Latin. However, inscriptions do not tell us anything about the language spoken by the community and St Luke's definition of the inhabitants of Malta as 'barbarians' is not very helpful, either, since it does not specify whether in 60 AD they spoke Punic or a local variety of vulgar Latin or Greek. The six hundred years of Roman rule would have been more than enough to change the language of a small

213

Marble Cippus of the second century BC in Phoenician and Greek, indicating bilingualism in Malta

G. F. Abela (1582-1655) was aware of the Arabic origins of Maltese (Photo: Heritage Collection)

community (5000-10,000 people) and the same may be said of the succeeding Byzantine period which was 350 years long.

The most mystifying linguistic aspect of the Maltese language is that there is no perceivable substratum (the old language's influence on the newly-acquired one), neither Punic, nor Roman nor Greek. The only plausible explanation for this is a sudden and crushing intrusion, and such an event is related by an Arab historian who had access to documents that were contemporary with the events recorded. Al-Himyari, in the longest and most detailed account of the two main events in the Arab period in Malta, describes a violent attack in 870 which left the island in ruins and, after a period of relative neglect, a fresh settlement in 1048-49 composed of Muslims (400 combatants with families) and their more numerous slaves. He also says that the city was rebuilt, becoming more splendid than before. From the linguistic viewpoint these facts are very significant. The year 870 marks the end or drastic reduction of the Byzantine society, which may have been Greek-speaking, and the introduction of Arabic as an acrolect with the use of Berber as the more likely spoken dialect of the invaders. The period of neglect may have witnessed two small communities, the survivors and the conquerors' garrison, speaking two different languages and perhaps intermingling in 150 years. In 1048-49 the sudden influx of a 5000-strong community of Arabic-speakers must have absorbed the few former inhabitants whose language did not leave its mark on the new one. Had the slaves not been Arabic-speaking their mother-tongue would certainly have given the Arabic of Malta a very strong local flavour. Comparative studies, however, show marked similarities with the Maghreb variety which had evolved in Sicily under Arab rule and which was still spoken under the Normans. It is quite possible then that Maltese is the only survivor of a linguistic situation which prevailed in most of Sicily and large parts of Spain, and this gives it considerable historical value.

Although the Spanish *reconquista* and the Norman invasion of Sicily were achieved by military action, there was a long period of religious, cultural and linguistic co-existence, and this is reflected in the substantial Arabic substrate that survives in both Spanish and the Sicilian dialects. In Malta and Pantelleria, both cut off from the larger island of Sicily by about 90 km, this coexistence lasted for a longer time and Arabic did not become a substrate in Malta while in the less populated Pantelleria it resisted till the eighteenth century when the Sicilian dialect of Trapani took over. In Malta romanisation kept increasing by complementing, rather than substituting, the fundamental elements of the local variety of Arabic. The decisive factor was that, unlike the rapid and full re-Christianisation, linguistic romanisation was slow, first of all because Christianity never imposed Latin on the faithful but used the local dialects in evangelisation, and then because the authorities did not bother to effect a linguistic policy. The Sicilian viceroys in the Anjevin, Aragonese and Castilian periods, and later the Knights, were only interested in the acrolect (high language) which, in agricultural societies everywhere, was only available to a very small percentage of the population (1-5 percent). The first documents received and written in Malta were in Latin (the first known dates back to 1198, with an Arabic version) but various Romance dialects were spoken, due to the presence of Genoese counts (1191-1123), exiles from Abruzzi (1224), French and Catalan soldiers (1268 and 1283 respectively), while for geographical, administrative and practical reasons the largest and most consistent presence was Sicilian. Maltese soldiers and sailors were employed by the rulers and rubbed shoulders with the foreigners, initiating the symbiotic process of Arabic and Sicilian. Frederick II's expulsion of Muslims in 1224 caused a certain shift in population but, as in Sicily, most of them preferred conversion to banishment. In 1241 they still made up a third of the islands' population but the year 1249 saw the end of the Muslim religion in Malta. The main religious orders established monasteries between 1371 and 1452 and churches mushroomed from ten in 1350 to 430 in 1575. While Latin was the formal language in liturgy, the local tongue was used for evangelisation and for interaction with the faithful. This practice helped in no small way to ensure the survival of Maltese.

The chancery koiné of the Sicilian dialect was introduced into Malta, and during the fourteenth and fifteenth centuries documents produced in Malta could be either in Latin or Sicilian or both. When the Knights of St John took possession in 1530 the written use of Sicilian rapidly declined and the Tuscan variety, which was now establishing itself as the new written medium all over Italy, was introduced in the administrative and cultural spheres by the Order and became the high language of educated locals. Actually the first poems known to have been composed in Malta were three *cansos-sirventes* written in Provencal by Peire Vidal in 1204-05, and although Jacopo Mostacci visited the island in 1240, it is not known whether he composed any poems in '*siciliano illustre*' here. A sentence spoken in Tuscan is documented as early as 1453 but the first formal document I traced is dated 1550 (CEM 30) and we know that poems were composed by a Maltese in Italian as early as 1584. Unfortunately these did not survive. Neither did the verses written in Maltese by the same Pasquale Vassallo and others. However, a Cantilena written by Pietro Caxaro around 1470 did survive and is considered as the first full text written in Maltese (actually in the pre-standard variety). Occasionally Maltese words of a practical nature appear before that, mainly in legal and administrative documents, the first ones being quoted in Abbate's report of 1241. The use of Maltese in formal situations is witnessed by references to the notaries' practice of explaining Latin documents in the local tongue and by hints at its use during the local council's meetings.

A striking fact is that although these uses are always oral, not written, local documents generally specify that the medium is '*lingua melitea*', '*maltensi*' or '*melitensi*', stressing its individuality, while foreigners usually called it '*lingua moresca*', '*africana*' or '*arabica*', at best '*sive vulgari melitensi*'. Apparently it was Jean Quintin who in 1536 launched the myth that Maltese was a survivor of the ancient, lost Punic language after observing Punic inscriptions in Malta. His conjecture was picked up by various visitors, including the famed Hieronymus Megiser, who drew up a list of 121 fundamental Maltese words in 1606. The connection with a great ancient civilisation pleased the locals who could now claim both uniqueness and prestige, and was asserted by De Soldanis, Vassalli (for a time), Manwel Magri and Lord Strickland, but in actual fact it was built on vague impressions, for Punic script was not deciphered before 1758 and no serious comparative studies were ever made. It is to Gio. Francesco Abela's credit that he was already aware of the real origins of Maltese in 1647: he knew that Arabic was spoken in medieval Sicily, that it survived as a substrate there and that the situation in Pantelleria was similar to Malta's in his time.

The Knights' contribution to the linguistic history of Malta is not limited to the introduction of Italian, which now forms part of more than half the lexicon of Maltese. It is certainly significant that their adoption of Tuscan as the language for interaction between its multilingual members made it possible for many Maltese to obtain a fine command of Italian and thus gain international circulation and respect: A. Bosio, G. and V. Cassar, L. Gafà, G. F. Abela, G. F. Buonamico, C. and D. Magri, E. Magi, G. Farrugia, G. A. Ciantar, G. F. Agius De Soldanis, M. A. Grima, N. Isouard and M. A. Vassalli. However, the Knights also created the right conditions for the survival of Maltese and for its standardisation. The composition of the Order, with its eight Langues, and the succession of Grand Masters speaking different languages, did not allow the Order's identification with one nation, and therefore with one language. They were happy with diglossia and did not bother to eradicate the local tongue. Another important indirect result of their presence was the social and economic development of the area around the Grand Harbour. The old capital, Mdina, had a very limited influence on the rest of the island because the original Arabic dialect had branched out into four different area varieties that were described by Vassalli in 1796. The huge building projects in Cottonera and later in Valletta attracted large numbers of workers from all over the island who now settled in an area which, having been uninhabited, did not have its own linguistic variety. The rapid growth of this area produced a koiné which shed most of the regional peculiarities and formed the basis for standard Maltese. In this new area internal migrants mixed with foreigners employed by the Order as sailors, soldiers and builders as well as the ensuing artisans and artists, many of whom settled permanently. From 1530 to 1797 the population of the Maltese islands rose from 17,000 to 96,000 and the percentage of the inhabitants of the harbour area rose from six percent to forty percent. Marriages between the local girls and male settlers bonded linguistic contacts even more strongly than employment and commerce, while ensuring that the 'mother' tongue absorbed new words without abandoning the fundamental lexicon and grammar, just as the community absorbed the large influx in small, successive waves. This process is confirmed by the present stratigraphy of the Maltese lexicon as well as by the ratios of traditional (pre-1530), Italian and English surnames.

On the academic plane a few knights expressed an early interest in the Maltese language and some could even speak it. Foreign scholars included Maltese in their collections of linguistic samples, and at least three dictionaries were compiled in

The cosmopolitan atmosphere of the harbour area led to the standardisation of Maltese (Photo: Malta Maritime Museum)

Pietro Caxaro's Cantilena of the second half of the fifteenth century (Photo: Notarial Archives)

the seventeenth century. Unfortunately they were not printed and were subsequently lost, although the Provencal knight Thezan's dictionary and short grammar seem to have survived in the Vallicelliana manuscript. Maltese scholars followed suit, and more comprehensive dictionaries and grammars were produced by De Soldanis (1750 and 1759), padre Pelagio and Vassalli (1790, 1791, 1796), while a bilingual catechism was printed in 1752, I. S. Mifsud wrote sermons in Italian and in Maltese in the 1740s, De Soldanis wrote dialogues around 1755 and, after Buonamico's eulogistic verses (1672), religious, humorous and folk poems became common. The medium of these writings was the urban variety that had developed in the harbour area, and thus the stage was set for the standardisation of Maltese and for its rise to the status of a language.

Before the 1870s the main criterion that distinguished a language from a dialect was the existence of literary texts. Consequently the locals' main preoccupation was the creation of a literature in Maltese. After Napoleon's brief occupation of the island, and his aborted attempts at introducing French into local culture, the British lost no time in declaring an equally drastic linguistic policy. In 1813 the governor received instructions to introduce English at the expense of Italian as early as possible. However the local educated class, who obviously knew no English then, strongly resisted these attempts. The main opponents were the clergy, who feared the introduction of Protestantism, and the legal profession, who suspected upheaval in the administration of justice. However, it is also clear that most educated Maltese honestly felt that Italian was their language of culture. In the meantime Italian liberals sought refuge in the island and fostered the Romantic seeds of nationalism in patriotic poems and novels. These became very popular and soon many translations and imitations were written in the local language, boosting literacy.

Within the cultural framework of the Romantic age and the political scenario of colonialism, three large-scale processes were set into motion and got inextricably intertwined for a hundred years of turmoil between the mid-nineteenth and the mid-twentieth century: anglicisation, nationalism and the defence of Italian culture, and the promotion and standardisation of the Maltese language.

Anglicisation was strongly resisted by the local inhabitants who stuck to their Roman Catholic religion, their Italian culture and legal system, and their own variety of Arabic. Understandably, the British felt uncomfortable governing an island in Italian. All official communications had to be translated into Italian and publications and notices were bilingual, and yet the British pressed the issue of anglicisation only after the Unification of Italy. Their apprehension over the strength of a new large neighbour urged them to build new forts all over the island because, by conquering Malta, Italy could cut off access to the newly-built Suez Canal. Knowing that the educated Maltese considered Italy their cultural and spiritual parent, they strove to offset this loyalty by gaining support among all the inhabitants and so they sent over Patrick Keenan, an Irish educationalist, to reform the local school system. A long-drawn-out controversy ensued, with a series of moves and counter-moves introducing English and Maltese and curtailing or restoring the teaching of Italian in the schools. A remarkable side-issue was the choice of language at the Council of Government, later the House of Representatives, where for some seventy years members addressed the meeting in Italian or English according to their stand in favour of the Nation or the Empire. Actually very few locals learned English in the nineteenth century but, after a slow start, English overtook Italian in 1911, when 13.1 percent of the population declared that they could read, write or speak it, against 11.5 percent who knew Italian. Obviously literacy was low in those days and the figures overlap because most educated people learned both languages. But when the fascists seized power in Italy and war loomed ahead, the British stepped up their efforts and by 1931 the number of persons knowing English was almost double that of those who knew Italian.

In the meantime Maltese, which had been promoted by the locals as a literary medium throughout the nineteenth century, was now in a position to claim a place in the institutions and advanced steadily. Thankfully neither the purists, who would have stifled the language, nor the denigrators had their way and so the empirical approach prevailed. On the one hand the high quality verses of Dun Karm conferred on it the prestige it formerly lacked. On the other hand the rise of the political parties in a democratic environment made the leaders realise that their message would not reach the monolingual masses, whose support was now indispensable, unless it were delivered in the local language. The use of Maltese was allowed in parliamentary debates in 1921, notarial deeds were written in the local language in 1927, parliamentary debates were recorded in it in 1933, and it was given the status of official language in 1934, next to English and Italian. In 1935 the matriculation exam in Maltese was introduced at the University and the Maltese channel of cable radio (Rediffusion) was set up and effectively spread standard Maltese to all the homes in Malta and Gozo. Italian was dropped in 1936. Public notices, street names and Christian names were changed, English became compulsory for employment in the Armed Forces and the Civil Service, and the war dealt a decisive blow to the prestige Italian enjoyed before 1939. Ironically, anglicisation spread after the war when it no longer interested the British government. After World War II Maltese society changed drastically: compulsory education was introduced in 1946 and strengthened the spread of standard Maltese together with the study of English, the cinema became the most popular form of entertainment, pop music became all the rage on radio stations, and English was associated with all things modern. In the meantime Maltese kept pace in administrative domains and in higher education, thanks to the institution of a chair of Maltese (Joseph Aquilina in 1937), its introduction as a compulsory subject for entry into University (1945), and the setting up of degree courses in 1948. Italian regained popularity in the late fifties when television came to Sicily and Italian channels could be followed in Malta, mending the image created by pre-war propaganda. In 1964 a local station started broadcasting home-produced programmes in Maltese and imported ones in English, but Italian channels continued to attract the majority of the audience up to 1996, when the major political parties set up their own stations. Together with the introduction of satellite and cable television, they brought Italian viewership down to around twenty per cent which still means, however, that from 40,000 to 70,000 persons are in touch with it every day during prime time.

These facts, seen in their historical perspective, have produced a community that has been exposed to different languages for a very long period of time. The census held in 1995 revealed that out of a total population of 324,386 aged sixteen and over, 317,311 speak Maltese, 246,157 learned English well and 118,213 know Italian, while languages studied only as school subjects follow at a certain distance: French (31,945), German (6,807), Arabic (5,955) and Spanish (1,955). The first result of this strong exposure and widespread use of different languages is the ongoing development of the native language. Under the cumulative effect of nine hundred years of contacts, not only with foreign rulers and their retinue but even more importantly with settlers at the lower social levels, the stratification of the Maltese language evolved rapidly and substantially. The lower and oldest layer, although it is still perceived as the main stratum (the one that proves its Arabic origins), only provides 32.41 percent of the lexemes in Joseph Aquilina's *Maltese-English Dictionary*. The Romance element, mostly from Sicilian and Italian, rose to 52.46 percent while the English element makes up 6.12 percent of the total of 41,000 lexemes. As a result, words of non-Arabic origin form no less than 60.23 percent of the lexicon, although the quantitative factor is offset by frequency. In fact Arabic words prevail in any text, because function words are repeated many times and basic terms are used more often than specific terms but, although one finds only six Romance words in the fundamental 100-word list, in the 1585 words of the threshold level these already go up to 52.8 percent. However, the lexical composition of texts varies greatly according to register (poetic, prose, journalistic, spoken) or domain (religious, administrative, legal, technical, scientific, rural, domestic, etc.).

On the whole the word count gives an idea of how the language has grown in the past nine hundred years in order to keep pace with the social and cultural development of the community that speaks it. Although the basic Arabic lexical core satisfies the communicative needs of a rural society and of most personal and domestic situations, the vocabulary acquired over the centuries kept growing together with the new skills that were acquired. In this way one finds that Sicilian words abound in traditional crafts like woodwork, fishing and building, while Italian words are mostly used in the spheres of education, culture, religion, administration and law. On top of this the terminology of new areas and activities that were introduced in the British period – the dockyards, aviation, accountancy and taxation – or which have been drastically renewed, like medicine, the sciences and technology, especially those involving electrical and electronic appliances and practices, is replete with English words.

Official policy in education and the public's awareness both agree on the need

Lord Gerald Strickland was of the opinion that Maltese descended from Punic

Prof. Joseph Aquilina: the first chair of Maltese at the University in 1937

to achieve bilingualism, while the EU policy on multilingualism, recommending the study of at least one other European language, has always been followed in Malta. Indeed, in certain ways Malta may be considered in the vanguard of linguistic trends, both as regards the use of English and the survival of the local language side by side with a major world language, a thought which is worrying linguists and politicians in many countries. Fellow EU members may therefore show interest in our linguistic situation as a relevant case study.

After Gibraltar, Malta was the first country in Europe to adopt English in its administration and its school system because here, since 1946, it is not only compulsory but also the main medium of instruction in most subjects, from kindergarten to university. In fact in the year 2003 (May session) no less than 5623 students sat for their SEC exam (O level) in English, 4943 sat for Maltese and 3027 sat for Italian. Besides, English is the preferred language for reading: the importation of books and newspapers in English stands at 4,665,623 Maltese Liri (10,731,000 euros), followed by those in Italian worth just over half a million Maltese Liri (1,150,000 euros), while books borrowed from the national and local libraries are mostly in English. The local cinemas all show English-language films, and over sixty percent of tourists come from Britain, keeping up the pre-Independence opportunities for the locals to practise conversation in English. On the other hand, few foreigners who have not visited Malta realise up to what extent

Maltese is a 'living' language. They are usually surprised to hear that it is used regularly in the institutions, that book publishing in Maltese is lively and that the media offer two daily newspapers in Maltese, next to another two in English, while no less than twenty-seven local radio stations broadcast programmes in Maltese (compared to two in English) and six local television channels produce programmes in Maltese and relay imported programmes in English. Even ATMs and the Google search engine offer the option of interaction in Maltese.

However, living with two or three languages does produce some problems, the most urgent one being code-switching. This is resorted to extensively by Maltese speakers, especially in certain domains and situations, but they only resort to it when conversing with persons who know both languages. Nobody alternates when speaking to Maltese monolinguals or to English people or foreigners. It is carefully avoided when writing, because one has time to reflect and choose the right word. It is therefore a kind of compromise between bilinguals, a means of speeding up an informal conversation, especially when one knows that an English technical term is more frequently used in a certain environment.

On the whole, Maltese citizens succeed in communicating efficiently for their own particular needs, obviously in varying degrees according to one's linguistic competence. As to the future there are pessimists and optimists, but it is not easy to perceive a trend since conditions are nowadays very different to the past. Maltese has survived for nine centuries as a spoken language in a state of diglossia but, in actual fact, up to the 1950s the majority of the islands' inhabitants were monolingual. As a result the language expanded thanks to the influx of first Sicilian, then Italian and later English words which were passed on orally from foreign settlers or servicemen and from the few literate Maltese to the illiterate population in a very slow but steady process. Since the 1950s literacy figures have been inverted, with ninety percent being able to read and write Maltese and English and only about ten percent showing problems. However, even the latter enjoy daily exposure to English for they have attended school for about ten years and must have picked up something; moreover they always watch English films at the cinema or on television, and thousands of fans follow the Premier League or *Campionato* matches or both every weekend and the midweek games for the European cups.

Language switching will certainly increase the number of English words that are absorbed into the Maltese language but will English words erode the core vocabulary? Or will the schools and social awareness manage to keep the two codes apart? At present Maltese is still spoken regularly by over ninety percent of the inhabitants although most of them consider English as indispensable in today's world. Interest in Italian is still very much alive, but it is obviously no longer seen as a threat to Maltese. The latter has strengthened its position by penetrating areas that a few decades ago were considered as the domains of English, namely the written register and official use. Maltese is used regularly in Parliament, the Law courts, the Church and all government offices, in banks and private firms and it has just reached a new prestigious peak by being recognised as one of the official languages of the European Union. If official policy succeeds in achieving bilingualism with a good competence in both languages, although at present the system is not perfect, Maltese will survive, although (or because) it is changing, so long as it is still considered important and efficient by its speakers. The community's knowledge of English may even ensure the survival of the local language, since the use of English for international communication will ease off the pressures on Maltese to change and grow too rapidly.

References

G. Brincat, *Malta. Una storia linguistica* (Genova, 2004). (An English version is in preparation).
J. M. Brincat, *Il-Malti. Elf sena ta' storja* (Malta, 2000).

Charles Briffa

A BRIEF HISTORY OF MALTESE LITERATURE

This paper will undertake a historical sweep of literary genres and varieties to examine the development of Maltese literature, most particularly in three consecutive centuries. It will reveal a tradition of Maltese writing but it is not exhaustive. Experimentation with early forms established stylistic conventions some of which are still retained in present-day writing.

A language reflects the mentality of its people, a mentality that eventually comes out in literature, and it is a generally accepted fact that the language of a past era gathers its identity from the character and quality of its literature. Official documents and notarial deeds yield shelves of secrets to the researcher, be he a historian, a philologist, or a lexicographer, but it is in literature that a language manifests its potential to transform a people's emotions and thoughts into an expressive form conveying a memorable experience.

Medieval Maltese Literature

Unfortunately literature written in Maltese does not have a very long life-story despite the fact that Maltese in its spoken form is a very old language[1] and despite the historical fact that Malta had been in close contact with literary civilisations since classical times.[2] Maltese writers had to make use of a foreign language for the expression of their feelings and thoughts. The first known Maltese poets flourished in the early part of the twelfth century when the dominant literary medium was Arabic despite the Norman presence on the islands.[3] Three Maltese poets, identified as Ibn as-Samanti, Rahman Ibn Ramadan, and Utman Ibn Abd ar-Rahman, wrote from Palermo in Arabic and their surviving works consist of literary

Ġużè Muscat Azzopardi (1853-1927)

Anton E. Caruana (1838-1907)

Ninu Cremona (1880-1972), Ġużè Aquilina (1911-97) and Ġużè Galea (1901-78)

fragments and epigrammatic pieces.[4] They sang of experiences that left a deep impression on them: the girl whose heavenly beauty sends hearts dancing - it is a beauty that contemplates the richness of the spheres; the proud overlord who lays great honours at the poet's feet but does not heed the latter's pleas - the poet is therefore left dejected, wishing he were dead and blaming his lord for all his misfortunes. Another epigram talks of distrust and hypocrisy: one should not trust friends because even their smiles may kill. Utman's elegy on the death of a Sicilian nobleman (of which only a fragment survives) celebrates with philosophical fervour the death of a hero. In these few twelfth century verses, Maltese poems in Arabic reveal the outlook and temper of the Mediterranean mind.

This Maltese-Arabic poetry shows much of the characteristics of contemporary Eastern poetry. It often flourished under the patronage of a nobleman. Poets were generally dependent for their livelihood on the generosity of their lord whose praises they sang, so that their poetry often took the form of a panegyric full of extravagant description. Yet Arabic poetry in the central Mediterranean was modified by the amalgamation of Semitic and European elements. It reveals a Christian sensibility in the face of death. Eventually the influx of Latin culture ousted Arabic as the dominant literary medium.

Oliver Friggieri contends that in the cultural development of medieval Malta there was a significant twin process which he terms 'a historical dualism'.[5] Maltese, basically Semitic, survived as an aural medium of an illiterate nation whose visual medium for formal communication, however, was often a Romance language.[6] In Friggieri's historical and philosophical perception this dualism, a major defining characteristic of Maltese culture, contained two independent and fundamental systems: (a) the system of the spoken Semitic mode, and (b) the system of the written Romance mode.[7] This leads him to hypothesise that Pietru Caxaro's *Cantilena*, a poem in medieval Maltese composed probably around the mid-fifteenth century and which is the only instance of medieval literature in the vernacular, is an attempt at challenging the assumption in contemporary culture of a monolithic or univocal Italianism.[8] In this view, Caxaro's poem works to uncover the literary potential of the submitting mentality and thus it becomes a marginal voice that ignores the dominant Italianate mode. It attains a remarkable flexibility through its predominantly Semitic vocabulary and through the bold use of figurative expressions.

The *Cantilena* is a lament in which the poet expresses his misfortune that an ungovernable heart had thrown him into a sea of despair. It is a personal experience that expresses solitude but moves towards self-determination in a ray of hope. Caxaro uses the metaphors of the collapsed building, the deep well, the broken stairway, death by drowning, and the stormy sea to design his allegory whose source was the Bible.[9] But the poem has stylistic and thematic similarities with Arabo-Spanish and Portuguese medieval poetry.[10] And one scholarly interpretation makes the lyric's desperate situation a feminine invocation: the poet assumes a fictional female role to lament 'the lack of love because of her lover's indifference, his absence or his preference for another woman'.[11] Another interpretation could be that it is 'a reference to some project' the poet might have had, a project – 'perhaps an ambition concerning his career' - that has finally collapsed.[12] Whether it is a contribution to the literary convention of the demands and characteristics of love, a strong allegorical expression of solitude, or a reference to a collapsed professional scheme, the poem remains a unique experience in a literary desert.

In the later middle ages, when the Normans consolidated their political position in Malta, the language of administration was Latin, which also replaced Arabic as the language of culture and learning. Gradually Italian in its Sicilian form made itself felt about the time of the *Cantilena*, but in the following centuries the language of culture in Malta was Italian in its Tuscan form. The language of Tuscany expanded and influenced the entire Italian peninsula. Since the fourteenth century the diffusion of Tuscan literature and the dispersal of Tuscans in search of commercial possibilities all over Italy left their literary and non-literary effects. The penetration of Tuscan into non-literary documents was unchallenged and became more common after the middle of the fifteenth century when political, commercial, and cultural activities interacted and left an indelible mark on the language of written usage.[13] It was not surprising, therefore, that Tuscan also crept into Maltese administrative activities since there were traditionally close political, commercial, and cultural links with Italy. Nobody ever raised a voice in favour of written Maltese or against the threat of Italian domination. The Maltese language was disregarded as the medium of culture and it survived only as the spoken medium of the illiterate folk. The next step forward belongs to the early writers who dared to adapt the vernacular to the visual medium.

The Seventeenth and Eighteenth Centuries

It was only in the seventeenth century that Maltese started to be written down, and then very scantily. The wordlists compiled by Megiser (1611) and Skippon (1664) and the number of Maltese words included in Gio. Francesco Abela's *Descrittione di Malta* (1647) are valuable sources for lexical studies. But in the field of literature we only have Giacomo Bosio's couplet (1602) on the value of land and G. F. Bonamico's (1639-80) poem, *Sonetto* (1672/75), in honour of Grand Master Nicholas Cotoner (1663-80). This poem starts with a description of nature in spring and moves on to stress the national importance of the Grand Master so as to define his authority. The association of Cotoner with the beauty of spring presents a vision of political stability and consolidates the Order's role by welding its identity and direction into a cohesive economy. This literary view also incorporates the concept of a divine plan in the Order's protective function and a nation's destiny. The *Sonetto*, thus, glorifies the Grand Master and surrounds him with a divine aura. Loyalty to this adored leader is implied as Bonamico appeals to the people's sentiment in presenting Cotoner as being sanctioned by God to be the protector and organiser of the nation. The poem expresses a political ideal as it seeks to channel the legitimate authority of the Order in directions consonant with the political needs of the country.

In the eighteenth century the language is mobilised for personal and social pursuits. In the development of literature prose generally comes after poetry since verse was often considered to be more expressive in an oral delivery and more easily memorised. It is therefore a rather remarkable feature of Maltese literature that eighteenth century writers produced a considerable body of written prose at a time which may be taken as the incubation period of Maltese literature. This unusual accomplishment was due mainly to the religious fervour of the preacher Ignazio Saverio Mifsud (1722-?), to the linguistic vehemence of Can. Gian Frangisk Agius De Soldanis (1712-70), and to the idealistic vision of Mikiel Anton Vassalli (1764-1829). Certainly in this century there was a firm consciousness of the past service the vernacular rendered to the simple country folk and of its present function and future mission. These writers realised that Maltese had the essential means of achieving its own progress and (in the case of Vassalli) of attaining a proper national dignity.

Mifsud's oratorical skills produced homiletic prose which achieves literary value through its style and imagination.[14] Agius De Soldanis' keen sense of observation gave us a series of dialogues whose linguistic and folkloristic importance has often been noted but on the literary level they introduced conversational prose into Maltese literature. And Vassalli's idealism encouraged the writing of Maltese in all spheres. As regards poetry, contributions are still scanty.

Fr Frangisk Uzzino, who lived in the first half of the eighteenth century, wrote three short prayers in verse to be recited by the people: *Lil Sant' Anna* (1730), *Lill-Glorjuż Arkanġlu San Mikiel* (1741), and *L-Att ta' l-Indiema* (1741?). Uzzino uses stylistic features for psycho-religious purposes. These religious poems turn on the virtues of the saints in question and the quality of the language tends to be euphonious to make it pleasing to the ear. The rhyming couplets he used in the religious poems to St Ann and St Michael, and the alternating rhyme in the act of contrition contribute to the melodic atmosphere that makes them almost song-lyrics. The aim, of course, was to make them popular among the people.

Agius De Soldanis tried his hand at versification also. Under the instigation of a friend he composed *Sonetto Punico-Maltese in Onore Dell'Illmo. Signr. Dr Ludovico Coltellini* (1758). Coltellini was the secretary of a botanical society in Cortona for whom De Soldanis had great intellectual respect.[15] This Petrarchan sonnet, structured on an ABAB ABAB CDC DCD rhyming string, is a true acrostic that employs a vertical reading of the initial letters of the lines, spelling out the name of Coltellini. It is an instance of light verse displaying obvious stylistic characteristics of rhyme and structure, and is intended to entertain with its wit and grace. But it is significant in its unique rhythmical variation that approximates speech rhythms. Fr Felic Demarco (1713 -?) wrote *Żwieġ La Maltija* (1760) which is also light verse.

It is light-hearted in tone intended for carnival and merry-making festivals. It is heavily rhymed and full of humorous juxtaposition that makes it almost a jingle.

However, the greatest achievement of the eighteenth century was in prose. It is understandable that the early writers had to be mainly people of the cloth and individuals engaged in notarial and administrative affairs. These were the literate native few, and since their education was mainly based on Latin and the Romance languages their Maltese came under the increasing influence of these languages. The language underwent lexical, morphological, syntactic, and semantic development and the early writers eventually found they could adapt it to a written Latin alphabet.

The eighteenth century marks the beginning of the first attempts of written Maltese prose. The list of works includes:
- Fr Frangisk Uzzino's *Taghlim Nisrani* (1752) - the first catechism in Maltese translated from Italian and commissioned by the Bishop of Malta, F. Paolo Alpheran de Bussan.
- Fr Ignazio Saverio Mifsud's *Discorsi e Panegirici* (1752) - a collection of 41 sermons (31 of them in Maltese and 10 in Italian) which he composed between the years 1739 and 1746 (that is, when he was 17 to 24 years).
- Thezan's *Taghlim ghal Suldat* (1719?) - a set of military instructions in Maltese.
- Can. Gian Frangisk Agius De Soldanis' *Id-Djalogi* (1750) - a collection of eight conversational pieces in Maltese depicting common customs and attitudes.
- Mikiel Anton Vassalli's *Alfabett Malti Mfisser bil-Malti u bit-Taljan* (1790) - a sort of manifesto on the orthography of the Maltese language.

Apart from these there were various attempts at compiling a grammar of the language and a suitable dictionary[16] most particularly by De Soldanis and Vassalli, and (according to De Soldanis) there were many who wrote in Maltese in his times.[17] These early steps concentrated mainly on non-fictional prose, and produced at least three forms of prose: baroque, plain, and conversational. Baroque prose suited well the type of homiletic writing found at the time because the early devotional prose is characterised by ornament and persuasion. The secular prose of the eighteenth century, on the other hand, was generally plain, that is free from rhetorical devices, from Italianised vocabulary, and from Latin quotations. The representation of military instructions and common people's dialogues contributed further to the conversational aspects of prose. One can reasonably say that these early attempts shaped modern prose as they established a milieu that included subjective, objective, evocative, and persuasive prose styles whose essential qualities persisted ever since.

What emerged, therefore, from the writing of eighteenth century authors are the diversity and capability of non-literary prose. The contexts of writing and the subject matter had already started dictating their own variation, and this led to a range of prose forms that had their own stylistic structures. In the subsequent centuries the preacher was displaced by the creative writer who continued to capture the required tone and weave it into the prose with relatively effortless ease.

One may say that the eighteenth century formed the starting-point for the development of literary prose.

The Nineteenth Century

The essential feature of nineteenth century prose is the continuing emergence of Maltese as a written medium that contributed to the perceptual reorientation of the times. Vassalli's exhortation in favour of the mother tongue had far-reaching implications, and his solicitation for writing in Maltese coincided with a social need for improving the local standards of education, making them suitable for the common people. This accompanied the emerging collective attitude as European romanticism encouraged the use of the national language as an affirmation of personal individuality and national identity within the consciousness of a community. The Maltese, under the influence of the Italian *Risorgimento*, developed a sense of national awareness that brought about a wider use of the vernacular which in turn led to the growth of an indigenous literature, most particularly poetry and narrative prose.

The nineteenth century is littered with Maltese writers who wrote in Italian:[18]

POETS:	Marquis Giuseppe Testaferrata Viani (1767-1837)
	Marquis Gioacchino Ermolao Barbaro (d. 1844)
	Carlo di Cristoforo (1769-1851)
	Giovanni Antonio Micallef (1787-1840)
	Cesare Vassallo (1800-1882)
	Giuseppe Zammit Brighella (1801-1890)
	Lorenzo de Caro (1817-1853)
	Gananton Vassallo (1817-1868)
	Baron Augusto Testaferrata Abela (1826-1885)
	Ramiro Barbaro (1840-1920)
	Zaccaria Roncali (1840-1918)
	Paolo Cesareo (1844-1928)
	Ġużè Muscat Azzopardi (1853-1927)
	Salvatore Castaldi (1857-1904)
	Alfonso Giglio (1860-1934)
HISTORY WRITERS:	Onorato Bres (1753-1818)
	G. A. Micallef (1787- 1840)
	Fortunato Panzavecchia (1797-1850)
	Baron Vincenzo Azzopardi (1783-1857)
	Giuseppe Depiro (1794-1870)
	Ferdinando Giglio (lived in Malta between 1848 and 1860)
	Antonio Schembri (1811-1872)
	Achille Ferris (1838-1907)

<table>
<tr><td>NOVELISTS/
SHORT-STORY WRITERS:</td><td>R. Barbaro, Un Martire (1878)
Ferdinando Giglio, La Bella Maltea (1872)
G. A. Vassallo, Alessandro Inguanez (1861),
    Wignacourt (1862)
Carmela Agusta Cassar, Leonilda (?)
N. Zammit, Angelica (1862, 1880)</td></tr>
</table>

Some of these even wrote in Maltese. For instance, Gananton Vassallo wrote both poetry and history, A. Testaferrata wrote drama, Ġużè Muscat Azzopardi poetry and narrative prose, F. Panzavecchia history, and A. Ferris history and instructional essays. Most of those who wrote Maltese verse during the nineteenth century followed the rules of Italian prosody, and the most popular metrical form of the period was the eight-syllabled line, considered to be the most congenial structure for emotive themes.[19] However, octosyllabic verse is a form very well suited to narrative verse since its length approaches natural thought units and even the span of conversational rhythms. The six-syllabled line was also quite popular at the time. These were the metres for what was called in mid-nineteenth century 'traditional poetry'[20] that dealt with historical, heroic, humorous, romantic, moral, and religious subjects. For instance, Vincenzo Caruana (d. 1824) wrote *Fuq il-Mewt ta' Napuljun il-Kbir* (1821) which uses the six-syllabled line and an alternate rhyme scheme to express the power of Napoleon; and Ludovico Mifsud Tommasi (1795-1879) wrote a poem in octosyllabic verse in honour of Queen Adelaide's visit to Malta, *Għall-Miġja f'Malta tar-Regina Adelaide* (1838). Patri Fidiel in 1822 wrote a religious poem addressed to the Holy Spirit and structured on the rising rhythm of the *Veni Creator Spiritus*, and F. Vella and G. Montebello Pulis in 1824 published some moral verse. And the anonymous *Għanja ta' Tfajla Bidwija* (1847) is a humorous love lyric about a country girl who can rejoice and plan her marriage since the political situation has improved.

However, the major nineteenth century poets who sought to raise poetry to the national level were Ludovico Mifsud Tommasi and Gananton Vassallo. Mifsud Tommasi's many versified prayers and hymns expressed religious thought in simple memorable words. Although he mainly employed octosyllabic verse he also used a variety of metrical forms that helped the faithful to become accustomed to Maltese verse rhythms. The cause of their popularity was religious and they are instances of didactic poetry adorned with imaginative power displaying essential Christian values. The diction he uses appears capable of being set to music or of being recited. Often the composer's art records plangently a religious experience without clogging the sense. And at times he increases his dramatic content to imitate the nuances of the admonishing preacher. Other verse writers of religious works were influenced by Mifsud Tommasi's almost dramatic style. Among these we may mention Fr Luigi Daniele Debono who wrote a hymn to St Philomena in 1840, Richard Taylor (1818-68) whose religious lyrics composed between 1843 and

1864 exhibit great imagination that adds their dramatic value, and Fr Indri Schembri (1805-72) who more than others associated religious themes with the workings of nature – Schembri's best known work is the Christmas carol *Ninni, la tibkix iżjed*.

Gananton Vassallo is perhaps the greatest poet of the first half of the nineteenth century. In his poetry he represented man as a psychological being seeking self-fulfilment and emotional completion through love. His lyrics are often sentimental in tone and sometimes even pathetic. His poetic vision is propped by a mental frame wrought by a sense of real nationalism which dredges up themes relating to patriotism that reveals the characteristics of his ancestors (*Mannarino, La Valette, Wignacourt, Il-Ġifen Tork, Tifħira lil Malta*), emigration as a social evil that leaves its scars on the individual (*Safar, L-Imsiefer, L-Għarus Imsiefer lill-Għarusa, L-Għarusa lill-Għarus Imsiefer, It-Turufnat*), and a didactic attitude mingled with a sense of humour (*Ktieb Sabiħ, Il-Musbieħ il-Lejl, Ix-Xhiħ u x-Xitan*).[21] Undoubtedly Vassallo's masterpiece is *Il-Ġifen Tork* (1842) which is a long narrative poem that seeks to glorify the heroic past. A group of Christian slaves on a Turkish galley succeed to set themselves free and return to Malta. Vassallo introduces epic elements in this narrative poem whose main functions are to entertain and to teach the common people. [22]

Other poets, like Ġuże Muscat Azzopardi, who wrote several religious and patriotic poems, and Dwardu Cachia (1858-1907) whose best known poem is *Katrin ta' l-Imdina*, followed in the footsteps of Mifsud Tommasi and Vassallo. Apart from religious poetry Richard Taylor composed also some light verse whose folkloristic content makes them rather important: *L-Istrina, Il-Festa ta' San Girgor, Il-Festa ta' San Ġorġ*). Some of his poems (*Talba tal-Fqajjar, Ir-Ragħaj u l-Lupu*), however, exhibit a sympathetic heart that is always ready to put in a good word in favour of the underdog. He even translated part of Dante's *Divina Commedia* (*Il-Konti Ugolino*). The greatest achievements of these was the fact that they established poetic diction and introduced literary forms into Maltese literature, thus paving the way to Dun Karm's poetic creativity.

In the meantime prose became a social need. Political demands and social reforms (and most particularly the introduction of press freedom in 1839) extended the general need for written Maltese. The people had always spoken Maltese; now they wanted to write it and read it. They realised that written Maltese prose was no longer an impossibility. The main efforts of literary composition during the period may be seen in terms of three interrelated activities that contributed to the varieties of prose.

    a. First of all, there were the attempts by anecdotists to reproduce the common speech of the people. The language which had always been orally transmitted and preserved was being conveyed onto paper, sometimes verbatim, in the style of the De Soldanis's dialogues. Mention is here made of the short compositions that make extensive use of conversational forms written by Annibale Preca (1832-1901) in 1885: *Mill-Qotna sal-Maktur* and *Disgħa, Għaxra, Ħdax*.

Rużar Briffa (1906-63)

George Zammit (1908-90)

Mgr Carmelo Psaila (1871-1961), the National Poet

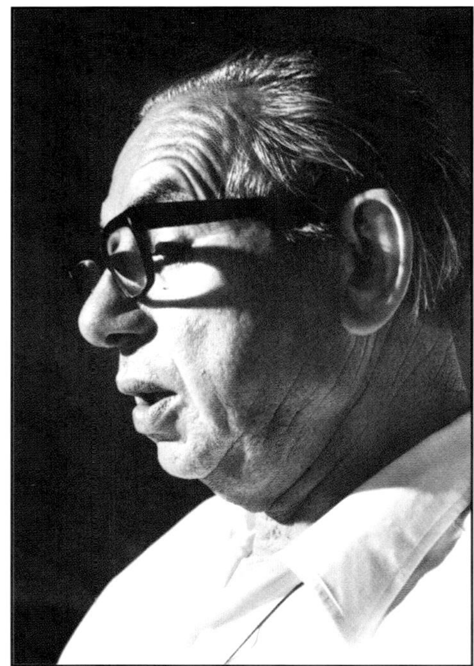

Anton Buttigieg (1912-83)

b. There was also a considerable amount of translation. These translated works could not help carrying the imprint of the source language. But they still contributed to the development of Maltese prose. Vassalli, for instance, translated the Gospels (1829) from Latin and the history and travels of Cyrus (1831) from French.

c. Finally, there were the writings of the literary men who consciously sought to create a proper style in prose. Among these cultured stylists there were Gananton Vassallo, Richard Taylor, Anton E. Caruana (1838-1907), Napuljun Tagliaferro (1843-1915), and Pawlu Bellanti (1851-1927) who composed fiction and non-fiction relating to historical and religious matters. They were all aware that Maltese prose lacked a style of its own and they experimented with written forms to create a proper one.

The talents of prose writers in all three categories were boosted by journalism. Their attempts, therefore, led to the development of modes of writing that gave information, discussed and reported events, and told a story.

The Maltese prose writers also aimed at reaching the common people who could understand only Maltese. They had to treat simple subjects but at the same time they aimed at instruction as well as entertainment. Their style, therefore, could not be baroque. It had to be plainer to reach more people and encourage learning. Even the cultured stylists did not write with the massive elaboration of baroque decoration. Furthermore, the promotion of the plain style reflected the general trend of the times. Realism in European literature and art made the environment more intelligible, and as the Maltese prose writers expressed a new reverence for their language, the feelings and experiences they depicted added new dimensions to social perception.

The pattern of experimentation that characterises the eighteenth and nineteenth centuries are evidence enough that written prose had to develop in response to social and psychological needs. The earlier demand for homiletic speeches, sermons, prayers, and saints' lives proceeded even into the twentieth century but now the general tone became less baroque and more secular because it was directed to the common reader. In the first part of the twentieth century the public still needed the ventures of prose chronicles which recovered aspects of Maltese history often integrated with creative narration as a 'national mythology'.[23] On the other hand, creative narration manifested conceptual and perceptual visions in the authors' mind styles. Maltese prose had reached the shores of the islands and was useful, especially since it grew side by side with journalism, from which it might have taken its professional pretension that eventually led to omniscience in the novel.

So by the beginning of the twentieth century there were at least four major varieties of prose:

1. the prose mode that narrated a story or an event, incorporating narration and description in the fields of literature, religion, journalism, and history;

2. the prose mode that interpreted material, comprising argumentation, commentary, and moralising in the fields of religion and journalism;

3. the prose mode that echoed conversation, embracing dialogue, conversation, thought presentation, and instructions in the fields of literature and (military) education;

4. the prose mode that gave information on a topic, including exposition, report, and chronicle in the fields of history, folklore, religion, and journalism.

In the course of literary output these modes intermingled as the nineteenth century prose writer was faced with the consciousness of creating an appropriate style. Turning to foreign authors provided part of the solution, but the Maltese writers who gained a sense of prose from the better European models had a mine of linguistic resources in their native environment and all they needed was to tap the wealth of stylistic material and deliberately explore the great power of colloquial prose. The adaptation of foreign stylistic conventions led to creativity, experimentation, and originality.

While the eighteenth century can be termed the age of awareness or the incubation period of Maltese prose, one can think of the nineteenth century as an age of ferment because the yeast in Maltese prose was undergoing steady changes as the translators brought foreign matters to the Maltese readers and the stylists experimented with technical elements and saw new conceptions of sentences. It was the century that encouraged several cultured elements[24] to pick up the pen to transfer their ideas from speech to paper in Maltese. By the end of the century Maltese prose could be written in a polished and ornate way or in the free movements of simple spoken norms. It was reaching out to meet the challenges of the twentieth century novel, but only after A. E. Caruana's major attempt in *Inez Farruġ* (1889), which is considered to be the first literary novel. The great stylistic strides of the twentieth century novel were made possible partly because of educational progress and social change and partly because of the nineteenth century attempts at written prose.

The Twentieth Century

The twentieth century then saw two major groups: the Academy of Maltese Writers[25] (founded in 1920) and the Movement for the Promotion of Literature[26] (founded in 1967). The latter was short-lived but its impact was more lasting. The Academy, however, survived and its functions and aims received the government's support during the 1980s and 1990s, and it entered the twenty-first century fully confident that it could face globalisation.

In the first two decades the Maltese language was still without a standard orthography. A group of Maltese writers got together to form an association that later became known as the Academy of Maltese Writers. The Academy's aims were to establish a standardised orthography for the language (which would facilitate matters for all writers) and to advance Maltese literature. The success of the Academy was largely due to its journal, *Il-Malti* (Maltese), which started publication in 1925, and to the fact that it has had in its fold every writer of note throughout the rest of the century. At the same time it often acted as training ground for the younger generations of writers. Through the Academy's efforts great strides were made in literature, and its task was facilitated because of educational progress and social change. The twentieth century, therefore, may be called the ripening period of literature in Maltese.

Political independence from Britain was attained in 1964 and this serves as a convenient dividing line. Pre-independence literature was mainly concerned with the search for a national identity and therefore veered towards traditional elements. It is dominated by a spirit of romanticism and by the figure of Mgr Carmelo Psaila (1871-1961), commonly known as Dun Karm and Malta's national poet. Post-independence literature, on the other hand, dealt largely with the conflict between the individual and society and steered towards the fundamental needs of the self. It is characterised mainly by a spirit of radicalism and modernism, and dominated largely by the Movement for the Promotion of Literature.

Poetry

Twentieth century romantic poetry is dominated by Dun Karm, a pillar of the Academy. His poetry transcends the particular to perceive the universal and in the process thoughts become unmediated perception. Dun Karm often found poetic expression in his solitude, which was eventually accompanied by a high degree of spiritual balance. His poetry reflects a background of village life crowned with an atmosphere of family feeling and it also portrays the Maltese countryside with a perceptive imagination. It synthesises the popular culture of the Maltese, which is quite evident from its rural characteristics that furnish a local identity. Dun Karm also explored poetically Malta's history to confirm its cultural and national identity. At the same time some of his best poems illustrate an inner journey of sentimental and moral experience. Thus his poetry exhibits great subjectivity but it also expresses his country's collective aspirations. Both the personal and the national sentiments are treated from a deep religious viewpoint that discusses existentialism. The spiritual crisis in his masterpiece *Il-Jien u Lilhinn Minnu* (1938, The self and beyond it) is analysed in universal human terms that illuminate man's existence and insist on the inexplicability of the relations between God and man except for the latter's absolute acceptance of the former's hidden power.

A group of poets, most of them active members of the Academy, came under his influence as regards theme, subject matter, as well as in style (mostly imagery, meter, and diction). The main figures of this school are: Ġużè Delia (1900-1980), Ġorġ Pisani (1909-99), Ġorġ Chetcuti (1914-), Mattew Sultana (1918-86), Vincent

Temi Zammit (1864-1935)

Ġużè Ellul Mercer (1897-1961)

Ġużè Galea (centre) as President of the Akkadeja tal-Malti 1944-45. Also in the picture are other known authors such as Ġużè Ellul Mercer, Ġużè Cassar Pullicino, Dun Frans Camilleri, Ninu Cremona and Ġużè Chetcuti

Ungaro (1919-96), Dun Frans Camilleri (1919-90), Ġużè Chetcuti (1921-), Ġużè Cardona (1922-88), and Pawlu Aquilina (1929-). Romanticism, as a broad movement in the history of Maltese consciousness, finds another outlet in another group of poets (most of whom Academy members also) who do not fall under the direct influence of Dun Karm. Chief among these are Rużar Briffa (1906-63), Karmenu Vassallo (1913-87), Anton Buttigieg (1912-83), and Ġorġ Żammit (1908-1990). Their poetry is characterised by a unique form of sensibility, each poet with his own peculiar form: Briffa's poetry represents spontaneity and raw feelings; Vassallo's excitability and at times even irascibility; Buttigieg's affectability and tenderness; and Żammit's realisation and understanding. In a very broad sense the works of the first two is poetry of anguished sentiment and that of the last two poetry of intimate descriptions. They are all engaged in the extraordinary enterprise of seeking the deep yearnings of man's heart. The power of the creative mind is autonomous. Each of these poets assumes that the imagination can perceive reality and re-create it as truth.[27]

With these came others most of whom are Academy members: Wallace P. Gulia (1926-2000), Amante Buontempo (1920-), Alfred Massa (1938 -), Mary Meylak (1905-75), Alfred Palma (1939-), V.M. Pellegrini (1911-97), Michael Buttigieg (1916-97), and the Maltese living in Australia. Most of these poets continued writing well into the last years of the twentieth century despite the new wave of poetry. Self-consciousness very often is a central characteristic of these romantics. Their subjectivity, grounded in common experience, poetically exalts the ordinary decencies that hold people together. Such romanticism, prevalent in human nature, is an aesthetic phenomenon whose achievement is imposing in twentieth century Maltese literature.

With the arrival of the Movement poets, like Victor Fenech (1935-), Daniel Massa (1936-), Achille Mizzi (1939-), Mario Azzopardi (1944-), Philip Sciberras (1945-), Oliver Friggieri (1947-), and Doreen Micallef (1949 -2001), poetry took a different tack because they shared a different set of principles about the nature of poetry and a new attitude to their readers. Most of the time they were anti-romantic and anti-sentimental and no longer believed in the power of the Muse as did the romantics. They did not write for a poetry-loving audience, and neither did they act as the people's spokesmen - except for Friggieri later on. They adopted a conscious unaffectedness in their tone which often invited the reader to agree with their judgement. Movement poems, however, were full of ambiguity and rather thin in images, yet the few images they had still presented a perception that dragged its own associational appeal. In the 1970s the Movement was already disbanded but the poets continued writing in isolation into the 1990s, each with his own characteristics. Most of them joined the Academy which had by now an aura of permanency because of its literary tradition. At first some of this poetry revealed an ironic distrust of all that was traditional, but that distrust was mingled with sentiments of direct experience as if the new poets' personal engagement was showing the inadequacy of conventional language.

These poets all use distinctly individual voices. Their poetry does not avoid experimentation but generally eschews the cultivation of stylistic idiosyncrasy. In the decades following the 1960s they set forth in divergent directions, but still they represent the continuation of the modernist tradition. Alongside come other poets such as Marjanu Vella (1927-88), Lilian Sciberras (1946-), Jane Micallef (1945-), Raymond Mahoney (1949-), Joe Friġġieri (1946-), Charles Flores (1948-), Charles Coleiro (1935-), Ġorġ Borġ (1946-), Trevor Zahra (1947-), and Joe Żammit Ciantar (1942-). Also in the last years of the century there was some interest in narrative verse with Oliver Friggieri's *Pawlu ta' Malta* (1985, Malta's Paul), and *L-Għanja ta' Malta* (1989, The Song of Malta) in which the poet raises a voice for the nation. Translations too became rather popular.

Drama

In drama the twentieth century inherited (from the previous century) the *teatrin* or the village theatre in which melodrama and the farce flourished. But the *teatrin* became divorced from literature. It flourished during the first decades of the century, hurling the theatre down the crag towards melodrama. Consequently, drama could not develop with the same pace as the other genres. It had to wait till the middle of the century to see some remarkable improvement, and it was only then that literary maturity could start prevailing over the taste for melodrama, farces, and extravaganzas.[28]

Not all scriptwriters, however, abandoned serious themes on the stage. One of the promoters of the *teatrin* was Ninu Cremona (1880-1972) who in 1913 moved to classical drama. His poetic play, *Il-Fidwa tal-Bdiewa* (1913, The Farmers' Ransom), is set in fifteenth century Malta when the islands were under a feudal lord who was a greedy despot. Excessive oppression led to the inhabitants' insurrection which overthrew the despot's government. As a consequence the poor locals had to refund in full the money paid for the possession of the islands. But all this is only the socio-historical backdrop of the love drama of the village girl, Roża - young, beautiful, respectable, and loyal - who is engaged to be married to the patriotic seaman, Pietru - strong, heroic, devoted, and altruistic. The bride-to-be is abducted by a brutish landlord and Pietru must save her. He does so and all evil elements are romantically destroyed. The love drama, however, merges into the nationalistic crisis so that Pietru's rescue of the helpless heroine on the white steed symbolises the farmers' redemption from the oppressor's yoke.

The next exponent of classical drama is Erin Serracino Inglott (1904-83). His three poetic plays *Ir-Raheb* (1941, The Monk), *Il-Barrani* (1942, The Outsider), and *Il-Kerjoti* (1942, The Iscariot) highlight the aspect of the outsider in him: as a creative artist he considers himself to be outside the cultural society of his times. In the 1940s Maltese writers were generally treating contemporary social themes. Serracino Inglott, however, treated universal themes. Finally classical drama continues with Oliver Friggieri who takes up the national issue again, this time with *Rewwixta* (1990, Rebellion) which depicts the Maltese uprising against the formidable French at the end of the eighteenth century.

By the middle of the twentieth century ranting melodrama is firmly removed from the scene and a type of social realism is allowed to make itself at home, at first intermingled with subjectivity and romanticism and later in a more objective manner. Ninu Cremona, Ivo Muscat Azzopardi (1893-1965), Ġorġ Pisani, Ġużè Aquilina (1911-97), and Ġużè Chetcuti all claim as dramatists to grapple with society's problems but they do so in a rather subjective manner to present a sublime idealisation (though Chetcuti is less subjective and romantic than the others). Their works exploit the social implications of realism as they aim to rid the stage of histrionics replacing them with a more natural style. However, they allow their own subjective consciousness to intrude into the action.

Objective reality is effectively dealt with in the plays of Ġużè Diacono (1912-2002). As a realist playwright Diacono aims at home-truth and the presentation of concrete facts. His plays *Salib Ħaddiehor* (1960, Other People's Troubles), *Erwieħ Marbuta* (1965, Chained Souls), *L-Ewwel Jien* (1972, I Come First), among others and his television serial *Il-Madonna taċ-Ċoqqa* (1978, Our Lady of the Hood) are not intellectual and they are unromantic and objective in their treatment of the themes. Diacono's intention is to analyse not man's hidden motives but the tangible results of those hidden motives, and he skilfully avoids over-sentimentalism. Consequently, his language is full of self-control and it lacks emotive values. There is very little inner spiritual tension and emotional relationship among his characters. He is not interested in speculation but it is the concrete world that provides him with material for his dramatic performances. He manifests a mind style based firmly on this concrete world. And therefore Diacono's realism does not allow the characters to control their own context. It turns them into objects and thus his theatre presents types and not individuals, emphasising the context and not the characters.

But the fifties also saw the birth of psychological realism in the modern literary theatre with the dramatic output of Francis Ebejer (1925-93), who wrote in Maltese and English, and attained international esteem. His ideas were upheld by both the Academy (to which he belonged) and the Movement. He wrote many plays from 1950 till his death, the best known being *Vaganzi tas-Sajf* (1962, Summer Holidays), *Boulevard* (1964, Boulevard), *Menz* (1967, Menz), *Il-Ħadd fuq il-Bejt* (1973, Sunday on the Roof), *L-Imnarja Żmien il-Qtil* (1973, *Imnarja* is a Time for Killing), *L-Imwarrbin* (1973, The Cliffhangers), *Ħitan* (1974, Walls), and *Il-Ġaħan ta' Binġemma* (1985, The Jester of Bingemma). He wrote many radio and television plays, and the televised serial *Id-Dar tas-Soru* (1977-78, The Nun's House) was a great hit.

The emergence of other playwrights, like Oreste Calleja (1946-) and Alfred Sant (1948-), both members of the Movement for the Promotion of Literature, and Joe Vella Bondin (1934-) and Vince Vella (1950-) ensures dramatic continuity in the last years of the twentieth century. They provide new efforts on stage that involve unique debates on man's condition.

Francis Ebejer (1925-93)

Fiction

The novel came to the Maltese shores via Italy in the form of the historical romantic novel which was compatible with the local mentality. History was a source of national pride and fiction (including novels and short-stories) gave vent to wishful thinking, so the historical novel was an obvious favourite form of literary expression. In the beginning of the century the novel had two branches: the popular (which appealed to and was comprehensible to the simple folk) and the literary (which was involved in healthy experimentation that withstood the test of time and scholarship. The literary novel ushered in the social novel that often assumed a reformist role and later developed into the political, psychological, and socio-psychological novels.[29]

The literary historical novel in Maltese has three structurally distinct kinds: the fictionalised history, the romantic fantasy, and the historical fiction.[30] The period novel that represents fictionalised history makes historical characters and actions form the basis of the novel. Ġużè Muscat Azzopardi (1853-1927) is the great exponent of this type of fiction. His best known novel is *Nazju Ellul* (1909, Ignatius Ellul) which emphasises the political situation during the French period in Malta by revealing social preoccupation and national concern, but it includes a fictionalised love tragedy. Agostino Levanzin (1872-1955) is another such novelist. His *Is-Saħħar Falzun* (1908-1912, Falzon the Wizard) aims at historical instruction through literary means. The romantic fantasy, on the other hand, is a period novel that depicts a historical romance in which the past is simply used as a sensational and dramatic backdrop for adventurous exploits. Ġużè Galea (1901-78) in his *Raġel bil-Għaqal* (1943, A Witty Man) depicts the hero's adventures on the Mdina bastions and in his hideout on Comino as the Maltese islands are being threatened by pirates. And Ninu Muscat Fenech (1854-1910) in his *Ġorġ il-Bdot* (1927, George the Navigator) presents a plot based during the era of the Knights of Malta. Finally, historical fiction includes the period novel that puts fictitious characters and actions within a historical background. The difference between the romantic fantasy and historical fiction is that in the former history is represented in an exciting and exotic way, whereas in the latter it is authentic. A. E. Caruana's *Ineż Farruġ* (1889, Agnes Farrug), Galea's *San Ġwann* (1939, St John's Co-Cathedral), and Ġużè Aquilina's *Taħt Tliet Saltniet* (1938, Under three Dominions) are all examples of historical fiction. Eliciting patterns from history was full of significance and it aroused a sense of patriotism.

After the historical novel came the social novel with novelists and short-story writers[31] like Victor Apap (1913 -2001), Ġużè Bonnici (1907-40), Paul P. Borg (1949-), Wistin Born (1910-86), Lina Brockdorff (1918-), Joseph J. Camilleri (1928-), Albert M. Cassola (1915-74), Ġużè Chetcuti, Ġwann Mamo (1886-1941), Alfred Massa (1938-), Mary Meylak (1905-75), Ivo Muscat Azzopardi, Ġużè Orlando (1898-1962), Ġorġ Pisani, Alfred Sant, Michael Spiteri (1917-), Paul Xuereb (1923-95), Ġorġ Żammit (1908-90), and Temi Zammit (1864-1935). The essential interest of the literary historical novel is nationalism, and the general aim of the contemporary social novel is awareness of the present. One glorifies the past to understand the present, the other tries to understand the present as a preparation for the future. Eventually the dwelling on the collective political theme for patriotic involvement gave way to a preoccupation with social hardships, and the social novel started demanding more interpenetration of plot, character, and moral theme. And as the social novel's offshoot developed into a psychological inquiry the interpenetration of character and theme became an essentiality. Novelists like Rena Balzan (1946 -), Ġużè Ellul Mercer (1897-1961), Oliver Friggieri, Frans Sammut (1945-), Francis Ebejer, Lino Spiteri (1938-), and Trevor Zahra all explored the socio-psychological novel.

Serious Maltese fiction has often been concerned with portraying life, and its audience was mainly recruited from among those who were chiefly interested in social change and in qualifying human conditions. Looking at the efforts of the century it becomes plain that local fiction has been depicting the spread of insecurity among the Maltese people: the historical and social novels reproduce most of the anxiety and fear that result from a nation's political fate, and the socio-psychological novel renders an aura of uncertainty and worry which are part of human nature. Even on a small island like Malta the novel does not prosper only in a stable and harmonious society: insecurity is often thematically productive. However, most modern novelists view life sharply and critically but they do not want to distort or caricature it. Their work is more of a comment and when they view the past of Maltese society (as some of the novels written in the 1980s did) their aim is mainly to lay judgement by their point of view or attitude.

Even children's fiction flourished especially through the indefatigable efforts of Trevor Zahra. Other juvenile writers include: Charles Casha (1943-), Carmel G. Cauchi (1944-), Charles Briffa (1951-), Ġorġ Mallia (1957-), Mary Puli (1930-), George Peresso (1939-), and Joe Żammit Ciantar.[32]

Into the Twenty-First Century

Maltese literature after the 1990s still carried the imprint of the Academy and the Movement intermingled with a measure of updating as it scanned the times for current trends. By the end of the twentieth century Maltese literature took an unpredictable course, depending not on any corporate intellectual and/or artistic effort but on individual genius. Thus, Maltese literature in the beginning of the twenty-first century must content itself with a moderate amount of scattered talents. Each genre tends to stress something. The poetry of the last decades reveals an important fact: the Maltese poet is utterly aware that he is a full-time member of the global community. He has to be sensitive to the events and moods experienced outside his shores but at the same time he has to confirm his Mediterranean identity. The environment and the self are, therefore, still very relevant as the twenty-first century sees Malta as a full member of the European Union. The novelist, on his part, becomes very sensitive too and finds himself in solidarity against a structure of social injustice. At the end of the century theatregoers still seek entertainment, but they have come to appreciate the lasting work of thoughtful, serious writers. Furthermore, it must be noted that it was in the beginning of the twenty-first century that the Maltese Academy recognised officially children's literature as a distinct genre. On the whole, Maltese literature since the 1990s shows a tiny nation trying to cope with European standards to remain literary significant. The giants are few but there are lesser beings walking in their shadow and having much to offer. And all of them try to show that literature is a lively art that may contribute to man's satisfaction of his curiosity and his own fascination towards life: a lively literature as developed by a tiny nation in a globalised world.

Notes

1   See J. M. Brincat, *Il-Malti: Elf Sena ta' Storja* (Malta, 2000).

2   See H. C. Vella, *Malta u Ghawdex fl-Era Klassika* (Malta, 2002).

3   As early as the middle of the ninth century the Bishop of Cordova was complaining that 'all young Christians' were acquainting themselves 'only with the language and writings of the Arabs', and many were 'capable of expressing themselves exquisitely in Arabic and of composing poems': R. A. Nicholson, *A Literary History of the Arabs* (Cambridge, 1907, reprinted 1976), 414-15.

4   J. Cassar Pullicino, *Il-Kitba bil-Malti sa l-1870* (Malta, 2001), 5-7.

5   O. Friġġieri, *L-Istudji Kritici Miġbura* (Malta, 1995), 1-2.

6   C. Briffa, *Il-Bilingwiżmu f'Malta* (Malta, 1994), Section B, 6-25.

7   Friġġieri actually calls these not 'systems' but 'traditions'. I prefer 'systems' because both modes have their own particular structure.

8   Friġġieri, *L-Istudji Kritici*, 4.

9   Ibid., 5-6.

10   Ibid., 11; T. Bonnici, 'Galician-Portuguese Traits in Caxaro's *Cantilena*' in O. Friggieri (ed.), *Journal of Maltese Studies*, 19-20 (1989-90), 46-51. A detailed stylistic analysis of the poem is found in C. Briffa, 'Investigazzjoni Stilistika tal-*Kantilena*', in Cassar Pullicino, 183-206.

11   Bonnici, 47.

12   G. Wettinger, and M. Fsadni, *Peter Caxaro's 'Cantilena': A Poem in Medieval Maltese* (Malta, 1968), 39.

13   E. F. Jacob (ed.), *Italian Renaissance Studies* (London, 1960), 414-15.

14   Cassar Pullicino, 21

15   Ibid., 59-64.

16   Ibid., 65.

17   Ibid. For a full exposition of the development of Maltese prose the reader is referred to C. Briffa, *Rhythmic Patterns in Maltese Literature* (Malta, 2001).

18   The following list is taken from Cassar Pullicino, 87; and O. Friġġieri, 'In Search of a National Identity', in K. Hopkins, and R. van Roekel (eds), *Crosswinds* (Scotland, 1980), iv-v.

19   Ibid., 7.

20   Ibid., 10-11.

21   Cassar Pullicino, ch. 16.

22   Friġġieri, *L-Istudji Kritici*, 29. An excellent exposition on Ġananton Vassallo and these other poets is to be found in O. Friġġieri, *Storja tal-Letteratura Maltija* (Malta, 1979), ch. 4.

23   O. Friġġieri, 'In Search of a National Identity: A Survey of Maltese Literature', in Hopkins and van Roekel, (eds), iv.

24   Ġananton Vassallo was a professor of Italian at the University of Malta; Annibale Preca was a state school teacher; and Napuljun Tagliaferro was a University rector.

25   Known today as the *Akkademja tal-Malti*.

26   Known in Maltese as *Moviment Qawmien Letterarju*.

27   See O. Friġġieri, *L-Istorja tal-Poeżija Maltija* (Malta, 2001).

28   See M. Azzopardi, *It-Teatru f'Malta* (Malta, 2003).

29   See C. Briffa, *Ir-Rumanz Malti sa Nofs is-Seklu Għoxrin* (Malta, 2003).

30   See C. Briffa, *Id-Dinja ta' Ineż Farruġ* (Malta, 2001).

31   See C. Briffa, *In-Novella Maltija* (Malta, 1999).

32   See T. Zahra, C. Briffa, and G. Mallia, *Il-Kotba għat-Tfal* (Malta, 2003).

PART FIVE

HISTORICAL ASPECTS

Joseph Bezzina

THE CHURCH IN MALTA:
AN INDELIBLE IMPRINT UPON THE NATION'S HISTORY AND CHARACTER

'Once we had come safely through, we discovered that the island was called Malta. The inhabitants treated us with unusual kindness. They made us all welcome'. So runs a memoir in the first two lines of chapter twenty eight of the Acts of the Apostles, one of the books of the Bible. It records the first encounter of the islanders with the apostle of the Gentiles Paul, the beginning of the relationship of the Maltese with Christianity, that religious movement destined to mould European culture for the next two millennia.

The Early Christians (60-455)

The shipwreck of Saint Paul on the mid-Mediterranean island of Malta around November of the year 59 has been questioned for half a millennium. However, it cannot be questioned seriously any longer. The unknown writer of the apocryphal Greek *Acts of Peter and Paul*, dated to the early sixth century, had no doubt. He began his acts with Paul's journey from the island of *Gaudomelete*, the Roman-Byzantine name for Gozo-Malta, to Rome.

During his over three month-long stay in Malta, Saint Paul definitely worked a number of miracles. The Acts do not refer to the Apostle's teaching, but this can be induced fairly easily from the whole narrative. Paul had been confided with the mission to preach salvation to the Gentiles. Indeed, the Acts were redacted to record that mission. The whole context of the narrative presupposes and postulates that Paul did preach to the Maltese.

The islanders were no foreigners to the gods. Since prehistoric times (c.5000–725BC), a number of impressive megalithic temples dotted the Maltese islands.

The Ġgantija Temples in Gozo and the Tarxien complex in Malta, both of world-wide fame, demonstrate without any doubt the deep religiosity of the inhabitants.

During Punic times (725–218 BC), other places of worship were raised to honour the Phoenician and Carthaginian gods. With the advent of the Romans in 218 BC, at the beginning of the second Punic war, several of the Punic temples were re-dedicated to Roman deities, a fact proved by both literary and archaeological sources.

The arrival of Paul was marked by a mishap. Paul collected a bundle of sticks to put them on the fire when a viper attached itself to his hand. The natives first thought that he must have been a murderer for divine nature would not let him live; when he came to no harm they changed their minds and began to say he was a god. This episode leaves no doubt about the deep religiosity of the Maltese during Roman times.

So it is no wonder that when the islanders were confronted with new more credible solutions about the eternal problem of humankind – its origin and destiny – they embraced the new faith. Indeed many of the miracles were probably worked to confirm this faith. The account of the departure of Paul from Malta and the generosity proffered to him and to his fellow travellers on the occasion, is highly indicative that such a community had been duly established. This is also the conclusion reached by Saint John Chrysostom (c.354–407), the great Christian writer of Constantinople, who in his commentary on the shipwreck episode affirms that the comportment of the islanders before the Apostle left for Rome testifies to the fact that many of them had by then accepted the Gospel of Christ.

There is no further documentation of an early Christian community in Malta. However, as elsewhere, palaeochristian archaeology provides a considerable amount of information on the early Christians. And in the palaeochristian world, Malta and Gozo are very highly ranked.

Malta's earliest underground places of burial belong to the third century and later. Their simultaneous appearance in both Malta and Gozo suggests that the christianisation of the islands took place at roughly the same time. These hypogea are usually referred to as funerary *triclinia*, an underground dining-room where the *agape*, a communal dinner, was held. They are so called as they are endowed with a *triclinium*, a dining table of four sides, three of which were provided with low couches.

In several instances, in the vicinity of the table there is a niche that probably used to serve as an altar-table for the celebration of the Eucharist. In the early centuries, the *agape* and the *eucharistia*, the shared dinner and the breaking of the Eucharistic bread, were two basic rituals of liturgical meetings. When the former fell in disuse during the fourth century, the *triclinia* began to disappear from underground burial sites. The niche, an original local altar-mensa, continued to survive until the arrival of a new altar pattern that may have brought with it liturgical modifications originating from Eastern Christianity.

The Byzantine Connection (455–870)

Malta and Gozo remained under Roman rule until the middle of the fifth century. By the year 455, and perhaps even some time before, the islands passed under the Vandals, a Germanic tribe. It is presumed that the islands remained in Vandal hands until 476, when they passed within the sphere of influence of Odoacer of the Sciri, who founded the first Germanic kingdom in Italy. When in 493 Odoacer was defeated by king Theodoric of the Ostrogoths, still another Germanic tribe, Malta and Gozo must have passed under the Ostrogoths and remained in their hands until 535. These Germanic or *barbarian* tribes, judging from archaeological evidence, caused no obvious break in the social or religious life of the Maltese.

Around 535 Malta and Gozo passed, with nearby Sicily, under the Byzantine sphere of influence. Emperor Justinian I (527–565) carried out extensive reforms in both the civil and the religious field. From 545 onwards, so as to strengthen Christianity and to unify the Empire through its official religion, he re-organised the metropolitan structure and founded many bishoprics to extend his reforms to the four corners of the Empire. Possibly it was around this time that he established a bishopric in Malta.

It cannot be a mere coincidence that the first reference to a bishop of Malta is of the year 553. That year a certain *Iulianus episcopus Melitensis*, Julian, bishop of Malta, was at Constantinople, where he signed the *Constitutum de tribus Capitulis* of Pope Vigilius anathematising Monophysitism.

A clearer unequivocal reference to two other bishops of Byzantine Malta is known from the registers of Pope Gregory I: Lucillus in 592 and 598, and Traianus, a Benedictine monk from Syracuse, in late 599. In the last mention, the pope proposes that four or five monks from the Syracuse monastery of which Traianus had been the head should be allowed to accompany him. It is unknown whether this eventually happened and whether monasticism became rooted in Malta at that time. Yet due to the close bonds between Malta and Sicily in the ecclesiastical sphere, it is not far fetched to imagine that monasticism was also established in Malta when closer bonds were forged between the Syracusian and Maltese Sees.

At the beginning of Byzantine rule, Maltese Christians probably worshipped in a *domus ecclesiae*, a house converted into a place of worship. They probably also prayed in their hypogea, where most ornamental features are iconographically and stylistically datable to the fourth, fifth, and sixth century. However it is not impossible that they even had a church or two. At tas-Silġ, Marsaxlokk, there are the remains of what was possibly a palaeochristian basilica. The scanty remains of a church outside tad-Dejr at Rabat, Malta, are also indicative of an early medieval church built on a basilica plan.

The bishopric of Malta, as referred to, was probably founded as a result of the politico-religious reforms of Emperor Justinian in 545. However, from the papal letters referring to the bishops of Malta, it seems that the Church of Malta, as that

St Paul's Grotto in Rabat: crucial for the development of the cult of St Paul in Malta (Photo: MTA)

The medieval chapel of Ħal Millieri: evidence of the consolidation of Christianity in the late middle ages (Photo: Heritage Collection)

of nearby Sicily, was within the sphere of influence of the Patriarchate of Rome rather than that of Constantinople.

The situation changed around 756 when Sicily and Calabria were transferred from the Patriarchate of Rome to that of Constantinople. At the same time or shortly afterwards, Syracuse was elevated to metropolitan status with Malta as one of its suffragan Sees. It is first referred to as such in a document prior to 780.

The Church of *Gaudomelete* continued to participate more and more fully in the religious milieu of Sicily and the central Mediterranean until the last quarter of the ninth century.

The Fate under the Arabs (870–1127)

It was the time when the Muslims, after having conquered most of the North African coast, turned their attention to the countries on the other side of the Mediterranean littoral and the islands in between. Malta and Gozo passed definitely under the Aghlabid Arabs in August 870.

The scantily documented period leaves a lot of guesswork on the continuity or otherwise of Christian life and worship under the Muslims. It is known that in 878 an unnamed bishop of Malta was in prison in Palermo, possibly because his faithful had broken their *(gh)ahd* or treaty of submission to the Muslims by helping a Byzantine relief force that attempted a reconquest. He was still in chains five years later. On 3 April 883, Pope Marinus I implored the great Emir of Sicily to release the bishop of Malta together with the archbishop of Syracuse and other men, among whom there might have been Maltese Christians, whom the Muslims had captured and enslaved in Palermo.

This episode attests to a definite disruption in Christian worship. This is further corroborated by archaeological discoveries at tas-Silġ and the San Pawl Milqi area that point to signs of destruction at levels corresponding to the arrival of the Muslims. The level of persecution for religious or merely political reasons cannot be determined with precision. It is neither possible to fathom its adverse effects on the practice of religion. It is possible that, with the Aghlabid invasion, Maltese Christians followed on the footsteps of their Sicilian counterparts and fled before or soon after the Muslim invasion to safer places on the mainland.

The problem is further complicated by the fact that research on the period seems to indicate that the Aghlabids did not actually colonise the island. There is hardly any documentary or archaeological proof of their active presence up to the middle of the eleventh century. A complete break between the Byzantine and the Arab period is especially evident in the post-Byzantine language of Malta that is wanting of elements from previous times.

After an unknown number of years, a group of Saracens, that is Arab-speaking Muslims, came over from Sicily and recolonised the island and they were definitely in possession of the archipelago by 1048–49. In 1054, they repelled a Byzantine attack. A census of the population prior to the attack of 1054 refers only to Muslims and *ghabîd,* slaves. There is no reference to *dhimmi* or people of the Book, Christians. These *ghabîd* reaped a reward for supporting the Muslims during the attack; the Muslims raised them to the status of *ahrar,* freemen, and gave them their daughters in marriage. The origins of the post-Byzantine Maltese race lays with this group; and it must have been this group of Arab-speaking Muslims that laid the base of what is now the Maltese language.

The survival of Christianity during this whole period is tied to the physical fate of the inhabitants that might have remained after the 870 invasion and their resistance or assimilation to the culture, language, and religion to their conquerors. There is no literary or archaeological proof of the practice of Christianity during these more than two and half centuries of Muslim predominance. However there is neither definite proof that the Islamisation of the archipelago stamped out every form of Christian belief.

Revival under the European Catholic Powers (1127–1530)

In July 1091 Count Roger the Norman attacked Malta and devastated Gozo but the inhabitants soon agreed on the terms of peace. The Muslim rulers were left in control but had to recognise him as their sovereign and surrender all Christian captives, who eventually left with Roger. There is no mention of Christian natives in the narrative.

The Normans reconquered the islands in July 1127 and this time they came to stay. Through marriage and maneuver, in 1194 they were succeeded by the Swabians, who were in turn ousted from power by the Angevins in 1266. These were in turn replaced by the Aragonese between 1282–83.

Under the Normans Malta and Gozo were part and parcel of the royal demesne. Around the end of the Norman rule, the archipelago began to be granted to a feudal lord and this alienation from the royal *demanium* to non-Maltese counts was to continue for most of the next two hundred years. On 7 October 1350, at the inhabitants' request, Malta and Gozo were returned to the royal *demanium* by King Ludovico of Sicily. However, between 1357 and 1397, except for short intervals, the archipelago was once again in the hands of feudal lords. On 16 November 1397 King Martin the Elder re-incorporated Malta and Gozo into the *demanium* in perpetuity. From 1397 to 1530 Malta was not granted out as a county, though it was alienated in other ways.

Slowly but surely, these Catholic powers brought about the re-christianisation of Malta and Gozo. The Normans must have left an administrator with a garrison and some members of the clergy to cater for their spiritual needs. The diocese of Malta in the post-Arabic era is recorded for the first time in 1143, when it was suffragan to Syracuse. It was not destined to remain so for long, for on 10 July 1156, Adrian IV, the only British Pope, declared Malta, with Girgenti and Mazara, suffragan to the metropolitan See of Palermo. John, the first known bishop of Norman times, is first recorded active in Sicily in February 1168. It is unknown whether he ever came to Malta.

Very little is known about the actual process of Christianisation. As in nearby Sicily, two rites were probably introduced in Malta: the Latin rite, promoted by the Normans and encouraged by the popes; and the Greek rite. The former must have been reserved to the Norman administration, while the latter, probably in the hands of monks, served mainly other Christian immigrants. When proselytism gained the first converts from the indigenous Muslims, they must have preferred, as in Sicily, the Greek to the Latin rite.

The process of re-christianisation was definitely slow. In 1133, a Greek-Sicilian referred to the inhabitants as *Agarenes*, descendants of Hagar, faithless, in other words Muslims. In 1175, a chronicle by Buchard, bishop of Strasbourg, refers to them as *Sarraceni*, a term referring to Muslim Arab speakers. A census of 1241 shows that there was still a considerable number of Muslim families in Malta and Gozo. In 1249 Muslims were expelled from Malta and Sicily by Emperor Frederick II. Many probably accepted a formal baptism to escape exile. Thus by the middle of the thirteenth century, Christianity formally became the religion of the whole population again.

The first churches were probably raised between the end of the twelfth and the beginning of the thirteenth century. A crude apsed church was possibly built at tas-Silġ on the ruins of the former church and some time later another one might have been raised at San Pawl Milqi. By the middle of the thirteenth century, there must have been a cathedral in *Mdina* and a church in the *Castrum* of Gozo, on the sites where the present cathedral churches stand. By 1274 there was another church at *Castellum maris*, the third fortified town of the archipelago, and by 1296 still another on the island of Comino. Some natural caves, especially in the Rabat area in Malta, were also adapted as chapels, but they are difficult to date. The Byzantine style paintings in some of them suggest a prolonged predominance of the Greek rites.

The appointments to the bishopric of Malta became more and more steady, though it was only after 1400 that their presence is attested on the island. By about 1270 there was an organised Roman diocese, with a chapter that included an archdeacon and a cantor, functioning as a suffragan of Palermo. By 1299 the Cathedral of Mdina was dedicated to Saint Paul. In 1299 too, a church within the Gozo *Castello* was functioning as a parish church. By 1436 the Mdina Cathedral had a chapter of sixteen canons and at least thirteen priests. There were besides 144 benefices in the islands, many of which were endowments for the celebration of mass. Otherwise, little is known on the number, the quality, and the organisation of the clergy at the time. In 1436 there were also twelve *cappelle* or parishes in Malta, including one at Rabat and another at Birgu. In 1435 the *Ecclesia matrice* within the Gozo *Castello* had a *cappellano* and other priests, and by 1450 there were three other parishes in Rabat, Gozo.

The Conventual Church of the Order of St John became a symbol of flowering ecclesiastical art in early modern Malta (Photo: MTA)

The number of places of worship multiplied by the passage of years. A survey of 1575 but reflecting to a great extent the pre-1530 situation lists about 380 churches, chapels and shrines in Malta and fifty in Gozo – a very large number considering that the population was around 20,000. Their quality was inevitably uneven but the embellishments in quite a number reveal the dedication that the inhabitants showed to their church.

The religious orders, somewhat inexplicably, did not come to Malta until much later. The first recorded are the Augustinians around 1370, followed by the Tertiary Regular Franciscans in 1372, the Carmelites around 1441, the Dominicans around 1450, the Franciscan Conventuals in 1494; and the Franciscan Observants around 1500. By 1443 there were also Benedictine nuns in Mdina. The friars with a greater possibility to study abroad were instrumental in raising the level of instruction among the Maltese.

The vitality of the Maltese church at the time is best perceived from the repeated claims made by the *Universitas,* the local municipal council, to the Aragonese authorities to provide the people with ministers of the Word and of the Eucharist who can dialogue with the people in their language, that is ministers who can speak Maltese. Despite the difficult times that priests and people must have gone through under these foreign powers, the social and ecclesiastical life of the island manifests a lot of vitality.

The Church under the Knights of Saint John (1530–1798)

On 23 March 1530 Malta and Gozo were handed over to the Sovereign, Military, and Hospitaller Order of the Knights of Saint John of Jerusalem by the mightiest monarch of the age, the Holy Roman Emperor, Charles V.

The Knights found that the people were very devoted to their religion, that it was practised in the whole island both privately and publicly, and that they cherished a special devotion to Saint Paul to whom the island was consecrated. The Cathedral church, also dedicated to Paul, had grown to a temple of considerable proportions and the bishop's residence was attached to it. The inhabitants were also great devotees of the Blessed Virgin Mary. A large number of churches, including the *Matrice* of Gozo and the church on Comino, were dedicated to her.

Initially the Knights brought no significant changes to the civil and religious life. It was only after the end of the Great Siege of 1565 – when the Knights with the help of the Maltese overcame a mightier Turkish attacking force – that new times dawned for Malta. These were ushered in by the building of the new city of Valletta, initiated the year after the siege. Three years earlier, in 1563, the great Council of Trent had come to a successful conclusion and the reform it decreed in ecclesiastical affairs coincided with the islands' renaissance.

The revival in the ecclesiastical field was the result of several factors. With the arrival of the Knights and a stepped-up security against the marauding Turks, the bishops of Malta became residents on the island also in line with the legislation of Trent. As a result, pastoral visitations became more and more regular. The first recorded took place in 1528, and in 1545 Bishop Domenico Cubelles carried out the first visit since the arrival of the Knights. Of major significance is the apostolic visitation of 1575 conducted by Pietro Dusina, sent for that purpose by Pope Gregory XIII. Its detailed report marked the beginning of the execution of Trent's decrees in Malta and served as a model for all future visits. Another important Tridentine decree prescribed bishops to hold diocesan synods regularly. Bishop Martin Rojas convoked the first synod in April 1575. The residence of bishops, the regular pastoral visitations, and the periodical synods were instrumental in upgrading the quality and organisation of both the clergy as well of the places of worship themselves.

Before 1530, there were twelve parishes in Malta and four in Gozo, though two in Malta and another two in Gozo lost all parishioners. An enactment by Trent to erect parishes in inhabited centres was immediately applied in Malta with the erection of the parish of Our Lady of Porto Salvo in the new city Valletta on 2 July 1571. With the steady rise in population and an increase in the number of settlements, many more parishes were erected. The need was less felt in Gozo, where the people lived mainly in the Citadel and in its suburb, Rabat. The first parish outside Rabat was erected in Xewkija on 27 November 1678. With the establishment of parishes throughout Malta and Gozo, the faithful were better cared after and religious life made significant steps forward.

It is clear from the apostolic visitation of 1575 that the majority of churches and chapels on the island left much to be desired. In the meantime, the Knights brought over from Europe the wealth and the know-how to revolutionise local church building. The indigenous plain rectangular churches were soon enlarged and rebuilt with a mixture of imported alien styles. The extravagant baroque became dominant in both towns and countryside. Local and foreign artists and sculptors were engaged to perfect the job. St John in Valletta, the Conventual Church of the Order of Saint John – dedicated on 20 February 1578 – is perhaps the best example of the flowering ecclesiastical art and architecture from the end of the sixteenth century onwards. In Gozo, the Matrice Church within the Citadel – dedicated on 11 October 1716 – set the pattern for all churches on that island.

The quality of the clergy and their organisation was also tackled by the bishops. In the reports of the first visits and synods, bishops harp time and again on the necessity of a more learned clergy. Attempts to open a seminary began as early as 1575. Philosophical and theological instruction to candidates for the priesthood was first imparted at the Jesuit College in Valletta, founded in 1592. Due to this partial solution, the opening of a seminary was postponed decade after decade, and it was through the toil of Bishop Davide Cocco-Palmeri that it was finally inaugurated in 1703. The two institutions did a lot to upgrade the erudition of the clergy. As a result, the choice of pastors became more and more exacting and only the best succeeded to the post.

More religious orders had by then settled in Malta: the Franciscan Capuchins in 1588; the Jesuits in 1592; the Discalced Carmelites in 1625; and the Oratorians of St Philip Neri in 1652. There were also new foundations of nuns: the Order of Jerusalem in 1583, the Franciscan *Ripentiti* in 1594, the Augustinians in 1611, and the Discalced Carmelites in 1731. They all played a significant role in the Maltese Church.

Pastoral life in Malta and Gozo also made big strides forward. Parish priests and their assistants imparted religious instruction on a regular basis to both children and grown-ups. The administration of sacraments was better prepared. The establishment of confraternities in all parish churches led to a greater participation of lay persons in the pastoral life of the church. The mainly agricultural community of Malta and Gozo usually worked hand in hand with their priests – a collaboration attested to this day in the monumental churches and in their embellishments in all the towns and villages across the islands.

Through the offerings of the faithful, the Church succeeded to carry out a considerable amount of charitable and assistential work. The church-run Santo Spirito Hospital in Rabat, Malta, the Saint Julian Hospital in Rabat, Gozo, and other charitable foundations did a lot to alleviate the suffering of the sick, the aged, and the poor. The Church promoted the foundation of marriage legacies to provide a dowry to poor women making it possible for them to marry. Poor and orphan children were cared after in special homes.

These achievements in no way mean that the ecclesiastical establishment was plain sailing all the time. During this period Malta and Gozo were practically under a tripartite authority: the Grandmaster, the sovereign and hence head of the military and the civil establishment but head also of a religious Order; the Inquisitor General and Apostolic Delegate, responsible for the protection of faith and the official representative of the Holy See; and the Bishop. The three had their sphere of jurisdiction and their courts. Many times their authority overlapped and this inevitably led to friction. During such times the pastoral and spiritual life of the island suffered and sometimes it took years before life could return back to normal.

Nonetheless, under the Knights of Saint John and not without their help, the Church succeeded in organising herself in all spheres and permeated the life of all the Maltese.

The Turbulence under the French (1798–1800)

On 10 June 1798 Napoleon Bonaparte, on his way to conquer Egypt, invaded Malta and Gozo and brought the Knights' rule to an abrupt end. He promised to respect the religion of the people; yet few, if any, ever succeeded to disturb so many and so much in such a short time.

Bonaparte launched a reform in both the civil and the religious sphere during his six day-long stay on the island. The French rule was however destined to be short-lived. Fed up of their despotism, the Maltese rose against them. The insurrection exploded on 2 September 1798 and was sparkled off by the intended sale by auction of the gold and silver articles, the tapestries, and other sacred objects in some of the convents of Rabat and Mdina.

The French retreated behind the Valletta fortifications where, with British help, they were blockaded and isolated from the rest of the world. Two priests played a leading role in this blockade, Francesco Saverio Caruana in Malta and Saverio Cassar in Gozo. Indeed people sought the clergy not only for spiritual help, but also for political leadership. The blockade was lifted on 5 September 1800, when Malta and Gozo passed under British protection.

The Church in an Island Colony (1800–1964)

The British took Malta under circumstances bearing no analogy in the history of the empire. They likewise discovered that few, if any, of their colonies had a strategic value in the expansion of the empire as this mid-Mediterranean island. It was thus of the utmost importance for them to maintain a good feeling among the inhabitants and this necessarily meant gentleness and benevolence towards their religion and Church.

In one of their first proclamations, the British promised the people of Malta

The three Maltese beatified by Pope John Paul II in 2001: Nazju Falzon, Dun Ġorġ Preca and Adeodata Pisani

that their religion would be confirmed, maintained, and respected. This promise was, more or less, enshrined in the twelve constitutions granted to Malta between 1813 and 1964. With the grant of self-government in 1921, these relations entered a new phase: the colonial powers retreated in the background and the front position was taken by the political parties and the Legislative Assembly or parliament of Malta.

Church-State relations were not free of all discord. Disputes ranged from the right of presentation to the Malta Bishopric, to the presence and role of priests in the Council of Government and the Legislative Assembly, to the integration of Malta with Britain, and to a host of other questions. Relations did become strained at times, but commonsense and the common good of the body politic led to the restoration of healthy relations.

The first important change in the local Church took place on 18 September 1807, when Ferdinando Mattei became the first Maltese to be elected Bishop of Malta. Since then all bishops have been Maltese. On 20 June 1831 the pope conceded a British request to separate Malta from the Metropolitan See of Palermo – under which it had been placed by Pope Adrian IV. On 16 September 1864 Pope Pius IX separated the islands of Gozo and Comino from Malta and established them a separate diocese. On 1 January 1944 Malta was raised to metropolitan status with Gozo as its suffragan see.

During the British period the population of Malta, after an initial drop, began increasing steadily and this necessarily led to a rapid expansion in all church activities. During the nineteenth century thirteen new parishes were established, nine in Malta and four in Gozo, and between 1901 and 1964, ten more were established in Malta and three in Gozo. Churches were enlarged to accommodate the increasing number of parishioners and many new ones were built.

The secular and regular clergy increased in both quality and numbers. In this field the seminary proceeded to give a major contribution. A second seminary was opened in Gozo on 4 November 1866. More male and female religious Orders settled in Malta: the Benedictines in 1883, but only for two years; the De La Salle Brothers in 1903; the Salesians of Don Bosco in 1903; and the Missionary Society of Saint Paul was founded in Malta in 1910. Twenty-one female congregations commenced their activity in Malta between 1800 and 1964. Of these two were founded in Gozo and three in Malta: the Franciscans of the Heart of Jesus in 1880; the Ursulines of Saint Angela Merici in 1887; the Dominicans of Saint Catherine of Siena in 1889; the Daughters of the Sacred Heart in 1903; and the Missionaries of Jesus of Nazareth in 1913.

In March 1907, Blessed Ġorġ Preca founded the Society of Christian Doctrine, known as 'Museum' from the acronym of its motto – a society of lay consecrated men and women to train themselves as catechists so as to impart catechism to others.

Englishmen, observed a British resident, were apt to point critically at the number of priests, monks, and nuns to be seen in the street. Few of them understood that these people were the doctors, lawyers, nurses, welfare workers, teachers, and civil servants and the like, who operated a welfare state based upon voluntary offerings and dedicated service.

The slowly-recovering economy had in fact also led to a great expansion of the Church's activity in the educational, charitable, and social fields. For the good of the whole community, the Church had opened many kindergarten, primary, secondary, and trade schools; increased the number of homes for poor and abandoned orphans; and ran two modern well-equipped hospitals. The help and support extended by the Church, its establishments, and their personnel during the Second World War was of no mean value for the Allies' victory.

The British at the very beginning had promised respect to Malta's religion and they kept their word. During the 164 years of British rule, the ecclesiastical establishment developed by leaps and bounds. Secularism had also crept in and the number of Maltese Catholics that were not practising had grown. However, it cannot be denied that the Christianity forms an integral part of the national identity of Malta.

The Church after Independence (1964–2004)

On 21 September 1964 Malta and Gozo became an independent, sovereign state within the Commonwealth and were declared a Republic on 13 December 1974. On 8 December 1965 the second Vatican Council, with a clearly set programme of *aggiornamento* came to an end. Independent Malta and the Vatican established full diplomatic relations on 15 December 1965. The Church in Malta entered a new era.

In the post-war years Malta witnessed a demographic explosion and a slow economic revival. These changes gained momentum after independence and caused a social upheaval in all sectors of Maltese life. Slowly but surely, the Church embarked on the mammoth task to bring the local ecclesiastical structures in line with the teachings of the Vatican Council and the demands of modern society.

A host of new pastoral structures were set up to shoulder the task. Resistance from centuries-old institutions was not lacking, but the Church was determined to achieve its goal. Nineteen more parishes were established in Malta after 1964. There is a total of some 320 churches and chapels in Malta, fifty in Gozo, and one on Comino – a visible sign of the presence of Jesus Christ among the Maltese.

The vital spiritual energy of a particular church is especially manifest in the missionary spirit pulsating through its members. The Church of Malta and Gozo, notwithstanding its minute proportions, is proud to be in the forefront in the evangelisation of the world-wide church. Priests and religious, male and female, have since time immemorial sailed from these shores to announce Christ's message of love and repentance to the four corners of the world. These have lately been joined by a significant legion of lay people.

Malta's missionary movement can be traced back hundreds of years but it increased substantially at the beginning of the nineteenth century with the growing number of Maltese who sought work in the major ports of the Mediterranean littoral. When emigration crossed the Atlantic and Pacific oceans towards the Americas and Australia, missionary activity quickly followed suit. Maltese missionaries also laboured in other countries around the globe where the message of Christ had not yet penetrated. From Abyssinia to Zambia in Africa, from India to Taiwan in Asia, and from Brazil to Chile in South America, Maltese born missionaries converted thousands to the fold of Christ. The Maltese at home were not unconscious of the sterling work carried out by fellow brethren for Christ, and they backed them through prayers and offerings. The essential commitment of evangelisation given by Christ to his followers has been taken seriously by many.

> For almost two thousand years, since the very dawn of the Christian era, the gospel
> of Jesus Christ has been preached and has taken root among the Maltese people ...
> the arrival of the Apostle of the Gentiles was to prove of decisive importance for the
> entire future of Malta and its people. Through Paul's preaching, the Christian faith
> was first implanted. In the centuries that followed, the faith was to leave an indelible
> imprint upon your Nation's history and character.

This is how Pope John Paul II summarised the history of the Church in Malta in an address to Ċensu Tabone, President of Republic, during his state visit to the Vatican on 18 December 1989. Pope John-Paul proceeded how:

> today too, 'the Catholic faith that comes from the Apostles' continues to inspire and
> foster in Malta's people a commitment to those spiritual and moral values which are
> indispensable for the authentic well-being and growth of the Nation.

Twenty-five and a half years after independence, the island evangelised by Paul was honoured with a visit by the successor of Peter. Between 25 and 27 May 1990, Pope John Paul II became the first pontiff to set foot on Malta. He returned for the beatification of the first three Maltese on 8 and 9 May 2001. He came, as he himself affirmed, so as 'to confirm (the Maltese) in faith and love' and to invite the Church in Malta and the Maltese to translate that faith 'in building a society worthy of Malta's distinguished tradition of Christian faith and virtue!'

The post-Vatican Maltese Church is still in the making, and it is hoped that in the future, as in the past, it will continue to raise to the challenges being offered to her within the European Union. One challenge has been clearly pointed out by Pope John-Paul during his concluding speech to the Maltese on 27 May 1990:

> More than once in her history, Malta has been admired and praised for her uncompromising defence of the Christian faith and her willingness to endure heroic sacrifices for the sake of the culture which that faith nourished and sustained. In our own days, as Europe prepares to enter a new period of its history, a period filled with fresh hopes and challenges, Malta is called to contribute to the spiritual unity of the Old Continent by offering her treasures of Christian faith and value. Europe needs Malta's faithful witness too!

References

Abela, G. F., *Della descrittione di Malta, isola nel mare siciliano con le sue antichità et altre notizie* (Malta, 1647).

Acta Iuratorum et Consilii Civitatis et insulae Maltae, ed. G. Wettinger (Palermo, 1993).

Agius de Soldanis, G. P. F., *Il Gozo Antico-Moderno e Sacro-Profano*, 1746: National Archives (Gozo), *Miscellanea*, 1, 453-950.

Balbi da Correggio, F., 'Una verdadera relación de todo lo que el anno de mdlxv ha succedidio en la isla de Malta' (Barcelona, 1566); Engl. trans. *The Siege of Malta* (Copenhagen, 1961).

Bezzina, J., 'Church and State in an Island Colony (1800-1964)', in V. Mallia Milanes (ed.), *The British Colonial Experience 1800-1964: The Impact on Maltese Society* (Malta, 1988), 47-78.

Bezzina, J., *Church history, including an account of the Church in Malta* (Gozo, 1994).

Bezzina, J., *Is-Sinodi Djoċesani f'Malta u Ghawdex (1558-1975)* (Malta, 1979).

Bezzina, J., *L-Istorja tal-Knisja f'Malta* (Malta, 2002).

Bezzina, J., *Religion and Politics in a Crown Colony. The Gozo-Malta story (1798-1864)*, (Malta,1985).

Bezzina, J., *The Veneration of Our Lady in Gozo (1600–1800)* in V. Borg (ed.), *Marian Devotions in the Islands of St Paul, 1600–1800* (Malta, 1983), 215-48.

Bonnici, A., 'Maltese society under the Hospitallers in the light of Inquisition documents', in V. Mallia Milanes (ed.), *Hospitaller Malta* (Malta, 1993), 311-49.

Bonnici, A., *Medieval and Roman Inquisition in Malta* (Malta, 1998).

Bonnici, A., *History of the Church in Malta*, I-III (Malta, 1967-75).

Borg, A. J., *The reform of the Council of Trent in Malta and Gozo* (Malta, 1975).

Borg, V., 'Malta and its Palaeochristian heritage', in *Malta, studies of its heritage and history* (Malta, 1986), 47–86.

Bosio, G., *Dell'Istoria della Sacra Religione et Illustrissima Militia di San Giovanni Gierosolimitano*, I-III (Rome 1594-1602).

Brincat, J. M., *Malta 870–1054. Al-Himyarî's account and its linguistic implications* (Malta, 1995).

Brown, T. S., 'Byzantine Malta: a discussion of sources', in A.T. Luttrell (ed.), *Medieval Malta. Studies on Malta before the Knights* (London, 1975), 71-87.

Buhagiar, M., *Late Roman and Byzantine catacombs and related burial places in the Maltese Islands* (Oxford, 1986).

Buhagiar, M., 'Medieval Churches in Malta', in A.T. Luttrell (ed.), *Medieval Malta* (London, 1975), 163-80.

Buhagiar, M., *The iconography of the Maltese Islands (1400-1900)*, (Malta, 1988).

Buhagiar, M., 'The Maltese Palaeochristian Hypogea - a reassessment of the archaeological, iconographic, and epigraphic source material', in S. Fiorini and R. Ellul Micallef (eds), *Collegium Melitense Quaterncentenary Celebrations (1592–1992). Collected Papers* (Malta, 1992), 133-202.

Cagiano de Azevedo, M., 'La villa detta di Publio', in *Missione Archeologica Italiana a Malta. Rapporto preliminare della campagna 1963* (Rome, 1964), 139-42.

Cagiano de Azevedo, M., 'Medieval buildings excavated at Tas-Silg and San Pawl Milqi in Malta', in A.T. Luttrell (ed.), *Medieval Malta*, 88-95.

Cassar, C., 'Popular perceptions and values in Hospitaller Malta', in V. Mallia Milanes (ed.), *Hospitaller Malta* (Malta, 1993), 311–49.

Ciantar, G., *Malta Illustrata ovvero descrizione di Malta isola del mare siciliano e adriatico con le sue antichità ed altre notizie* (Malta, 1772).

Ciappara, F., *Society and the Inquisition in Early Modern Malta* (Malta, 2001).

Coleiro, E., 'Fonti Patristiche', in *Missione Archeologica Italiana*, IV (Rome, 1967), 17–21.

Documentary sources of Maltese History, I, 1, Notarial Documents. Notary Giacomo Zabbara, R494/1 (I) (1486-1488), ed. Stanley Fiorini (Malta, 1996).

Documentary sources of Maltese History, I, 2, Notarial Documents. Notary Giacomo Zabbara, R494/1 (II–IV) (1494-1497), ed. S. Fiorini (Malta, 1999).

Documentary sources of Maltese History, II, 1, Documents in the State Archives of Palermo. Cancelleria Regia (1259-1400), ed. S. Fiorini (Malta, 1999).

Documentary sources of Maltese History, III, 1, Documents of the Maltese Universitas. Archivum Cathedralis Melitae, Miscellanea 33 (1405–1542), ed. J. del Amo García, S. Fiorini and G. Wettinger (Malta, 2001).

Dokumenti dwar problemi u tilwim bejn Knisja – Stat f'Malta mit-23 ta' Dicembru 1976 sat-30 ta' Mejju, 1983, u mis-16 sa 23 ta' Gunju 1983 (Malta, 1983).

Dusina, P., Visitatio Apostolica (1575): ASV, Cong. Vescovi e Regolari, Malta 51: Documentary sources of Maltese History, IV, 1, Documents at the Vatican, Visitatio Apostolica Dusina 1575, ed. G. Aquilina and S. Fiorini (Malta, 2001).

Ferris, A., *Descrizione storica delle Chiese di Malta e Gozo* (Malta, 1866).

Ferris, A., *Storia Ecclesiastica di Malta raccontata in compendio* (Malta, 1877).

Ganado, H., *Rajt Malta Tinbidel*, I-IV (Malta, 1974-77).

Lee, H., 'British policy towards religion, ancient laws, and customs in Malta (1824–1851)', *Melita Historica*, III, 4 (1963), 1-14; IV (1964–67), 1–13.

Mifsud Piscopo, P., *Notitiae Gozo, 1755*: Archivum Cathedrale Melitense, *Miscellanea*, 55.

Pertusi, A., 'Le isole Maltesi dall'epoca Bizantina al periodo Normanno e Svevo (Secc. VI–XIII) e descrizioni di esse dal secolo XII al Secolo XVI', in *Byzantinische Forschungen*, 5 (1977), 253-306.

Peter on the island of Paul. Pietru fil-gzira ta' Pawlu, I-III (Malta, 1990).

Pietru fil-gzira ta' Pawlu, il-pellegrinagg tal-Qdusija Tieghu l-Papa Gwanni Pawlu II fuq il-passi ta' San Pawl, 8-9 ta' Mejju, 2001 (Malta, 2001).

Wettinger, G., *Il-Grajja bikrija tal-Knisja Matrici ta' Ghawdex (1435–1551)* (Malta, 1975).

Wettinger, G., 'The Arabs in Malta', in *Malta, studies of its heritage and history* (Malta, 1986), 87-104.

Wettinger, G., *The Jews of Malta in the Late Middle Ages* (Malta, 1985).

Winklemann, E., *Acta Imperii inedita saeculi XIII* (Innsbruck, 1880).

Joseph Muscat

THE MARITIME HISTORY OF MALTA

The Ancient Period

Ancient man in Malta, like anyone else who lived on small islands, loved to live by the sea and consequently had some type of boat or ship to work with. In an attempt to give portraits of the ancient vessels that sailed round Malta one must refer to the ship graffiti found on the island. The primordial contact of men with the sea might be interpreted as being one of the reasons why so many ship graffiti are found in Malta.

It is possible that the first sea people to influence Malta in the second millenium BC were the inhabitants of the Cyclades, who came from the Aegean. Later, maybe, the Minoans and Myceneans followed and set up a trading base in Malta. One may say that Malta was in contact with Crete, Greece and Egypt and their ships must have entered the natural harbour of the island.

The Tarxien Temples ship graffiti dating to circa 1600 BC were investigated for the first time in 1957 by Diana Woolner, who interpreted a number of them as representing an Egyptian wooden ship, the Bull's Horns profile of the ship found in the Iliad, the ship depicted in early Cycladic pottery, the vessel found on Greek vases and on a Cretan seal, and an Egyptian or Phoenician spoon-shaped ship.[1] Unfortunately the state of the two stone-slabs with the ship graffiti leave much to be desired; most of the incisions have faded out almost completely.[2]

The Hal Far Neo-Punic tomb number 3 is dated between the first century BC and the first century AD. A stone block was found there showing a badly damaged ship graffito. It shows a type of an Althiburus mosaic ship with a stern rudder, a highly raised decorated stern, a square sail and a ram at the bows. The horizontal lines might indicate a bank of oars.[3]

265

The Tas-Silġ temples graffito possibly represents a Roman ship with a rectilinear freeboard, a raised forestem and oars. The ship graffito found on the walls of St Paul's catacombs in Rabat, dating most probably to the fourth or fifth century AD, shows a double ended open type of boat which represents most probably a mechant ship. It shows a *sperone* or cutwater on the bows and what looks like side wooden washboards. No rigging is represented, an omission which further complicates any attempts at identification.[4]

The boat graffito found on the right hand side wall as you enter the chapel of Tad-Dejr Catacombs at Rabat is quite interesting, although unfortunately its state of preservation is poor. It shows high stems fore and aft, side rudder and two masts. The graffito might represent a merchantship of the early middle ages.[5]

At the Roman Domus in Rabat, Malta one may see an onyx boat shaped ex-voto offering. An almost identical one can be found at the Archaeological Museum in Gozo. Both seem to refer to a certain type of incense powder container or an object of a similar utility related to a sacred place.

A gold ring representing a ship is found in a private collection in Malta; the Archaeological Museum in Valletta holds a copper replica. The ring, made up of two parts fitting each other in the shape of a ship, was possibly kept by two partners as a means of identification. Otherwise it could also be classified as a seal. It shows six oars on each side, a side rudder, a roofed cabin at the stern, a square sail and a ram at the bows.

An enigmatic, enourmous lead stock of a Roman anchor was found at Qawra, Malta in 1963. It is thirteen feet six inches long and defined as *'anima di legno'* type as the melted lead was poured round a wooden core. Similar stocks were not found as yet anywhere in the Mediterranean and no explanation can be given for its possible employment, stowage on a ship and the manner of lowering or hoisting such a huge anchor.[6]

On Corradino Heights, overlooking the Grand Harbour of Malta, one may see a boat shaped stone recipient which might have been an offering as it is found in an ancient temple.[7]

The Middle Ages

The period known as the Dark Ages is almost a complete blank page in the maritime history of Malta. The Byzantines first and later the Arabs occupied the island for a long stretch of time. The short visit of the Vandals in Malta is greatly challenged as they left no signs of their occupation if ever they stayed on the island.

The dromon first and the *scelandia* were the fruit of the technical naval superiority of the Byzantines. The Arabs were able to copy them and with their light, swift galleots soon controlled the whole of the Mediterranean. The Arabs in Malta influenced the social, religious, economic, as well as naval affairs, as evinced by the linguistic affinities of the Maltese language. A twelfth century ceramic plate shows an Arab influenced boat having certain characteristics found on Maltese boats.[8]

During the eleventh century the Normans were very active in the Mediterranean. They drove the Arabs out of Malta but the island had to experience the rule of various dynasties until the Aragonese, who were very strong in the Western Mediterranean region, imposed a government which was the same for Sicily. Venice, Pisa and Genoa struggled for the mercantile supremacy in the Mediterranean and Malta was involved in their activities. More warships than merchant ships visited Malta in the struggle between these maritime cities who sought to ensure a base on the island.

The Mediterranean witnessed a great impetus for travel by sea which proved to be the quickest, cheapest and safest method. People started to travel and merchandise to circulate in the Mediterranean at a much greater rate when compared with previous periods in history. The great movement of the Crusaders required great merchant ships which necessitated better navigational aids and sailors.

It has been noticed that the medieval period under consideration was to witness great changes affecting ships and seamen. The skeleton-first techniques were preferred to the shell-first construction methods. The lateen sail, apparently introduced by the Arabs in the Mediterranean, was found to be of utmost importance and increased the sailing performance in general, especially of small ships. There was a general trend to adopt three masts or more instead of the normal rule when vessels were rigged with a single mast. The stern rudder replaced the side ones with greater efficiency and simplicity of operation. Better firing machines necessitated better ships; the discovery of gunpowder required adequate measure to be implemented on warships.

There was a general advance in the technology of shipbuilding. Navigational instruments provided the required aid to masters of ships. Together with the emergence of the art of chartography they contributed to safe passages at sea, thus rendering possible the great movement of discovery during the late middle ages.

While in Rhodes the Order of St John operated with various types of ships, showing perhaps western influences rather than eastern ones, as the Knights opted for European standards. The most common fifteenth century ship typologies included the galley, galleot, *barcia* or round ship, *fusta* and *saettia*. But Maltese *padroni* were sailing with their brigantine, *fregata*, *felucca*, *grippo* and *usciere*. The great carracks, which were intended as merchant ships but were heavily armed, also evolved in the Middle Ages. They were considered the answer against the threat represented by corsairs.

Tarxien temples ship graffiti (Photo: Joseph Muscat)

A Siculo-Maghreb boat of the thirteenth century. Note the use of the lateen sail and high stem posts (Photo: Joseph Muscat)

Post Medieval Period

The post medieval period in shipbuilding should be considered as being the transition period to modern times. The evolution of the ship was advancing steadily as a consequence of the fast changing social and economical changes prevalent in the Mediterranean and elsewhere.

The carrack was replaced by the smaller and more manoueverable galleon. The high stern of the galleon was found to be badly affected by winds which sometimes determined the outcome of battle at sea or the correct reckoning of a course. By 1650 the frigate evolved from the galleon, which was a warship with a low stern, guns on one or two batteries and a sail arrangement on three masts which was to remain in service for long years.

By the end of the seventeenth century the rule of thumb in building warships was to be replaced by scientific approaches experimented with success first in France and later in England. French experts in the field studied the best successful warships of various countries built by the old method of the rule of thumb, comparing measurements and achievements in combat and under sailing conditions. Consequently it was possible to lay down certain rules in planning warships and in formulating proportions, measurements, tonnage and rating. Each warship was rated by the number of guns carried.

The battle of Lepanto in 1571 was to be the last great sea combat between great Christian and Muslim galley squadrons in the Mediteranean. Subsequently small galley squadrons were engaged on corsairing activities. Galleys were effective for such a type of warfare on a small scale but the great warships were soon to replace them.

While Venice was struggling to maintain peace with the Turk and a hold on mercantile activities, France managed to dominate the Mediterranean with her mercantile activities, especially in the Levant through her 'scandalous' alliances with the Turk. English and Dutch ships entered the Mediterranean, challenging the monopoly of French and Venetian mercantile interests, thus making possible the influence of Northern European ship-building technology on Mediterranean ones.

The period under consideration was characterised also by a prolific increase of merchantship typologies. Apart from English and Dutch vessels, there were others coming from France, various ports of the Italian western coastline and those from the Adriatic. Such merchantships were normally small, and were mostly employed on tramping voyages all along the coasts of the Mediterranean.

The lateen rigged brigantine, *fregata* and *tartana* remained the most popular Maltese merchant ships up to the eighteenth century. The swift *xprunara* remained the most popular passenger boat for trips to Sicily and Italy. Other typologies like the *pinco* and *pollacca* were operated by Maltese *padroni*, but on a much reduced scale.

The first shipyard, located near fort St Angelo at Birgu, was to develop into an important establishment when the knights of St John settled in Malta in 1530. A new era of shipbuilding dawned on Malta as the Knights required galleys for their perpetual operations against Muslim objectives. The galley arsenal at Birgu was constantly busy and the local workforce attained high standards of achievement in shipbuilding and other ancillary services.[9]

Private owners of merchant ships constructed their vessels on private slipways in the Grand Harbour. Indeed, they were to set up on the island a flourishing mercantile society which emerged primarily in the eighteenth century but was to develop in the following century.[10]

One can say that Malta acquired a good reputation under the order of St John when local people were employed as shipbuilders, sailors, soldiers and rowers.

The galleys of the Order of St John remained basically the same for centuries. However until the seventeenth century they had underwent certain minor changes. Galleys were fitted with a foremast by 1580 and a mizzen one was added early in the eighteenth century. The number of oars was increased to a total of twenty-six on each side for a common galley, twenty-eight for a *padrona* and thirty for a *capitana*. Another important change was effected on Maltese galleys when by 1540 the rowing system was changed from that known as *a sensile* to that of *a scaloccio*. The first system required three rowers on the same bench pulling three separate oars, while by the second system three men on the same bench pulled the same oar. A Maltese *capitana* was painted black after 1625 in imitation to that of Spain.[11]

The Eighteenth and Nineteenth Centuries

Shipbuilding in Malta during the eighteenth century followed French standards. The great majority of the Knights were French and their influence was affecting all aspects of life in Malta, including that of shipbuilding. The first two frigates of the Order were built in Toulon while two other third-rates were built in Malta. A French master ship-constructor, Coulomb, worked for the Order of St John while Blaise, his son, actually worked in Malta for a period of time.[12] Local apprentices were also sent to Toulon to learn naval architecture and gunfounding techniques.[13]

A nautical school was founded in Valletta and young Knights were obliged to attend three days per week to qualify for promotion. The galley squadron of the Order was reputed as being the nursery for future naval officers of various countries. The commercial connections with Venice were strengthened as the Order imported almost all shipbuilding material requirements from there.[14]

During the eighteenth century the shipbuilding industry in Malta was catering for the Order of St John by providing galleys and warships. The merchant ships were built exclusively for local masters; only a few were sold outside Malta. It should be noted that the local workforce employed with the Order of St John transmitted the experience gained at the arsenals to other local ship- and boat-builders.

It has been observed that the Maltese population depended too much on the Treasury of the Order and corsairing activities. Early in the eighteenth century, however, such a situation was changing rapidly. The Order was facing financial difficulties as Turkey was brought down to her knees.[15] Consequently there were hardly any corso activities in the Levant and this meant a drastic loss of income for Maltese armateurs.

By 1750 the Barbary regencies were at war with each other, a situation which affected their activities at sea. As a direct consequence Maltese mercantile activities increased as never before. When the Barbary corsairs decreased their actions at the beginning of the eighteenth century Maltese merchants increased their activities and people were moving more freely in the Mediterranean.[16]

French influence was great and Malta was serving as an emporium for the distribution of French products in the Mediterranean.[17] While Maltese merchant ships kept the island supplied with all kinds of provisions, by the first half of the eighteenth century Maltese merchants were operating to all parts of the Mediterranean carrying local and French products.

Such an increase in mercantile activities necessitated an adequate increase in merchant ships. Maltese masters preferred the Maltese *tartana*, brigantine and *xprunara* for their activities. With such vessels local armateurs sailed to Marseilles, Spain and Lisbon carrying local and foreign products.[18]

British rule in Malta introduced new ideas in mercantile activities. Maltese shipwrights gained a lot of shipbuilding experience. There was a general trend to adopt new information as regards typologies of ships and boats and their building technologies. After 1798, with the French occupying Malta, local commerce was utterly destroyed. The Napoleonic Wars produced far reaching upheavals in the Mediterranean and elsewhere but to some extent they also curbed the Barbary corsairing activities.

The first two decades of the nineteenth century were characterised by local masters acquiring ship prizes caught by British ships and sold at public auctions. Some ships were built locally at the French Creek shipyard and at Kalkara. Many others which were built in Venice, Ragusa, Genoa, Sicily, Naples, Trieste, America, Greece, Denmark and Sweden were bought by Maltese merchants. It is important to note that such foreign-built ships offered an opportunity to local shipwrights to widen their experience in respect of the technology of new typologies.[19]

By 1869 Maltese shipyards dispersed round French Creek were fully employed launching bombards, brigs, barks, ships, schooners and other typologies of foreign origin like the *bovo, mistico, paranza, balancella, trabaccolo*, pink and *pollacca*. Indeed, those were the golden years for Maltese merchantship production.

The decline of local shipbuilding can be traced to the unpopular decision to move all shipbuilding facilities from French Creek to Porto Novo at Marsa. But there were other factors which precipitated the final collapse of all wooden shipbuilding in Malta. The Industrial Revolution facilitated the production of steam ships, and steam power was preferred to wind force. Even as early as 1844

The Birgu galley arsenal in the late seventeenth century (Photo: Joseph Muscat)

A Bark anchored in the Great Harbour at the end of the nineteenth century (Photo: Joseph Muscat)

a local merchant was operating with a steam propelled schooner. Evidently local merchants saw the advantages of steel and steam and turned to steamers rather than continuing to operate with wooden ships.

Shipbuilding Material

Malta never had any forests. All shipbuilding timber therefore had to be imported. For that reason construction costs of ships were high and local boat-builders developed a system whereby they made good for reduced use of timbers by developing their carpentry expertise, thus cutting costs on wood.

The Order of St John possessed great extensions of landed property all over Europe and was able to administer the forests as necessary to meet her shipbuilding programmes.[20] Great quantities of timber were acquired annually from Calabria, and by the beginning of the eighteenth century Venice provided the Order with all its requirements. Venice was a centre for the export of wood for Christian and Muslim countries.[21] Compass and square timber was ordered from Venice. Sometimes moulds for supplies of *baccalas,* stems, *madieri* and *staminali* were sent with the order forms. Strakes sixteen feet long were quite a normal order, but on certain occasions timber forty feet long was ordered for some type of special application. It has been noticed that great quantities of straight timber were occasionally ordered reaching the figure of 12,000 units of planks and scantlings of various thicknesses and types of wood in one order. The most popular timber in use was the white and red deal, pine, oak and larch. Ash, elm and walnut was ordered for special use as in the making of rudders of galleys.[22]

Denmark, Norway and Sweden had inexhaustible supplies of timber and the Order bought great quantities from there especially for mast making.[23] Sometimes substantial amounts of timber were obtained on the high seas from captured Muslim prizes. The Muslim convoy route from Alexandria to Constantinople or vice versa was purposely patrolled by the galleys of the Order for possible shiploads of timber that might be carried.[24]

Oak was normally kept in wood basins for seasoning purposes. There was a basin at Cospicua and another one at Senglea *dietro l'Isola;* they were guarded day and night.[25] Masts and spars were kept in the *fossa degl'alberi* in salt water to avoid twisting, splitting and for better preservation.[26] Although timber was most important in shipbuilding there were various other items which were required like iron fittings, nails of all sizes, resin, tar and paint ingredients. All such material had to be imported, mainly from Venice.

In the nineteenth century all shipbuilding material for the Dockyard came from British sources; the docks never experienced any defeciences. But when referring to private shipyards one must remember that all material had to be imported. The same situation as that experienced in the previous century persisted. Quantities of compass and straight timber came from Venice, Albania and from ex-Yugoslavia.

Old craftsmen still recall the days when they chose their requirements of compass timber from great heaps amassed on the Marsa quays.

'Cannibalism' was widely practised, especially by boat-builders who availed themselves of discarded surplus supplies or abandoned vessels of the Dockyard. It is an open secret that boat-builders found it quite easy to acquire pieces of teak for the stems of boats from the Dockyard.

The last few schooners and xprunaras continued to operate on wine routes, and the last shipyards at Marsa provided maintenance facilities and the building of pontoons. Malta under British rule enjoyed a privileged position in the centre of the Mediterranean - but lost its wooden shipbuilding tradition perhaps earlier that other countries.

Notes

1   See D. Woolner, 'Graffiti of ships at Tarxien, Malta', *Antiquity*, XXXI (1957).

2   J. Muscat, 'The Tarxien ship graffiti revisited', *Melita Historica*, XIII, 1 (2000), 49-57.

3   *Id., Il-Graffiti Marittimi Maltin* (Malta, 2002), 54-55.

4   Ibid., 54-58.

5   Ibid., 60.

6   *Museum Department Annual Report* (Malta, 1963), 7, fig. 6.

7   L. Basch, *Le Musee imaginaire de la marine antique* (Athens, 1987), 395.

8   Information kindly provided by Honor Frost.

9   For more information see J. Muscat, 'The Arsenal: 1530-1798', in Bugeja, L., Buhagiar, M., and Fiorini, S., (eds), *Birgu – A Maltese Maritime City*, I (Malta, 1993), 257-325.

10   NLM plan 156 indicates the place where local merchant ships were built.

11   B. Dal Pozzo, *Historia della Sacra Religione di Malta*, I (Verona, 1703), 744.

12   J. Muscat, *The Maltese Vaxxell* (Malta, 1999), 5.

13   *L' Arte*, No. 24, Sabato 7 Novembre 1863; NLM, AOM 127, ff.277-77v.

14   J. Muscat, *The Birgu Galley Arsenal* (Malta, 2001), 15-17.

15   NLM, AOM 1934A, f.12.

16   NAM, *Libretto delle Prattiche de Bastimenti*, passim.

17   A. Plaice, *Le Rouge de Malte* (Rennes, 1991), 67.

18   NAM, *Consolato del Mare*, passim mentions the *tartana*, brigantine and *xprunara* more frequently than other typologies.

19   NAM, *Chief Secretary to Government*, gives a series of registers of Maltese ships, and refers to the many prizes taken by British warships and sold in Malta.

20   Dal Pozzo, I, 62; G. Bosio, *Historia della Sacra Religione et Illustrissima Militia di S. Giovanni Gierosolimitano* (Venice, 1695), 199.

21   F. Chapin Lane, *Venetian Ships and Shipbuilders of the Renaissance* (Baltimore, 1934), 218.

22   Archivio Gran Priorato di Venezia 40 *Nota di legnami da provedersi da Venezia*. As the document is unpaginated the first line is given instead of the folio number.

23   G. Fournier, *Hydrographie contenant la Theorie et la Pratique de toutes les parties de la Navigation* (Paris, 1667), 169.

24   Dal Pozzo, I, 540, 653.

25   NLM, AOM 1823, ff.266, 273; NLM AOM 1000, f.122.

26   NLM, Lib. 223 s.v. *Fossa degl'Alberi*.

Ugo Mifsud Bonnici

GOVERNING AN ISLAND:
HISTORY OF GOVERNMENT IN MALTA

We have often heard repeated that our islands, throughout most of our known history, have been under the dominion of the most important world power of the particular time. In fact our history books generally divided the chapters according to different dominations. When one looks closer however, one has to say that on the internal level Malta and Gozo have always been, to a very large extent, run by the islanders themselves, under varying degrees of restriction and constriction. Given the geographical position of our archipelago, before the discovery of means of distance communication, it could not have been otherwise; surrounded as we are by not very placid waters, direct rule from abroad was not very easy. The retrieval of coins of the Maltese and Gozitan *Municipia* in Roman times is an expression of considerable latitude in self rule. Closer to us, the *Acta Iuratorum et Consilii Civitatis et Insulae Maltae*, which contain the records of the deliberations and decisions of the *Università* at Mdina for the years 1450-1498, are ample proof that during those years, though ostensibly the name of the distant King Alphonse of Aragon was invoked, these islands were being run by our forefathers, even if the king's foreign officials might at times, and very inconveniently, intervene.

During the Order of St John's stay in Malta, a substantial part of this relative autonomy was progressively lost as the grand masters and their 'government' was very present and active. Indeed the Hospitallers increasingly asserted their independence from the titular sovereigns, the Kings of the Two Sicilies who had succeeded the Emperor, grantor of their fief, and even, at times, from the Pope. The old Maltese Commune's rights and privileges were eroded. However a second way of Maltese self-rule crept in as the government of the Order engaged an increasing number of Maltese as the officials actually running most affairs under the titular direction of the highest dignitaries of the Order's hierarchy. The Maltese

Sir Filippo Sciberras, President of the Assemblea Nazionale *of 1919*

Joseph Howard, Prime Minister 1921-23

Sir Ugo Mifsud, Prime Minister 1924-27 and 1932-33

Sir Paul Boffa, Prime Minister 1947-50

Uditori stood in for the grand master, advised him, and wielded considerable influence. By the end of the Order's stay it was said that they ran most of the daily affairs of State. Maltese judges sat in disputes between knights, and heard ordinary cases in the Order's Courts, Maltese doctors administered the Order's hospitals, Maltese priors ran St John's Co-Cathedral, Maltese officials ran what services the State offered, and increasingly Maltese architects erected their churches and auberges.

When the Maltese rose up against the French occupying forces in 1798, the rural areas outside Valletta and the three cities were run by representatives of the towns and villages, who in effect re-established a State, at first unfurling the flag of His Sicilian Majesty as its titular head. However my ancestor Clemente Mifsud Bonnici was sent to Sicily on a *Speronara* together with Luqa Briffa, to ask for grain, not political direction or government. The Maltese Congress asked for and accepted British protection, but made the famous Declaration of Rights of 1802, in effect affirming self-determination. However the brief period of complete self-rule which began in September 1798 was soon subsumed into a state of subjection to British rule, with much the same pattern being developed as that of the previous late period of the Order's rule. Sir Alexander Ball acted the role of a benevolent *quasi-*grandmaster. The administration of Malta never carried the salary of more than a handful of British officials. When in the beginning there was an attempt to bring in British Chief Justices and Crown Attorneys, the experiment failed dismally. It so continued for all the period of British sovereignty up till 1964. The whole machinery of the administration of government was in Maltese hands, though the ultimate power rested with the few British high officials who were sent here for the purpose. However we also have evidence that during certain periods of time some Maltese officials became so deeply trusted by the imperial government in London that they were *de facto* the governors of the islands.

This of course did not mean real self-government: on the contrary it meant arbitrary government on matters which really mattered for the whole country. A very eloquent letter by Giorgio Mitrovich and others in 1833 expressed the need to have a Council of Government. The first council, set up on 1 May 1835, was a wholly nominated council, consisting of five official and three unofficial members. Once again Mitrovich, this time writing directly from London, on 31 July of that year, remonstrated against the fact that the handful of foreign officials who were pocketing high salaries were not in fact rendering good service, and when in November he addressed a pamphlet to his countrymen in Malta he emphasised the fact that what Malta really needed was government by the Maltese, as they had had with the old *Consiglio Popolare*. The next constitution did provide for a partially elected Council of Government, but the elected members were in a minority, and were elected by and from a very restricted electoral list. Moreover the council examined the proposed legislation and the budget, but was impotent in the face of an official 'No' from a distant Colonial Office. The records of the meetings of the council are eloquent proof of a responsible, enlightened and 'mature' group of elected members making the most sensible suggestions, and an official side trying to justify patently wrong or retrograde decisions.

Subsequently, under the 1887 Constitution, the council was formed with an elected majority and one of the elected members was to take a seat in the executive council. But that experiment was aborted when the imperial government failed to respect the will of the majority on education matters. Henceforth the politics of Malta evolved by moving out of the august Council Chamber and into the streets and square *fuori dei bastioni,* of political mass agitation. The disfranchised masses could take part in the 'monstre meetings' together with brass bands with their richly embroidered *stendardi,* to hear Fortunato Mizzi or Sigismondo Savona and show disapproval of the Colonial Office and/or the 'palace clique'. Though Mizzi and Savona might have differed on the 'Language Question' both were seeking a greater measure of home rule, and in the case of Mizzi, ultimately Malta's independence.

The first years of the twentieth century saw a peculiar type of agitation through caricaturing elections to the council. Notoriously 'ridiculous' characters were returned to the council and paraded down *Strada Reale* in triumph, demonstrating very clearly that the Maltese had not been duped by the restoration of a constitution which gave them no further right than that of criticising a government not responsible to public opinion or to the elected representatives in council but simply complacent to faraway London and imperial interests. During the First World War, the local government was found to be quite insensible to the hardships suffered by the majority of the Maltese population through the highly inflated prices for most daily necessities regarding food, fuel, clothes and house rent. While in Britain rents were frozen, in Malta the matter, though raised in the press, was left unattended. Bread was scarce and the provision inadequate, which made most Maltese suspect that those in the Palace were in league with the importers of grain, who were perceived as having made fortunes on the common man's hardship. Wages and salaries had not moved substantially from their pre-war levels. When in 1919, in addition to all this, demobilisation deprived thousands of families of their meagre remunerations with no possibility of alternative employment or possible earnings, the pot was set boiling. The Maltese were fed up with foreign and bad government and were clamouring for self rule. A National Assembly was called where the representatives of all Maltese Civil Societies, which to-day would be known as NGOs, elaborated a self-governing constitution. The official nonchalance in the face of political agitation, which had not budged when during a students' demonstration in May, the Union Jack had been torn down from its mast at the University and at the *Bibliotheca,* was made to react crudely and savagely to the bread and liberty riots of the famous three days of June 1919. British troops fired upon and killed four demonstrators. The situation could scarcely be contained and the British Government asked the Church to help in calming down the people, and then, taking stock of the political and social tensions, proceeded to promise through a new Governor, Lord Plumer, the grant of self-government.

With the 1921 Constitution Malta and Gozo returned at least to the old, pre-1530 position of an autochthonous self government of local affairs, while the external affairs (including security and coinage) were dealt with by the imperial government. The experiment had some success until the imperial government began to intervene in matters strictly local, ostensibly to help those Maltese parties deemed to be more pro-British. Elections were suspended in 1930 when it appeared that the politico-religious complications would result in an electoral defeat for those parties. However all Maltese Governments (Nationalist or formed by Compact between the Constitutional and Labour Parties) responsible to the Legislative Assembly and the Senate during the years 1921-30 and 1932-33, performed well in the way they ran the country, building its schools, its hospital, improving its communications and general infrastructure, and also making a start of a democratic political culture of alternation in power. Bi-polarisation was achieved, even though the chosen system of proportional representation was initially seen as leading to a divisive multiplicity of parties. Reading the debates of the Assembly and the Senate of these years one must pay tribute to Maltese politicians who improved the state of Malta considerably in all fields while acting within the scenario of a world economy characterised by unemployment, inflation and after a few years of buoyancy, the crash of 1929.

The constitution was again suspended in 1933, the British imperial government opting to remove any possible suspected irredentist movement, and acting high handedly, assuming the reins of government in 'official' non-democratically elected hands. It was the security and intelligence aspects that were entrusted to non-Maltese, while most of the usual daily administration continued to be handled by the same Maltese Civil Service. In addition, even a Nationalist ex-minister, the former Minister of Agriculture, Dr Micallef, was asked to return as director of his former ministry. In a partly nominated Executive Council in the years 1936-39, the Maltese members continued to press for the measures in internal matters which were needed in a situation of a threatened new world war. In the now elected Council under the 1939 Constitution, it was the Maltese members, as expected, that actually prodded the executive to undergo measures of civil protection from attack, by providing air raid shelters and from scarcity profiteering and black marketing, through proper food provision and the control of prices. If Malta survived throughout the ordeal of continuous aerial bombardment and enforced embargo, it is owed most decidedly to the collaboration that was established between the Maltese population and an informed and largely non-discriminatory wartime administration. Although by far the finest page in the records of the 1939-45 Council of Government is provided by the spirited and enlightened condemnation by Sir Ugo Mifsud of the internment and banishment of other Nationalists by the British Government, and although the imperial authorities and the military command had not adequately provided for the defence of these islands, yet the Maltese never wavered in their choice of fighting against Fascism and Nazism and resisting the German-Italian onslaught. It must be said that most of the mistakes of 1914-18 were not repeated, and the deprivations and hardships were borne equally by all, Maltese and British. Food was delivered by

Lord Strickland, Prime Minister 1927-32

Dr Enrico Mizzi, Prime Minister 1950

*Dr George Borg Olivier, Prime Minister
1950-55 and 1962-71*

*Mr Dom Mintoff, Prime Minister 1955-58
and 1971-84*

convoy at great cost of men and ships, and then strictly rationed; relief was given to families who lost their breadwinners; a guarantee was given and honoured of providing funds for War Damage Reconstruction.

When self-government was returned in 1947, the Labour Party was elected to government by a landslide, but it had not only to attend to the material reconstruction of devastated towns and villages, but also to the construction of a welfare state, in a country which had no old age pensions, no unemployment cover, and whose health services had been under great strain during the war. In the first two years that government introduced income tax, old age pensions and set about the reconstruction of private housing, as well as the building of new housing, in great earnest. It was soon to realise, however, that War Damage Funds could not cover either the repair or restoration of the historical monuments and fortifications damaged or destroyed during the war or, very important at that juncture, with demobilisation and mounting unemployment, the investment money to build an economy out of one solely propped up by dwindling British Defence expenditure. Malta was refused access to Marshall Aid, so that while its former enemies and allies on the continent were planting their apple-seed and planning for the post war economic resurrection, the Maltese were plunged into political crisis with a division within the Labour Government and the emergence of a more radical leader for the Labour Party in Dom Mintoff. The erstwhile leader of twenty-two years standing, Dr Paul Boffa, was ousted. A period of unstable minority and coalition governments led by the Nationalist Party could not produce much government of any sort but the Borg Olivier/Boffa coalition of 1952 did produce in the Conditions of Employment Regulation Act the bedrock legislation for all subsequent labour legislation in these islands.

Mr Mintoff was elected with a good majority in 1955 and set out to modernise the administration, to build an economic base through tourism, as well as some light industry, and sought to finance his programme by moving forward on a proposal of integration with Great Britain. He hoped to be able to approximate Maltese living standards to those obtaining in the British Isles through the funds made available by the Government in Westminster precisely for this object. Though he managed to obtain some substantial subvention in the initial years, his government realised in late 1957 and early 1958 that Britain was also very interested in being relieved of the burden of continuing to maintain the Naval Dockyard, still a mainstay of the Maltese economy in employment and in the earning of foreign currency. The determination shown by the British Government in this direction, and the Mintoff government's resistance thereto, eventually scuttled the Integration proposal and brought about the suspension of the constitution and four years of direct colonial rule. One can say that though at times the Labour Government of 1955-58 adopted, internally, arrogant and high handed methods, occasionally verging on illegality, it had indeed striven to bring about an improvement of living standards, and had stood up to the cavalier attitude displayed at times by the British Government.

In 1962 the constitution of 1947 was restored, and in the first elections which ensued the Nationalist Party was elected to govern with a marginal majority of seats, with no clear-cut majority of votes but facing a divided opposition. The Prime Minister, Giorgio Borg Olivier, declared that his aim was the achievement of full independence at the shortest possible time. Before and after the actual proclamation on 21 September 1964, the Nationalist Government, during the nine year period it was in power (1962-71) set about, with some good advice and assistance, to build the physical infrastructure (new power station, desalination plant for potable water production) the economic infrastructure (Central Bank, the Malta Pound, the Development Corporation), the tourist infrastructure (the first five star hotels, the restaurants and hotels grading machinery), and after the 1966 election with a more comfortable working majority, a stable and poised style of political exchange and debate. Malta's foreign policy was aligned with the West and Malta's defence and security were seen as safe within the NATO web. Malta joined the Council of Europe in 1965, and entered into an association agreement with the then Common Market in 1970.

The next stage in the country's evolution of its way of governance came with Mr Mintoff's return to power in 1971. Speed, dynamism, challenge, and no squeamishness about the strict observance of the niceties, were now the order of the day. The NATO headquarters in Malta was no longer welcome, and fresh arrangements for the continuance of the British Defence base were to be arrived at after new negotiations. After negotiations conducted with extreme brinksmanship, the payments made by NATO were considerably augmented. Then Mr Mintoff turned his attention to changes in the constitution which again were arrived at by negotiations characterised by pressure followed by accommodation and compromise. For the continuation of the sixteen years of Labour government (1971-87) one could see an intensification of the State's intrusion into the economy (nationalisation of banks, radio and television, Enemalta, Sea Malta, Air Malta), trade (control of imports and management of consumption), health (elimination of private hospitals and restriction of private medical practice), education (harassment of Church schools and other private educational institutions), and employment (labour corps and government employment). The foreign policy of Malta became neutralist and non-aligned but somewhat alienated from the West. In the end however, even though the climate became as heavy as was possible, Mr Mintoff himself recoiled from venturing forward into dictatorship, and at first relinquished his premiership and later was instrumental in arriving at an agreed constitutional amendment removing the possibility of a repeat of the 1981 election (perverse or gerrymandered) result whereby the Opposition, with more than fifty percent of the vote, was denied access to power.

In the 1987 election the Nationalist Party was returned to power and there was a gradual redirection of the economy towards less government intervention and towards a less confrontational style in the conduct of public affairs. In addition there was a further strengthening of the infrastructure (new power station, extension of reverse osmosis plants, communication systems). The years since then have also seen expansion in tourism, financial services, and streamlining of government procedures. A massive investment in education and in the health services, as well as in many collateral welfare services, could also be observed. A major constitutional change was the introduction of local government in 1992. No notable departure from the general direction of government could be discerned when Labour was again in power between 1996 and 1998. What distinguished the Nationalist governments in 1987-96 as well as 1998-2004 was the concentration of efforts so as to reach the goal of accession to the European Union.

What level of democracy, rule of law, safeguard of human rights, and what standards of efficiency have been achieved in these islands as of 2004? One can say that democracy is now very firmly established and has withstood the difficulties encountered in the first decades after Independence very well. The rule of law and our fundamental rights and liberties seem to be safeguarded by our Courts and by our participation in the European Human Rights Court in Strasbourg, to which Maltese citizens can since 1997 address their individual petitions. The average Maltese citizen participates in State (above ninety percent) and local (around seventy percent) elections. Political debate can be passionate but is far more restrained now than ever before. The machinery of public service could be more efficient, but throughout history, and especially during the Order's (1530-1798) and British (1800-1964) rule, it was the Maltese bureaucracy that really governed, even if under foreign direction, and the proper relationship between the civil servant and the holder of political office is only now coming into its normal position. The standards of integrity and efficiency in the bureaucracy are high, and those of the political milieu are not low by European standards.

Malta's accession to the European Union presents a challenge. The human resources will be further stretched by the country's participation in the governance of the Union. There might be some brain drain towards the Union's bureaucratic set-up, and all Maltese participating in the art of government will have to extend their knowledge and skill to cover extensive new areas. This will however be an enrichment, and one is entitled to hope that the ability of the machinery of State in Malta to satisfy the needs of its people will be further enhanced by the enlarged experience.

References

Cassar, C., *A Concise History of Malta* (Malta, 2000).

Debono, P., *Sommario della Storia della Legislazione in Malta* (Malta, 1897).

Frendo, H., *Malta's Quest for Independence. Reflections on the course of Maltese History* (Malta, 1989).

Frendo, H., *Party Politics in a Fortress Colony: The Maltese Experience* (Malta, 1991).

Mallia-Milanes, V., (ed.), *Hospitaller Malta 1530-1798. Studies on early modern Malta and the Order of St John of Jerusalem* (Malta, 1993).

Mallia-Milanes, V., (ed.), *The British Colonial Experience 1800-1964: The Impact on Maltese Society* (Malta, 1988).

Grand Masters of the Order of St John in Malta

L'Isle Adam, Philippe Villiers de (French)	1530-1534
Ponte, Pierino del (Italian)	1534-1535
Saint Jaille, Didier de (French)	1535-1536
Homedes, Juan d' (Spanish)	1536-1553
Sengle, Claude de la (French)	1553-1557
Valette, Jean Parisot de la (French)	1557-1568
Monte, Pietro del (Italian)	1568-1572
Cassiere, Jean l'Eveque de la (French)	1572-1581
Verdalle, Hughes Loubenx de (French)	1581-1595
Garzes, Martino (Spanish)	1595-1601
Wignacourt, Alof de (French)	1601-1622
Vasconcellos, Luis Mendez de (Spanish)	1622-1623
Paule, Antoine de (French)	1623-1636
Lascaris Castellar, Jean Paul (French)	1636-1657
Redin, Martin de (Spanish)	1657-1660
Chattes Gessan, Annet Clermot de (French)	1660
Cotoner, Rafael (Spanish)	1660-1663
Cotoner, Nicolas (Spanish)	1663-1680
Carafa, Gregorio (Italian)	1680-1690
Wignacourt, Adrien de (French)	1690-1697
Perellos y Roccaful, Ramon (Spanish)	1697-1720
Zondadari, Marc'Antonio (Italian)	1720-1722
Vihena, Antonio Manoel de (Portuguese)	1722-1736
Despuig, Ramon (Spanish)	1736-1741
Pinto de Fonseca, Manuel (Portuguese)	1741-1773
Ximenes de Texada, Francisco (Spanish)	1773-1775
Rohan Polduc, Emmanuel de (French)	1775-1797
Hompesch, Ferdinand von (German)	1797-1798

APPENDIX II
British Civil Commissioners and Governors

Civil Commissioners

Ball, Captain Alexander, R.N.	1799-1801
Pigot, Major-General Henry	1801
Cameron, Sir Charles	1801-1802
Ball, Rear-Admiral Sir Alexander	1802-1809
Oakes, Lieutenant-General Sir Hildebrand	1810-1813

Governors

Maitland, Lieutenant-General Sir Thomas	1813-1824
General the Marquess of Hastings	1824-1826
Ponsonby, Major-General Sir Frederic	1827-1836
Bouverie, Lieutenant-General Sir Henry F.	1836-1843
Stuart, Lieutenant-General Sir Patrick	1843-1847
More O'Ferrall, The Right Honourable Richard	1847-1851
Reid, Major-General Sir William	1851-1858
Le Marchand, Lieutenant-General Sir John Gaspard	1858-1864
Storks, Lieutenant-General Sir Henry	1864-1867
Grant, General Sir Patrick	1867-1872
Straubenzee, General Sir Charles T.	1872-1878
Borton, General Sir Arthur	1878-1884
Simmons, General Sir Lintorn	1884-1888
Torrens, Lieutenant-General Sir Henry D.	1888-1890
Smyth, Lieutenant-General Sir Henry A.	1890-1893
Fremantle, General Sir Arthur J.L.	1893-1899
Grenfell, Lieutenant-General Lord	1899-1903
Mansfield Clarke, General Sir Charles	1903-1907
Grant, Lieutenant-General Sir Henry F.	1907-1909
Rundle, General Sir Leslie	1909-1915
Methuen, Field-Marshal Lord	1915-1919
Plumer, Field-Marshal Viscount	1919-1924
Congreve, General Sir Walter N.	1924-1927
Du Cane, General Sir John P.	1927-1931
Campbell, General Sir David G.M.	1931-1936
Bonham-Carter, General Sir Charles	1936-1940
Dobbie, Lieutenant-General Sir William G.S.	1940-1942

Gort, Field-Marshal Viscount	1943-1944
Schreiber, Lieutenant-General Sir Edmond C.A.	1944-1946
Douglas, Sir Francis (later lord)	1946-1949
Creasy, Sir Gerald H.	1949-1954
Laycock, Major-General Sir Robert	1954-1959
Grantham, Admiral Sir Guy	1959-1962
Dorman, Sir Maurice	1962-1964

Governors General

Dorman, Sir Maurice	1964-1971
Mamo, Sir Anthony	1971-1974

APPENDIX III
Maltese Prime Ministers

Howard, Mr Joseph	1921-1923
Buhagiar, Dr Francesco	1923-1924
Mifsud, Sir Ugo	1924-1927
Strickland, Sir Gerald (late Lord)	1927-1932
Mifsud, Sir Ugo	1932-1933
Boffa, Dr (later Sir) Paul	1947-1950
Mizzi, Dr Enrico	1950
Borg Olivier, Dr Giorgio	1950-1955
Mintoff, Mr Dominic	1955-1958
Borg Olivier, Dr Giorgio	1962-1971
Mintoff, Mr Dominic	1971-1984
Mifsud Bonnici, Dr Carmelo	1984-1987
Fenech Adami, Dr Eddie	1987-1996
Sant, Dr Alfred	1996-1998
Fenech Adami, Dr Eddie	1998-2004
Gonzi, Dr Lawrence	2004-

APPENDIX IV
Presidents of the Republic of Malta

Mamo, Sir Anthony	1974-1976
Buttigieg, Dr Anton	1976-1981
Barbara, Ms Agatha	1982-1986
Xuereb, Mr Paul (Acting President)	1987-1989
Tabone, Dr Vincent	1989-1994
Mifsud Bonnici, Dr Ugo	1994-1999
De Marco, Professor Guido	1999-2004
Fenech Adami, Dr Eddie	2004-

APPENDIX V
Notes on Contributors

CARMEL ATTARD has read for a BA (Gen.) in Communication Studies, BA (Educ.) Hons and MA in European Studies. He joined the Malta-EU Information Centre (MIC) in July 2000 as Media Officer and he is presently the Acting Head of MIC. Previously Mr Attard worked at the Media Centre as editor of the Maltese language weekly newspaper *Il-Ġens* (1991-2000) and as News Manager of RTK Radio Station (1992-2000). Before joining Media Centre Mr Attard had spent ten years teaching in State schools.
E-mail: <u>carmel.a.attard@gov.mt</u>

JOSEPH BEZZINA was born in Rabat, Gozo. He studied at the University of Malta and the Pontifical Gregorian University, Rome, and was ordained priest by Pope Paul VI in 1975. He holds three history degrees, including a First-class Honours Doctorate in Church History, and has also received the Pope's Award, his University's highest honour, after being placed first in the 1982 finals. He is Head of Department of Church History at the University of Malta and Senior Lecturer in history in the Faculty of Theology at the same University; at the Sacred Heart Seminary, Gozo; and at the Interdiocesan Seminary of Albania, Shkodèr. He wrote extensively about Church history, including a book under the British, *Religion and Politics in a Crown Colony. The Gozo-Malta Story. 1798-1864;* a short general history, *Church history, including an account of the Church in Malta;* and the first history of the church in Malta, *L-Istorja tal-Knisja f'Malta.* He is also the author of several guidebooks as well as of other books in English, Maltese, German, and Italian. He has slowly established himself as Gozo's leading historian.
E-mail: <u>joseph.bezzina@um.edu.mt</u>

ANTHONY BONANNO, B.A. (Hons) (Malta), D. Litt. (Palermo), Ph.D. (London), is Professor of Archaeology and Head of Department of Classics and Archaeology at the University of Malta. He convened two international conferences, one in 1985 and one in 1988. He edited the papers of the first one in a volume entitled *Archaeology and Fertility Cult in the Ancient Mediterranean* (Amsterdam, 1986) and a selection of papers from the second one in the *Journal of Mediterranean Studies* I, 2 (Malta, Mediterranean Institute, 1991). He has also authored various publications on Roman art and Maltese archaeology, such as, *Portraits and Other Heads on Roman Historical Relief up to the Age of Septimius Severus* (Oxford, 1976); *Roman Malta. The Archaeological Heritage of the Maltese Islands*

(Rome, 1992) and *Il-Preistorja* (Malta, 2001). He has served on a number of national and academic committees related to cultural heritage.
E-mail: anthony.bonanno@um.edu.mt

JOHN J. BORG joined the ranks of the Museums Department as Custodian and Guide in 1995, where he spent most of the latter half of the 1990s assisting the Curator at Għar Dalam. In 2000 he was appointed Museum Officer responsible for the running of the National Museum of Natural History. He started a series of long-term studies on the breeding seabirds of the Maltese islands, now in their 23rd year, and he published his results in local as well as foreign scientific journals. He served on various posts in the BirdLife Malta Council and is the newsletter editor of MEDMARAVIS: the Mediterranean Association of Researchers on Marine Birds and Cetaceans. Mammalogy is another branch of science in which he carried out a number of studies, mainly on the Chiropterafauna (bats).
E-mail: john.j.borg@gov.mt

CHARLES BRIFFA, born at Birkirkara (Malta) in 1951), is a lecturer in Maltese Literature and Literary Criticism at the University of Malta and the Principal Subject Area Officer for Languages with the Matsec Board at the same University. He also lectures on the practical aspects of translation with the Faculty of Arts. He is a literary critic himself and wrote extensively on the stylistic qualities of Maltese literary prose works. He is the President of the *Akkademja tal-Malti*, member of the Poetics and Linguistics Association (UK), and member of The Association of Literary Scholars and Critics (Boston). His publications include the following: *L-Analiżi Kritika tal-Proża* (2001), *Trevor Zahra: A Childhood of Delight* (1992), *Il-Proża tal-Femminiżmu* (1998 awarded the literary prize for 1999), *Il-Proża fl-Arti Drammatika* (1998), *In-Novella Maltija* (1999 awarded first literary prize for 2000), *Rhythmic Patterns in Maltese Literature* (2001), *Id-Dinja ta' Ineż Farruġ* (2001), and *Ir-Rumanz Malti sa Nofs is-Seklu Għoxrin* (2003).
E-mail: charles.briffa@um.edu.mt

Professor **JOSEPH M. BRINCAT** teaches Italian Linguistics and Medieval Literature at the University of Malta. He holds degrees from the universities of Malta, London and Florence and has published books on Italian philology: *Giovan Matteo di Meglio, Rime*, (Florence, 1977), a history of linguistics: *La linguistica prestrutturale*, (Bologna, 1986) and a history of the Maltese language in Maltese: *Il-Malti. Elf sena ta' storja* (Malta, 2000). He is vice-president of the *Società di Linguistica Italiana* (1998-2000), member of the editorial boards of Al-Masaq (Leeds) and Aljamìa (Oviedo), he organised and edited the proceedings of two international conferences in Malta and co-edited *Purism in Minor Languages* (Bochum, 2003). His *Malta. Una storia linguistica*, has just been

published as part of the activities of Genoa, Cultural Capital of Europe 2004 (Le Mani, 2004).
E-mail: joseph.m.brincat@um.edu.mt

CARMEL CASSAR, Ph.D (Cantab), M.Phil (Cantab), BA, FRHist.S, FCCS, MRAI has published extensively on Maltese and Mediterranean culture and history. His books include: *Society, Culture and Identity in Early Modern Malta*; *A Concise History of Malta*; *Daughters of Eve. Women, Gender Roles, and the Impact of the Council of Trent in Catholic Malta*; *Il Senso dell'Onore*; *Witchcraft, Sorcery and the Inquisition*; *Sex, Magic and the Periwinkle*; *Fenkata. An Emblem of Maltese Peasant Resistance?* He was awarded an ODA (full) Scholarship by the Cambridge Commonwealth Trust to read Anthropology, a Holland Rose Scholarship from the Faculty of History (Cambridge), and several other studentships and bursaries by Cambridge institutions. Cassar was visiting post-doctoral Fellow at the University of Durham; a University of Wales Visiting Research Fellow, and a Mary Aylwin Cotton Foundation Fellow, besides receiving other post-doctoral awards. He was also responsible for the development of an Ethnography Section within the Museums Department. Dr Cassar has read papers and participated in research seminars and conferences in Italy, Britain, Ireland, France, Rumania, and Algeria and his papers appeared in learned journals in Italy, Britain, Spain, the USA and Malta. At present he serves as Senior Lecturer at the University of Malta Junior College.
E-mail: carmel.cassar@um.edu.mt

After having studied at the Lyceum and the Teachers' Training College of Education, **FRANS CIAPPARA** graduated M.A. from the University of Malta and Ph.D. from the University of Durham (UK). He is a specialist in the late eighteenth century, his areas of interest being the Enlightenment, church history in general and the Roman Inquisition in particular. His research has been published both locally and abroad and includes: *Mill-Qighan ta' l-Istorja. Il-Kappillani fis-Seklu Tmintax* (Malta, 1987), *Marriage in Malta in the Late Eighteenth Century* (Malta, 1988), *The Roman Inquisition in Enlightened Malta* (Malta, 2000), *Society and the Inquisition in Early Modern Malta* (2001), 'Perceptions of Marriage in late-eighteenth-century Malta', *Continuity and Change* 16, no. 3 (Cambridge, 2001), 'The Financial Condition of Parish Priests in late Eighteenth-Century Malta', *Journal of Ecclesiastical History* 53, 1 (Cambridge, 2002), 'The Roman Inquisition and the Jews in seventeenth- and eighteenth-century Malta', in *Le Inquisizioni Cristiane e gli Ebrei*, Atti dei Convegni Lincei 191 (Rome, 2003).
E-mail: francis.ciappara@um.edu.mt

NATHANIEL CUTAJAR has graduated in History and Archaeology from the University of Malta and furthered his studies at the University of York in

Archaeological Heritage Management. He has participated in excavations on various sites in Malta, Sicily and the UK and has been involved in heritage management projects at a number of Maltese sites, including the World Heritage Sites of Ħaġar Qim, Mnajdra, Tarxien and Ħal Saflieni. He has published works on Maltese archaeology and on cultural heritage management and lectures on 'Material Culture of the Medieval World' and 'Archaeological Heritage Management' at the University of Malta. Mr Cutajar has held the post of Curator at the National Museum of Archaeology from 1996 to 2002 and since 2003 is a leading member of the Superintendence of Cultural Heritage of Malta.
E-mail: nathaniel.cutajar@gov.mt

CHARLES DALLI is a member of the Department of History at the University of Malta, where he lectures in medieval history. He studied history at the University of Malta and specialised in Medieval History at the University of Cambridge, England. He has researched the late medieval history of Malta, Sicily and the central Mediterranean region in Maltese, Italian and Spanish archives. He has presented studies in international conferences in Italy, Spain and the United Kingdom. He is the author of *Iż-Żmien Nofsani Malti* [The Maltese Middle Ages] (Malta, 2002) as well as a number of articles in scholarly publications.
E-mail: charles.dalli@um.edu.mt

Professor **DENIS DE LUCCA** was born in Malta in 1952 and graduated in architecture from the University of Malta in 1975. He afterwards practised his profession, lectured in architecture and carried out primary source research on various aspects of architectural history and theory. Since 1989 the author has occupied the posts of dean of the Faculty of Architecture and Civil Engineering, heads the Department of Architecture and Urban Design and directs the very active International Institute for Baroque Studies at the University of Malta. He also chairs the Mdina Rehabilitation Committee in the Resources and Infrastructure Ministry. Prof. de Lucca also authored and designed four books, entitled *Mdina: A History of its Urban Space and Architecture* (1995); *Carapecchia: Master of Baroque Architecture in early eighteenth century Malta* (1999); *Giovanni Battista Vertova: Diplomacy, Warfare and Military Engineering Practice in early 17th century Malta* (2001) and *Mondion - The achievement of a French military engineer in early eighteenth century Malta* (2003). In addition he has contributed a series of studies to a number of books including: *The British Colonial Experience: The Impact on Maltese Society* (1988); *Gozo - the Roots of an Island* (1990); *Collected Papers* (1992); *Birgu: A Maltese Maritime City* (1993); *Companion to Contemporary Architectural Thought* (1993); *Mosta: The Heart of Malta* (1996); *Evangelista Menga: Dal Castello di Copertino al Grande Assedio di Malta* (1999); *Annali del Barocco in Sicilia* (1999, 2001) and *Matteo Perez d'Aleccio - Pittore Ufficiale del Grande Assedio di Malta* (2000).
E-mail: monica.floridia@um.edu.mt

ANTONIO ESPINOSA RODRIGUEZ was born in 1949. He holds a BA (Hons) degree from the University of London, an MA degree and a Diploma in Librarianship and Information Studies from the University of Malta. In 1976 he joined the Museums Department; since then he has served as Assistant Curator of Fine Arts, Curator of Fine Arts and Curator of the Maritime Museum. He is currently detailed with Heritage Malta and holds the post of Manager of Collections and Conservation. He is also a part time lecturer in History of Art at the University of Malta. Mr Espinosa Rodriguez is the author of various articles and publications. He was also awarded the *Premio Castore e Pulluce agli Uomini del Mare by* the Lega Navale Italiana, the *Premio Vicente Azzopardi* for promoting Hispanic-Maltese cultural relationships, and *La Croce dell'Ordine al Merito Melitense* by the Sovereign Military Order of Malta.
E-mail: antonio.espinosa-rodriguez@gov.mt

A doctoral graduate of Oxford University, where he was in residence at University College, and an elected life member of Clare Hall, Cambridge, where he was a Visiting Fellow, **HENRY FRENDO** has been Professor of History at Malta since 1992. The author of several books since 1970, some of them published in translation, Prof. Frendo has taught in European, Australian and American universities as well as held various awards as a Commonwealth Scholar, a Salzburg Fellow, a Fulbright Scholar; he has been an International Visitor to the UK, the USA, Germany and the EU. In addition to his academic interests relating to European history and culture, European expansion, nationalism and decolonisation in the Mediterranean, migration, and journalism, Prof. Frendo served with UNHCR in Europe, Africa and Asia in the 1970s and 1980s; he was active in the Council of Europe's Congress of Local and Regional Authorities, and led the Maltese delegation in the 1990s, where he chaired the Euro-Med group. He chaired the Malta branch of the European Cultural Foundation until 1996, as well as the Local Councils Association, and the College of Mayors until 1998. He is now chairman of the Refugee Appeals Board in Valletta, and vice-president of the Council of Europe's committee of experts on local government in Strasbourg. His most recent book is *Miċ-Ċensura ghall-Pluraliżmu: Il-Ġurnaliżmu f'Malta 1798-2002* (2003). The first volume of a general history of Malta during the British period is in the press.
E-mail: henry.frendo@um.edu.mt

UGO MIFSUD BONNICI was born at Cospicua, Malta in 1932. He is the son of the late Professor Carmelo Mifsud Bonnici and the late Maria *nee* Ross. After studying at the Lyceum and the University of Malta, he graduated BA (1952) and LL.D. (1955), and practised Law in the Courts of Malta from 1956 to 1987. Dr Mifsud Bonnici was elected to Parliament on behalf of the Nationalist Party from the Second Electoral Division in 1966, 1971, 1976, 1981, 1987 and 1992. He was appointed Minister of Education (1987-90), Minister of Education and the Interior (1990-92), Minister of Education and Human Resources (1992-94). During that time (1987-94) he was responsible for a new Education Law (1988), The Law for the Protection of the Environment (1990), the National Archives Act (1990), the new Broadcasting Law (1991), the Law for the transfer to the State of Church property (1992), and the Law for the Protection of Health and Safety at Work (1994). He was elected President of the Republic of Malta on 4 April 1994. He edited *Malta Letteraria* (1950-55) and authored *Biex il-futur jerġa jibda* (1976); *Il-linja t-tajba* (1981); *Biex il-futur reġa beda* (1992); *Il-Manwal tal-President* (1997) and *Kif sirna Repubblika* (1999).

Dr **GEORGE MIFSUD-CHIRCOP** is an anthropological folklorist and ethnologist and lecturer at the University of Malta. He is well known for his ethnographic research and assiduous fieldwork in Malta and Gozo. His special areas of research include narratology, paremiology, riddles, material culture, and folk singing. He is a regular radio- and television- programme producer and presenter and has published monographs and studies in Malta and abroad and participated actively in various international conferences (Göttingen, 1994; Ittiri, Sardinia, 1999; Arles, Gibellina, and Oxford, 2000; London, 2001; Cardiff and Sheffield, 2002; Visby, 2003; Glasgow and Marseille, 2004). Mifsud-Chircop has been literary adviser, editor and analytical indexer since 1972. He is on the editorial board of *Archivio Antropologico Mediterraneo* published by the University of Palermo.
E-mail: george.mifsud-chircop@um.edu.mt

JOHN A. MIZZI started life as a journalist when he was 15 in the dramatic days of Malta's second siege, writing about his experiences for *The War Illustrated*, edited by Sir John Hammerton. Mizzi was the youngest person to write about the war from any front and was the youngest holder of a restricted press pass in Malta. He joined the *Times of Malta* in 1947 where he spent 25 years at various appointments, including picture editor, features editor, and news editor, as well as acting editor of both the *Times of Malta* and the *Sunday Times* of Malta. He was also the correspondent for the British United Press from 1959-65 and has been the representative of the *Daily Telegraph* of London since 1955. He has reported extensively on military and naval matters, having among many assignments, flown one of the last R.A.F. Lancaster bombers, been down in the submarine which made the deepest dive, landed and taken off as a passenger from Royal Navy and US Navy carriers, crossed the Libyan Desert with the Royal Marine Commandos and reported on stories round the world, including from North and South America, Australia, South Korea and on the disintegration of the Soviet Union during the Gorbachev era. He is still busy as a journalist and is presently publishing what is in essence the definite history of Malta and its people during the Second World War.

Born in Rabat, Malta in 1934, **JOSEPH MUSCAT** received his education at the Lyceum and at St Michael College for Teachers, and is an active member of the Society of Christian Doctrine (M.U.S.E.U.M.), the Malta Historical Society, Sacra Militia Foundation, Friends of the Maritime Museum, the Society for Nautical Research (England), the Naval Drydocks Society (England), and the *Association des Amis du Musee de la Marine*, Paris. In 1988 he was appointed secretary to the provisional committee of the Maritime Museum and assisted in the setting up of the museum. He has a lifelong interest in the maritime history of Malta with particular emphasis on the navy of the Order of St John and the development of traditional Maltese ship and boat technology and iconography. Besides carrying out extensive archival research he studied other related subjects such as ship graffiti and votive paintings. He has also produced numerous writings on maritime subjects in both Maltese and foreign publications besides being a ship model maker and restorer. Among his publications are *The Dghajsa and other Traditional Maltese Boats* (1999), *The Carracks of the Order* (2000), *The Birgu Galley Arsenal* (2001), *Graffiti Marittimi Maltin* (2002), *Maltese Ports (1400-1800)* (2002), co-authored *Naval Activities of the Knights of St John (1530-1798)* with A. Cuschieri (2002), and *Kwadri Ex-Voto Marittimi Maltin* (2003).
E-mail: <u>tacsum@nextgen.net.mt</u>

ANTHONY PACE trained as an archaeologist and historian. Throughout a long career in the heritage sector, he has served in various national and international positions. In Malta, he has served as the last Director of the Museums Department before becoming the country's first Superintendent of Cultural Heritage, in 2003. He has represented Malta at the Council of Europe, UNESCO and at various international cultural heritage gatherings. His research interests cover Maltese prehistory, cultural heritage policy, the presentation of cultural heritage, public heritage, cultural landscapes and intangible cultural heritage. In the field of international exhibitions, he has successfully directed an acclaimed display of Maltese prehistoric art which has travelled to Florence, Prague, San Marino and Brussels. As a field scholar, he has directed a number of excavation projects and undertaken extensive field research in the Maltese islands. His publications include *Melit et Gaul* (1996), *Maltese Prehistoric Art* (1996), *The Hal Saflieni Hypogeum* (2000), contributions to *Malta Before History* (2004), and a number of articles on cultural heritage.
E-mail: <u>anthony.pace@gov.mt</u>

JOE SULTANA was born in Xagħra, Gozo in 1939. After eighteen years teaching in primary and secondary schools, he was appointed head at Villa Psaigon Field Studies Centre (1977-80), Conservation Officer (1981-92), Head/Environment Manager of Reserves, Sites and Habitats (1993-94), Principal Environment Officer (1995-2000), and adviser to the Minister for the Environment on nature reserves (2001-02). Other posts held included Member of the Board of Directors of the Planning Authority (1992-97), President of the Malta Ornithological Society (now BirdLife Malta) (1976-87), and World Council Member of BirdLife International (1994-99). Sultana was also Chairman of Naturopa Centre (1987-88), Malta's representative on the Steering Committee on Conservation and Management of the Environment and Natural Habitats (1982-94), and Member of the Organising Committee for European Conservation year 1995 (1993-95). He authored, co-authored or edited various publications, including *Bird Studies on Filfla* (1970), *L-Agħsafar* (1975), *A New Guide to the Birds of Malta* (1982), *Red Data Book for the Maltese Islands* (1989), *Wildlife of the Maltese Islands* (1996) *Monitoring and Conservation of Birds, Mammals and sea Turtles of the Mediterranean and Black Seas* (2000), *L-Ghasafar ta' Malta* (2001), as well as several ornithological and nature conservation papers. Among others he was awarded the Gouden Lepelaar by Vogelbescherming of the Netherlands (1993), the Royal Society for the Protection of Birds Medal (1996), and Membership of Honour by BirdLife International (1999) for outstanding service to ornithology and bird conservation.
E-mail: joe.sultana@maltanet.net

Initially trained as a bass singer, **JOSEPH VELLA BONDIN** won the approbation of both critics and audiences through his interpretation of leading roles in operas and oratorios. His musicological interests were furthered by theoretical studies with composer Carmelo Pace and concentrate mainly on the history of Maltese music on which he has written widely. He is a contributor to the Second Edition of *The New Grove Dictionary of Music and Musicians*, ed. Stanley Sadie. His history of Maltese music in two volumes, *Il-Mużika ta' Malta sa l-Aħħar tas-Seklu Tmintax* and *Il-Mużika ta' Malta fis-Sekli Dsatax u Għoxrin*, published in 2000, is the first such study to be written. The first volume, *Il-Mużika ta' Malta sa l-Aħħar tas-Seklu Tmintax*, won the Malta Government Literary Prize in the Research Category for the Year 2000. His modern edition of the *Stabat Mater* (1750) by the Maltese composer Girolamo Abos was published in the USA by A-R Editions of Middleton, Wisconsin, in 2003.